Kinship to Kingship

Texas Press Sourcebooks in Anthropology, No. 14

Kinship to Kingship

*Gender Hierarchy and State
Formation in the Tongan Islands*

Christine Ward Gailey

UNIVERSITY OF TEXAS PRESS   AUSTIN

First edition, 1987

Requests for permission to reproduce material from this work should be
sent to:
    Permissions
    University of Texas Press
    Box 7819
    Austin, Texas 78713-7819

Library of Congress Cataloging-in-Publication Data

Gailey, Christine Ward, 1950–
    Kinship to kingship.

    (Texas Press sourcebooks in anthropology ; no. 14)
    Bibliography: p.
    Includes index.
    1. Kinship—Tonga.   2. Sex role—Tonga.
3. Acculturation—Tonga.   4. Tonga—Politics and
government.   5. Tonga—Social conditions.   I. Title.
II. Series.
BN671.T5G35   1987   306.8'3'099612   87-10804
ISBN 0-292-72456-X
ISBN 0-292-72458-6 (pbk.)

Title page: Woman of the Friendly Islands. Engraved by Springsguth. From
Labilliardière 1800.

Contents

Figures

Acknowledgments

WRITING DEVELOPED out of census and tax records and retains a sense of alienated communication. We write in isolation, but cannot write critically without the love and support of others. My mother, Margaret Pearsall Gailey, transcended her ambivalence about her childless daughter and provided open arms, wonderful stories, and steady encouragement until her death. Learning about Tongan people helped me appreciate my other "parents." Stanley Diamond guided my graduate work, and in subsequent years he has always "been there" for me in terms of theoretical discussions, political analysis, and inimitable caring. Eleanor Burke Leacock gave me a sense of anthropology as a life-long commitment to understanding and conveying the social and historical origins of exploitation, and of the obligation to apply that knowledge in practical ways to oppose class, race, and gender stratification. Both of them have helped me to avoid the trap of disciplinary and linear thinking and have led me to perceive the potential of anthropology as a critique of civil society.

A number of other friends and colleagues also have read chapters and given useful criticisms. I want to thank Laura Anker, Louise Berndt, Mona Etienne, Viana Muller, Timothy Parrish, Betty Potash, Michael Schwartz, and Irene Silverblatt for their efforts to keep me from waxing hopelessly obscure or repetitious. Tom Patterson has been especially generous and insightful in reviewing the manuscript, far beyond the call of friendship.

The College of Arts and Sciences at Northeastern University provided funding for the fall 1986 field research in Tonga. My colleagues in the Sociology and Anthropology Department, especially Debra Kaufman, Alan Klein, Elliott Krause, and Carol Owen, have been consistently supportive. Students at Northeastern gave me a forum for working out some of the arguments about class and gender. The people of Isle au Haut, Maine, gave me encouragement and weekly nudges about finishing the book.

I could not have completed this book without my family. Meg and Tim Gailey, with characteristic thoughtfulness, provided me with a gentle and happy atmosphere in which to write. Adam and Eleanor saved me from hermitage with their humor and exuberance. C. K. and Stephanie, keen and interested always, lent me the money to buy a sorely needed word processor.

Suliana 'Ulu'Ave, Tupou Taufa, Laki Kafovalu Tonga, Manisela and Pilisita Ta'ufo'ou, Soane Uata, Lafaele Vaipuna, the women of the

Friendly Islands Co-operative, and their families made the field research exciting and enjoyable. I thank them for their wisdom, generosity, kindness, patience, laughter, and invaluable assistance.

I dedicate this book to my cherished mother, who wanted her children to "work for the benefit of humanity"; to Eleanor Burke Leacock, who forged my appreciation of the sources of authority held by women in kinship societies; and, with respect and 'ofa, to the women and men of the Tongan Islands, whose lives and struggles can inform our own.

C.W.G.
Boston, 1987

Introduction

WOMEN'S AUTHORITY and status necessarily decline with class and state formation. Class formation is a process in which groups that cut across age and gender distinctions come to have differential control over what is produced in a society and how it is distributed. At least one group—the largest numerically—loses control over at least part of its own production or labor. In the process, one or more groups become divorced from direct engagement in the making of goods needed to reproduce the existing society. This unproductive group is dependent upon labor or goods supplied by other groups; class relations emerge if those who supply the goods and services lose the ability to determine what is produced and what is supplied. State formation is a closely related process, namely, the emergence of institutions that mediate between the dependent but dominant class(es) and the producing class(es), while orchestrating the extraction of goods and labor used to support the continuation of class relations.

The conflict between producing people, orienting their work toward subsistence,[1] and civil authority, protecting the classes that siphon off goods and labor, is a *continual, ongoing* process. Most theories of state origins consider the state as a *thing*, with a life of its own. Further, most consider the state as a *stable* force in society. Profound social change—especially state origins or revolution—becomes difficult to explain.

Conceptualizing state formation as a *process* rather than a type or a category helps us to analyze historical changes and transformations of political institutions. The character of those states emerging out of kinship societies is thrown into high relief: unsystematic, often unstable sets of mediations between producing and dominant classes, that nevertheless serve to bolster the existence of the nonproducing class(es). Similarly, class formation is also an inconclusive process, a changing configuration; classes can emerge, proliferate, shrink, and disappear, depending on shifts in political and economic alignments. In other words, neither class nor state formation is a one-way street. Their inherent instability creates a ground for social change, including revolutionary change.

The dynamics of class and state formation, and the declining authority and status of women, can be examined through the experiences of people in the Tongan Islands in Polynesia, a society that shifted from kinship to class relations in the course of the past 250 years. In so-called primitive or kinship societies,[2] such as Tongan society in the period before European contact, tax, administrative, legal, and military institutions—collectively considered to be "the state"—do not exist. Instead, social life is ordered through kinship relations. Societies may be associated with a territory, but rights to use the resources are determined by kin and quasi-kin connections. Kinship indicates a social relationship—fictive, blood, or both. What is important is the content of the relationship, rather than its source or how it is phrased. The connection may or may not be seen as kinship: it might include such institutions as age groups and age sets, trade-friends, and other persons entering into a nexus of labor claims and expectations of reciprocity. In this definition, kinship involves reciprocal support, in the form of goods, services, and aid in life transitions. This support is generally not an equivalency; instead, the inequalities are offset through time, or through claims established by other relationships. Kinship relations are many-faceted and encompass functions that would be housed in separate religious, economic, and political institutions in our own society.

Why do class and state formation entail the subordination of women? The dynamics are explored in Chapter 1. Briefly, the ability of local, kin-based communities to remain autonomous must be constrained for institutions of state to emerge. Community or kin group autonomy is based upon the ability to reproduce a way of life, that is, *social reproduction*. This broad sense of reproduction includes, but is not limited to, the biological reproduction of kin group members (Gailey 1985b).[3] Both people and their social relations must be maintained and continuously re-created. Women, by virtue of their involvement in subsistence work and their ability to create other people, represent both aspects of reproduction (Leacock 1983).

In state formation, however, community reproduction becomes contingent. Kin groups must provide material and labor support for a politically dominant, unproductive class. The two aspects of reproduction then become arenas of conflict between the needs of the kin communities and the emerging sphere of class relations. In the long-term conflict between kin communities and an emerging civil authority, the ability to work and the ability to reproduce in the narrower sense of childbearing become abstracted from other aspects of social identity. Both women and men of the producing class(es) provide the taxes, rent, or labor used to support the emerging dependent class(es). But women symbolize the ability of kin communities to control their own reproduction. In their dual capacity, as both producers of subsistence goods and reproducers of kinspeople, women become the focus of attempts to reduce their relative authority and autonomy (Leacock 1983). In resisting the extraction of goods or labor, kin communities are themselves forced to emphasize the reproductive aspects of kinswomen, and women's authority and status may suffer as a result (Gailey 1985a).

Inequalities in authority exist in all human societies, and one form of inequality can crosscut another. Various forms of inequality have been identified in contemporary and past societies: class, caste, estates or orders, age or life experience, achieved prestige, descent-based rank. Inequality in state societies is supported by the institutions of government. Other forms of inequality also can exist in state societies, such as estates or castes, but class relations characterize all state societies.

State formation is unique in the support of systematic inequality along class lines and the creation of systematic hierarchy along gender lines.[4] *Gender hierarchy* refers to the association of what is culturally considered to be "maleness," although not necessarily men only, with social power. The term is preferable to *patriarchy*, since it can encompass situations where both women and men in a ruling class are categorized as "male" vis-à-vis the producing people, as in Inca relations toward conquered Andean communities (Silverblatt 1978).

In kinship societies, people may be ranked according to their life experiences or age status, position in social networks, position in a descent group, achievements, or some combination. The significance of such kin-based inequalities for the status of women has been debated for more than a century in Western countries. The resurgence of the women's movement in the early 1970's has sparked new, cross-cultural research into women's status. The position taken here is that the authority and status of women in kinship societies varies with forms of inequality, but no single form of inequality is based upon gender.

In state formation, authority and status become partially detached from kin considerations and increasingly linked to abstract qualities such as gender. The subordination of women—their association as women with less authority—emerges as an integral part of the emergence of both class relations and the state. Class and gender stratification are related, but derive from different dynamics. Class stratification is rooted in the way production is organized, that is, how necessary goods are made or gathered, distributed, and consumed. *Class* refers to a social group whose continuity derives from a specific relationship to the resources used in production and to the labor needed to change raw materials into usable forms (known as use-values). Gender stratification is created through changes in the political process, the forging of institutional means of ensuring the survival of class relations. As classes and state institutions emerge, the relative authority of women declines, but some women come to have social power through their class position.

The central issue is how kin-based inequalities, such as rank, can be transformed into political and economic control. Any group which is removed from the provision of goods and services needed for reproducing a culture, that is, socially necessary production,[5] is dependent. But how does dependency become domination? The transformation is explored in Chapter 2, on state formation.

The transition from kinship to class involves fundamental social upheaval. In kinship societies, what is made, given, traded, and so on is embedded in a division of labor by gender, age, and kin role. Where a dependent but dominant class emerges, the division of labor must change, and so, too, must gender relations. The shift from kin to class relations is necessarily exploitative of the producing communities, since goods and labor are extracted regardless of the makers' self-determined needs. Changes from kinship to class and the relationship of class to state formation are examined in Chapter 2. In this context, the state is considered as a set of changing legal-judicial, administrative, taxation, and often military and religious institutions created to mediate an intense and long-term struggle between kinship-based, autonomous communities and a nonproducing class or classes. The civil authority, composed of groups from within and outside the kin communities, attempts to institute means of obtaining labor and goods needed to support those removed from direct production. Kin-organized communities may be placed in a position where they cannot continue without forfeiting services and goods, even where the surface relations between producers and civil authorities appear peaceable. In their attempts to continue production to serve kin-determined ends, community members come into opposition to the civil authority, whether or not this opposition is recognized. In other words, the very efforts to reproduce kin-based relations become resistance to state penetration.

Among ranked and stratified kinship societies, chieftainships exhibit the potential for the dependent, high-ranking groups to become dominant classes. Chieftainship is a form of social authority found in some kinship societies. The position of chief is constituted, and generally involves some control over initiating certain types of activities. Typically, a chief has a call on the labor and some goods of lower-ranking kin, but he or she is constrained by the reciprocal expectations of generosity and material return (Sahlins 1963). Where the authority of a chief is marked, successors are selected from a pool of persons of appropriate inherited rank. Who becomes the next titled chief, however, is a matter of achievement and local support.

In the chieftainships of Polynesia prior to Western colonization, high-ranking people were dependent for the maintenance of their positions on lower-ranking people's labor and goods. The tensions within such stratified kin relations can be reproduced; class relations are not inevitable. But the relationship of high-ranking to low-ranking people can come to involve a threat of coercion if products and labor support are not forthcoming. The analysis of Tongan society over the past 450 years centers on how the dependency of "chiefly" groups shifted to political power and class-based economic control, and how the transformation involved and affected women.

Why Tonga?

The Tongan Islands of Polynesia, located south of Samoa and east of Fiji, present an opportunity to investigate the tensions in stratified kinship societies which can generate movements for and against class and state formation. Women from both chiefly and nonchiefly[6] strata have been deeply involved in state formation and in processes associated with Western influence. To analyze the significance of their involvement and the impact of these processes on Tongan women, we need to understand gender relations, the relations between chiefly and nonchiefly people in the precontact era, and how these relations persisted or were altered in the context of European influences.

Analysis of changing gender relations is possible, for much information is available with regard to kin-based inequality in the society prior to extensive European contact. The case is of particular interest, since Tonga is one of the so-called native kingdoms—including Hawaii and Tahiti—which developed in Polynesia in the course of the nineteenth century. In Tonga, the formation of governmental structures is said to be an indigenous response to the perceived threat of European imperial expansion. The chiefs' efforts to avoid annexation were not entirely successful: the islands were made a British protectorate in 1900 and were returned to political independence only in 1954.

The emergence of state institutions is fairly recent, and well documented in a variety of primary sources.[7] Written accounts begin in 1643 and document a range of European views of the Tongans. For the precontact period, we have evidence from oral histories (recorded later), genealogies taken from a range of high-ranking families, and collections of myths and legends. From the late 1700's on, there are a

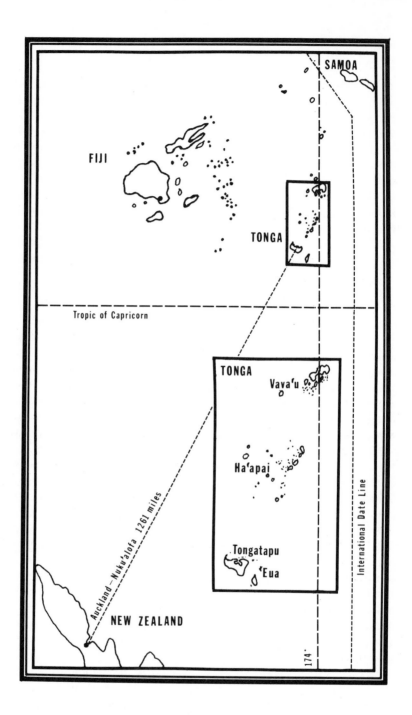

Figure 1. The Tongan Islands.

number of ships' logs and early travelers' accounts. From the late 1820's there are missionary journals and, still later, colonial administrators' records and memoirs. In the twentieth century, ethnographic accounts begin in the 1920's; and much research has been done by anthropologists since the mid-1960's. The disparate primary and secondary sources are discussed in the appendix on ethnohistorical methods.

The Tongans' experiences over the last few centuries support the theory that gender hierarchy emerges in association with class relations and state structures. Women were once the only creators of wealth in Tonga. The valuable objects made by women often were utilitarian, but whether or not they were used in everyday life, the finely woven mats, satiny bark cloth (*tapa* and *ngatu*), and decorated baskets were crucial in the re-creation of precontact Tongan society as a kinship society characterized by chieftainships. In each kindred or lineage, sisters and their children had claims to the products and labor of brothers and brothers' children. Today, wealth is no longer created exclusively by women; rank considerations have been superseded by class prerogatives; and material and labor claims by sisters are illegal. These changes accompanied the emergence of state institutions—administrative, legal, fiscal, military—in the 250 years following Tongans' first contact with Europeans.

In the precontact society, kinship and gender together determined the allocation of authority, the division of labor, and the distribution of products and services. Kinship ranking created chiefly and nonchiefly strata; chiefly and nonchiefly people had differential claims to goods and services. Those chiefly people who held titled positions had the greatest claims, and acquisition of titled positions depended on the demonstration of rank. Rank had to be validated through the presentation of valuable objects, by definition the result of women's work.

Rank was, in theory, hereditary. But the principles of superiority and inferiority used to determine rank were contradictory. So, while kin-based ranking was crucial to social authority, kinship was structured to be ambiguous. The argument in Chapter 3, on kinship in the precontact society, is that structural ambiguity helped to prevent class relations from emerging prior to European intervention. To reduce to systematic order the contradictions in the principles of ranking, for example, would project into the past a set of relations that developed only recently. There were attempts in the precontact period by chiefly groups to reduce ambiguity, but the pivotal role of women as sisters and nonchiefly people's insistence on customary chiefly conduct undercut their efforts. These dynamics are explored in Chapter 4, on the reproduction of ambiguity.

The division of labor—by gender and kinship, including rank—embodied tensions toward and away from class formation in the pre-contact period. The limitations placed on kin-based authority and the relationship of rank to the division of labor support the argument that Tonga was not a class-organized society at the time of contact. Changes in the division of labor following European contact show a critical shift from kin-based to class relations.

Gender relations in Tonga were crucial in both production and the reproduction of Tonga as a kin-based society. Women's responsibility for making the goods which validated the rank and position of all Tongans is analyzed in Chapter 5, on the division of labor. The significance of women's and men's spheres of exchange, and the importance of gender and rank considerations in the determination of the value of objects are discussed in Chapter 6. Gender relations—the relative autonomy of women and men in their various roles, the meanings attached to sex differences and to sexuality in the pre-contact society—are analyzed in Chapter 7.

Two processes, usually identified with expansion by capitalist countries, were central in changing Tongan women's status. The period of early contact with European explorers and merchant seamen introduced commodity exchange for the first time and exacerbated interchiefly warfare (Chapter 8). The promotion of Christian religion and of commodities and markets (mercantile relations) in stratified, but still kinship-organized societies frequently has catalyzed the formation of state structures. Both processes heightened existing tensions in Tonga and helped to precipitate the emergence of class relations and a centralized government. The imposition of Christianity in the Islands, accomplished primarily through military conquest, had a profound effect on women's status. Missionaries were in a position to enforce Western notions of appropriate female behavior, since they provided advice and arms to groups pressing for political centralization and expanded commercial trade. The crusade for Christian civilization, the integration of proselytizing with the imposition of political centralization through military conquest, and efforts by Christian missionaries to "domesticate" Tongan women are analyzed in Chapter 9.

Because of the quasi-colonial context, the Tongan case acquires another importance: state formation, while catalyzed by European intervention, was not imposed. The role of the emerging state structure in fostering class formation and gender hierarchy is analyzed in Chapter 10. The Tongan case can help us understand the tensions toward and against class formation that are evident in neo-colonial countries today.[8] Where state formation has been encouraged through commodity production and marketing operations—usually dimensions of capitalist colonialism—another aspect of the potential shift from dependency into domination becomes evident.

The relationship between colonizer and colonized has been investigated in depth, as has the way the image of the colonizers and their culture becomes internalized (e.g., Memmi 1967; Fanon 1967). What is not so apparent is the dramatic shift in gender relations within the society experiencing this upheaval. As commodity production becomes emphasized, women of the emerging producing class(es) typically become removed from more lucrative types of production—both traditional *and* imposed. The locus and control of that production tends to become associated primarily with men (Etienne 1980; Leacock 1954; Van Allen 1972). Of course, the major control of commodity production is in the hands of the outsiders, but when colonial rule is broken, the association of strategic production with men continues. The impact of commodity production and trade on Tongan women and men is explored in Chapter 11. Tonga was never colonized in a technical sense—colonial administrators were officially advisors, not governors, and land was not seized or purchased by foreigners. But processes associated with colonialism deeply influenced the development of class and state structures, and the changing status of women.

Tongan state formation, as a process independent of direct colonization but in a context of capitalist expansion in the Pacific, involved a double transformation of the kinship society. On the one hand, one of the chiefly groups which had been dependent upon kinship relations for its continuity, and whose capacity to organize some types of production rested on kin connections, came to control appropriation of those products and services independently of obligations to producing people. This change demanded the removal of high-ranking women from direct involvement in making necessary goods. Succession has come to be validated through legal codes, rather than through the presentation of women's wealth objects.

On the other hand, women in the producing classes have lost use-rights to resources they once could claim through the role of sister; their involvement in subsistence production remains important, but commodities have undercut their control of necessary products. The diffuse dependency of people on a wide range of kin—the source of personal autonomy—has become narrowed, particularly for nonchiefly women. Through the combined effects of missionary pressure, commodity production, and legal restrictions, nonchiefly women have become—for the first time—partially dependent upon their husbands. This process is not concluded, but at present the trajectory is toward greater dependency and less social authority.

The kinship sphere, which had constituted the entire society, has become circumscribed. Crucial kin relations have become either extraneous or illegal in the state society. This double transformation—of the dependency of Tongan chiefly people into political domination by some, and of nonchiefly Tongan women into partial dependents—provides a perspective on the emergence of women's oppression.

PART ONE

The Quest for Origins

1. The Subordination of Women: Gender in Transitions from Kinship to Class

Nisa, *a !Kung woman* (quoted in Shostak 1981:206)	*"Nisa has given birth! How well she has done!" They praised Nai (her newborn daughter) and they praised me, calling our names in affectionate greetings.*
Fu Hsuan, *China* (quoted in Hinton 1966:157)	*How sad it is to be a woman! Nothing on earth is held so cheap. . . . No one is glad when a girl is born: By her the family sets no store.*

THE QUESTION of the subordination of women has been an aspect of the problem of state formation since the second half of the nineteenth century (Morgan 1877/1964; Engels 1884/1972). In all state societies, femaleness is associated with lower status and women, as women, have less social authority. But while state origins have attracted much attention in recent years, reasons for the universality of women's subordination in all state societies has attracted little attention in the state formation literature. Apart from feminist works, few of the recent writings even mention women; even fewer consider gender relations as a major dynamic in the development of classes or state structures. Outside of the Marxist tradition, women's subordination generally is assumed to be rooted either in nature or in cultural constructs. In the recent Marxist works,[1] subordination of women usually is acknowledged but it is presented as a tangential effect—a kind of fallout—of state formation. It is the view here that state and class formation cannot be understood as processes without concomitantly analyzing gender and the status of women (cf. Rapp 1978a).

Gender hierarchy describes the association of social power with maleness, that is, with characteristics associated culturally with masculinity. Most feminists have argued that gender hierarchy is, in one way or another, cultural. The persistent disagreement about reasons for women's subordination parallels antagonistic perspectives in Western social science in general. But although the feminist movement has not resolved the basic problems in Western civilization, the resurgence of feminism in anthropology, and particularly Marxist anthropology, has contributed importantly to the destruction of ideological supports for institutional sexism.[2]

Both within and outside feminist anthropology, debates continue about the origins and character of women's subordination (Gailey 1987). Theories that postulate natural causes for subordination usually center around issues of biological reproduction; they range from "biology as destiny" to "but technology can set us free."[3] "Universal but cultural" subordination theories revolve around issues of authority and the division of labor by gender in kinship societies. Historical development arguments hinge on the relationship of gender-based stratification to other processes of systematic social hierarchy.

A number of scholars have argued that subordination is cultural, but also that it is a structural feature of kinship societies. One group of these theories holds that women have lower status and less social authority as a result of a putative domestic/public split in human societies (Rosaldo 1974). Women are associated to a greater or lesser extent with the domestic realm, because of the mothering role. The degree to which women are associated with the public sphere and men with the domestic sphere reflects the relative social authority of women.

The existence of separate public and domestic spheres in kinship societies has been questioned on historical and empirical grounds, particularly because the same relations organize both production and the activities needed to ensure the continuity of the people as constituted. In other words, where production is for communal use and organized and controlled through reproductive relationships, there is no public/domestic split. Mona Etienne and Eleanor B. Leacock (1980) examine a range of kinship societies that contradict such a "split"; they point to the emergence of such spheres with capitalist colonization especially. Seeing separate domains in kin societies seems to derive from the British structural-functionalist tendency to project jural and domestic domains onto the (colonized) peoples they studied (see Asad 1973). Louise Lamphere's formulation (1974) is more accurate than Michelle Rosaldo's (1974): Lamphere draws the distinction between egalitarian or corporate kin societies and peasant societies. She orients the study of strategies of women's cooperation and conflict around the existence of a "political" versus a "domestic" sphere. Such a separation of domestic and civil domains can be seen in precapitalist state societies, and a growing association of women with domestic work is related frequently to a decline in social authority (Sacks 1979).

The other group of "cultural but universal" theories is structuralist, drawing from the work of Claude Lévi-Strauss (1969), particularly his model of marriage in kinship societies: the exchange of women by men is viewed as a means of inter-group communication. According to the structuralist view, women's status is subordinate in kinship societies, where the division of labor is by sex and age. This is because, according to the model, male is superior to female in the nexus of isomorphic, logical oppositions—derived from a universal, hierarchical opposition of culture over nature—that together comprise the cultural "code." Purportedly, female is associated with nature, while male is associated with culture and thus superiority (Ortner 1974). Subordination is said to be shown, and replicated, in the exchange of women in marriage (Rubin 1975).

The theory of universal subordination through exchange of women has been criticized from the perspective of exchange theory by Annette B. Weiner (1976). She maintains the association of women with reproduction, and agrees that marriage may involve the exchange of women. But she argues that women are not subordinate in kinship societies, such as the Trobriand Islands in the southern Pacific. According to Weiner, Trobrianders consider the essential qualities of being a woman ("womanness") to include the power to procreate, and the cultural emphasis placed upon this type of power is considered by Weiner to indicate different qualities of authority held by men and women in the Trobriands (Weiner 1976; 1980). In "womanness" women in a sense embody, and in funerary exchanges they "recapitulate," kin identity for all people. Since this role is essential in the reproduction of the matrilineal kin groups and, thus, all of society, women are highly valued. Indeed, their capacity to reproduce people, as well as to recapture kin identity through exchanges of women's goods, provides them with a timeless, transcendent power. This power is beyond the mundane efforts of men to build renown during their lifetimes.

The structuralist position has been refined by Sherry Ortner (1981). She follows through on Lévi-Strauss' distinction of "cold" (unchanging) and "hot" (where change is part of the cultural code) societies in her focus on what she terms "hierarchical" rather than kin societies. In doing so, she glosses societies characterized by castes with those having estates or orders (cf. Rousseau 1978; Gailey 1980). She argues that the partial dissolution of a division of labor based on "sex and age" can lead to the elevation of women's status even though men remain politically dominant (Ortner 1978; 1981). Stratification (which remains vaguely defined as "hierarchical") apparently becomes progressive for women. Catharine MacKinnon and Ruby Rohrlich do not share Ortner's view (MacKinnon 1982; 1983; Rohrlich 1980). They argue, along with Gerda Lerner (1986), that the subordination of women was a necessary prerequisite to the formation of classes and the state. Their congruence in this view derives from decidedly different positions on the condition of women in prestate societies: widespread subordination (Lerner) or universal subjugation (MacKinnon), versus patriarchal overthrow of a putative matriarchal civilization (Rohrlich).

The possibility that women form part of an exploited class in some kinship societies has been postulated by a number of French Marxist anthropologists,[4] who are mostly men and debatably feminist. They have argued that women and junior men form a subordinate class exploited by (male) elders, especially in societies having a "lineage mode of production."[5] Feminist anthropologists in the Marxist tradition have disagreed about the relative status of women in kinship societies. Some concur with the structuralists and the French Marxists that marriage exchanges and marital relations in general indicate subordination in kinship societies, since purportedly women exercise little control over their own allocation and production as wives (Edholm, Harris, and Young 1977).

Most Marxist scholars who are involved in the question, however, hold that the inequities in (uncolonized) kinship societies are not, on the whole, equivalent to subordination of women.[6] Institutionalized gender hierarchy in this view is created historically with class relations and state formative processes, whether these emerge independently, through colonization, or indirectly through capital penetration.[7] To comprehend the emergence of gender hierarchy, we must consider the sources and limitations of authority in kinship relations.

Kinship and Authority

Authority in so-called primitive societies is embedded in kinship relations. The relative authority of women and men in such societies rests on the claims to others' labor time or products implied by relations through birth, adoption, and marriage. Kinship structures, particularly ranked ones, allow for unequal exercise of authority. The dimensions of these inequalities provide a backdrop for changes in women's authority during state formation.

No kin relationship is neutral with regard to authority (cf. Service 1975). But, as can be shown in the Tongan case, these "hierarchies"

are never consistent with gender, age, or any other single consideration. Some relationships continue throughout life, such as those between siblings, parents and children, and so on. Other relationships
develop as partial markers of maturation or increased status, such as
becoming an in-law, a spouse, or a grandparent (cf. Bunzel 1938 : 360).
There exists a complex offsetting of relationships in which one has
claims to another's labor or products, and vice versa. Some relationships entail deference, still others prestige but no labor claims, and
so on.

These kinship relations (fictive or not), in association with gender
and age, determine not only what one does, but with whom, for
whom, and at what time. The complexity and simultaneity of these
relationships allow no one an unambiguous status. The nexus of
roles can be juggled by all parties, since each has claims to others
who can mediate the deference or obligations involved in the problematic relationship. Thus, no one can claim unlimited authority;
no one is without authority.

To understand the relative status of women in any particular kinship society, one has to be especially careful not to gloss the meaning
of a specific action or behavior in our own, or any other class society,
with its meaning in the kin context. The meanings may be similar,
but the similarity must be demonstrated, not assumed. Deference
behavior is one arena where many confusions have arisen.

The etiquette of deference may not indicate dependency or significant claims to the deferent one's labor. Ruth Bunzel provides a description of wifely behavior among the Zuñi that invites our projec-
tions of male dominance. A Zuñi wife is weaving in a house; her
husband returns from the fields with an armful of produce. She
drops her work, takes the goods from him and sets about preparing a
meal for him. Bunzel then explains the meaning of the action, which
indicates mutual aid, daily affirmation of married status, and an absence of control by husbands, where married men are viewed as
guests in the matrilineal households (1938 : 307). The tendency to assume that deference by women indicates powerlessness is under-
standable, since it generally does in this society. But deference in a
kinship context may cloak a *fragile* or highly charged connection between two relatively autonomous people or groups. This was the
case in Tongan marriages (Gailey 1980). Indeed, deference behavior
may even indicate a reverse dependency, as is perhaps the case for the
relations of lower-ranking kin to chiefs among several Amazonian
peoples (Clastres 1977 : Ch. 11). As gender distinctions became hierarchy in Tonga, the deference behavior of wives was transformed into

dependency upon husbands. Today the meaning of deference has changed: a relative autonomy of spouses no longer underlies a wife's deferential behavior.

For women to exercise less socially recognized authority *as women*, both women and men must be identified apart from other factors. In other words, gender identity must be abstracted in some way from other aspects of social personhood. For women's status to be overall less than men's, there must be a distinctive status to discern. The roles that women and men grow into and change throughout life must be unbalanced with regard to authority. Here also, the roles must be identified primarily in gender terms. Kin relations must be made authoritative, less multifaceted and less flexible. One way in which this can occur is through a partial divorce of the division of labor from kinship considerations.

Gender and the Division of Labor in Kinship Societies

In kinship societies, the relationships that determine who is to make goods (or plant or fish or hunt), with whom and when, are the same connections that organize the recruitment or creation of group members, socialization, and passages of members through life transitions. The relationships that organize productive activities provide the means for people to reproduce the society in all its complexity. For this reason, the division of labor in kinship societies is the meeting point of social reproduction and socially necessary production. Anthropologists have categorized classless (primitive) divisions of labor as on a "natural" basis, meaning one of age and sex, with skill injected in some cases. Gender, the cultural interpretation of physiological differences of males and females related to reproduction, as a rule is not considered apart from sex differences. There are societies where gender is seen as substance that flows through life among people, turning them from women to men and vice versa (see, e.g., Meigs 1976). But in spite of a growing literature on the complexities of gender categories in kinship societies, writers persist in referring to activities done by males and females, rather than men or women.

Age, too, is misleading: life status is a better phrase, since chronology rarely is the primary focus. Passage through culturally identified critical experiences is more important than physical aging, since such transitions involve becoming more fully human (Radin 1971; Landes 1971; Diamond 1974). In addition, some societies organize certain types of work along age-group or age-grade lines; these typically parallel gender categories, while they cross-cut kinship connections. The analytical abstraction of gender from life status has led frequently to distortion, to the fragmentation of an undifferentiated fusion of statuses. A number of researchers have emphasized the importance of life cycle in analyzing women's authority in kinship societies (Bell 1980; Etienne and Leacock 1980).

The division of labor by gender and age in kinship societies sets up separate spheres of productive activity for women and men *during certain periods of their respective life cycles.* In most cases, these periods are roughly congruent with the culturally determined ways of becoming a parent and rearing children. Often overlooked are those periods when the gender distinctions are inoperative or transcended. The emphasis on gender categories and, in some societies, the selection of a gender may be an aspect of certain life crises, such as puberty (Clastres 1977: Ch. 5; Radin 1971). Gender considerations may be inactive during childhood, in such cases. Certain life transitions, such as the time after one's children have children, may provide transcendence from effective gender identity. There are many examples of older persons being accorded a special status independently of gender (e.g., Bell and Ditton 1980). In addition, gender identification may change through time (Meigs 1976) or an age status may replace the gender associations of earlier life stages.

Sensitivity to these factors is not sufficient, for there is another critical dimension to the division of labor, namely, kin connections. Age and gender are commonly assumed to be the two determinants of classless divisions of labor. But people exercise claims to specific relatives' labor or products, and work efforts may be organized on a relationship basis. Anthropologists frequently do not identify kinship connections when they describe the division of labor, giving one the impression that gender and age are the preeminent factors. For instance, Janet Siskind describes the relationships of those who work together at different tasks, and she implies that kinship connections are vital in the Sharanahua division of labor, but this dimension is not a focus of her discussion (Siskind 1973).

Gender relations rarely are abstracted from other aspects of one's social identity in kinship societies. To know that someone is a woman tells one of some of the potential tasks she may perform, since gender is one of the key dimensions of a kin-based division of labor. But one cannot know what she actually does without reference to her particular roles—e.g., as a mother, sister, mother-in-law, wife—as well as the particular status she has at that time in her life cycle. To my knowledge, there is no dimension of the division of labor in so-called primitive societies that persists through all passages from one life status to another. Also, the same person simultaneously occupies more than one role and tasks vary with the shifts from one role to another. For example, Mbuti women cannot be said to fix leaky roofs; sisters and daughters do not—only wives perform this activity (Turnbull 1962).

Typically, ethnographers collapse these roles into the division of labor by gender. Usually there is a further reduction, from gender to sex differences (Oakley 1972). Such glosses may be a consequence of the researchers' ethnocentrism. In capitalist societies the division of labor by gender *is* unmitigated by age in the sense of life experiences, or kin considerations. Regardless of age, women and men are expected to perform different tasks, associated with a split between public and domestic spheres.[8] We may unwittingly project such an unsubtle categorization onto kinship societies. The division of labor in classless societies includes gender as a major dimension, but kinship connections, life cycle, and skill interact with gender in a complex and often irreducible manner.

Marriage, Exchange, and Social Authority

Structuralists have argued that women have less social authority in kinship societies, because of their identity with nature and because they are said to be exchanged in marriage by their fathers or brothers as a way of ensuring continued communication with other men (Lévi-Strauss 1969; Ortner 1974). If these scholars are correct, to focus on class and state formation is somewhat irrelevant. However, the putative identification of men with culture and women with nature in so-called primitive societies has been dismissed as ignoring the historical creation of nature and culture as categories in Western civilization; thus the dichotomy is projected onto peoples who are shown not to have such rigid concepts (Leacock and Nash 1977). Indeed, the identification of women with nature is culturally specific and recent in Western civilization: in middle-class Victorian life, women were considered the "civilizing" influence, as maternity was seen as less animal-like than the siring of offspring. The task, then, to evaluate the meanings of marriage and marriage exchange in kinship societies. In doing so, other problems with the structuralist model can be appreciated.

Several structuralist assumptions about marriage in kinship societies derive from our own, or precapitalist state societies. For instance, the division of labor by gender is said to make marriage a necessity (Rubin 1975; Lévi-Strauss 1969). This claim seems to be related to situations where the married people form the core of a household unit (a problematic assumption in many societies, including our own), and where the household is the primary unit of production. While this is the case in many kin-ordered societies and most peasant societies, there are numerous exceptions (Gough 1968).

In Dobu the household is an important, but not the sole unit of production (Fortune 1963). Married couples have certain claims to one another's labor. But the core of the household is not a married couple: the *susu* consists of a married woman, her children, and her brother. The husband lives with his sister and her children. The division of labor by gender in no way makes marriage essential for this arrangement to succeed. In other societies, the men's work necessary for a woman because of the interdependence of the gender division of labor may not involve her husband to any significant extent and vice versa. These exigencies may be discharged by siblings, as in the (pre-contact) Tongan and Trobriand Islands (Gailey 1980; Weiner 1976).

Marriage is by no means the occasion for major social attention in all kinship societies. Other transitions, particularly first-time parenthood, may be the elaborated ceremonial (as in the Amazonian societies that practice the couvade). Where marriage is accorded great significance, it can be understood in the context of other life crisis rites. In such important changes in life status, people who already are kin and some who are becoming kin establish new and unique claims to the person who is changing status.

Unlike other life crisis rites, marriages may represent the indivisibility of production and reproduction in kinship societies. In marrying, a person acknowledges his or her responsibility to the group as a whole to help continue the group, in terms of both provisions and demographic replacement; the responsibilities show a fusion characteristic of kinship societies between public and domestic activities. In the establishment of at least potentially a new household, the new couple *owe their adulthood to their kin*. They can only reciprocate over time by providing products and productivity—fecundity and labor time—to the nexus of people who validated and made possible their growing personhood.

Marriage concerns continuity of status changes and of the kin group as a whole; production is related to this end. The exchanges which are initiated upon marriage must be placed in a context of exchanges initiated or reinforced in every life crisis. Marriage is the entry into adult status in many societies; in others, the critical rite may be the transition to parenting or becoming a potential spouse after puberty (Radin 1971). But marriage creates neither the sole unit of production, nor necessarily the primary unit of consumption, nor even the primary locus of demographic replacement. Rather, upon marriage a person can begin to activate and extend his or her material and symbolic claims to other people. Weiner discusses the network of exchanges of products established with marriage in the Trobriands (1976). These claims may transcend the life of the particular marriage. In any case, the division of labor by gender does not explain why people marry in kinship societies.

Marriage involves an exchange of people, but should not be reduced to a timeless form of exchange, as in Lévi-Strauss (1969). Young women are exchanged, in their first marriage at least, in many kinship societies, but not in all. The act of marrying involves an increase in individual status and autonomy, and an extension of obligations to a new range of women and men, one's in-laws. It is reasonable to assume that such women and men might have to concur in the selection or acceptance of the new spouse. In their focus on the exchange of women by men, structuralists miss this aspect.

It was long assumed that Australian aboriginal peoples not only practiced the exchange of women by older men, but the appropriation of young women as wives by male elders (Hart and Pilling 1960). Jane Goodale pointed out that a Tiwi son-in-law provided labor service to his mother-in-law throughout her life and the duration of the marriage; the mother-in-law also exercised some control over the duration of the marriage (Goodale 1971). Diane Bell has shown that constraints upon marriageable people among the Warlpiri were not reducible to the gender of the people involved (Bell 1980). She argues that the selection of spouses has been misunderstood as being in the hands of men. Potential mothers-in-law decided their children's initial spouses and relayed the decision to their husbands, who then demonstrated the selection; only the latter part of the ceremony was "noticed" by ethnographers (ibid.: 255–257). Older men often did marry young women, but Phyllis Kaberry and Goodale describe such marriages for young wives as similar to their earlier homes, in terms of affection and care (Kaberry 1939; Goodale 1971). The "other side" of older men/younger women marriages is shown by Bell: the marriage of older women to young men (1980:260–261).

The focus almost exclusively on first marriages is another profound problem in exchange theory. Subsequent marriages—which were the rule in most Australian societies—involved *increasing* control over the selection of a spouse, or the decision not to remarry in the event of divorce or widow(er)hood. In addition, the incidence of de facto plural marriages for women (without the wife residing simultaneously with the husbands) in some societies has been virtually ignored (see, e.g., J. Muller 1980). The quality of ethnographic descriptions is highly uneven. Many of the categorization schemes are extremely misleading: Karla Poewe discusses the inadequacy of descriptions of postnuptial residence. She describes verbiage that transforms extremely flexible arrangements—such as among the precolonial Lovedu, women at times marrying their brothers' daughters—into a technically correct, but highly misleading patrilineality and virilocality (residence with the husband) (Poewe 1980). The authority of older female relatives, as well as, in this case, female-female marriage, is lost—or buried—in the manner of description.

It has been argued that in some West African societies, elders (said to be men only) control the allocation of women through their control of bridewealth needed for validating the marriage; in this way, the elders are said to control the labor of younger men. Again, the attentiveness of the ethnographers to older women's authority and alternative forms of marriage must be questioned. It seems highly unlikely that unofficial or less prestigious forms of marriage are unknown or that elopements do not occur (Kathleen Gough establishes this for the Nuer/Dinka peoples of the Sudan [Gough 1971]). It also seems highly unlikely that older women who, as lineage co-wives, have become the de facto future founders of patrilineages, have no involvement in the marriage arrangements of their grown sons and daughters. It is reasonable to assume that elders would provide a ethnographer with an ideology of control; it is not reasonable to then make their version the model for marriage exchange (as in Meillassoux 1975; 1979).

Marriage exchanges, like household arrangements, are not the "core" of any kin-based culture. Even in patrilineal societies where women do leave their natal groups upon marriage, ties to the natal group are not necessarily broken with marriage: they can be transformed, expanded, or activated at strategic times (Goody and Tambiah 1973; Paulmé 1971). The claims established with marriage are far more complex than structuralists have indicated. Claims are material as well as symbolic, and the symbolism has as much to do with personal status transcendence as it does with intergroup communication.

The claims established in marriage vary widely from society to society—the affiliation of children is not always decided at the time (Goody and Tambiah 1973), sexual relations may not be necessary (Shostak 1981), expected services or provision of products may have little to do with the spouse, and so on. To reduce this complexity to women mediating men's communication does not help our understanding of this range of claims. The more important point is perhaps that it is impossible to achieve adulthood in kinship societies without becoming obligated to others; it is impossible to retain high status without enabling others to grow. The continuity of the kin group is impossible without the social recognition of individual growth and transcendence. The personal changes and the heightened status which accompany such transitions are symbolized and demonstrated through the assumption of broader and more intense responsibilities.

But marriage, like other institutions of kinship societies, changes radically in content in situations of increasing stratification. "Generalized exchange" or matrilateral cross-cousin marriage is found in some ranked and stratified societies (Leach 1951). This form of marriage underscores rank—the inequality of intermarrying groups—and the "flow" of women may be to groups distant from their natal ones. But even in those cases where women clearly are exchanged, it is unwise to presume that such exchange has always been the case, or that the reason for the exchange is male-oriented communication (as in Ortner 1981). The structuralists' assumption is that men arrange the marriages and thus promote a communication system they presumably control. The evidence is slender. In the Tongan case, the highest-ranking *women* had interests in instituting generalized exchange *and were in a position to do so,* as can be seen in Chapter 4, on the re-creation of ambiguity in kinship.

With class formation, personal status becomes increasingly estranged from wider kin-based obligations. The meaning of marriage—crucial as it is in the replication of kin-based relations—reflects this critical shift. Among the Kwakiutl of the Northwest coast, marrying involved the acquisition of a new name, which marked an expanded social identity. The fur trade and later contact with European merchant houses encouraged a shift from ranking to class stratification—inconclusively in the precontact period. Plural marriages had been a mark of high rank, but in the social crisis that accompanied the introduction of commodity trade (in furs and slaves), the marriage pattern shifted. Before, the contracting of polygynous unions demonstrated a man's high rank and, at the same time, assured that a broad range of kin would have claims on his kin group. Later, the act of marrying many times to increase personal status *without* incurring kin claims came to be emphasized. How could this be done? High-ranking Kwakiutl men at times married (named) parts of their own bodies (Bunzel 1938:360). (The named parts were not exchanged by men.) Kwakiutl women who attempted to build renown could be said to become polyandrous. A high-ranking woman could acquire new names and heightened personal status by marrying the same man a number of times (ibid.). Obviously, the division of labor by gender has little to do with marriage in this case. But the fragmentation of the self into parts is a striking metaphor for what happens to social personhood in class formation.

It might be argued that, since the Kwakiutl were stratified, the partial dissolution of the division of labor by gender with the use of slaves allowed such a freeing-up of marriage (cf. Ortner 1981). Such an argument assumes that exchange is a result of the division of labor by gender, which we have questioned above. It also assumes that marriage exchanges were a medium of men's communication.

In cases where stratification involves descent-based inheritance of rank, marriage rules tend to become more rigid, rather than more flexible. In the case of the Kwakiutl, the act of marrying one's self or one's spouse signals a *closing of ranks*. There is a refusal to broaden the network of kin obligations that had been inherent in high rank. Kinship obligations are implicitly narrowed in the close-in marriages characteristic of stratification within kin societies (Sahlins 1963). An alternative form the rejection of kin claims can take is found in proto-state Dahomey (Diamond 1951). Succession to the kingship was a denial of marriage as important in the replication of the society. The heir would be selected from the children of the king by his concubines, not the royal wives. Thus, kin claims established with marriage did not last past a single generation. One also can see the implicit diminution of the role of wife, as she no longer could become the founder of a patrilineage as before. With stratification, exchange of women becomes prominent. The structuralist dilemma is the refusal to appreciate historical change and the fundamentally unoppressive nature of kinship societies (Diamond 1974; Gailey 1983; Poewe 1980).

Why Women?

What remains is the knotty problem of the historical emergence of gender hierarchy, which has been defined as the association of social power with maleness, or masculine attributes. What relationship do class and state formation have with the oppression of women? Why is it that where gender hierarchy has developed, women have always been the dominated gender?

Engels associated state formation with the declining status of women; his work was based on Johann J. Bachofen (1859/1967) and Lewis Henry Morgan (1877/1964). *The Origin of the Family, Private Property, and the State* is marred by such unreliable ethnographic information, a linear evolutionist quality of argumentation, and an absence of attention to the complexities of gender relations both in kinship societies and within the classes of precapitalist states. Recent research has been attentive to differences in the dynamics of precapitalist state societies, while taking up the questions posed by Engels. Several works have indicated that state formation generates systematic gender hierarchy.[9] Included in the processes associated with state formation that most affect women's status are the restriction of use-rights, commoditization—prominent where state formation is catalyzed through capitalist colonization—and tribute extraction in the form of taxes, rents, or labor service.

Women's authority, even more than that of non-elite people in general, is circumscribed as state structures emerge. Here we need to comprehend not only the dynamics of societal conflict in the imposition of tribute or tax/rent modes of production, but also the meanings of women's participation in kinship production and reproduction. For example, prior to European intervention, the labor of Tongan women reproduced Tongan society as kin-organized. Men's work provided most of the food, but women's production reproduced kin relations, rank, and so on, as will be demonstrated. The reproduction symbolized by Tongan women was far more than biological replication in the aboriginal context. Women continuously created the kin-ordered relations, oftentimes as concretized in the goods women made and distributed at critical moments in their relatives' lives. In such a situation, there was no effective split between productive and reproductive labor.

Weiner argues that in the Trobriand Islands (southern Pacific), women are associated in exchanges and, symbolically, with kin group continuity (1976). Women restore lineage identity when it is threatened by a member's death; exchanges of goods known as "women's wealth" during funerary ceremonies recapture the fragmented identity and ensure the lineage. Correlatively, Mary Douglas argues that giving birth is a "natural symbol" of group continuity (1973). Both birth and menstruation are powerful symbols of regeneration (Douglas 1966; 1973).

One needs to recall at this juncture that in such kin societies, a person's social authority and claims to labor and products cannot be determined solely on the basis of birthing or other sex-associated functions. The role of mother may be vital for growing authority (although other roles may provide more authority, as Sacks 1979 and Gailey 1980 point out). But the status of being a mother need not involve giving birth; "social maternity"—adoption, fosterage, and so on—may be a readily available alternative (Etienne 1979).

In class and state formation, people's functions in the division of labor come to be discernible with reference to categories of gender, age, and skill, *abstracted from their particular kinship connections and meanings.* Gender and age in kinship societies are as a rule loosely associated with (but not determined by) physical differences or changes in life (cf. Radin 1971; Diamond 1974). But where people become identified independently of kinship—for instance, as constituents of a class—biological differences or functions (as defined in the culture), rather than social identities, become increasingly important. This can be seen in the emergence of institutionalized gender hierarchy as well as in the development of ethnicity in state formation and consequent racism (Gailey 1985b).

The partial abstraction of gender identity from social personhood makes it easier to discuss the status of women in a peasant society than in a primitive society. Peasant or artisan women are apt to be involved in fewer kin roles, and those roles are apt to have fewer facets. In addition, the kin roles in peasant, artisan, or elite sectors of precapitalist state societies tend to emphasize biologically distinctive aspects of femaleness, particularly culturally determined sexual characteristics and reproductive capacities.

In the attempt to ensure the survival of a division of labor that provides for fundamental differences in social power—the existence of ruling groups permanently removed from direct production, etc.— all aspects of social life are called into question, but especially the relations that organize the maintenance and continuity (production and social reproduction) of the kin communities. In understanding this dynamic, we can come to understand why women would become the particular focus of ideological and lived-through status diminution.

The kin/civil conflict inherent in state formation politicizes and thus redefines a range of kinship relations (Diamond 1951). Many kinship relations become detached from traditional functions and crystallized in non-kin-based state institutions, as where a given relative is designated as a tax collector or corvée leader. To effect the systematic extraction of goods and labor, the control kin groups exercise over the determination of what is produced and how it is distributed must be denied. The continuity of kin-based communities must be made dependent upon the emerging state institutions.

To effect subordination of community reproduction to that of the state-associated relations, there is an ongoing attempt of the emerging dominant classes to split the unity and autonomy of the local kin groups (see Diamond 1951). Kin relations in general are the focus of legal and ideological diminution, and circumscription by non-kin institutions. All persons whose prestige derives from kin connections are threatened: chiefs may be transformed into tax collectors, older people into magistrates, household heads (women and men) into overseers of production. The variations are marked, but the underlying attempt is to redefine kin relations in the interests of surplus generation to support the nonproducing class(es). State and class formation alter kinship relations most often through the claims made on labor time.

The emerging state society is reproduced partly through kin-ordered production (including distribution and consumption patterns). But the reproduction of class relations depends upon non-kin institutions (such as military or religious structures) that ensure or orchestrate political control. Such domination is needed to generate, extract, and distribute the goods and services that support the non-producing class(es). Thus, productive and reproductive activities become separated. How work is done for the civil sphere remains organized partly through kinship, but kinship as a component in a class-based division of labor.

Work oriented to the maintenance of the kin community remains simultaneously productive and reproductive; the same relations organizing production in the kinship sphere also help to maintain the group over time. But they no longer comprise the sole reproductive relations. Should the kin communities not provide products or labor, the survival of the producers as a community is jeopardized. The Inca reacted to the withdrawal of tribute with political pressure and military conquest; members of reconquered communities frequently were scattered to distant parts of the empire (Silverblatt 1978; 1980). Numerous examples exist of unsuccessfully rebellious communities being slaughtered, sacrificed, or enslaved; at times, women were reserved for concubinage. Social reproduction, thus, depended on the subordination of kinship considerations to those of class.

The nature of kinship within each of the emerging classes changes, since kinship relations no longer re-create the entire society. In the producing class(es), kin relations continue to determine remaining use-rights to lands, the organization of subsistence production, household and familial composition, and often the technical division of labor in corvée projects and tribute production. But each of these arenas is either created or constrained to an extent by demands from the civil sphere.

Legal codes, taxes or rent, forced labor, and so on rely on and relate to kin structures, but redefine the claims and expectations inherent in them. In the ruling class and the class(es) associated with the reproduction of state institutions (e.g., priesthoods, merchants such as the Aztecan *pochteca,* or warriors), kinship has a different meaning. Here, the regulation of succession (Goody 1976), alliances with other elite classes, and claims to the surpluses and labor extracted predominate. Marriage in these nonproducing classes becomes more strictly political alliance or the demonstration of political power through the exchange of women (by women and men). Marriage tends to become defined by procreation, since inheritance of title, position, or wealth becomes a paramount concern within a non-producing elite.

Kinship relations and identities persist in less altered ways in those arenas that are not in service to the emerging civil order. But the range of responsibilities and prerogatives associated with kinship connections is narrowed. Indeed, the number of kin roles within the producing class(es) typically is reduced. Thus restricted and, in the case of producing communities, defensive vis-à-vis the inroads of civil authorities, kin relations that survive can become distorted. This encapsulation of kin groups and curtailment of their autonomy differentially affects women and men.

The mental versus manual labor split emerges with state formation (as has been noted widely); the association of inferior nature with working and culture with not being engaged in direct production is fostered in early states and continues in all class societies. Women of the producing class(es) receive the ideological debasement of doing manual labor, of being engaged in direct production. But they also produce other workers and so most represent the fundamental dependency of the nonproducing classes. Those who must represent potential autonomy receive the brunt of ideological denial.

Another distinction develops within productive labor, between work for the support of the emerging class relations and work within the kin community. The extraction of goods and services for the state-associated elite creates discernible kin-defined (domestic) and civil domains. Production oriented toward kin continuity is consigned to a necessary, but ideologically devalued, domestic realm. By way of contrast, the relations associated with the generation of tribute, taxes, or labor service and the regulation of class relations (as in law) are in the so-called public realm. The degree to which kinship tasks are made domestic or private varies greatly.

Privatization depends primarily on the way production, including distribution, is organized; where this is done largely through existing kin forms, that is, where the kin communities are stronger, kin-defined tasks are less likely to be relegated to a domestic sphere. One can see the privatization of some of women's work in precapitalist societies—in Islamic and Hindu states, the degree of seclusion varied with class, where high position was demonstrated by seclusion. But privatization of women's work accelerates with capital penetration. The association of women's work with housework is most marked in capitalist societies—whether or not women are in the labor force.

In early states, providing for a nonproducing elite places unprecedented stress on the acquisition and control of labor. Women not only can work, but also can produce new producers. Thus, they become a special focus for control (Leacock 1983). New producers also can be obtained through conquest. The identity of women, captives, or slaves vis-à-vis the state-classes is not as kin but as producers (of food, of crafts, of construction projects), as service workers who support the life-style of the elite (servants, porters, etc.), or as producers of both goods and people (concubines, slave women, secondary wives, etc.). Thus, the incorporation of new groups into tribute production or labor service often becomes the occasion for an ideology of separate, "biologically distinctive," and purportedly inferior humanity—the ethnic group or race. Racism and sexism emerge concomitantly; women of the producing classes—which often are conquered communities—are typed from above in the strongest sexual or reproductive terms and experience the greatest reduction of identity to what is considered by the dominant classes to constitute femaleness.

Class relations and the (state) institutions that may develop to ensure their survival draw and freeze a range of functions out of the context of kin responsibilities, among them sexuality and the capacity to give birth. These so-called natural functions become the focus of efforts to limit the autonomy of the kin-based communities (Gailey 1984). The argument is not "biology as destiny." Rather, narrowly defined reproductive functions become abstracted because they represent both control over present and future workers and the subordination of local kin group reproduction to the reproduction of the emerging class-based society. Institutions that stand apart from and out of the control of the kin communities reduce identity in strategic ways to functions or features defined as "natural."

In general, civil/religious ideologies highlight women's role in sexual reproduction as a primary determinant of their social identity, just as local deities are split into forces of nature or dualities when incorporated into state pantheons. While female deities' sexual and birth-related potential may be emphasized as powerful, the type of power is ambivalent: sexual potential must be controlled or it can kill. (MacKinnon stresses the control of sexuality as part and parcel of state patriarchy [1982; 1983].) State ideologies may debase women as less sacred or worthy than men, but at the same time exalt women whose sexual and reproductive potential is controlled by the state class(es).

Producing-class women in many precapitalist state societies could attain high status, but solely through the alliance of their (sexual) reproductive capacities—willingly or not—with the ruling elite (see

Gailey 1984). Ortner drew attention to cults of virginity in certain early states (1978). She has argued with regard to Tongan society that the emergence of stratification allowed for greater status mobility for women, through the exaltation of virginity or controlled sexuality (Ortner 1981). Certainly class stratification in Tonga was linked to a greater emphasis on the control of women's sexuality, particularly in the emerging dominant class, but the exalted status was accompanied by a severe restriction of customary sources of women's social authority. The mobility involved an assumption that one's identity was in fact isomorphic with reproductive potential in the narrow sense: virginity came to be carefully guarded among unmarried chiefly women, while bearing children to chiefly men meant rank mobility for unmarried nonchiefly women.

In Dahomey, some girls taken from their natal kin to become wives to the king—again, status mobility through a loss of control over reproductive potential—committed suicide (Bosman 1705, quoted in Diamond 1951:68). Irene Silverblatt analyzes the linkage of exalted status with permanent alienation from kin affiliation for Andean women in the Inca empire (Silverblatt 1978). In the latter case, status mobility demanded that local women relinquish all kin ties to their natal communities when they were drafted into service as either state-associated weavers and officiants or secondary wives of elite men.

Patriarchy, in the sense of associating social power with the kin roles of father and husband, may not emerge for millennia in state-formative situations. Gender hierarchy is more typical of early states (as well as industrial capitalist ones). Patriarchy does not emerge first within the elite or the producing classes, but characterizes the relationship of rulers to subjects, using gender and kin roles as metaphors of politicized relations. Women of the producing classes experience this debasement first vis-à-vis the dominant class(es)—as quasi-wives or virgin-wives—not their own kinsmen. Put simply, class relations emerge concomitantly with gender hierarchy, but class relations precede patriarchy.

In the defense of kin communities against the extractions and exactions of the emerging dominant classes, kinship relations become strained and can become oppressive (Gailey 1985b). State penetration may include, as in ancient Babylonia, the determination of marriages among persons of the producing class(es) by agents of a state religion. Alternatively, kinship relations may become debased due to demands placed on kin inserted into state-associated roles. For example, elders who were lineage heads in Dahomey were responsible—under threat of execution—for recruiting sufficient numbers of kinsmen for the annual conscription. The exercise of strategic kin roles may be made impossible or illegal, as will be shown for Tonga. Or, as the community's capacity to continue as a kin group is threatened, there may be an accentuated effort to control the allocation of people sought for service to the state-classes. This can involve greater regulation of kin group membership, a more rigid definition of use-rights to kin-held lands, and in general, more emphasis on the control of younger men and women. In Africa, such changes also have deeply affected the status and options of other unmarried people, particularly widows (Potash 1986).

State ideology may press a sexual/mother identification for women in the larger society; in the kin communities, the very threat to continuity posed by the denial of autonomous, social reproduction can lead to a parallel emphasis on women as bearers of children. The content of kinship roles typically changes—and can become burdensome—while the forms can remain similar. It invites distortion to assume that the persistence of form indicates identity of content of those relationships with the past.

The idiom of kinship is used by all constituencies, but the meaning changes in ways detrimental to generalized or balanced reciprocal (material) obligations. Control over the determination and allocation of labor and products is the battleground of kin/civil conflict. The autonomy of the kin communities is at stake. One of the arenas of struggle therefore becomes how communities are reproduced, and control over biological reproduction necessarily becomes an issue. The injection of political power into community continuity—the crisis of social reproduction in state formation—creates the emphasis on women's role in sexual reproduction, which ordinarily is only a facet of their social identity and status. The control over women's potential as both makers of goods and makers of people becomes an issue in both the state-associated classes and the kin communities. The heightened emphasis on sexuality and fecundity as power in state ideologies is paralleled on the local level, but for opposite reasons.

The civil sphere depends upon the suppression of local autonomy and a politically imposed dependency of kin groups upon the emerging state-associated institutions and classes. Control of women's dual potential becomes an obvious metaphor for the appropriation of kin group continuity. Kin communities are confronted with the unprecedented difference between continuity and survival. They are forced into fragmenting women's social personhood and reducing women's identities at least partially to the exigencies of sexual reproduction. In this setting, women are actors in both kin and civil arenas; their interests lie with those of their class. While state formation reduces the status of producers in general, the process by which emerging classes are bolstered creates a reductive association of women with the narrow sense of reproduction. Since the reproduction of kin relations is necessary but inimical to class relations, those most closely associated with the capacity of kin groups to reproduce are most disparaged.

2. State Formation

MOST OF human existence has been spent in kin-organized societies. Class relations and the state structures that support them have emerged only in the past six thousand years. Each known civilization has tried to justify the existence of social classes and the institutions of state. The Aztecs, for example, promoted a myth that far antedates our own myth of the "social contract" (Wolf 1959). Most early civilizations portrayed people who were not state-associated as barbarians or subhumans, uncivilized in culture and society (see Sahlins 1972: Ch. 1). The peasants and artisans—sources of the food and other goods that ultimately supported the class structure—were presented in several state ideologies as superior to nomadic peoples. But in all precapitalist state ideologies, those who were nonproducing were presented as purer, more sacred, more learned, more advanced, or more cultivated—as opposed to cultivating—than the direct producers.

Every civilization has proposed at least one theory of state origins, generally proposing that a ruling class is crucial for order, harmony, or prosperity. Every civilization has offered the populace an explanation for how classes emerged, or how the hierarchical social relations echo the order of the universe. At times, the implications of a hierarchical cosmology were made explicit: disruption of the social order invited destruction; the alternative to state control was chaos. Today, the prevailing theories of the state still present views that justify the persistence of both class and state structures (see Gailey 1985a). The theories of origins disagree about causes, but most consider classes and the state either as inevitable or as necessary for human prosperity, even survival.

How kin-based societies become class-structured and how state institutions emerge have been the concerns of anthropologists and historians since Sir Henry Maine (1861/1963) and, before him, social philosophers such as Jean-Jacques Rousseau (1754, 1762/1950), Thomas Hobbes (1651/1958), Michel de Montaigne (1580/1946), and Ibn Khaldun (1377/1958). The problem has been addressed in various dimensions, each associated with distinctions between kinship or "primitive" societies and so-called civilizations. The nineteenth- and twentieth-century literature abounds with trait lists of such differentiations between state and nonstate societies: legal codes and judicial structures versus customary ways of assuring social order, territorial versus kin-associated demarcation of groups, bureaucratic administrative structures or theocratic elites versus alliance or descent connections as means of organizing production and distribution, and variations on autocratic versus *primus inter pares* leadership and authority. These contrasts are largely correct, but the task is to explain why the distinctions developed.

In the nineteenth century, most of the explanations cited the advancements of state societies and ranked state societies according to their resemblance to the researcher's society (Tylor 1888; Maine 1861/1963; 1872). They presented a single line of development from foraging through industrial capitalist societies: all societies were seen as progressing through each stage, or being arrested at a given stage for reasons varying from societal exhaustion or cyclical degeneration to innate backwardness (Tylor 1904; Spencer 1896/1967).

Since World War II, theories of state formation have again taken up evolutionary models. In keeping with modernization theory, they usually propose multiple causes and a range of pathways to "societal complexity" (Steward 1972; Service 1971). Most present state institutions as developing in response to presumed ecological constraints or population pressure—seen as "natural laws"—or to ease internal social tensions (Fried 1960; cf. Gailey 1985a). Demographic, social, or ecological dilemmas become triggers (White 1959; cf.

Cowgill 1975); alternatively, direct causation is shunned, but a state apparatus is seen as providing a rational solution to imbalances (Service 1975). Systems approaches, the most elaborate of the recent theories, map a complex series of positive and negative feedback loops which presumably initiate and then strengthen the emerging administrative institutions (Wright and Johnson 1975; H. Wright 1977; Habermas 1975).

Most contemporary theories in the mainstream social science literature have at base such a functionalist model, and the variations reflect, in one form or another, models of capitalist society and the role of the capitalist state during different periods of accumulation (Gailey 1985a).[1] All present state structures as creating or ensuring social stability. Reflection on the researcher's own civilization has taken the form of an explanation for existing states.

Many authors treat the state as an entity: "it" comes into being and exists somehow beyond human intervention (White 1959; Fried 1967:226). Before there was no state; then the state influences human existence, regardless of the fate of particular state societies (Service 1975). If a state "collapses," it is seen in some way as due to either conflict within the elite or the concomitant development of more powerful states in the region (e.g., Willey and Shimkin 1973). While these tensions can create crises, they are not the sole causes of the breakup of state institutions. Resistance by the producing class or classes, through institutionalized, cultural means or active rebellion, also can be seen if one looks.

Few scholars have presented state formation as an ongoing process. There has been no complete state, although all state societies tend toward totalitarianism, including all capitalist states (Diamond 1974:17). State formation as a process is not necessarily one-way, nor is it an inevitable outgrowth of, for instance, stratified kinship relations.

If we view state formation as a process, contingencies of historical change become visible (cf. Thompson 1975). Human activities— conscious or not—may precipitate new social arrangements which may include class formation; similar actions may conserve or reconstruct kinship-defined relations. These human activities are only effective if they are organized, but the organization need not be planned consciously: replication of customary use-rights, for example, may be revolutionary in state formative situations. In other words, to understand state formation as a process, we must have reference to the particular historical circumstances in which institutions emerge that provide for the systematic extraction of goods and services, for governance by a nonproducing elite, and for the repression of direct producers, that together support the replication of a class structure.

Class, as described in the introduction, refers to the source of one's subsistence, not necessarily one's occupation or income level. In a capitalist society, for instance, a retiree, a unionized construction worker, and a middle-level manager may all have similar incomes, but the retiree is the only person of property of the three. To be retired with such an income, one must be living on interest or rental income or own other sources of income-generating property. The salaried manager and the construction worker are in the same class— both sell their labor power for a living. The white collar/blue collar distinction is irrelevant to class, but not to social status. Class, then, refers to the relationship a person or social group has to the resources and labor needed for subsistence. The group may retain partial control over tools and land, over tools but not land, over land through its position as the nobility from which the rulers are chosen, and so on. In many precapitalist societies, one's class position entails either producing goods or providing services for those who live off those goods and services, but who are not directly involved in production. They may be overseers or landlords, but they gain their income through their relationship to the state. An elite, by comparison, is generally a social group comprised of fragments from wealthy sectors of two or more classes, that has political ascendancy in a region or a state at a given time (Parrish 1984).

Among state formative dynamics explored in the Tongan case, there is a struggle over time between elite classes, or an emerging civil administration, and local kin or quasi-kin groups, notably over assertions of control over local labor, goods, and social continuity (Diamond 1951; Gailey 1985a; 1985b). The development of historical civilizations has involved the restriction of rights to use so-called subsistence resources such as land, products needed for maintaining the producers, or labor needed for subsistence. This restriction of use-rights, which can take many forms, is connected with the imposition of occupational specialization and class formation (Thompson 1975). Most precapitalist states were not characterized by widespread private property; instead, the use of resources was made contingent upon payment of taxes in kind, labor, or cash.

The argument here is that state formation embodies an instrumental logic, but states are not rational. As statescraft approaches instrumental rationality, it approaches maximum repression of human potential, totalitarianism in the structural, not the Cold War, sense.

Complete bureaucratic rationality, if possible, would reduce the human to his or her labor power, anticipated in the cooperation between state and private industry in organizing forced labor and extermination in Nazi concentration camps.

In precapitalist states, such bureaucratic rationality is minimal: the institutionalization of forced extraction of goods and services creates ecological disasters, demographic and social dislocations, that cannot be resolved through techniques of rulership because they originate from the interests of particular nonproducing elites in preserving the conditions that brought about the conflicts and disjunctures. What appears as stability or prosperity is at some points volatile and at others merely repressive. Productivity may increase—fueling civil projects or the expansion of state borders—at the same time as the local standard of living may decrease. Alternatively, the standard of living for those in the heartland may increase, but at the expense of those more recently annexed or captured, or of local autonomy.

The *state*, then, represents a rough, crisis-ridden series of institutional mediations between producers, on the one hand, and those who benefit from the forcible extraction of goods and labor, on the other. The mediating institutions aim at containing discontent while ensuring the continuance of a class structure, although not necessarily the existing class structure. The state cannot provide a long-lasting resolution to the disruptions created from the extraction process, because it would challenge the very basis on which the state institutions and functionaries depend. Most theories of the state ignore this dynamic; they adopt the rationale of rulership, namely, that the state is crucial for orderly social progress.

Critical and Marxist Perspectives

The analysis of state formation offered in this volume fits into the Marxist dialectical tradition (Diamond 1975). The historical emergence of exploitation and the possibilities for redressing oppression have been an aspect of theories of the state in the critical tradition since Montaigne and, especially, Rousseau. The work of Marx and Engels in the nineteenth century drew such observations into social analysis.

In the mid-nineteenth century, a critic of United States policy toward American Indian peoples, Lewis Henry Morgan, postulated an origin for the state in the trade-based institution of private property (Morgan 1877/1964). He also stressed that the emergence of private property spelled the demise of the "gens" or kin group, and of kinship society in general, and identified this replacement with the origins of exploitative relations. Morgan was not a Marxist. But his *Ancient Society* heavily influenced Engels' theory of state origins, Marx's work on the so-called Asiatic, and other precapitalist state societies (Engels 1884/1972; Marx 1858/1964; 1881/1974). The political reaction of social theorists in the United States against Morgan and the Marxist adoption of his fundamental point—that exploitation is historical, not natural, and that state formation is oppressive to producing people—continues to characterize much U.S. anthropological research into state origins.

Robert Harry Lowie headed the liberal reaction in his attack on Morgan (1927). The state, he argued, was implicit in all human societies. In primitive societies one could find private property, classes, government, legal codes, and the other features considered by Morgan (as well as Maine and Tylor) to be particular to state societies. In a monumental effort to discredit Morgan's evolutionism—which can be accomplished without assailing his appreciation of the distinctiveness of kin-based societies—Lowie managed to confuse property with possessions, custom with law, rank with both status and class.[2] Lowie's work on the state has been relegated to a rather deserved obscurity. But in one way or another, the conceptual muddle he introduced still plagues anthropological research into class and state formation.

Scholars in the Marxist tradition continued to refine this early research into the origins of the state. During the McCarthy era in the United States, and before the Soviet and other denunciations of Stalin, there were few U.S. anthropologists in the Marxist tradition who were not also functionalists or linear evolutionists. While V. Gordon Childe—one of the more subtle of the archaeologists—assumed that state formation was fundamentally progressive, he also stressed the oppressive and exploitative consequences of the "rise of the state" for the producing populations (Childe 1951a; 1951b; 1952). This progressivism was, at base, in keeping with the positivist and nondialectical character of Western social science. Stanley Diamond and Eleanor Leacock stand out as exceptions to this nondialectical tendency. Diamond's dissertation on Dahomey focused on the dialectics of state formation (Diamond 1951). Leacock's work on the fur trade and the Montagnais-Naskapi peoples considered the related process of commoditization and its impact on kinship, use-rights to resources, and gender relations (Leacock 1954).

Since the mid-1960's, and especially since the end of the Vietnam War, there has been a proliferation of Marxist research into state origins. In the United States, Great Britain, France, Eastern Europe, the

Soviet Union, and elsewhere, Marxist scholars have reformulated questions about state origins.[3] The feminist movement has provided a needed corrective in its stress on gender in stratification,[4] as has been shown. Nevertheless, the work integrating gender—one of the pivotal dimensions of the division of labor in all precapitalist societies—continues to be marginal to the Marxist (and other) state formation literature. The present work is intended to show how state formation cannot be analyzed clearly without focus on the intricacies of gender as central in the shift from a kin-defined to a class-based division of labor.

There remains a great debt, sometimes unrecognized, to Engels, as Leacock points out (1972). Engels relied heavily on Morgan's *Ancient Society*, and both scholars' work has been criticized in the light of better ethnographic, ethnohistorical, and archaeological information available today. Engels' search for an ultimate cause for the state ended in "greed." But despite this reductionist tendency, Engels outlined major areas for investigation and provided valuable insights into state formative processes. For instance, he associated conquest with domestic repression as part and parcel of what Darcy Ribeiro would later call the "civilization process" (1968). Engels also noted that urbanization and the opposed interests of town and countryside developed with state formation. Although later studies have documented the existence of "stateless" cities (see Kohl and Wright 1977), the opposition of urban and rural areas in state contexts has been amply documented. Engels identified the development of a nonproducing class involved in commodity exchange with the first institutionalized exploitation.[5] Engels also—and the Marxist tradition is unique in exploring this point—proposed that the systematic oppression of women appeared with state formation.

Perhaps most important, he perceived that institutional exploitation *has a history*, that is, exploitation is not timeless, and thus it is not natural. For exploitation to emerge, kin-based relations of work, distribution, and consumption—i.e., the relations of production—must be subordinated to class relations, a point Engels took from Morgan. Further, this new, class-based division of labor must be politically imposed, since it contradicts decisions based upon custom and consensus. Later ethnohistorical and archaeological research supports many of his contentions: the control of redistribution—through storage, transportation, marketplaces, etc.—is linked to the development of exploitation; political authority accompanies changes in the relations of production from kinship- to class-based; and state institutions attempt to legitimate and protect the interests of at least one class that has no functional kin ties with the producing class(es).

Recent works have discarded the functionalism or unilinear evolutionism found in most of the earlier Marxist literature. For example, necessary, directional change from kinship to class and class to state—implicit in Engels—has been abandoned. The notion of progress as applied to the development of state institutions—and backwardness as applied to kinship or "primitive" societies—has been criticized in many of the works (e.g., Diamond 1974). Crude materialism of the sort practiced by Karl Wittfogel (1957) or Marvin Harris (1974) also has been repudiated empirically and theoretically (Friedman 1974; Nonini 1985). The recent scholarship is more attuned to the importance of the symbolic—of cultural forms and meanings—in both class formation and resistance to the emergence of state structures (Abélès 1981; Bonte 1981). Most have emphasized process rather than inevitability in the emergence of classes and state institutions (Maretina 1978). Debates have developed over the nature of inequalities in kin-based societies, the role of kin groups in class formation, and the role of indigenous, precapitalist class relations in colonial and capital penetration.[6] What has been retained is the reason for social analysis, namely, to inform efforts to eliminate forms of exploitation. The basic analytical categories have been retained and refined: mode of production, social formation, and the relations and means of production.

Precapitalist Modes of Production

The concept *mode of production* is an abstraction that expresses the relationships between the organization of property and work, on the one hand, and the material conditions in which production, distribution, and consumption take place, on the other (Gailey and Patterson in press). The concept has the utility of being parsimonious: relatively few modes of production have existed historically. The concept also provides a basis for evaluating parallels and differences among societies removed in time and space: comparative and historical research is facilitated.

The first and most prevalent mode of production in the precapitalist world has been the communal mode. In this mode, property needed for subsistence production is held in common by people self-identified as kin through blood, marriage, or adoption. Production is for use, that is, for maintenance of the group through time, whether or not this involves exchanges with outsiders. Use-rights and labor claims are obtained through a combination of one's gender, age or life status, and kin connection, including rank in some cases. Labor, authority, and leadership are also divided along these lines. There may be significant status differentials, but no real exploitation exists, because every person, by reason of his or her membership in the resource-holding group, has the right to subsist. Wealth differences also may exist, but classes do not, since wealth does not entitle one to deny another the products or labor needed to subsist. There are variants of the communal mode that develop in response to either proximity to state societies or penetration by capital (Gailey and Patterson in press): they have been called the Germanic mode (after the Germanic tribes on the periphery of the Roman empire) and the lineage mode of production (Meillassoux 1975; cf. Hobsbawm 1964).

The most widespread form of precapitalist class society was identified by Marx as the Asiatic mode of production, because the examples at the time were from India and China (1858/1964; 1881/1974). In recent years the term has been corrected for its inappropriate emphasis on geography rather than internal structure; Samir Amin called it a tribute-paying mode of production (1976). In fact, most precapitalist state societies had this mode. The state claimed the land, and peasants had to pay taxes to continue using their hereditary lands (Krader 1975). The dominant form of tribute extracted from the peasantry was tax-rent (Skalník 1981:348). In Tonga and many other state formative situations, labor service as well as "in-kind" and cash tax-rents were extracted (Gailey 1980; cf. Van Binsbergen and Geschiere, eds. 1985).

In tribute-based state societies, the dominant classes depend for their sustenance on goods and services extracted directly from local communities that remain, for the most part, organized through kinship relations. These kin groups may be agglomerated into villages or, as in Tonga, reside in dispersed hamlets throughout a region. The social formation would include the kin communities, the emerging classes, the means of tribute extraction and of subsistence production, and the institutions that help to reproduce the entire set of relations.

Production in this setting is bifurcate, and the mutually antagonistic spheres are linked ultimately through the threat of force. Some production is destined for a civil sphere and the support of nonproducers. The nonproducers include the rulers, their kin, retainers, attendants, and so on. In some cases, where state control is more consolidated, the peasants' production also supports craftworkers attached in service to the elite. The degree to which production is organized apart from the kin communities, as through regional corvée along gender and age lines, indicates the relative strength of the state structures. The other type of production remains oriented to the maintenance of kin communities, and accomplished through kinship relations. Tribute production depends largely upon the way kin communities organize work. But the continuation—in some cases the survival—of kin communities is subordinated to the requirements of the state-associated classes. Where the institutions of repression and extraction are stronger, crises in production can result in famines for those who are not allied with the state classes, as happened periodically in precapitalist China (Skinner 1971).

Kin communities and kinship relations remain necessary for the production of the "surplus" goods and labor used to support the emerging class structure.[7] So the partial persistence of a communal mode of production is necessary for the continuity of class relations. But the communal mode of production is subordinated to tribute production for the civil sphere. In the process of encapsulation, the content of kinship relations within the producing communities changes, since kin relations no longer can organize the creation and reproduction of an autonomous way of life. In cases where the state institutions that ensure the tribute extraction do not fall apart, there is a tendency for commodity production to develop in some degree; where it does emerge, kin relations are dissolved further (Krader 1975; Claessen and Skalník, eds. 1981).

The second major precapitalist mode of production involving class relations is slave-based, and is known to us through ancient Greek city-states and the Roman Empire (G. Thomson 1949; 1955). The use of war captives and unsuccessfully rebellious peoples to produce goods and perform services for dominant classes is not restricted to these states, of course. What is unique is how much of the food and other necessities was produced through such captive labor.

There is a tendency for this type of slavery to shift from a temporary to a hereditary status, or for the slaves to become commodities. The possibilities for change are different from the dynamics of tribute-based states, but slaves can be transformed into peasants where the state penetration is weaker. The difference is that the kin communities of tributary modes retain possession of the lands, although the sovereign claims rights to tax-rents by virtue of an asserted overall ownership. There is no such hereditary connection between slaves and the soil they till.

The citizenry in slave-based social formations as a rule is taxed little; conscription into military forces is a form of labor service associated with this kind of state society. Often, citizens become urban populations, supporting themselves through slave production in rural and urban areas, and goods acquired through taxation and raiding abroad. Generally, there is at least some tribute extraction from the citizenry, but this tends to be less than the extraction from conquered provinces. The Roman Empire, for example, represents a slave-based mode of production at home; in the provinces, slavery was combined with tribute-paying by the conquered, noncitizen communities. The dynamics with regard to gender relations and women's status vary (Pomeroy 1976), depending on the disjunctures between the modes of production and the relative strength of the kin communities.

Where states emerge out of kin-based societies, or where an expanding state or political economy comes to dominate others, a new social formation also develops. The concept *social formation* refers to one or more societies and their modes of production, absorbed into an overarching political and economic structure in which one of the modes is dominant. In the case of a state emerging out of a kin-based setting, the resulting social formation would include both a communal and a tribute-paying mode of production, the means of linking the modes of production, and the ideological structures that serve to encourage the reproduction of class relations. If the state society is reproduced, the communal mode is encapsulated and subordinated to the tribute-paying mode. In other words, to survive, the direct producers must pay tax-rents regardless of kin-based obligations. Since state formation prevents the continuity of a way of life—the culture of the kin communities that once were autonomous—the process is ethnocidal (Gailey 1985b).

Uneven Development and Articulation

The anticolonial movements of the postwar period, the promotion of "economic development" and the impact of multinational corporations on neocolonial countries have prompted efforts to understand the relationship of an imposed, global capitalist market and precapitalist relations of production (e.g., Banaji 1972; 1977). Louis Althusser proposed that capitalist and precapitalist modes of production can coexist in an antagonistic way in colonial and neocolonial situations (Althusser 1969). The capitalist mode of production will be dominant, but others can persist to aid in the reproduction of the political economy as constituted; Althusser called this antagonistic coexistence *articulation* (see also Rey 1973; Van Binsbergen and Geschiere, eds. 1985; Levine 1981). The concept is useful with regard to societies such as Tonga, where relations today are neither fully capitalist nor distinctively kin-based.

"Modernization" or industrialization in the neocolonial world did not involve a uniform shift to capitalist relations of property or labor. Amin called the process through which economic sectors with various types of property and production relations emerged and were reproduced *unequal development.* The absence of a complete transition to a capitalist economy required more nuanced explanations than "traditional conservatism" or "cultural differences" (Amin 1976). Analyzing the reasons for precolonial political and economic relations that were used within a dominant capitalist sphere revived interest in precapitalist modes of production (Marx 1858/1964; Hindess and Hirst 1975; Terray 1972).

The questions that remain require empirical research, since modes of production and social formations are expressed in given historical cases. How do different, antagonistic modes of production become articulated, and why do the ways they are joined take the form they do? How are the social relations that organize work and the replication of the society altered in situations of capital penetration *apart from* direct colonization? The questions posed have importance for understanding the range of resistance movements throughout the neocolonial world.

State and Class Formation

One of the unifying concerns in the recent wave of Marxist scholarship has been class and state formation. The recent studies are more empirically grounded than the earlier, stagial works. They use archaeological, ethnohistorical, and ethnographic data to document the structural antagonisms and human actions that shape the emergence of class, the consolidation or obviation of state institutions. One of the first examples of this sort of dialectical analysis is Diamond's work on precolonial Dahomey (1951).

Diamond stressed the long-term struggle between kin-ordered communities and an emerging civil authority, which he termed *kin/civil conflict* (Diamond 1951). The civil authority attempted to redefine the functions of kinship while using the idiom of kinship as legitimation. At the same time, when customary kin forms were rendered ineffective, local kin groups devised alternative forms which, as much as conditions allowed, fulfilled the responsibilities of the earlier kin connections. The society-wide struggle between kin groups and the central administration was not armed, in this case, but each institution of the kinship society and the emerging civil structure was involved. His creation of the term "proto-state" to describe the Dahomey situation reflects the concern for state formation as an inconclusive process.

The question arises, do states that develop out of kinship societies differ from those that emerge out of other state societies, and, if so, how and why? Morton Fried made a distinction between "pristine" and "secondary" states (1967:231–242). He considered only those states that emerged in the absence of other states as "pristine"; all other state societies developed, in one manner or another—conquest, colonization, reconstruction—in relation to other state societies. Fried's pristine and secondary distinction, like his definition of stratification, has been adopted by most American anthropologists concerned with state origins. The implicit argument, that the historical context of state formation influences the character of social relations, is vital. But his categories draw attention away from the kin/civil struggle.

A distinction can be made between state societies that develop out of preexisting, usually precapitalist, class and civil relations, and those which involve the development of class relations *for the first time*. In the latter instances—and there have been few in the absence of colonization—all institutions and relations are called into question (see Diamond 1951; Rapp 1978a). There is a profound complexity in the type of resistance and the forms of symbolic mediation that characterize situations where the kin communities are challenged for the first time, whether this occurs under colonial pressure or autochthonously. Thus, some "secondary" state formation is more similar to "pristine" situations than to situations where one set of state institutions replaces or is imposed upon the ruins of a previous state and class society.

For example, the imposition of colonial rule in British India demanded a shift in the class structure from that of the precapitalist Hindu and Buddhist state societies. The precapitalist mediations of class, such as caste and religious ideology in general, had to be redefined to fit the new form of class and state relations (Cohn 1981). Yet, disruptive and destructive as these impositions were, kin relations in the precolonial period has been only one sphere in societies that included systematic extraction of goods and labor from peasants and artisans. Far more brutal was the British conquest and forcible annexation of those peoples who had avoided incorporation into the precapitalist states (e.g., Maretina 1978).

"Secondary" state formation such as that in Tonga entails the processes discussed above. One can trace the partial dissolution or encapsulation of kin relations; the imposition of a political division of labor; the development of class relations; the creation and siphoning of social product and labor to support nonproducing, but dominant, ruling, administrative, and landlord classes. In Tonga, the process was catalyzed by merchants' capital and the introduction of Christian ideology. However, the transformations of kinship, the subsistence-oriented sphere—that is, the surviving communal mode of production—are comparable to situations of other state societies developing out of kin relations.

The crucial issue is the character of a social formation created through efforts, on the one hand, to generate and extract a surplus and, on the other hand, to continue kin-organized relations of production, distribution and consumption. These efforts may eventuate, and did in the Tongan case, in the emergence of a new mode of production alongside, and inimical to, the continuation of a kinship-based order. In Tonga, the communal mode of production persisted, but it was encapsulated and dominated by new class relations and the necessity of providing surplus products and labor. The insertion of the islands into a capitalist market subordinated an emerging, tribute-based mode of production to the requirements of the overarching capitalist relations. In the development and maintenance of tribute extraction from kin communities, Tonga is comparable to other precapitalist, tribute-based state societies. In the subordination of a tribute-based mode of production to the needs of a capitalist system, Tonga is comparable to other colonial and neocolonial societies (see Banaji 1972; 1977; Lonsdale 1981).

The extent and depth of transformation is profound in societies where class relations were only a potentiality, as in Tonga in the later eighteenth century. State formation in Tonga involved a double transformation: a shift from kinship to class relations, and a partial shift from communal and tributary modes of production to a capitalist one.

The brittle accommodation between political authorities and kin communities can be seen also in the proto-states of precolonial West Africa. Emmanuel Terray describes the transformation of nonclass, domestic slavery into class relations to support an emerging ruling class in the Abron kingdom of Gyaman (Terray 1979a). In my interpretation, the local kin communities were too powerful for sufficient surplus to be extracted to support a civil sphere. The accommodation lay in the conscription of local kinspeople for the annual slave raids needed to reproduce the class relations. The unique form of the state in this case derives from the articulation of kinship, tribute-paying, and slave modes of production—and the emergence of the latter two derived from the resistance of the kin communities and the internal tensions of the emerging state classes.

Silverblatt's studies of Inca transformations of Andean gender relations document the manipulation of Andean kinship forms by the conquering Inca state classes (Silverblatt 1978; 1980; 1987). Prior to the Inca takeover, Andean ranking systems reordered intercommunity relations following warfare. The "conquest hierarchy" rewarded victorious people with prestige, but no claims to the defeated group's lands, labor, or women apart from the traditional claims of kinship. The Inca redefined this hierarchy to include claims to resources and to women and men. Inca state ideology is shown to have differently affected women in peasant, artisan, and elite sectors. The studies also analyze opposed ideologies and interests of local Andean groups and the Inca elite, and of women and men within the Inca elite. Silverblatt points out inconsistencies in state ideology: Inca notions of "sexual parallelism" in status and authority contradicted male importance in the "conquest hierarchy." The Inca also actively fostered ambivalence in local communities toward the extraction of tribute, especially the tribute in young women. The young women selected for service to the state as *aclla* were permanently alienated from their natal communities and lost control over their reproductive potential, but they were highly honored in their state-associated roles.

In focusing on process and shifts in the content of cultural forms, each of these analyses implicitly criticizes structuralist definitions of cultural meaning and opposition in precapitalist state societies (cf. Geertz 1980; Sahlins 1976; 1981; see also Leacock 1981). The fundamental and oppressive changes in social relations during state formation can be analyzed only if one accepts that symbols can change in meaning over time and can have contradictory meanings for structurally opposed groups during any particular time. Forms may remain the same, but their substance or functions change in the political struggle. By the same token, the emerging state classes may create new institutions or forms to mediate the conflict, as occurred with the creation of widespread slavery in precolonial Gyaman (Terray 1979a). Correlatively, local kin groups may create new forms in an attempt to conserve the content of productive and reproductive relations that have been trivialized, coopted, or made illegal in their customary forms. The Tongan case embodies the full range of these cultural, social, political, and economic conflicts.

Resistance

There is another side to the ethnocide inherent in state formation, namely, *ethnogenesis,* a concept originating in Diamond's work (1970; see also Sider 1976; cf. Gailey 1985b). Ethnogenesis is one possible consequence of resistance. Groups forcibly integrated into expanding state societies generally experience, over time, class formation within their communities. Peoples who have come from different cultures originally may come to share a historical experience of oppression, and a new people may emerge from this new condition. The meanings created by people to make sense of their shared condition of life and the shared resistance to domination can become the basis for a critique of the dominant society and its values and the forging of a new culture. Such movements may, of course, be defeated; but the process can be documented in virtually every known state society. We know little of this process, in part because the prevailing imagery of state societies is that of omnipotence or inevitability, and in part because of the fear or despair of profound social change—rooted in a mistrust of the producing classes—found among so many scholars of all political persuasions.

Resistance is chronic and sustained in state formation, but one has to look beyond armed conflict. Little attention has been focused outside the Marxist tradition on the role of popular or peasant resistance. But resistance as a process is crucial in the limitation of power in the face of customary authority. The relative success of producing people's resistance determines, in part, the content of class relations, the degree and means of state penetration, and the relative autonomy of the peasant community.

The bias toward state institutions as progressive[8] has converted the producing classes—predominantly peasants in precapitalist states—into those who largely adopt, or are complicit in, the dominant values of the state society. Some writers have ignored that such aspects of a state ideology generally reflect the interests of the ruling class(es). Others, like Robert Redfield, accord the peasantry, the "folk society," a role in creating culture—the "little tradition." But Redfield tended to neutralize the need for the dominant classes to use the kin-associated symbolic universe in the forging of a state ideology (1971). No ruling class can maintain itself indefinitely by force alone. Coercion is omnipresent as an assertion or a threat, but attempts are made to defuse resistance or deflect community hostility by the adoption of customary forms while redefining their content.

State ideologies promote concepts of rulership as essential to prosperity and social hierarchy as legitimate. These assertions, in the form of religious or other propaganda, have frequently been assumed to reflect the cosmology of the society as a whole. Clifford Geertz in particular seems to assume a shared cultural code between ruler and ruled (1980). One of the hallmarks of the recent Marxist scholarship is attention to changing meaning, as seen in ritual, belief structures, and world views. Ideas are not causative in these works; they are dialectically related to the relations of production and reproduction; but the authors avoid the reduction of meaning to political and economic structures (e.g. Abélès 1981; Bonte 1981).

In contrast to the few symbolic or structuralist anthropologists who have written about the state (Geertz 1980; Sahlins 1981), Marxist scholars do not divorce the world of meaning from the world of everyday endeavors. Also unlike the symbolic and structuralist researchers, they do not (in most cases) take the position of the elite (Gailey 1983). Instead, in their works the cosmologies and ideologies promoted by the state or state classes are compared and contrasted with local "traditions" that emerge alongside and in opposition to them. Of course, there is some shared meaning, but the Marxist analyses emphasize disjunctures, arenas of disputed meaning.

The symbolic order promoted in state ceremonials is derived from customary images of the universe, but the forms are decanted of the range of ambiguous meanings typical of a kin context. The forms are made to serve political ends: they become dichotomies, hierarchies, immutable. But, fortunately for the possibilities of social change, this symbolic universe is an assertion from the top, only partially adopted by the peasantry.[9] Accelerations of ritual events generally mark a relatively powerless center—the symbolic, class-based order must be enacted again and again: it reveals how little the model was part of the local consciousness, or at least, affected local action (cf. Gailey 1983). Such elaboration would not be needed for reproduction otherwise, regardless of cognitive structures in the elite classes.

In the Marxist tradition, meaning is considered as socially constituted out of human action in given circumstances—thus mutable and irreducible. People *make sense* out of lived-through reality; cultural meanings are continuously created (cf. Radin 1971; 1973; Diamond 1974). The "common sense" may not reflect the relationships that underlie the empirical reality. But the understanding may be transformed into what Antonio Gramsci called "good sense," that is, awareness of the social reality, complete with internal contradictions (1971). The transformation may be effected, for instance, through engagement in attempts to preserve or ameliorate everyday conditions.

The meanings created through direct involvement in the world are denied in the symbolic and structuralist formulations.

Gramsci, among others, has provided ways of conceptualizing both resistance and the partial adoption of dominant explanations for the social order. The hegemony of civil society he characterizes as:

> The "spontaneous" consent given by the great masses of the population to the general direction imposed on social life by the dominant fundamental group; this consent is "historically" caused by the prestige (and consequent confidence) which the dominant group enjoys because of its position and function in the world of production. (1971:12)

But this hegemony should not be confused with isomorphic belief systems or institutional stability. For behind the pervasive ideology, the promotion of certain beliefs as "common sense," there is the repressive power of state institutions. The state

> "legally" enforces discipline on those groups who do not "consent" either actively or passively. This [state] apparatus is, however, constituted for the whole society in anticipation of moments of crisis of command and direction when spontaneous consent has failed. (Ibid.)

The successful penetration of hegemonic structures into academic halls of this society has resulted in the assumption by some researchers that written accounts from precapitalist civilizations— almost uniquely sponsored by the ruling class—are, in fact, the history of the state or the society. For example, it remains "common knowledge" that the Great Wall in China was built (through corvée and slave labor) to keep marauding tribal nomads out of the "Middle Kingdom" (see, e.g., *New York Times*, July 24, 1984: C1). Owen Lattimore, however, pointed out that peasants could not flee the more institutionalized depredations of state tax collectors after the wall prevented them from returning to a nomadic life (1937/1962). Lattimore's thesis has not been discredited, and yet the "marauding barbarian" imagery continues to prevail.

The revolutionary role of the peasantry has been analytically resurrected, primarily because the major revolutionary movements in the twentieth century have been in predominantly agrarian societies that, prior to colonial pressures, were characterized by such class and state relations.[10] Armed struggle between local, kin-identified groups and state-associated classes has been documented, primarily through the interested lens of state documents. Archaeologists have unearthed few examples of violent struggle, at least of the sort that would leave traces centuries later. Where these are apparent, conquest is invoked as an explanation, rather than insurrection or a combination. The Mayan case, where state buildings were burnt, posed a "mystery" for many years.[11] Recent archaeological research has indicated the existence of an extensive irrigation system in the area that had been "abandoned" for less intensive cultivation, at approximately the same time as were the ceremonial centers (*New York Times*, June 1980). When the Spanish arrived, the Mayan were swidden agriculturists living in dispersed hamlets throughout the region.

The history of passive resistance to state penetration rarely is addressed as a form of struggle (but see Bodley 1982; Scott 1985). It is uncommon for communities impressed into state societies to abandon efforts to deceive and manipulate state agents, even when active resistance has been crushed (see Hobsbawm 1959). The evasion of surplus production and the avoidance of yielding goods, labor, or information—as in census-taking—is widely recognized in slave or peasant societies. Indeed, one can see similar forms of evasion in contemporary capitalist countries, on the part of working-class people at home and at the workplace.

The use of direct and indirect forms of terrorism by the state representatives can be seen as indirect evidence of chronic community resistance. In Dahomey, for instance, in exchange for tolls and marketplace fees, travelers were promised safe conduct. The need for state "protection" was created through the deployment of state-sponsored goons (Diamond 1951). The Aztecs punished defeated rebels through massive public human sacrifices to the god of conquest. Overt conflict in extracting products or labor can be documented. Pierre Philippe Rey cites Bazin's work on the Segou kingdom in precolonial West Africa:

> . . . the central state could only extract surplus from the villages by waging constant war against the village communities, even those which were in the center of the kingdom. (Rey 1979:49)

Resistance also can be seen in the necessity for *indirect* forms of surplus extraction in place of or alongside taxation and labor service. The proliferation of tithing or propitiations to state-sponsored deities can be viewed as indirect taxation; other forms may include tolls, court fees, fines, and so on. Kin/civil conflict includes, on the part of political authorities, attempts to coopt local authorities or entire kin groups.

Conversely, local communities periodically take advantage of divisiveness among the state-associated classes. Local communities have been known to support pretenders or rival claimants to state positions. Potential conquerors also have attracted popular support (viz. Cortés). The peasantry in these cases has been viewed as ignorant or blind to their own interests. Alternatively, the people are seen as having been dragooned or merely expected to participate in the warfare. In many cases, this is certainly true. But other, perhaps concomitant possibilities often are not considered. For example, if contention is successful, the burden on communities might be lighter, even if central control persists. Wars of succession may significantly weaken or even destroy central control. The "traitorous" Indian support for Cortés—including that of La Malinche, his indigenous consort, guide, and advisor, and regardless of the eventual result—must be seen as popular resistance to Aztec rule. Similarly, in a feudal structure, the peasant support for Alexander Nevsky was a move against the Russian landed nobility.

The results of this kin/civil conflict are not predictable and still are unresolved. In precapitalist state societies, the accommodation of peasants to state and class structures is incomplete, contingent, and not what any of the parties intended, even where surplus extraction has been institutionalized for hundreds of years. In fact, kin relations still have not been dissolved completely, even in capitalist society: there remain sectors of generalized reciprocity, pooling of resources, and anti-civil action, even in ostensibly quiet times (Stack 1974; Susser 1982).

The periodic explosion of such tensions, the baring of the lie of peaceful accommodation, has sometimes meant the demise of civil authority. Precolonial highland Burma showed an almost cyclical pattern of imposition of political control and uprisings that broke Shan state incorporation of Kachin communities (Leach 1954). Such an occurrence typically is masked in mainstream presentations through neutral or progressivist phrases that anticipate the reemergence of state structures. Thus, the collapse of the archaic Egyptian state through elite-led peasant rebellions or popularly supported invasions is termed a "period of local reintegration" in the New York Metropolitan Museum of Art. If the emperor is stripped of his clothes, it becomes an interregnum rather than a revolt. The realized potential for kin-ordered communities to reassert their autonomy is obscured.

State formation emerging out of a kin-based society is a continuing struggle between the encapsulated communities and the civil authorities over control, on the one hand, of property, relations of work, distribution, and consumption and, on the other hand, of the conditions of social and cultural continuity. There are no given outcomes, but the relationship between property, work, reproduction, and the generation of meaning are called into question. Where class relations do emerge, and where institutions develop to effect their reproduction, the consequences for the communal division of labor by gender, life status, and kin role are profoundly deleterious. Their forms may be retained, but the control and authority conveyed by those dimensions of kin-based personhood are not.

PART TWO

Gender and Kinship Relations in Precontact Tonga

3. Authority and Ambiguity: Rethinking Tongan Kinship

Edward Winslow Gifford
(1929:90)

In Tonga, a woman is always the highest chief.

IN PRECONTACT Tonga, contradictions between the descent scheme and sibling-linked rank, coupled with shifting marriage arrangements, prevented any permanent political hierarchy. Succession to chiefly title—and consequently, to the labor and products of lower-ranking people—depended upon the social recognition of hereditary rank. While this seems ascriptive and rigid, in fact ranking principles created ambiguity. So long as rank remained ambiguous and claims to labor and products remained linked to rank, movements by the highest-ranking chiefly kin groups to redefine customary relations between themselves and lower-ranking people could not remain unified or effective for any significant period.

All Tongans were ranked according to three inconsistent relations of superiority and inferiority. The relations were not reducible, nor were the three considerations internally ranked. Older was superior to younger; maleness was superior to femaleness; sisterhood was superior to brotherhood. "Older" as a category included genealogical as well as chronological age. Maleness and femaleness were sex categories which did not reflect the relationship of men to women: for instance, the male side of a canoe was superior to the female side, but higher-ranking women sat on the male side.

It seems clear from the three principles that no one's status could be determined solely on the basis of gender—or any other single factor—since one's sibling's gender and seniority were just as important. These complexities of rank make any association of "sacredness" or "profanity" with gender or age impossible in Tonga, in contrast to some characterizations of Polynesian kinship. In Tonga, as could be shown in other ranked, kinship-based societies, the principles of ranking were inherently inconsistent—it is not simply one researcher's attempt to avoid the difficult work of reducing three terms to two. Structuralist interpretations of Polynesian kinship emphasize binary oppositions and reduce the three sets of relations to two (e.g., Sahlins 1981; Ortner 1981); in reducing the complexity, they convert a historical process into a categorical scheme (Gailey 1983). In precontact Tonga, the context of particular relationships, rather than any abstract factor, determined personal status. Contradictory ranking principles created a situation where claims to others' labor had to be justified through the establishment of higher rank in the eyes of the society. This process demanded the exchange of valuables—made by women and in their control. Permanent hierarchical relations of production, including distribution and consumption, between kin groups were effectively thwarted by the intersection of women's productive and reproductive roles.

Rank provided the basis for contention for chiefly title. But the ambiguity created through the ranking system provided grounds for a number of chiefly kin to contend for title. Irving Goldman presents this ambiguity and contention as "status rivalry" (1970). He excludes chiefly women from the contention as representing instead—or being intergenerational conduits of—high rank and honor. Ortner has adopted Goldman's formulation in her structuralist interpretation of gender in "hierarchical societies" such as Tonga (1981). The split between high rank and social authority was a potentiality in precontact Tonga—certainly tensions are evident, and in retrospect the split appears as incipient, because it did occur. But the argument here is that women were directly involved in the contention; their engagement, as well as men's, derived from the cross-cutting ranking principles.

All relationships were charged with unequal authority, but the network of relationships left much room for maneuvering and, thus, a considerable degree of personal autonomy. For example, although wives were supposed to defer to husbands, sisters had authority over their brothers; because of this connection, a wife could obtain something requested by her spouse from one of her brothers' wives or her own lower-ranking sisters. Similarly, although chiefly men were supposed to hold titles and discharge administrative functions, the rank which justified a man's title-holding was inherited through his mother, and was inferior to that of his sisters and their sons (Mariner 1827 : 1 : 89). Rather than impose a post hoc regularity onto the precontact society, the focus here is on the reasons for both flexible authority and stratified kin relations in the prestate society (Gailey 1980; Urbanowicz 1979). Kin-based ranking legitimized social authority, but the ranking was structured in an ambiguous or contradictory fashion.

The ambiguity of status in stratified kinship societies such as Tonga derives from the contradictions within kin-based ranking, coupled with the partial juxtaposition of rank and social authority. For example, it was debatable whether the children of a junior-born sister were less chiefly than those of a senior-born brother. Most people in Tonga bore the rank of their mothers, but how the rank of each mother was determined left considerable room for interpretation.

Kinship-Based Stratification

Tongan kinship in the precontact period has been characterized as a conical clan (Kirchhoff 1959; Sahlins 1958), a pyramidal ramage (Gifford 1929; Firth 1968), or a status lineage (Goldman 1970). While each of these models addresses aspects of ambiguity in kinship ranking, particularly the indeterminacy of hierarchies in chieftainships, all tend to overlook or dismiss the strategic importance of women in the re-creation of such ambiguity. Each tends to overemphasize patrilineal considerations in rank and descent. Even Goldman, whose formulation is otherwise extremely valuable,[1] does not discuss the involvement of women, as sisters especially, in rivalries within the chiefly ranks. Yet the pivotal position of women, inherent in the principles of kinship ranking, effectively prevented the transformation of Tongan society from kin-based to class-based prior to European intervention.

In the precontact period, people were ranked both personally and collectively. As has been noted throughout Polynesia, in Tonga every person was ranked vis-à-vis every other person: there were no "equal" statuses (see, e.g., Sahlins 1958). These inequalities of rank gave the higher-ranking person claims to the lower-ranking person's labor or products, at least in that context. In addition to this personal ranking, there were two overarching, relatively ranked strata, which I have called chiefly and nonchiefly.

The intricacies of Tongan kinship have been discussed at length by anthropologists,[2] as has Polynesian kinship in general.[3] Irrespective of the characterization of the kin structure as a pyramidal ramage, conical clan, status lineage, patrilineal, ambilineal, etc., all versions draw from certain verbalized characterizations by Tongans of their kin structure. Tongans saw themselves, in one of the origin myths, as one great clan descended from a trio of earthly brothers and godly and earthly women (Mariner 1827:2:353; see also pp. 84, 100).

Tongan people were ranked according to their closeness to a common ancestor, with preference given to patrilineal primogeniture, at least among chiefly kin groups (cf. Korn 1974). A diagram of the "ideal type" of pyramidal ramage or conical clan is shown in Figure 2. Most of the ethnographers have considered ties through mothers as necessary but "second best" (e.g., Goldman 1970:293), with the exception of Shulamit Dector Korn, who argues that matrilineal ties still figure large today (1974; cf. Marcus 1977a). Inheritance, especially of chiefly titles, is supposed to have passed from father to eldest son, although Marshall Sahlins and Goldman have discussed the vagaries of such ranking and inheritance with regard to high-ranking men (Sahlins 1958; 1963; Goldman 1970). Here the problem lies in periodization and sources of data. Edward Winslow Gifford (1929), who first proposed the existence of named, chiefly patrilineages (as he characterized what Tongans call the *ha'a* or "houses") drew much of his information from those chiefly people who had become part of the Tongan nobility (*nōpele*) in the early twentieth century.[4] Patrilineal primogeniture had been made the legal form of inheritance by this emerging noble class.

I suspect that much of the *patrilateral* bias in precontact Tongan kinship has been converted into patrilineality to support claims that the new nobility represents Tongan tradition. The succession disputes in modern Tonga center on the legal interpretation of precontact kinship (Marcus 1977a; 1977b); these kin relations have become more rigid in the new purpose to which they are put. Charles Urbanowicz, in contrast to Gifford, considers the term *ha'a* to refer to broader kin groups than patrilineages, at least in the precontact period. They were created at the point when the male sacred paramount chief (Tu'i Tonga)

> divided his lands between his kinsmen, his *'eiki* [people of chiefly rank, whether titled or not]. The various *'eiki* established and belonged to their own named groups of *'eiki* or *Ha'a*, a corporate descent group. (Urbanowicz 1979:232)

Korn's work (1974), which emphasizes matrilineal ties, was drawn from chiefly people who had reason to stress such customary—as opposed to legal—connections in their efforts to press claims to noble titles in the modern society. Thus she contributes a much-needed corrective to the patrilineal bias of most researchers. Who-

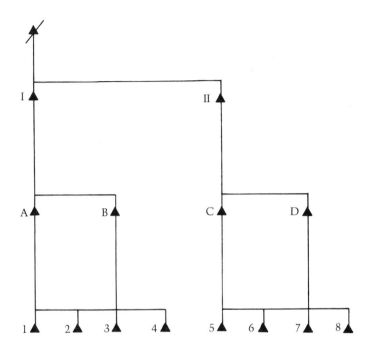

Figure 2. Schematic representation of a pyramidal ramage. Rank declines from left to right.

I: senior branch

II: junior branch

1: senior descendant of original older brother

5: senior descendant of original younger brother

ever studies the kin structure in the twentieth century receives a well-grounded version consistent with the contemporary interests of the group with whom he or she is primarily associated (and all ethnographers or outsiders must be associated with one group primarily—that much is customary for Tongans vis-à-vis strangers). All of the twentieth-century studies are, in that sense, correct.

Certain of the ranking principles favored patrilineal primogeniture. But tensions which derived from a contradictory principle should not be considered as disruptive of an otherwise patrilineal system. It is well recognized in ethnology that genealogies and myths can serve as charters for current practices; both can be interpreted, juggled, or otherwise manipulated to suit contemporary interests. To read backward from what eventuated in Tonga to a systematic precontact situation is unwarranted, especially considering the political struggles in the nineteenth century. Yet both structuralist and other accounts of Tongan kinship, with a few notable exceptions (e.g., Urbanowicz 1979), seem to take current practice as indicative of either similar or more consistent kinship relations in the past. But there could be no consistency in descent or succession, so long as either rank was not entirely removed from the allocation of authority, or the principles of rank continued to be at odds.

Tonga was stratified before the arrival of the first European vessels. Chiefly and nonchiefly people had differential access to basic resources (Fried 1967). The question becomes, if Tongan society was stratified, did the strata represent class relations? "Differential access" does not necessarily indicate class relations. There may be no capacity to prevent use of said resources. Sahlins has characterized chieftainships in general as societies where higher-ranking groups have "preferential," rather than exclusive, access to resources (1972: 92–94). This characterization is more accurate, but still somewhat aside from the salient differences between kinship and class relations. To understand the nature of chiefly and nonchiefly strata in Tongan society, we should consider the character of tensions within stratified kinship societies.

Use-Rights: The Limits of Kin-Based Stratification

Where everyone's access to labor and resources is through kin connections, no matter how ranked, there can be no class differences—so long as kinship determines use-rights. Only where a nonproducing group depends upon a producing one, *and can deny the producing group's continued subsistence*—its existence as a group—can class relations be discerned. In precontact Tonga, these conditions were only partly fulfilled.

The chiefly stratum was internally ranked, with the highest ranks being designated by titles. Title-holding gave the bearer claims to labor and products of lower-ranking kin. Most titled chiefly men were not directly involved in production, although even the highest-ranking, titled male chiefs at times took part in certain men's activities. But chiefly women—titled or not—were engaged in the creation of "valuables," *koloa*, an activity which was considered honorable and "chiefly"—a point that will be discussed further in Chapter 5. Chiefly people did not determine others' use-rights to labor and material resources. Chiefs allocated land and access to other resources in their capacity as guardians of Tongan fertility and prosperity (Gifford 1929:76, 144, 171); but they could not refuse to allocate such resources.

Land was traditionally in the possession of local extended kin groups. Each local kin group is said to have been headed by a man who "usually held an hereditary title" (Maude 1971 : 107). Alaric Maude considers these groups to have been patrilineal segments (ibid.: 108). The head of a local kin group, so far as male chiefs were concerned, may have been a man, but this does not mean local kin groups were patrilineal segments. One can infer that local kin groups were at least more cognatic in the precontact period, since nineteenth-century laws restricted cognatic use-rights to land. Further, material claims of sisters and their children were pivotal in both production and reproduction, and to exercise such claims, sisters and brothers had to reside in the same chiefly district. Local kindreds are cognatic today (Korn 1974). It is reasonable to suppose that local kin in the precontact society were kindreds centered on a brother-sister pair, rather than a patrilineal segment, regardless of a widespread tendency to consider cognatic forms as a degeneration from what is assumed to have been more orderly patrilineality in the precontact situation.[5]

Both chiefly and nonchiefly kin held lands hereditarily (Mariner 1827:2:93). A chief allocated land to kin group heads, and people within the kin groups claimed use-rights through their own kin connections (Maude 1971:108). Although the chiefs told early European visitors that people could be dispossessed at will, this seems an empty boast. The rare instances of group dispossession seem to have been during warfare (Williamson 1924:3:266).

Use-rights to land, claims to one another's labor, and other so-called subsistence resources were allocated according to kin-based rank, which was contextual to a considerable degree. The determination of rank, particularly for chiefly people, could become politicized. There were a number of kin connections between any two persons, allowing for many interpretations of rank. Regardless of rank, however, use-rights and necessary labor could not be denied any Tongan who had not violated kinship norms of tolerable conduct. What constituted a violation of the *tapus*—the customary term for forbidden actions or states of being—was a charged issue. The determination of *tapu* violations certainly became an arena of political struggle on occasion, especially after European contact.[6]

For class relations to emerge, a critical change in the control of labor and products must occur. The nonproducing group must have the capacity to deny subsistence if the surplus labor or products are not provided. So long as the kin group retains use-rights, the decision to provide or not to provide services and goods depends upon the perceived balance of return, in *both* material and symbolic terms.

The support can be withdrawn, a more suitable contender backed. Pressure may be forthcoming from the nonproducing group toward the people expected to contribute, but a harangue is qualitatively different from confiscation.

What constitutes an adequate return for a presentation or service is, of course, a moot point (see, e.g. Godelier 1980). Who decides upon the return and the consequences for those who do not concur are the basic parameters of kinship versus class. Perhaps the most striking political dynamic in class formation out of kinship, in Polynesia and elsewhere, is the attempt by emerging nonproducing classes to redefine what constitutes "balanced" reciprocity. Certain chiefs may risk rebellion by providing abstract returns, interspersed with periodic largesse. "Symbolic" return gifts—the prosperity-assurance of the Tongan sacred paramount chief, for instance—usually are embodied in material forms, but there may come to be a divorce from this demonstration of the symbol in a useful form. As such, the symbolic world becomes detached from—and antagonistic to—the continuity of kinship relations. The ideological degradation of production, of manual work, characteristic of class and state formation, is consistent with this assertion that meaning is independent of human transformation of the sensate world.[7]

Changing control over the allocation of resources may be the *one* means by which kin-defined groups lose the ability to reproduce themselves as autonomous groups. But the critical shift is from the determination of labor claims and use-rights through kin connections to non-kin considerations such as ownership. Production of goods to support nonproducers then ceases to be determined in accordance with reciprocally understood and agreed-upon obligations, with primacy given to local requirements.

In precontact Tonga, high rank entitled chiefly people to particular privileges, a greater call on labor and products, rather than ownership of resources or consistent control over nonchiefly people's labor. The critical absence of chiefly control over labor or the determination of production signaled the non-class nature of the hierarchy. Tongan society was stratified, but the relations of production were kinship-dominated prior to the arrival of Europeans.

Chiefly and Nonchiefly Strata: Transitional Forms from Kinship to Class

The strata in Tongan society were determined through kinship relations common to both and characterized by similar obligations.

Thus, the strata were not classes. Differences between chiefly and nonchiefly people were based on inherited rank, degree of close-in marriage, and the birth order of children. How were such differences reconciled with kin-determined claims to labor and products?

Chiefly and nonchiefly strata were transitional, a kind of mediation between kinship and class relations. At times in the precontact period, the tensions between nonchiefly and chiefly strata approximated class relations; at other times, the relations were more typical of ranking within kinship. The strata could, and historically did, eventuate in class relations, so they appear as transitional forms. But seen as a process, chiefly and nonchiefly relations retain some of the ambiguity of kin-based authority and labor claims. Today, there are still chiefly and nonchiefly strata, but they are not isomorphic with either precontact strata or contemporary class relations.

Chiefly and nonchiefly strata in precontact Tonga can best be conceptualized as estates or orders. Jérome Rousseau describes an estate system as

> A form of stratification in which the strata are jurally defined, and where the strata present a significant homology with the system of relations of production. (1978:87)

Estates, for Rousseau

> crystallize into a structure what is actually a political and economic process and they provide an ideology which justifies inequality as natural, inherited reality. (Ibid.: 93)

This "political and economic process" in Tonga was the potential formation of class relations. Rousseau is careful to indicate that estates or orders are not classes, nor are they castes. Classes may approximate estate membership, but one estate may contain several classes—as in the pre-revolutionary French Tiers Etat—or only a part of one—as in the nobility in feudal France.

Estates are usually distinguished by descent, with succession to rank and marriage patterns functioning to limit the size of the highest stratum. To use the criteria, one has to refine the concept for nonstate societies such as precontact Tonga. In those state societies where estates may persist, estates become jurally defined; in kinship societies estates may exist through customary descent and ranking principles. Estates in kinship societies may not be simply ideological constructs which crystallize inequality, for instance, through descent. Estates may emerge where inconsistencies in kin-based ranking and attendant labor claims *could* become the basis for class stratification.

The ideological utility of estate stratification might explain why, where class and state structures emerge, the transitional form often persists. Estates in this new circumstance *obscure the existence of classes,* because they emerged—at least in Tonga—prior to class formation. Estates or orders provide kinship-associated categories which misrepresent changes in the relations of production. The familiar idiom of kinship ranking serves to justify the new content, that is, class relations.

While estates, where they exist in kinship and state societies, are constructed on the basis of descent, the character of descent is qualitatively different where descent and recruitment have become codified, that is, legally determined. Customary descent rules in Tonga were quite flexible, in stark contrast to all known precapitalist state societies, where grounds for entry into higher strata were rigidly defined even where there was considerable mobility. Estates or orders may more appropriately describe the chiefly and nonchiefly strata in Tonga rather than either ranks or classes. But the descent basis for estate membership in state societies is more prescriptive, more ascriptive than in the kin context.

Mobility in Estates and Ranks

Tongan estates were hereditarily and relatively ranked; chiefly and nonchiefly strata also were internally ranked. Recruitment into the various ranks was through marriage, birth, or, rarely, appointment. Considerable mobility was possible.

Within the nonchiefly estate there were two or perhaps three ranks, each internally graded according to seniority, sibling gender, and ties to higher-ranking people. The chiefly estate consisted of highest-ranking titled chiefs (*hau*) and their untitled lineal and collateral kin (*'eiki*), who formed the top descent groups (the *ha'a*), as well as lower-ranking chiefly people. The nonchiefly estate consisted of the *matāpules*—almost all of whom were categorically foreign—and the conceptually indigenous, but lower-ranking *tu'as*. There also was a rather murky rank known as the *mu'as*. The relationship of the estates and ranks to the occupational structure and the division of labor is discussed in Chapter 5. Here the concern is recruitment and rank mobility.

Becoming Chiefly

Marriage arrangements limited succession to the highest chiefly ranks, but some marriages did occur across estates. Extramarital liaisons were commonplace, and children of such unions were accorded a higher rank than the nonchiefly parent. The highest-ranking male chiefs were not allowed to marry "commoner" (*tu'a*) women (Goldman 1970:307). One of Gifford's informants claimed that in former times a young chiefly man could be killed if he married a *tu'a* woman (1929:113). It is likely that this would apply only to the highest-ranking chiefly men: it certainly referred to marriage only, not to concubinage or other sexual liaisons. Chiefly women, however, gave their rank to their children, regardless of the father's rank. One of the earliest European residents in the Islands, William Mariner, explained:

> In every family nobility descends in the female line—where the mother is not noble, the children are not. All the children of a female noble ['*eiki*, high-ranking chiefly woman] are without exception, noble. (Mariner 1827:2:89)

Although technically chiefly, children of a chiefly woman by a *tu'a* man might have been called by the disparaging term "half-chiefs" (*mu'as*) by other chiefly people, but they were more highly regarded than the children of chiefly men by *tu'a* women (Gifford 1929:123).

Matāpules, the nonchiefly attendants and assistants retained by the chiefs, could marry chiefly or nonchiefly people. A *tu'a* woman who married a *matāpule* became one herself, as did their children (Mariner 1827:2:95). Such a marriage represented a considerable increment in social standing for the women. It is not clear what happened to *matāpule* women who married *tu'a* men, nor is it clear what rank the children of *matāpule* and chiefly marriages bore. According to Mariner's statement and custom, rank would depend on the mother.

Mu'as: *The Rank between Ranks*

The rank of *mu'a* perhaps embodies the complexities of rank mobility. The rank is disputed in the literature. Some claim the *mu'as* were the offspring of chiefly and *matāpule* parents. By the early twentieth century, a person was *mu'a* if one of his or her parents was chiefly ('*eiki*) and the other *matāpule* (Gifford 1929:109). If the chiefly parent was high ranking, the child was considered chiefly; if lower ranking, the child was *matāpule.*

The problem here is one of time, and indicates the danger of reading backward from contemporary practice. Traditionally, a child's rank derived from that of the mother. According to Mariner, *mu'as* were the children of chiefly men by *tu'a* women. These children were attached in service to their fathers and to their higher-ranking half-siblings. In this capacity, they were housed and fed as part of the chiefly retinue (Mariner 1827:2:95).

But Mariner also said the *mu'as* were the collateral kin of a *matāpule* (Mariner 1827:2:90). The *mu'as* included both the younger sons and brothers of *matāpules,* and their descendants. Over time, *mu'as* would slowly merge into the rank of *tu'a.* This paralleled dynamics in the chiefly ramage structure, where rank for collateral kin declined toward nonchiefly status. Mariner described the grading of *mu'a* into *tu'a* as follows:

> . . . no mooa [*mu'a*] can become a mataboole [*matāpule*] until his father or brother whom he is to succeed be dead so in like manner, the sons and brothers of mooas are only tooas [*tu'as*], and no tooa can become a mooa till his father or brother . . . be dead. (Ibid.)

The ranking of occupations provided by Mariner[8] seems to confirm the placement of the *mu'a,* implied above, as intermediary between the two nonchiefly ranks (*matāpule* and *tu'a*). The insertion of *mu'a* between the chiefly and *matāpule* ranks appears to be a later development, first reported in the mid-nineteenth century (Farmer 1855:139).

Tu'as who had a chance to inherit a *mu'a* position gained some respect from those who had no such connections. But there were other ways to accomplish *mu'a* status than the vagaries of inheritance. One's children or grandchildren might be born with *mu'a* or even higher rank. A father or his kin might proffer a lovely *tu'a* woman to a chief temporarily in order to introduce chiefly blood to a locality (Bain 1967:82). The resultant child resided with his or her mother's kin and was considered the child of the entire kindred. The baby was known as the "village child" and was highly regarded by the local kin (Gifford 1929:113; Collocott 1923b:226). The term "village child" is intriguing: since residence was dispersed prior to the warfare that followed contact, it is unclear if this valued *mu'a* child was called by a kin-associated term in former times. The possibility of a shift from a kindred-linked to a locality-linked term is another symptom of the shift from kin to territorial identification associated with state formation (Maine 1861/1963).

The *mu'as* thus represented upward rank mobility for *tu'as* and downward mobility for *matāpules.* In either case, the determining factor was how one forged or renewed kin ties to higher-ranking people. The change in how one become *mu'a* from the precontact period to the twentieth century underscores the declining authority of women: a mother's chiefly rank no longer was transmitted to all her children. By the twentieth century, entry into chiefly status was more restricted. But in the precontact period, rank was regulated largely through institutions controlled by women.

Rank and Cognatic Claims: The Distaff of Life

Both Sahlins and Goldman recognized that the idealized ramage or lineage (Figure 1) was not the lived kinship structure in Tonga, as elsewhere. In operation, even the chiefly groups were openly cognatic. But both attributed this cognatic reality to the exigencies of establishing closeness to a strategic relative, alive or dead, regardless of the quality of those linkages. Women are viewed as facilitating men's claims to male chiefly titles, primarily through the marriage alliance system (Sahlins 1958; 1963; Goldman 1970; see also Kirchhoff 1959).

These categorizations limit our understanding of inheritance, authority, and rank in Polynesia, and are particularly misleading in Tonga. Alliances through marriage were crucial for the chiefly estate: over time, a pattern of generalized exchange emerged among the highest-ranking chiefly descent groups (*ha'a*). But the implications of marriage exchanges were far more complex than the structuralist conception of chiefly women as being exchanged by their fathers and brothers (Lévi-Strauss 1969; Ortner 1981) for the sake of their male kin. The exchange of women in Tonga can be seen as deriving from the interests of the highest-ranking women; the importance of marriage exchanges in the reproduction of chiefly relations is analyzed in Chapter 4.

Chiefly men's roles are discussed in some detail in most accounts: their roles as fathers, brothers, brothers-in-law, sons, and husbands are well known. Women typically have been discussed only in terms of marriage (the daughter to be given, the wife to be taken) and motherhood, and only as these pertain to their purported role as facilitators of men's communication. In Tonga, wives deferred to husbands (Beaglehole, ed. 1969:3:945), and chiefly husbands tended to outrank their wives for reasons to be discussed below. Chiefly men also were polygynous. Evidence is quite contradictory for chiefly women. However, chiefly women had authority in their marital kin group in certain contexts, including at times, political disputes (ibid.: 117n; J. Wilson 1799/1968:104). But if wives could at times become authoritative, sisters simply were authoritative.

The Fahu: *Sisterhood Was Powerful*

A father's sister was never ignored. Tongan women—especially chiefly women—exercised social authority throughout life as *sisters.* The role is not to be confused with more informal sources of authority, such as personal influence, manipulation, etc. Nonchiefly women and nonchiefly men had no *political* authority, but chiefly women who bore titles had political authority in their natal "houses" or *ha'a.* This authority included command over the labor of women defined as inferior to them. It is likely that sisters and brothers had parallel lines of authority: sisters over lower-ranking women, brothers over lower-ranking men (see Mariner 1827:2:212); for chiefly people, this would be expressed in a call on lower-ranking people's labor and products.

Because the sister—especially the eldest sister—was ranked superior to her brother, sisters' children outranked brothers' children (Gifford 1929:22). For chiefly people this ranking involved political and material claims vis-à-vis maternal uncles and their children. These rights—often termed privileges in the literature—included the sister's call on her brother, his household, and his descendants. She and her children were *fahu* to the brother and his children. The term *fahu* subsumed the claims of sisters and sisters' children; it meant "above the law" (ibid.: 23) or, more correctly, "beyond custom."

The father's sister, the imposing *mehikitanga,* was the focus of avoidance by her brother and his children, particularly his sons. She arranged and vetoed her brother's children's marriages. She could command the labor and products of her brothers' spouses, and she had the right to adopt her brothers' children. A curse from the *mehikitanga* threatened a brother's children and spouse(s) with sterility or painful childbirth (Burrows 1970:64; Collocott 1923b:226–228). Women, considered as a medium of exchange between groups of men by structuralists, could, in fact, negate the purpose of marriage alliances. A women could threaten the reproduction of the lineage or kindred that ostensibly had "alienated" her, both through her supernatural control over fertility and through her quite concrete control over her brothers' children's marriages.

The *fahu* relationship brought benefits to a woman's sons as well as to herself and her daughters. For instance, the son of the titled sister (the Moheofo) of the administrative paramount chief (the Tu'i Kanokupolu)

> has the largest district of any chief at Tonga [Tongatapu, the main island]; and is not obliged to furnish Dugonagaboola [Tu'i Kanokupolu] with his produce. (J. Wilson 1799/1968:254)

Such benefits were recognized as emanating from a person's mother, rather than the mother's brother. Even today, Tongans appreciate that their *fahu* rights—for, although illegal, they are still exercised locally—derive from their mother's cognatic claims. Any presumption that the mother's brother is the "real" authority seems unwarranted.

Among chiefly people, there were wife-receiving and wife-giving relations between patrilineages. In the Tongan perception, wife-receiving was superior to wife-giving, since wives were also sisters and sisters were higher ranking than brothers. Benefits accruing to the husband's people, such as children and co-wives, were the result of the wife outranking her brother.

Chiefly people supposedly were more concerned with the political aspects of the *fahu* than with material benefits. But entire lineages (including the *ha'a*, the highest-ranking chiefly descent groups) were *fahu* to others, which entailed a tributary relationship as well as political inferiority (Gifford 1929:115). Because the *fahu* relationship was not restricted to single households, but included kin groups, the analysis of kinship to precontact Tonga should not allow women to "drop out" through a focus solely on their married or maternal roles.

The role of sister and *fahu* transcended lineage affiliation. Before, during, and after marriage a sister had the same claims to her brother and his children. The diagram of a ramage shown in Figure 1 appears to be a male realm, but a second kinship structure cross-cut it. This second kin-based ranking system was *the sibling group over time*. The second structure was inherently bilateral or cognatic; the point of convergence of the two structures (ramage and kindred), the sister, is obscured in typical representations of the ramage or conical clan. The sibling pair was extremely important in inheritance, alliance, and descent; the sibling-based descent group corrects one-sided representations of the lineage. The *fahu* as an institution marked the persistence of sister-brother claims over generations.

The *fahu* for chiefly people rested on the recognition of lines descended from sisters, which were, it seems, named. Sina'e was one branch of the male sacred paramount chief's (Tu'i Tonga) "house" or *ha'a*. E. E. V. Collocott claimed that this line was possibly composed of the children of the "female side" of the house (1928:153). The phrase is ambiguous, but related information supports an interpretation of "female side" as the children of sisters. The word Sina'e derives from one of the names of several Tu'i Tonga Fefines, that is, the female sacred paramounts. Children of the sister could benefit most from the *fahu* in material terms if they lived near their mother's brother, and Ernest Beaglehole and Pearl Beaglehole reported such a preferred residence pattern in the 1930's (1941). Finally, the *fahu* included generations of sisters' and brothers' children. So it seems reasonable that lines traced from strategic sisters would be recognized.

In addition, at least for the top chiefly positions, sisters of the paramount chiefs bore parallel titles: Tu'i Tonga Fefine (woman Tu'i Tonga) and Moheofo, the name of the "house" of the Tu'i Kanokupolu, the Ha'a Moheofo (Collocott 1928:134; Mariner 1827:2:184). The difference in the structure of these titles—exact parallel versus descent group title—perhaps indicates the disparity of time between the emergence of the two paramount titles. Moheofo also meant "Great Royal Wife" (bearing with those who project monarchy into precontact Tonga), which was the title of the Tu'i Tonga's principal wife. Whether this title existed prior to its marriage-associated meaning cannot be determined. Some claim the title Moheofo was used to refer to the principal wife of the sacred paramount chief prior to the creation of the Tu'i Kanokupolu title (and line), but this would mean that the latter kin group was named for its function of wife-giving. This seems doubtful, since the previous wife-giving line was not so named. It is tempting to speculate that the title was one associated with the Ha'a Moheofo prior to the marriage connection, but I have found no indication that this was the case.

It is clear in the precontact situation that a tension existed between the role of sister and that of wife (see Sacks 1979). Sisters had consistent authority; wives deferred to husbands. The tension reveals a contradiction in the chiefly stratum between authority based on cognatic kinship and that based on patrilineal kinship. Attempts to reduce this structured ambiguity can be discerned in some of the chiefly genealogies. Regardless of whether or not the actual disputes occurred, the existence of patterns in the genealogies at least points to structural tensions. The attempted resolutions of kin-based ambiguity underscore the critical importance of gender in the emergence of class stratification.

4. The Reproduction of Ambiguity: Succession Disputes, Marriage Patterns, and Foreigners

William Anderson,
1777 (quoted in
Beaglehole, ed.
1969:3:954)

Will Mariner
(1827:1:136)

*We . . . were told that when his Father [the Tu'i Tonga]
was alive the sister of his father . . . reigned jointly with
him at Tonga[tapu].*

*. . . the people of that island [Vava'u], at the instigation,
and under the guidance of their chief [Finau's father's
sister] . . . , had come to the resolution of freeing
themselves from the dominion of the king [Finau, a
paramount chief], and of erecting themselves under a
separate nation.*

KINSHIP RELATIONS in precontact Tonga were tension-filled. The tensions derived from contradictory ranking principles—the structural basis for ambiguity. The contradictory ranking principles ensured that cognatic ties, which involved women, were needed to validate high rank and to accede to chiefly title. Cognatic ties, which were institutionalized in the relationship of *fahu* between sisters and brothers, prevented the development of systematic patrilineal inheritance even within the highest chiefly ranks (Gailey 1980).

The ambiguity of kinship—in the determination of rank, in the reproduction of rank through generations, and in the relationship of rank to social authority—was recognized by the highest-ranking chiefly groups. Through time, various chiefly groups sought to reduce the contradictions within the ranking system, to consolidate chiefly titles in one person, or to dissociate rank from political power. Attempts to regularize chiefly succession to title included splitting administrative from fertility-assurance functions and creating new titles to placate disruptive junior lines and sisters' lines.

Marriage arrangements embodied strategies to consolidate rank or to support a title bid. Marital strategies at different times ranged from island exogamy for highest-ranking women to possible brother-sister incest, closed-circle generalized exchange, and, later, open-ended generalized exchange. The inherent opposition of the *fahu* to patrilineal succession spawned attempts to circumvent the claims of sisters and their children to succession and inheritance. A clear example of this is in the injection of non-kin foreigners to replace *fahu* kin.

Notably, all these attempts to narrow effective kin claims failed. The dependency of social power on the reproduction of cognatic claims persisted. Alongside these periodic attempts to concentrate control in the hands of a relatively small, cohesive, and patrilineally organized chiefly group were rebellions by lower-ranking chiefly and nonchiefly people. The relationships activated in each of the attempts were at cross-purposes and thus acted to re-create the tense, fundamentally kin-based network of responsibilities among higher- and lower-ranking chiefly people, and between the chiefly and non-chiefly strata.

Succession Disputes: Cognatic and Lineal Conflicts

Ideally, higher rank meant that the bearer was closer to the ancestors or gods, more *tapu* (filled with *mana* or impersonal power, sacred in this case) and thus more fit to exercise social authority. Over time, however, authority in Tonga became somewhat removed from rank considerations, though this process was not complete until the nineteenth century. The estrangement of authority from rank perhaps indicates one attempt to resolve the tensions arising from the contradictions in ranking. The failure to resolve the contradictions prior to European intervention can be attributed to the ways in which chiefly kin groups were reproduced through time.

Periodically, chiefs tried to avoid succession disputes by limiting arenas of authority for specific chiefly titles. New chiefly titles would be created to mimic the new division of labor. But after a few generations, the same contradictions would reemerge. The first instance was around 1450. After a series of assassinations of the paramount sacred chief, the Tu'i Tonga split his sacred, fertility-assurance functions from more "mundane" administrative authority. The Tu'i Tonga was thenceforth to be sacred chief "of the soil only," rather than of its products as well. The Tu'i Tonga's younger brother, the Tu'i Ha'a Takalaua, assumed administrative functions for all areas apart from the regions most closely associated with the sacred chief's "house" (*ha'a*) or the corporate-descent group.

Activities other than "planting and fishing"—primarily men's activities—were to be associated with the male sacred paramount. This shift was echoed later by the eclipse of the Tu'i Ha'a Takalaua by his own younger-brother line, headed by the Tu'i Kanokupolu. Cycles of splitting authority into sacred/ritual and administrative functions, and usurpation by junior branches of chiefly descent groups has been discussed for several Polynesian societies by Sahlins (1958), Goldman (1970), and Valeri (1972), among others. They are characteristic of pyramidal ramage organizations.

In situations where male title-holding and patrilineal bias are evident, there is an impending crisis for junior ranking kin. Through time, the children of younger brothers drift inexorably from the locus of both sacredness (*tapu*, derived from high rank) and administrative authority. According to the classic representation of the pyramidal ramage (Fig. 2), father-son succession would define the lines of rank and authority as 1-2-3-4-5 etc. But, as Sahlins (1963) pointed out, 5 and other sons descended from the original younger brother have little to anticipate but a gradual decline in chiefliness. However, 5 would have a good claim to title, being the eldest son of the cadet line. In Tonga, the ambiguity created by sibling rank versus preferred patrilineal primogeniture created circumstances in which the senior line's authority was at times challenged by the primary descendants of the original younger brother. Succession to Tonga's highest chiefly titles from approximately 1600 to the present can be seen in Figure 3; the creation of the younger-brother titles are indications of the dynamic discussed by Sahlins and others.

Following the logic of such ranking, the further one gets from the senior line, the more important become the "invisible" (in most representations) matrilateral links. If sisters either share their brothers' rank (as in Hawaii) or outrank them (as in Tonga), a high-ranking woman has much to gain in the way of support in succession disputes, through an alliance with a junior kinsman, especially if she has been overlooked for title herself. Oral histories, genealogies, and other, written accounts attest to attempts by lower-ranking kin to activate matrilateral linkages, or by senior lines to defuse contentious younger brothers or elder sisters.

Lines of succession were, thus, unclear. In theory, seniority and patrilineality were primary considerations in the allocation of chiefly titles. But tendencies toward patrilineal primogeniture were undercut by claims of collateral kin, in particular those who were *fahu* or "sisters' children." Where everyone was ranked according to sibling seniority, succession could fall to the title-holder's eldest child, in most cases the eldest son, given the preference for males holding male titles and the existence of certain parallel titles for females.

But seniority also could favor the title-holder's next-oldest sibling, particularly if the son were still a child.

This situation was complicated by the higher rank of sisters. If a sister were passed over because of the preference for male title-holding, then because of her much greater rank over her brother's children—and the claims she had to those children through the *fahu*—she would stand to succeed. Alternatively, by extension of her position as *fahu*, her eldest son would have strong claims to title, especially with the backing she could provide.

In fact, contention by father's sisters and sister's sons for chiefly titles did occur, even at the paramount level[1] (Gifford 1929:57; Williamson 1924:154–155; J. Wilson 1799/1968:252–253, 275). Claims were made on the basis of high-ranking mothers and the mothers' connections with other paramount chiefs. Women exercised claims as sisters and fathers' sisters to the title-bearer and, thus, *outranked* him. At the time of Cook's visits in the late eighteenth century, a younger half-brother became sacred paramount chief specifically because of the power of the Ha'a Moheofo, the kin group to whom his mother was *fahu* (Beaglehole, ed. 1969:3:177n). At the end of the eighteenth century, a female chief (sister of the administrative paramount and widow of the sacred paramount) made an unsuccessful effort to reunite the sacred and administrative functions in herself (J. Wilson 1799/1968:104).

Although matrilateral links were strategic in succession to chiefly title, Tonga was not matrilineal; similarly, the patrilateral bias in the descent system cannot be reduced to patrilineality. Viewed in this context, matrilateral links were not "second best," but followed from one of the basic principles of ranking. Tongan chiefly women were not "used" by their husbands, brothers, and sons in elaborate marriage exchange and succession intrigues. At least, they were no more used than they used their own male and female kin. Tongan chiefly women were engaged in these machinations because the kinship structure was ordered through contradictory ranking principles and because their children's futures depended on their actions. The ambiguity allowed women to enter into contention in their own right as sisters, as well as on behalf of their own children, as the children of fathers' sisters.

In general, however, high-ranking female chiefs were not as able to muster warriors as high-ranking male chiefs. This was due in part to the changing position of women in the chiefly marriage system as it developed from the fifteenth to the nineteenth century. If, for example, a chiefly woman were not defined out of contention through marriage, she could be quite disruptive. If she married a lower-ranking chiefly man, he gained use-rights to the land she brought to the marriage. If she bore a son to a contending junior chiefly branch, she could call on the resources of her husband's group, since she out-ranked her husband. In a succession bid, one female chief even called on the resources—warriors and supplies—of junior branches of her enemy brother's line (Collocott 1928:150). One of the major foci of attempts to resolve the ambiguities of succession and, at the same time, to consolidate rank through time and defuse the rank of chiefly women was through marriage arrangements.

Marriage Patterns: Problems of Rank and Authority

Chiefly women were intimately involved in succession disputes: chiefly genealogies were kept by older chiefly women. Personal names were not gender-linked, so there was room for creative inter-pretation. These women obviously would have recognized the grad-ual decline in rank of junior chiefly people. In addition, marriages were arranged or vetoed by the father's sister. It is reasonable, then, to assume that the highest-ranking chiefly women would be active in any attempts to consolidate rank through generations. A new per-spective on chiefly marriage exchanges in the precontact society can be gained by focusing on problems women chiefs might have en-countered in the attempt to consolidate rank over time. How might women chiefs have used both their privileged genealogical informa-tion and their right to arrange their lower-ranking brothers' chil-dren's marriages, to address the contradictions in the ranking system?

The Early Period: Deflecting Contradictions Abroad

Tongan society probably was more stratified in the twelfth and thir-teenth centuries than subsequently, at least until European contact. Tongans occupied and exercised tributary hegemony over parts of Samoa, Fiji, and other islands from the 1100's until about 1400.[2] Rea-sons for the creation of this tributary empire are not well under-stood. An early interchiefly struggle could have been temporarily resolved through conquest. This type of respite to internal tensions has been noted for other stratified kin societies in Polynesia (Hawaii, Marquesas). It presumes an increasing stratification at home.

Chiefly women appear to have been prominent during this early period. The mothers of the earlier Tu'i Tongas are known by name, as are some of the sisters (Gifford 1923:222). The female sacred paramount title, Tu'i Tonga Fefine, may not have existed prior to the seventeenth century. There is no way of knowing whether the title was created later and projected backward by subsequent generations, a commonplace and politically charged maneuver (cf. Gifford 1929: 79). But there is indirect evidence for prior periods (Collocott 1923a: 179). Perhaps one indication is that the names of the daughters of the earlier Tu'i Tongas (before 1450) also are known, from the tombs that were constructed for them.[3]

The attempt to consolidate rank at this early date can be seen in activities of the eleventh sacred paramount. Around 1200, at the height of Tongan dominion in the region and the power of the Tu'i Tonga kin group (Goldman 1970:283), he is said to have raped his virgin sister—the woman who would be the female sacred paramount. While this seems grim, it may express either the ultimate close-in marriage or a refusal to extend kinship alliances to other chiefly groups. What appears in one account as rape or incest could be a highly sacred marriage.

Brother-sister marriages marked the closest degree of "sacred marriage" in Hawaii (Davenport 1969). The existence of the institution in archaic states such as Incaic Peru and Egypt, and in a few stratified non-state situations, indicates the strategic importance of this most consolidated form of marriage. Sacredness and pollution are closely related (cf. Douglas 1966): because it is a mark of high rank, incest is sacred; because it violates marriage rules, it is an abomination. Incestuous rape might make the sister unmarriageable. It does not matter whether the intercourse actually occurred; it is sufficient that it is attributed to the sacred paramount chiefs—male and female—during a period of heightened power.

The consolidation of high/sacred rank implied in sister-brother intercourse (for our purposes, marriage) reveals an attempt by the highest-ranking chiefly kin group to divorce itself from marital obligations to lower-ranking chiefly people. Sacred marriage is a distinct possibility: there is mention of the son of a Tu'i Tonga (i.e., potentially Tu'i Tonga himself) who married a Tu'i Tonga Fefine, named Fatafehi Lapaha (Collocott and Havea 1922:76). But such brother-sister bonds are rare. The question becomes where most of the highest-ranking women married, during this period of regional power before the sacred paramount title split into fertility and administrative components.

Several sisters of Tu'i Tongas married into Samoa, one of the areas from which tribute was collected (Gifford 1929:54; Kramer 1936: 1:468). Such marriages are mentioned for the time of the seventeenth, eighteenth, and nineteenth Tu'i Tongas, that is, prior to the assassinations that led to the split in the paramount chieftainship around 1450. The record is not clear, but the twenty-sixth Tu'i Tonga appears to have married a Samoan, as his daughter may have done (Gifford 1929:56).

What might be involved in such external marriages is defusing of high-ranking women and, at the same time, forging of broader ties by the spouses. The Tongan chiefly women would assume paramount titles in the conquered areas. Marriage into local chiefly groups generally is a strategy in state formative situations: the initial relationship of conquest is transformed into ranked, formalized kin relations, which ostensibly facilitate tribute extraction. The children of these high-ranking Tongan chiefs would be assured of paramount titles in their mother's marital district.

Bringing the War Home: Contradictions Resurface

By the fifteenth century, Tongan control over other regions had been shaken. Perhaps the progeny of the high-ranking sisters refused—on the grounds of higher rank—to continue forwarding tribute. Marriages into other lands ceased; contradictions of rank and authority reemerged at home.

Assassinations of several Tu'i Tongas are reported in the years following. By 1450, the prominence of the Tu'i Tonga in political affairs was eclipsed by a younger-brother branch. In short, political authority was partially divorced from sacred rank. Marriages reflected the split. The Tu'i Tonga married at least one daughter of the administrative paramount. She is called Moheofo (the name of the "house" of the younger brother) in one of the chiefly genealogies, but this may be a backward projection of the title. The administrative paramount married the daughters of Tu'i Tongas, until the seventeenth century. The pattern of the highest-ranking chiefly succession and marriages can be seen in Figure 3.

But just as the Tu'i Tonga had been eclipsed in terms of administrative control, the Tu'i Ha'a Takalaua administrative paramount would face usurpation by another younger-brother line in the early seventeenth century. This time, the new title was Tu'i Kanokupolu, of the Ha'a Moheofo. But tensions that led to the later split also involved the creation of a new female chiefly title, the Tamaha (Gifford 1929:80; 1924a:29, 46).

The Tamaha was the "sacred child," the daughter of the Tu'i Tonga Fefine, the female sacred paramount. She was the highest-ranking

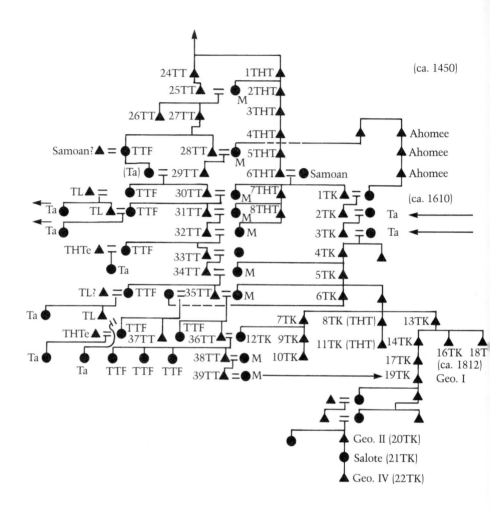

Figure 3. Paramount chiefly succession and marriages, fifteenth through twentieth centuries.

M: Moheofo

T: Tamaha

THT: Tu'i Ha'a Takalaua

THTe: Tu'i Ha'a Teiho (Fiji)

TK: Tu'i Kanokupolu

TL: Tu'i Lakepa (Fiji)

TT: Tu'i Tonga

TTF: Tu'i Tonga Fefine

person in Tonga, a transcendent status. Like her mother, the Tamaha was *fahu* to the sacred paramount kin group.

The first mention of the Tamaha title is in the generation prior to the creation of the new administrative paramount title (Gifford 1924a:48–49). The creation of this title signals an intense political struggle, since the rank of any children would be extremely high. The stakes appear even higher when we consider whom she married: her husband was her mother's brother's son, the sacred paramount.[4] The title seems to have been an attempt to shore up the sacred paramount's authority—and that of his sister—in the face of growing claims by the younger-brother branch. Again, the attempt failed, and the administrative paramount title came into being.

In the next generation, a migration of chiefly and nonchiefly people arrived from Fiji. These included the "House of Fiji" (Ha'a Fale Fisi) chiefly people, into which the female sacred paramount married subsequently. In light of the failure by the brother and sister sides of the sacred paramount house to consolidate administrative control, this migration takes on a particular significance. The Tu'i Tonga Fefine, the sacred female paramount, surrounded herself with foreigners, lest her own position deteriorate along with that of her brother. That her daughter, the Tamaha, by the immigrant Fijian paramount would become the principal wife of the administrative paramount (Tu'i Kanokupolu) reflects this shoring up of her position, independently of her sacred paramount brother's efforts.

The presence of purportedly foreign kin groups is reported throughout Polynesia. Their political significance has been examined by both Sahlins (1958; 1963) and Goldman (1970). Sahlins' view is that a high-ranking but foreign group provides a solution for where the highest-ranking women can marry without becoming politically disruptive in "regular" succession disputes. Whether or not the people were in fact Fijian, their foreignness would in theory exclude the sons of high-ranking women from contention for Tongan chiefly titles. Put another way, the introduction of another, foreign ramage creates another field for what Goldman (1970) calls "status rivalry." The highest-ranking Tongan "houses" and the introduced foreign chiefly ramages were articulated through women as sisters and wives.

Rank was inherited through the mother, but nationality was inherited through the father. This distinction between rank and nationality may have derived from the earlier alliance strategy in tributary regions; in the absence of an empire, sisters could marry high-ranking resident "foreigners." Sons then succeeded to chiefly titles within the House of Fiji. Daughters, however, remained a problem. They had extraordinarily high rank, since their mothers were

Tu'i Tonga Fefines. Although the highest-ranking daughter, the Tamaha, was ostensibly Fijian through her father, the rank she carried made marriage a highly charged issue.

There was an attempt to resolve this dilemma. In the generation following the creation of both the new administrative paramount title and the transcendent Tamaha title, a new marriage system was instituted among the topmost chiefly kin groups. The marriages contracted among the highest-ranking titled chiefs from about 1600 to 1800 can be seen in Figure 4 below.

Appearance and Disappearance of Generalized Exchange

Generalized exchange is a marriage pattern that can signal the emergence of stratification in kinship societies. In Tonga, generalized exchange emerged and was undermined twice, both reflecting and embodying the tensions toward and against permanent social hierarchy. The reasons for its development and abandonment reveal both patrilineal tendencies and the persistence of matrilateral claims within the chiefly stratum.

Generalized exchange involves at least three intermarrying groups. A man is supposed to marry his mother's brother's daughter or a woman who stands in that kind of relationship to him, a classificatory mother's brother's daughter; from a woman's view, marriage is to her father's sister's son.[5] The marriage ties among the three groups are repeated in every generation. There are two variants, so-called marriage-in-a-circle or closed-ended, and open-ended (Leach 1954). Generalized exchange in the closed-ended or marriage-in-a-circle form emphasizes the equivalency of the intermarrying groups; permanent ranking of kin groups through marriage is not possible. Open-ended arrangements, however, set up marriage alliances that are one-way. A hierarchy among intermarrying groups is possible. At different times, both forms developed and devolved in Tonga.

Generalized exchange is presented as a means of consolidating rank in situations where junior lines tend to decline in rank. At the same time, the repetition of the same marriages over generations can preserve the ranked order of the lineages (Lévi-Strauss 1969). The system is not completely effective where ambiguity in rank encourages jockeying for position. The reordering of an open-ended system after periodic succession disputes or "usurpations" by junior lines is typical where there is no institutionalized political authority.

In structuralist formulations, generalized exchange has come to symbolize the exchange of women. Women are presented as the ultimate gift, that is, the "gift that keeps on giving"—a person who can produce others. In marriage exchange, accordingly, women are considered as the living gifts that forge strategic links among brothers-in-law and other men (Lévi-Strauss 1969). In discussions of generalized exchange, wife-giving groups are said to be superior in rank to wife-takers (Leach 1954; Lévi-Strauss 1969).

Generalized exchange in an open-ended form only exists where ranking exists among marrying groups. But in Tonga, wife-receiving lines were superior in rank to wife-giving lines. Lower-ranking women accrued to higher-ranking kin groups through subsidiary marriages; in that sense, "wife-taking" is an accurate term. For chiefly people, the kin of the bride were inferior in rank to the kin of the groom. But this was due to the *fahu:* the groom and his kin were father's sister's children to the bride's group. In other words, the superiority of wife-receiving lines was attributed to the relationship of the groom's mother to the bride's kin: the bride's mother-in-law was her actual or categorical father's sister.

There were two periods when generalized exchange was instituted in Tonga. The circumstances in which the marriage pattern was attempted reveal tensions within the chiefly estate, the involvement of women in the creation and decline of the marriage pattern, and the limits of authority derived from kinship considerations.

The First Attempt: Female Chiefs as Sisters and Wives.   A closed-ended form of generalized exchange emerged in the early 1600's, during the crisis surrounding the creation of the new administrative paramount title, the Tamaha title, and the migration of Fijian chiefly people to Tonga. The so-called House of Fiji, or Ha'a Fale Fisi, became the female sacred paramount's marital group (Thomson 1904: 307). Closed-ended generalized exchange, because it underscores the relative equality among intermarrying groups, would appear to stabilize intergroup relations in this period of political crisis.

The system involved intermarriage among three sibling pairs. The female sacred paramount (Tu'i Tonga Fefine) married a "Fijian" paramount resident in Tonga. Her daughter (the Tamaha) became the principal wife of the newly created administrative paramount chief (Tu'i Kanokupolu). The Moheofo—a title taken from the name of the administrative paramount's "house"—was the mother's mother of the Tamaha, and, for our purposes, her classificatory daughter. The Moheofo became the principal wife of the sacred paramount chief (the Tu'i Tonga). In any single generation, the arrangement would look like this:

= Tu'i Tonga	Tu'i Tonga Fefine	= Tu'i Lakepa (Fiji)	Tamaha	= Tu'i Kanokupolu	Moheofo	=

What analysts who focus on generalized exchange from a male perspective miss is the impact of the pattern over time on succession to female chiefly title. Generalized exchange would *completely* consolidate the topmost female chiefs' rank over four generations. If other kin claims could be limited—which they could not for reasons explored below—a ruling class could emerge over time. The highest-ranking women's titles would cycle over four generations:

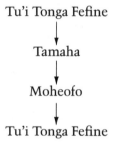

Tu'i Tonga Fefine

↓

Tamaha

↓

Moheofo

↓

Tu'i Tonga Fefine

Paramount female chiefly title passed from father's sister to brother's daughter. No term exists in anthropology to describe this pattern of succession, particularly where it coexists with tendencies toward patrilineal primogeniture for men. Despite women being presented as passive exchangees in the structuralist "male-male communication" model (cf. Ortner 1981), the marriage pattern appears especially attuned to the highest-ranking women's interests.[6] In fact, the institution of generalized exchange during this period better served the interests of the highest-ranking chiefly women than those of similarly ranked men. Certainly, the meaning of the pattern is more complex than the usual explanations, namely, that lower-ranking chiefly men demand that higher-ranking male kin distribute high-ranking women or that high-ranking male chiefs try to consolidate rank and ensure regular succession along patrilineal primogeniture lines. These were certainly factors, but the marriages critical to rank consolidation were arranged by women. It is tempting to describe the institution of generalized exchange in Tonga as one in which husbands were the means by which chiefly women assured the continuity of rank and title for their daughters. The statement is facetious, but to consider women as a medium of exchange also trivializes the content of marriage arrangements.

Chiefly women were not removed from political involvement by being married away from natal groups. The *fahu* provided them with authority—including the right to arrange their brothers' children's marriages—and claims to labor and material goods in their natal "houses." Similar prerogatives were passed to their children. Marriage broadened their network of alliances and helped the women to develop a retinue, the base of support for potential contention for title—for themselves, their children, or their husbands.

The relationship of wife-giving and wife-taking among the topmost chiefly houses was opposite to the relationship of *fahu* claims to labor, products, and political authority. In other words, part of the *fahu* claims set up by sisters' higher rank included the right to marry the mother's brother's daughter. The Tu'i Tonga house exercised *fahu* claims to the labor and products of the Tu'i Kanokupolu's descent group, even though, in terms of social power, the Tu'i Kanokupolu was effectively more authoritative. On the one hand, struggles between senior and junior branches of the "houses," typical of pyramidal ramage structures, called into question the rank basis of social authority. On the other hand, the *fahu* structure rooted claims to desirable marital connections, goods, and services in sister's higher rank. Schematically, the claims can be seen thus:

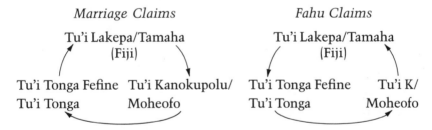

As father's sisters, chiefly women retained control over the reproduction of both marriage and *fahu* claims. As wives, the highest-ranking chiefly women stood as *fahu* to—that is, they outranked and could claim products and support from—those who were *fahu* to their husbands' people.

Abandonment: Structural and Political Contradictions.   Given that generalized exchange allowed the complete consolidation of the highest-ranking women's rank and authority over four generations, it seems surprising that it was abandoned after the first four-generation cycle. Generalized exchange in the closed-ended form consolidated female chiefly rank and maintained a relative balance among the chiefly kin groups. But the diametric opposition of claims

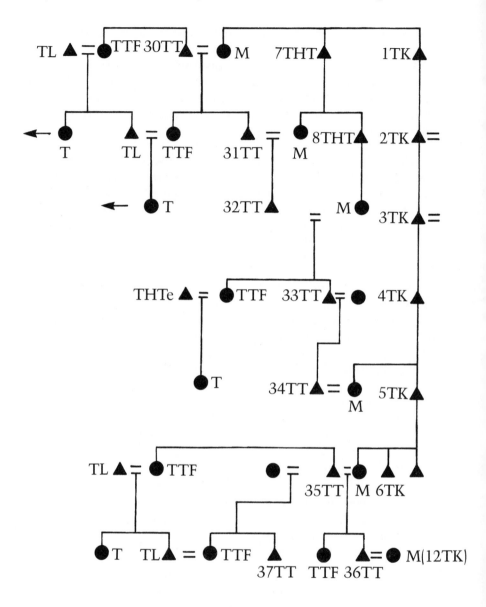

Figure 4. Paramount chiefly marriages, 1600–1800.

M: Moheofo
T: Tamaha
THT: Tu'i Ha'a Takalaua
THTe: Tu'i Ha'a Teiho (Fiji)

TK: Tu'i Kanokupolu
TL: Tu'i Lakepa (Fiji)
TT: Tu'i Tonga
TTF: Tu'i Tonga Fefine

through high rank based on descent and claims based on sibling gender threatened to concentrate both sacred and administrative power in the hands of the Tu'i Kanokupolu, through his marriage to the Tamaha. Ironically, generalized exchange in its closed form, structured to emphasize a rough equality between intermarrying groups, in this case underscored the necessity of contradictory forms of ranking to perpetuate kin-based authority.

Since fathers' sisters arranged the marriages, reasons for the contravention of generalized exchange must have involved the *fahu* prerogatives, the rights derived from sisters' higher rank. The difficulty with closed-ended marriage-in-a-circle lay in the threat it posed to the reproduction of the authority relations among the top chiefly houses, the *ha'a*. The problem was both political and structural. Politically, the marriage pattern denied close connection between the highest chiefly groups and lower-ranking chiefly people.

Structurally, closed-ended generalized exchange provided a dangerous coalescence of sacred rank-based authority in the position of the new administrative paramount chief, the Tu'i Kanokupolu. The threat derived from the rank and position of the Tamaha, as both the "sacred child" and wife of the Tu'i Kanokupolu. She was *fahu* to the sacred paramount house (the house of the Tu'i Tonga and the Tu'i Tonga Fefine). This, coupled with her own exalted rank—regardless of her supposed Fijian nationality—provided the Tu'i Kanokupolu house with well-grounded claims to sacred authority as well as administrative functions. Such a move would threaten the position not just of the Tu'i Tonga, but of all other high-ranking chiefs.

To eclipse the sacred paramount (Tu'i Tonga) entirely would threaten the titles of the very people who arranged marriages, that is, women as fathers' sisters. For the Tamaha to become the wife of the next administrative paramount, his father's sister (the Moheofo) had to make the arrangements with the Tamaha's father's sister (also Tamaha). The Moheofo also was wife to the Tu'i Tonga. If the Tu'i Tonga's sacred authority were absorbed, the sister of the administrative paramount would have no place to marry. In such a situation, her alliance to another chiefly group could be dangerous: she was both of Tongan nationality and high ranking.

In addition, the marriage of the Tamaha violated the prevailing inferiority of rank of bride's kin to groom's kin. The bride's Fijian nationality would seem to transcend the strictly Tongan ranking, yet she was simultaneously the highest-ranking person in Tonga, being the eldest daughter of the female sacred paramount. But the critical marriage denied the relative superiority of rank of the Tu'i Tonga

Fefine and her daughter; the significance of sacred rank would thus be challenged from another direction.

There was thus a double bind for the highest-ranking female chiefs: closed-ended generalized exchange that included the Tamaha would ensure the consolidation of rank, but the *fahu* claims—including the right to arrange marriages—would lead to the virtual destruction of one of the key marriages, that of the Moheofo (the Tu'i Kanokupolu's sister) to the sacred paramount. This marriage was essential, since it produced the Tu'i Tonga Fefine, mother of the Tamaha. It would be acceptable if a suitable position could be made for the Moheofo, but the issue was not resolved.

In addition, the administrative paramount chief's (Tu'i Kanokupolu's) claims to sacred rank would be based on that of his mother, a Tamaha, which depended in turn on her mother, the Tu'i Tonga Fefine, sister of the sacred paramount. The absorption of sacred and administrative authority would alienate all other chiefly groups, including the marriage group of the Tu'i Tonga Fefine, the House of Fiji. While the claim to sacredness could be made, unless it could be defended against other high-ranking chiefly claims, the political consequences would be disastrous.

The relative brevity of generalized exchange as a marriage pattern in this period reflects, in part, the brittle character of inter-chiefly alliances during what was in essence a power struggle. It is significant that the subsequent institution of generalized exchange in the early eighteenth century took an open-ended form and signaled the declining importance of sacred rank as a basis of social authority. The male sacred paramount married the sister of the administrative paramount; the resident Fijian paramount chiefs married the female sacred paramounts, that is, their mother's brother's daughters; but the Tu'i Kanokupolu did not close the circle. He married into a number of chiefly houses (see Fig. 4).

The Tamaha thus had nowhere to marry, as there was no foreign group other than her natal one into which she could take her dangerously exalted rank. Alliance with other Tongan groups would constitute rebellion. By the time of Cook's voyages in the late 1700's, the Tamaha "could have no recognized descendants" (Beaglehole, ed. 1969:3:136). She may have been one of the female chiefs who could take many lovers and bear children to them, but who could not marry.[7]

Open-ended generalized exchange persisted among the highest-ranking chiefly groups until the mid-nineteenth century, when the Tu'i Kanokupolu finally absorbed the Tu'i Tonga title as well as its functions. This chief, who became the first king of Tonga, dissolved generalized exchange as a pattern when he abducted for himself the principal wife of the sacred paramount. The consequences were indeed heavy—civil war. But in the nineteenth century, European assistance and weaponry contributed to the subjugation of kin considerations.

Chiefly women arranged their brothers' children's marriages and were the pivot of the *fahu* claims that directly contradicted the claims established through generalized exchange. Their critical importance in re-creating authority based upon kinship rank provides a reason why class relations could not emerge without constraining the prerogatives of father's sisters.

Subverting Fahu Claims: The Kindness of Strangers

The contradictions in the marriage alliances stemmed from the role of *fahu* claims. These contradictions served to reproduce a net of ambiguous claims to high rank and social authority. It should come as no surprise that, when paramount chiefs were most powerful, attempts were made to defuse the power of *fahu*. These involved the periodic introduction of ostensibly foreign kindreds in Tonga. The so-called House of Fiji was not the only group of resident foreigners. As discussed in Chapter 3, there also were *matāpules*, that is, nonchiefly ranks of foreigners who were attached to various Tongan chiefs.

The significance of *matāpules* in attempts to reduce the cognatic claims of chiefly kin seems to center on their being of foreign origin. Even though they were assimilated into Tongan culture (Gifford 1929 : 141)—as foreigners—and intermarried extensively with Tongan people, they remained categorized as foreigners (Goldman 1970 : 299). There was only one group of *matāpules* who were considered of Tongan origin, and this group was thought to have descended from one of the immortals who came with the sacred paramount from the sky (Gifford 1929 : 149). The changing functions of these attendants highlight three ways in which the highest-ranking chiefly people attempted to deny kin-based obligations, namely, through (1) restricting succession to chiefly title, (2) limiting transmission of wealth to collateral kin (cf. Collocott 1928 : 75), and (3) systematizing claims to the labor and products of nonchiefly people.

The *matāpules*, with the exception of the sky-born Tongan group, were supposed to have migrated at different times, from Fiji, Samoa, Tokelau, Rotuma, and other islands where Tonga had exercised tributary hegemony. The first in-migration came from Fiji, during the time of the eleventh Tu'i Tonga, at the height of Tongan influence in the region and the pinnacle of the Tu'i Tonga's power. The second influx, from Samoa around 1600, accompanied the Samoan wife of the Tu'i Ha'a Takalaua, the administrative paramount. She was the mother of the first Tu'i Kanokupolu, the administrative paramount title that would eclipse the other administrative paramount. The last major migration, from Fiji, marked the arrival of the Fijian paramount chief, the Tu'i Lakepa, head of the "House of Fiji," the marital house of the female sacred paramount (Hocart 1915:32). What did these foreign residents do? The use of non-kin retainers to discharge functions previously controlled by kin is symptomatic of class and state formative tensions (cf. Muller 1977; Diamond 1951; M. Smith 1960; Gailey 1985b). The chiefs who retained the foreigners used them to perform ceremonial, personal, and administrative functions without incurring the danger of conspiracy or title contention. Foreigners were interposed as buffers between the highest chiefs and their collateral and cognatic kin. Indeed, the word *matāpule* is said to derive from *mata*, "a cutting edge" and *pule*, "authority" (Churchward 1959); in other words, *matāpule* is the "face" of authority, the "surface" authority (Schneider 1977; Farmer 1855:139).

Foreigners were considered inappropriate to hold Tongan chiefly titles. Therefore, unlike higher-ranking *fahu* relatives or lower-ranking chiefly kin, in theory they would not be tempted to use their intimate association with titled chiefs to build local bases of support for rebellion, or to assassinate the paramount. The attraction of foreigners for high-ranking chiefs also centered on their immunity from the *tapus*, or customary restrictions. The only other people so exempted were Tongans who were *fahu* to the chiefs. In terms of political intrigue, being *fahu* meant being free to touch the chief's person. Where high-ranking chiefs attempted to limit obligations to collateral kin, this right spelled potential assassination.

The contrast between the practices of chiefly and nonchiefly Tongan people in life crisis rites reveal the significance of foreign officiants for limiting *fahu* claims. Where lower-ranking people's *fahu* presided over their life transitions, the chiefs injected the nonchiefly foreigners as much as politically feasible. In this, title-holding chiefly people used *matāpules* to try to dissociate themselves from responsibilities to their own collateral and cognatic relatives.

The oldest, Tongan *matāpules*, who surrounded the sacred male paramount, can be seen as the initial attempt to inject non-kin in place of *fahu* relatives. The first in-migration augmented this older group, which had supplemented the Tu'i Tonga's lower-ranking kin. The Tu'i Tonga gave the *matāpules* the responsibility of allotting his goods. They were to preside over his *kava* ring—the drinking ceremony that established protocol of rank in any group of chiefly people. In addition, *matāpules* were to distribute food at feasts and to direct funeral services for the paramount and his immediate family. In each arena, *matāpules* were to replace *fahu* relatives (cf. Collocott 1928 : 76).

Interposing *matāpule* attendants especially alienated the paramount's sister. Being the major *fahu* relative, she assumed responsibility for the funeral ceremonies. She would distribute her brother's goods and reserve the bulk of the wealth for herself and her kin. By the time of the nineteenth Tu'i Tonga, the functions of the *matāpules* had been redefined to include acting as bodyguards for the sacred paramount, which was wise, considering how deeply these actions alienated his *fahu*. Significantly, he was assassinated anyway.[8]

The second influx—from Samoa in the early 1600's—is perhaps associated with the creation of loyal, matrilaterally related support for the newly created Tu'i Kanokupolu, the administrative male paramount title. His *fahu*, the female sacred paramount, responded by augmenting her marital group, the "House of Fiji," with nonchiefly Fijian *matāpules* a few years later.

Foreigners had significance beyond the highest-ranking chiefly rivalries. *Matāpules* also acted as warriors and directors of productive activities. These roles also indicate an estrangement between the highest-ranking, titled chiefs and their lower-ranking chiefly kin. By the late eighteenth century, only district chiefs were nominated from the ranks of chiefly people: all others were titled, but nonchiefly, *matāpules*. The attenuation of kin connections between high- and low-ranking chiefs, and the absence of pertinent kin connections between high-ranking chiefs and their assistants, the *matāpules*, are two indications of class formation as a process.

Creation of a group of personally loyal retainers who claim elevated rank by virtue of extra-kin considerations demonstrates the pressures toward class formation before European contact. The insertion of a non-kin group, itself internally ordered through kinship, between high- and low-ranking chiefly people serves a dual purpose. On the one hand, the non-kin groups absorbed some of the functions previously associated with the chiefs' lower-ranking and *fahu* kin. On the other hand, the interpolation exhibits the only future possible—apart from rebellion—for both lower-ranking and *fahu* kin. Lower-ranking people could either absolve their connections to higher-ranking chiefs of authority claims, and continue to discharge administrative and ceremonial functions as *matāpules*, or they could slip for all practical purposes into the nonchiefly estate. The only way for junior kin to remain close to the paramount chiefs was through the suppression of kinship links, if the claims to close kinship were not strong. Such suppression was possible through marriage to foreigners. That all *matāpule* titles were male-held has a further significance. Lower-ranking chiefly women were defined out of this way to remain in the chief's retinue; their alternatives were marriage to *matāpules* or becoming secondary wives or concubines to higher-ranking chiefly men. The alternatives for higher-ranking, cognatic kin of the titled chiefs—the *fahu*—were to arrange strategic marriages or to contend for title.

Nonchiefly Tongans and Reproduction of Kin-Based Authority

Discerning the involvement of nonchiefly Tongans in these attempts to either limit or reproduce kinship relations is difficult. The genealogies, legends, and myths are the charters of chiefly groups. They tend to minimize or even disparage the capacity of nonchiefly Tongans to question chiefly actions. But nonchiefly Tongans were involved in chiefly succession disputes, as the quote at the beginning of this chapter indicates. If we consider kinship as the basis for social authority—sometimes challenged—and at the same time, sufficiently ambiguous to allow the emergence of stratification, then the limits of chiefly authority become pivotal. If the limitations are all derived from tensions within the chiefly estate, the nonchiefly estate becomes passive in the process of class formation out of kinship. How, then, did nonchiefly people help re-create kin-based relations between themselves and the chiefly estate?

For a lower-ranking chiefly person to contend for title and, thus, for the chiefly portion of people's labor and products, he or she had to enjoy the support of local kindreds. There are recorded instances of rebellion against chiefs considered oppressive by their nonchiefly kin (Gifford 1929:182; Goldman 1970:303; Thomson 1904:300–301). Successful rebellions must be viewed, at least in part, as local kindreds' insistence upon customary chieftainship: fertility-assurance, prosperity, largesse, limitations on intervention into production and everyday life, and so on.

Sahlins has noted the cycles of centralization and upheaval in Hawaiian "prehistory" as repetitive rebellion against particular chiefs which never became revolutionary. In other words, chieftainship itself was never questioned. In Hawaii, as in Tonga, the problem was not one of chieftainship per se. The problem was in certain chiefs' attempts to divorce authority (including claims to labor and products) from kin-associated obligations. The problem was the *denial* of chieftainship, of what it meant to be a chief. Revolution was unnecessary, because kin-based stratification was not exploitative. A chief who became oppressive *was not acting as a chief.* The actions were contrary to customary reciprocity. The expectation of reciprocity underlay the delegation of authority from local kindreds to the chiefly estate, through their donation of much of the products needed to provision the chiefly people (cf. Clastres 1977). The reassertion of customary mutual obligations between chiefly and nonchiefly groups, and between titled and untitled chiefly people, marked each successful contention for title, each popular rebellion.

Tongan kinship before European influence provided many chiefly people with claims to particular titles. Decisions about succession made within the *ha'a* or chiefly descent group were influenced heavily by the promise of popular support (cf. Urbanowicz 1979). Such support, considering the pool of contenders, could not be forced.

In granting support, local kindreds obligated the contender to act as a chief toward them. Liberty, equality, and fraternity were unnecessary, so long as chiefs could be replaced by others more mindful of chiefliness in a kinship universe. This is not to argue that the contending chiefly parties had the good of the people at heart. They could be contemptuous, but the contradictions between rank and authority, and the ambiguity within the ranking system, forced chiefly dependency upon lower-ranking people as the ultimate source of authority. The ambiguity of ranking provided nonchiefly kin with the means to assure the reproduction of a social structure that protected them from permanently exploitative relations.

5. Division of Labor

Will Mariner
(1827:2:82)

*To divide society into distinct classes . . . would be . . .
perhaps impossible in respect to the people of these
islands.*

THE DIVISION of labor in Tonga prior to contact was ordered along lines of rank, gender, age, and relationship, as well as skill. There was a rough congruence of the chiefly estate with nonproduction and dependency upon nonchiefly people for subsistence. The occupational differentiation and labor relations within each of the estates, chiefly and nonchiefly, underscore the importance of rank to the division of labor. But chiefly and nonchiefly strata were not isomorphic with nonproducers and producers, and therefore did not constitute classes. There was a degree of occupational specialization, and the highest ranks of chiefly people were partially dissociated from productive activities, but these indications of potential class formation were counteracted by the gender division of labor.

The society was provisioned through goods directly appropriated from the environment (fish, birds, certain plants) and goods created through more intense intervention in the environment, especially cultivated plants. Other subsistence necessities—clothing, shelter, tools and technology—were transformations of readily acquired materials. Services performed for higher-ranking persons—chiefly or nonchiefly—brought compensation. Compensation took the form of exchange labor, or provision of food products or "valuables" (wealth objects or *koloa*), depending upon the type of service and rank of the person for whom the service was performed. But rank did not entirely determine a person's productive activities.

For example, wealth objects, or *koloa*, were produced by chiefly and nonchiefly women. Most of these objects were not solely ceremonial; they also were used as everyday necessities. The distinction between ceremonial and subsistence uses does not really exist in the kin context, since both aspects are included in the concept of production for use.

The production of symbolically important goods, such as bark cloth (*tapa*) or finely plaited mats in precontact Tonga, was in fact the production of use-values. Reproductive labor—the labor which makes possible the maintenance of the society as constituted—was virtually indistinguishable from productive labor. The same activities and the same items embodied both the necessities of everyday life and the replication of everyone's social relations through time. Wealth objects, as much as the foodstuffs typically considered as subsistence items, such as taro and fish, embodied both production and the reproduction of the society.

Rank was perhaps the primary dimension of the division of labor. Each estate, chiefly and nonchiefly, consisted of several ranks. In turn, each of these ranks was internally graded and articulated with the division of labor.

Occupations: The Nonchiefly Estate

"Commoners": The Tu'as

The nonchiefly estate consisted of at least two ranks, *matāpule* and *tu'a*. The *mu'as*, discussed in the previous chapter under rank mobility, probably should be included in the nonchiefly estate as well. The lowest-ranking nonchiefly people were the *tu'as*. The word *tu'a* generally is translated as "commoner." The translation is taken from the perceptions of early European visitors and residents, particularly missionaries, who made analogies between their own monarchical and class societies and Tongan social relations. To call this rank "commoners" is to call the paramount chiefs "kings and queens," the higher chiefly ranks "nobility," and so on. The *tu'as* became commoners during the nineteenth century, but there is no satisfactory English term for their status prior to that time. In the early twentieth century, *tu'a* was used to describe anyone who was indelicate, rude, without manners, or ignorant of Tongan chiefly etiquette (Gifford 1929:108). The term parallels the connotations of "peasant" in English. Chiefly and titled *matāpule* people, even in the years of early contact, called the *tu'as* by a range of terms. Some were said to be complimentary, if objectifying, such as *matatangata*, "good-looking," said of a man (Gifford 1929:108). One rather common epithet was *kāinanga oe fonua*, "eaters of the land," which derived from the somewhat derisive *kāinanga*, "one who eats the leavings of others." Other terms were scornful—*puaka*, "pigs"—and belied the prosperity that rested with these producing people.

The *tu'as* constituted the largest group of Tongans in the Islands. They were responsible for most of the fishing, horticulture, and craft production. In times of war, *tu'a* men comprised the bulk of the fighting forces. This was said by district chiefs to be a form of labor service on behalf, usually, of the paramount, but where contention for chiefly title occurred (the usual occasion for warfare), it seems doubtful that such support could be demanded. In addition, *tu'a* people could be called upon by higher-ranking people, particularly those connected with the district in which they resided, for labor services at feasts, for the construction of chiefly dwellings, chiefly burial mounds, and so on. If other ranks called upon *tu'a* labor, it was to relay the requests of chiefs, not in their own right.

The *tu'as* had hereditary use-rights to land and other resources (Maude 1971:107). These use-rights were obtained through cognatic connections, through the *fahu* for the children of sisters, as well as through patrilineal ties. In theory the *tu'as* were bound to the land and could not change residence without the approval of the district chief. This assertion doubtless depended on the relative power of the district chief, and seems a linguistic inversion typical of chiefly parlance: people who have inalienable use-rights are therefore bound. At times, the chief probably asserted a control which merely mimicked the customary association of a cognatic kindred with the soil. People did change residence during times of warfare and when they visited other islands—visits which could be extended by local marriage. There is no indication that a chief's permission was required for such changes or, more important, that permission could be withheld.

Matāpules: Proto-Functionaries

The *matāpules* formed a rank within the nonchiefly estate, but in some ways they were a mediation between the chiefly and nonchiefly estates. They had no distinctive relationship to people's labor or products. Their significance as foreigners, with the exception of the sky-born Tongan *matāpules* associated with the sacred paramount, in Tongan chiefly tensions has been discussed in the previous chapter. *Matāpules* were predominantly ceremonial attendants, including such roles as speakers for the chiefs, or talking chiefs (Williamson 1924:3:135; Gifford 1929:135), counselors, and servants to the chiefs. But, as retainers of the chiefs, they also served as warriors, craft specialists, navigators, and low-level administrators (Mariner 1827:2:92; Gifford 1929:66). As administrators they dis-

charged police functions, oversaw production by *tu'a* people, and relayed chiefs' directives to the *tu'as.*

The paramount chief assigned these attendants to district chiefs,
although district chiefs also could nominate *matāpules*, subject to
the approval of the paramount (Gifford 1929 : 144). *Matāpules* were
hereditarily nonchiefly, but some were titled and all were higher in
status than the *tu'as.* The *matāpules* were ranked according to the
chiefs to whom they were attached. The occupations of the *matāpules* reflected their unusual intimacy with the chiefs. Certain *matāpules* were engaged in productive labor; others were nonproductive,
performing personal services for the chiefs—as funeral directors,
ceremonial attendants, and the like—or police or overseer functions.
Whether these *matāpules* were specialists or a social rank is unclear,
according to Goldman (1970:298). Gifford claims they were appointed officials, not a rank. The problem lies in the lack of consistency between hereditary rank and occupational differentiation—an
indication of tensions toward class formation, but not class relations.

Artisans were ranked by craft; the higher-ranking crafts were reserved for *matāpules* rather than *tu'as.* But *matāpules* who were
artisans were ranked lower than those who were attendants. *Matāpule* artisans could call on lower-ranking—especially *tu'a*—people
for help if the production was requested by a chief; workers were provided with food by the chief for the duration. Those who were attendants were dependent upon the chiefs for sustenance while they
were in service; this also was true for warriors, although being a war-
rior was not a full-time specialization until after contact. The relative wealth of those *matāpules* who were attendants upon the chiefs
depended on the capacity of the chiefs to extract wealth, food, and
services from *tu'as.* Perhaps as an indication of the uneven flow of
such extraction, the *matāpules* had "plantations of their own" (Mariner 1827 : 2 : 209), as did all other social ranks, both chiefly and nonchiefly. As in other nonchiefly ranks, the lands were allotted by the
district chiefs.

Matāpules were buffers between the lower-ranking nonchiefly
people and the chiefs. They would call local community assemblies,
or *fono,* to convey chiefly orders. Unlike the Samoan *fono,* there
could be no discussion or disagreement at these assemblies (Mariner
1827 : 1 : 289–290).[1] At the same time, the directives may well have
varied with the particular chief. *Matāpules* are depicted as ordering
"planting and fishing" (Gifford 1929 : 98) and as haranguing people to
work harder at gatherings called by chiefs. It is not clear if the chiefs,
via the *matāpule* talking chiefs, were ordering people to continue
to produce whatever they would produce anyway. To order people to

perform an activity they normally do is to assert the capacity to determine activities. This kind of assertion is typical of state formative tensions, particularly of early legal codes (Diamond 1974). But the exhortation to continue customary activities may indicate no more than an assertion, a potential to appropriate the determination of production, but not actual control.

Mu'as

The relationship of the *mu'as* to the division of labor was as convoluted as their position in the ranking scheme. They assisted at public ceremonies under *matāpule* direction, according to Mariner (1827:2:90). Except on important occasions, when *matāpules* would take over, they usually directed the sharing out of food or *kava*, the fermented drink so important in chiefly protocol.

Their responsibilities included haranguing violators of public order or flouters of customs and morality. In particular, since many *mu'as*—as collateral kin and heirs—were *matāpules* "in waiting," one of their duties was to look

> to the morals of the younger chiefs, who are apt to run to excesses, and oppress the lower orders (the tooas), in which case they admonish them, and if they pay no attention, they report them to the older chiefs, and advise that something should be done. . . . They [*mu'as*] are very much respected by all classes. (Mariner 1827:2:90)[2]

Like the *matāpules, mu'as* were considered part of the chiefly retinue and were ranked according to the chief to whom they were attached. Most of the *mu'as* were "professors of some art" (ibid.: 91).

Part-Time Specializations

All specializations in the precontact period were part-time. As Mariner put it, "Everybody knows how to cook and till the ground in a tolerable degree" (1827:2:93). Part-time specializations were associated primarily with nonchiefly people, particularly the *tu'as*. Most craft specializations were associated with men.

Craftsmen were known as *tufunga*, which was a title of respect rather than a rank (Mariner 1827:2:92). Some *tufungas* were hereditary and had designated titles, while others were not. Mariner listed the artisanal occupations (ibid.: 91), along with the rank of those who practiced the skill and whether or not the occupation was hereditary. Certain occupations—cooking and horticulture—not only were hereditary but were said to be restricted to *tu'a* people only, although this is contradicted by the allotment of land to all ranks. Those hereditary occupations associated only with *mu'a* and *tu'a* ranks included stonecutting, net-making, fishing, and the construction of large houses. No other occupations were restricted to *mu'a* and *tu'a* people. Hereditary crafts practiced by *mu'a* and *matāpule* ranks were canoe construction and whale tooth carving, both items associated with chiefly people.

Hereditary artisanry involved every son in the father's occupation, although if the artisan bore a title, only one son inherited the title. This son was chosen by the older *tufunga* (Gifford 1929 : 144). A skilled outsider might be preferred to sons if he presented appropriate gifts. The title, if any, would then shift to the outsider's line (ibid.: 145).

Rank considerations extended to the lowest-status occupations. Mariner claims there were two major reasons why several occupations were hereditary. Some skills were adjudged honorable and brought handsome gifts (valuables) as remuneration. These were not hereditary by compulsion, but through the artisan's "own interest, or the common custom" (Mariner 1927 : 2 : 92). Horticulture and cooking were hereditary through compulsion, at least according to the chiefs:

> . . . the chiefs . . . necessarily require their cooks' and "peasants'" services, and their children naturally succeed them, for neither of these arts require any great talent to learn. (Ibid.: 93)

Mariner ranks cooks above the "peasantry" as he refers to the *kai fonua,* those who cultivated the soil. The cooks were more closely associated with chiefly groups, even though the chiefs always spoke disparagingly of cooks. But cooks had more authority than other *tu'as.* The chief's head cook, according to Mariner,

> is generally not a little proud of himself, and is looked on with some respect by the cooks below him and the common peasants. . . . [He] sees to the supplying of provisions (for the chiefly compound), takes care of the storehouse, looks to the thatching and fences of the dwelling house, occasionally gives an eye to the plantation, and sometimes works upon it himself. (Ibid.)

The cook also had overseeing functions, to assure that chiefly retinues would have enough, although a *matāpule* or petty chief was responsible for reserving chiefly foods. However, within an assembly of *tu'as*, the relative ranking of kin overarched any occupational authority:

> . . . he that has the least to boast of in respect to family connections is sure to be made the cook, as it were servant to the rest. (Ibid.: 93–94)

Some occupations were not considered to be crafts. Several of these specializations were open to both genders. Doctors could be either women or men, and most were *tu'as*. The term for healer, *faito'o*, was not gender-linked, although the gender of the practitioner could be indicated by adding the word *tangata*, "man," or *fefine*, "woman," as a prefix (Gifford 1929: 148). The healing skill involved shamanic practice as well as herbal treatment. Healing expertise passed from parent to child. Doctors practiced some types of surgery, although certain operations could be performed by the patient (Mariner 1827: 2: cii). Captain James Cook described one woman doctor in 1777:

> . . . a Woman was dressing the eyes of a young child which was blind: the eyes were much inflamed and . . . covered with a thin film. The instruments she used were two slender wooden probes, with which she had probed round the eyes so as to make them bleed: she had almost finished the operation [*sic*] when I went in. (Cook in Beaglehole, ed. 1969: 3: 113)

Midwifery was distinguished from other forms of medicine. Like medical practitioners and the men who superincised boys at puberty, midwives received valuables, *koloa*, for their services (ibid.; see also Gifford 1929: 148, 188). A colonial administrator remarked in the late nineteenth century, "Nearly all the old women are medical practitioners . . . heavy fees in kind [are paid] for their services" (Thomson 1904: 134–135). The skill was hereditary, passed from mother to daughter (Thomson 1904: 375). If the midwife had no daughter, she would train her son.

The priesthood also was available to both genders. Tutelary deities were of either gender and some were androgynous. These deities were consulted by priests and by the highest-ranking chiefs, especially the male and female sacred paramounts, as guardians of Tongan fertility and well-being. Priests and priestesses were nonchiefly people, usually *tu'as*; none had the authority of their counterparts in Hawaii. Priestesses predicted the weather and could influence men's and women's activities thereby. Women in general were supposed to be more receptive than men to spirit- and god-possession, whether or not they were priestesses. In trances, they would foretell calamities (Mariner 1827:2:21) or speak of the deity's or spirit's anger and its causes (ibid.: 1:103).

Chiefly Estate and the Production Process

The chiefly estate, including even the highest ranks, was never completely removed from subsistence production. Most higher-ranking chiefly men were not engaged in either craftwork or agricultural pursuits. But, as will be shown in the section on the gender division of labor, chiefly women—even the highest titled women—remained engaged in the production of use-values, in the form of wealth objects or *koloa*.

Chiefly Tongans were internally ranked, in keeping with the model of a conical clan: titled chiefs (the *hau*), their kindreds (the *'eiki*), and lower-ranking, more distantly related chiefly people. The higher-ranking, titled chiefs did not produce their own food or shelter, but were dependent upon nonchiefly people, especially the so-called commoners or *tu'as*, for the maintenance of their life-style. Land was vested in the highest-ranking chiefs—theoretically in the Tu'i Tonga as the sacred protector of Tongan fertility and perhaps at one time in the sacred brother-sister dyad. The paramount chiefs (*hau*) delegated usufruct areas or use-rights to junior-branch district chiefs. District chiefs were known as *tu'a kaifonua* or *kauma'atu'a*, "ruling commoner eating the land" in chiefly parlance (Gifford 1929:286).

District chiefs were supposed to reciprocate by providing manpower during periods of warfare. In ordinary times, they were supposed to donate perishable and durable products, as well as labor of nonchiefly people associated with the district, periodically throughout the year. In addition, particular foods—certain yams decorated with dyed pandanus strips—and "valuables" were to be given during the large-scale annual first fruits ceremonial period, the *'inasi*. These petty chiefs were also responsible for estimating the crops, and the sizes of plantations, and for setting aside, through the use of the chiefly prerogative of *tapu* or forbidding, particular items or areas for the paramount chief. It is notable that the role was one of observing what was being done, rather than initiating new production—estimating what could be supplied, rather than determining what was to be produced.

The involvement of lower-ranking chiefly people, *matāpules* and others, in direct agricultural production varied with the relative power of the paramount chiefs. When the chief was relatively weak, there might be exhortations to enjoy the fruits of one's own labor. The bedrock control of the direct producers over their own subsistence is clear from a widely remembered speech by a paramount chief in the early nineteenth century. Mariner recorded the advice, based on the chief's memory of a famine when he was a boy:

> . . . during the great famine . . . more of these men (chiefs' dependents) had died than of the lower orders, who tilled the ground for their own support, as well as that of their chiefs, because they always found means to reserve food for themselves, however great might be the tax, while those who depended upon the bounty of their chiefs, got but a very scanty allowance. (Mariner 1827: 1:325)

The chief went on to suggest direct involvement in food production, revealing the relative weakness of his chieftaincy:

> Therefore let us (chiefs and attendants of chiefs) apply ourselves, as we have nothing else to do, to agriculture. Follow my example; I will order a piece of ground to be cleared, and, during the next rain, I will assist in planting it . . . (Ibid.: 325 – 326)

Who assigned district chiefs also depended on the relative power of the titled chiefs at a particular time. Until eclipsed by a junior relative or other contending chiefly people, the administrative paramount selected the district chiefs for all areas outside the regions that were hereditarily associated with the Tu'i Tonga, the Tu'i Tonga Fefine, the chiefly Fijians, and the Tamaha. At first the administrative paramount was the Tu'i Ha'a Takalaua, followed by the Tu'i Kanokupolu and, after European contact, a series of paramount chiefs on different Tongan islands.

But until the early nineteenth century, the first fruits or *'inasi* continued to be offered to the Tu'i Tonga and to the Tu'i Tonga Fefine.[3] Mariner, who lived under the protection of the chief who abolished the tributary donations, says that it was viewed as a hardship by the *tu'as* and they welcomed its end: "This measure [the abolition] . . . did not prove objectionable to the *wishes* of the multitude, as it relieved them of a very heavy tax [*sic*], and, in times of scarcity, one extremely oppressive" (1827:2:27).

Land was vested in the Tu'i Tonga and other paramount chiefs as the highest-ranking people in the Islands. Usufruct lands were allo-

cated to lower-ranking chiefly people (mostly men), who in turn designated plots to their attendants, the *matāpules* and *mu'as*, and to
tu'a people already residing in the district (Maude 1971 : 107). In return the chiefs were to have a call on lower-ranking kin, and on nonchiefly people's labor and products.

First Fruits and Labor Claims

The chiefly call on labor and products was direct for the *tu'as*. The
first results of any productive activity, the first fruits of any harvest—especially of yams—and unusual or high-quality products,
fish, other foods, and so on, were destined for the chiefs. Particular
varieties of vegetable foods, species or sizes of fish, turtles, types of
shellfish, and pigs over a certain size (Beaglehole, ed. 1969 : 1 : 169n)
were *tapu*, that is, reserved for chiefly use.

The great *'inasi* ceremony, held annually just before the yam harvest, expressed both the call chiefs had on nonchiefly people's labor
and products and the claims titled chiefs had on one another's products, that is, their relative rank. As a ritual, the *'inasi* served to reproduce the chiefly view of the social relations of production. It did
so by underscoring the division of labor by rank and gender: chiefly
people sat while the cultivators presented foods; men presented their
products, women theirs. But, at the same time, it underscored the
responsibility of even the highest-ranking kin to others: everyone received goods in return, and no one left the ceremony hungry or without a basket to take home (Mariner 1827 : 2 : 171). The ceremony was
ostensibly to offer a portion of the earth's bounty to the gods, in
the person of the male sacred paramount, to ensure prosperity (ibid.:
2 : 168; Anderson in Beaglehole, ed. 1969 : 3 : 948).

No one was to work on the day: until midnight the night before,
men and women sang and prepared the yams and other products in
the dispersed hamlets. Women prepared decorated bark cloth (*ngatu*)
and mats for presentation. Coastal people prepared baskets of fish.
The cultivators harvested the earliest yams, the most important
staple, and *kava* root, the base of the drink that expressed social
rank. Yams, ordinarily not a chiefly food, were wrapped in white and
red pandanus strips to make them presentable to chiefs (Mariner
1827 : 2 : 170).

Early in the morning, bundles of these yams were slung on poles
and carried by pairs of (male) cultivators to Mua, the seat of the male
and female Tu'i Tonga. In the ceremony described by James Cook,
there were 250 such men in procession (Cook 1784 : 1 : 337). Women
carried their valuables, mats and *ngatu*. The various paramount

Figure 5. '*Inasi* ceremony, as seen by Captain James Cook at Tongatapu,
1777. From Cook 1784:337.

chiefs and their entourages also assembled at Mu'a. The current Tu'i Tonga received the yams before the tomb of the last Tu'i Tonga; the yams were then taken to the village green, where the chiefs sat in a large circle, the people behind them. Then the *ngatu*, mats, and other foods were presented (Mariner 1827 : 2 : 171).

The goods were then shared out by one of the Tu'i Tonga's *matāpules:* one-fourth to the gods, accepted by the Tu'i Tonga and taken away by the priests; one-half to the Tu'i Kanokupolu, taken away by his *matāpules;* and one-fourth to the Tu'i Tonga, taken immediately to the Tu'i Tonga Fefine. A *kava* party then ensued, ranking every chief in order. Subsequently, prepared foods were distributed to each chief according to his/her rank, and to the mass of people. Wrestling and boxing matches followed, then dancing at night, involving large numbers of chiefly and nonchiefly participants. Mariner noted that the people considered the *'inasi* demands a burden and that the largesse involved in the distributions and feasting sometimes meant scarcity if the harvest was not "abundant" (ibid.: 2 : 173).

However, the first fruits and the portions saved to donate to chiefly people did not mean the *tu'as* were malnourished. The yams used for the *'inasi* were a special, early-ripening variety; they were not the only variety grown. Similarly, seafoods not reserved for chiefly consumption were plentiful: there were exchange relations between seashore and inland people within the same district. The *tu'as* also ate rats (Anderson in Beaglehole, ed. 1969 : 3 : 942), which they considered tasty,[4] smaller pigs, and, upon occasion, the less desirable parts of pigs eaten at chiefly-sponsored feasts.

The goods reserved for the chiefs—to be distributed to the chiefly, *mu'a*, and *matāpule* retinue—were relayed to the paramount via the district chief and his *matāpules* (Bain 1967 : 35). Offerings for the Tu'i Tonga and Tu'i Tonga Fefine (the sacred paramounts) were relayed from the Tu'i Kanokupolu to the Tu'i Ha'a Takalaua, then to the Tu'i Tonga, and then to the Tu'i Tonga Fefine (Gifford 1929 : 98, 103). The flow of donations, then, paralleled the ranking system from lower to higher. Paramount chiefly women—especially the Tu'i Tonga Fefine and her daughter, the Tamaha—had their own channels of first fruits offerings, donations of special foods and products (ibid.: 141). The line of product prestations in general marked the claims of the *fahu*, the claims derived from sisters' higher rank.

In return for these products and for the periodic labor service on chiefly-sponsored projects expected of all *tu'as*, women and men, the *tu'as* had use-rights to land, almost unrestricted fishing rights (Gifford 1929 : 146–147), and food during the period of labor service. Gifford says the paramount chief would present bark cloth (*tapa* or *masi)* or *kava* root to those who brought baskets of fish (ibid.: 10). *Tu'as* who transgressed the chiefly prerogatives or violated the *tapus* on chiefly foods risked beatings, and possibly death (ibid.: 104, 127). However, there were sanctuaries—known as god-houses—scattered throughout the Islands for anyone who had seriously violated the *tapus* (ibid.: 324).

The *matāpules'* relationship to the production process, and to the distribution of goods encompassed by the term, was similar to the *tu'as'*. Some provided goods, while others performed services for the chiefs in the form of assistance or attendance. In return for such services and goods, the *matāpules* received use-rights to land for their kindreds, and they also received valuables which could be exchanged for foods, other men's work items, and other valuables. *Matāpules* who transgressed chiefly prerogatives might be beaten, but they were not killed (Gifford 1929:141).

Chiefly people could order activities of lower-ranking chiefly people, *matāpules* in their retinues, and *tu'as* in the district. Generally, this initiative was along gender lines. For the primary wife of a paramount chief—herself a paramount chief, as has been shown—the women to whose labor she had claims included her co-wives; her husband's concubines, who were her own attendants; the wives and daughters of lower-ranking chiefs and *matāpules*; and those *tu'as* living in both her marital and natal regions (Mariner 1827:2:212). Thus chiefly women had access to valuables and other subsistence products in their own right, through the *fahu* claims on their brothers, and through other aspects of their rank such as marital status. They were dependent on neither their brothers nor their husbands.

It is unclear if chiefly men could order production by *tu'a* women, or if chiefly women could order *tu'a* men, but both seem likely. Gifford (1929:98) says in this regard that the administrative paramount chief, the Tu'i Kanokupolu, could command "planting and fishing." Both of these were men's activities. If male chiefs could command *tu'a* women's labor at gender-specific tasks, leaving aside for the moment sexual services—and they could at undiscriminated tasks—the importance of estate over gender considerations would be indicated. What would *not* be indicated is a control of women's labor by men.

Rank and estate were not unrelated to the division of labor, nor were they mimicked in the division of labor. Both use-rights and labor claims were available to all by virtue of kin connections, but the level of claims to labor varied with rank. Occupational differentiation crossed rank and estate lines; all ranks were to some extent engaged in productive labor. The symbolism of high rank, of chiefly estate, was grounded in the relations that ordered the production process. Ultimately, changes in the division of labor during the nineteenth century also changed the conceptualization of rank and estate. Some chiefs asserted that first fruits and other donations were tribute. But they were compelled to reciprocate with material returns as well as symbolic assurances. The people who presented goods did so as much as possible in the form of gifts, which emphasized the need to reciprocate. The division of labor and the differential labor claims by rank indicate potential class formation, but other aspects—such as the necessity of return and the involvement in productive activities—indicate kin-associated relations of production.

In one critical aspect, however, subsistence production was not related to rank. This aspect, the division of labor by gender, substantially prevented the emergence of class relations prior to European intervention. The gender division of labor was the keystone of social reproduction and the replication of tense, but kin-based relations of production.

Gender Division of Labor

All things made by women were considered *koloa*, valuables, wealth objects (Gifford 1929:148). *Koloa* were stored in the rafters of a house (Collocott and Havea 1922:69). In myth women were equated at times with the ridgepoles of a house (ibid.:169; Collocott 1928: 16–17). In other words, women supported and guarded the wealth of a household. In birth ceremonies, the newborn actually was called *koloa* (Collocott and Havea 1922:169; Beaglehole and Beaglehole 1941:81). In a sense, the baby was the product of the mother's labor. Valuables were always superior to things made by men; men's objects and women's objects formed separate and unequal spheres. Men's products usually were not acceptable as a return for a presentation of valuables, regardless of the relative quantities involved (Goldman 1970:301). The articulation of men's and women's spheres of exchange is discussed further in the next chapter, on exchange and value.

Chiefly women's production of valuables validated other chiefly persons' status throughout life. For instance, a contender had to present goods of appropriate value, that is, higher rank, in order to be granted a title. To become a titled chief, then, a chiefly Tongan had to persuade women of higher rank to provide goods, since no one could commandeer the goods of a higher-ranking kinsperson. Chiefly women engaged in direct production of valuables both because the goods were needed to validate status changes, including the reproduction of chiefly titles, and because their own influence over which contender became the titled chief depended on their labor.

All women, chiefly and nonchiefly, plaited mats of various types and made bark cloth. Generically bark cloth is known as *tapa*, although this may not have been a Tongan term; the Tongan generic term probably was *masi*.[5] There were terms for different types of mats—based on intended use, plaiting techniques, and materials used[6]—and a wide variety of bark cloth, both plain and decorated. The finest mats were known as *ngafi ngafi*. Some fine mats were interwoven with red feathers, obtained in chiefly-sponsored expeditions to Fiji. These trading parties often began with warfare between Tongans and Fijians; the conclusion of hostilities involved exchanges of indigenous valuables. Women also wove baskets, which were used in exchanges and presentations to chiefly people. Some of these were functional, while others were decorative or purposefully functionless (Gifford 1929: 148).

Nonchiefly women gathered shellfish and octopi on the reefs and netted fish in the lagoons; these items, since they were obtained by women, were considered to be chiefly foods (Gifford 1929: 106). Other marine creatures, with the exception of turtles, which were associated in myth with women, were considered nonchiefly. Men were responsible for such deep-sea fishing. Nonchiefly women crafted clothing, bedding, bags, and ornamental aprons. Nonchiefly women also prepared certain chiefly specialty dishes and extracted coconut oil (West 1846/1865:267; Collocott 1928:165; Mariner 1827:1:122). Coconut oil was blended with flowers and used as a perfumed skin salve; certain scents were reserved for chiefly people, notably sandalwood, which was not native to Tonga.

Chiefly women, particularly young and unmarried women, chewed the *kava* root and prepared the slightly intoxicating brew.[7] Cook mentions that both women and men prepared *kava* for the chiefs (Beaglehole, ed. 1969:3:123), and there are indications in Tongan oral histories that even older *tu'a* men could be called upon to chew tough *kava* roots as punishment for infractions of chiefly privileges. But to chew and brew the *kava* was considered an honor by young women, not a hardship.

Tu'a women were expected to contribute labor to chiefly-sponsored projects. Mixed-gender work groups were known in situations where appropriate tasks within the overall project could be delegated to women or men (Gifford 1929:145, 146). House construction and lagoon fishing were perhaps the most common activities so organized. Chiefly people could call upon *tu'a* women for mat-making and *tapa*-

Figure 6. Vava'u woman weaving a basket for the Friendly Islands
Cooperative. Photo by the author.

making as well. The manufacture of bark cloth is described in several sources: it involved cooperative labor and seems also to have been an occasion for the exchange of information and social planning.[8]

Women plaited mats and made *tapa* in a house constructed especially for such purposes. This women's house was located in the chiefly compound if the women involved were chiefly or *matāpule* in rank. If the women were *tu'as*, the house was built in a central location, since prior to contact and the subsequent "civil wars" cultivating households were scattered throughout the districts in hamlets. After contact, the women's house occupied the center of the village on the *malae* or village green—a place considered to be chiefly. These houses were the only community houses used by Tongans: there were no men's houses. *Tu'a* women worked under the direction of an older woman (Gifford 1929:147).

Gatherings called by chiefly women to beat the bark into cloth were termed *kautaha*; gatherings to stamp and finish the cloth were called *kokanga* (Kooijman 1972:319). Chiefly women made and kept the design stamps, *kobechi*, used to mark the decorated variety of cloth, *ngatu*.[9] The designs were associated with particular chiefly houses and, since the cloth was exchanged to mark significant status changes, such as marriage, the relationship of the various chiefly houses to each other was reflected in the possession of these cloths.

Even the highest-ranking chiefly women were involved in the production of *koloa*, the making of wealth objects needed in everyday life. Mariner writes of mat-making:

> The women employ themselves (particularly nobles [*sic*]) in making a variety of articles chiefly ornamental; these employments, however, are considered accomplishments, not professions. Some of the higher class [rank] of women not only make these . . . but actually make a sort of trade of it, without prejudice to their rank; which is what the lower class [nonchiefly] of women could not do, because what they make is not their own property, but is done by the order of their superiors. (Mariner 1827:2:97)

Nothing chiefly people did would be considered a profession, since all specialists were *matāpules*. In addition, nonchiefly women also exchanged labor with relatives and neighbors to make *tapa* and mats for their own household uses, gifts, life crisis ceremonies, and so on (Gifford 1929:147). Chiefly people had first call on mats and on bark cloth. It is not clear from the literature, but since chiefly women designed and sewed the stamps, it seems likely that prior to contact *ngatu*—the stamped, stained, and decorated variety—might well have been reserved for chiefly use. All people had access to some forms of bark cloth, but early European travelers noted that the *tu'as* appeared more scantily dressed than higher-ranking people. Since *tapa* was a wealth object, their relative lack of wealth would be obvious.

Men's products were *ngāue*, or work.[10] Before contact, *tu'a* men did all cooking, which bore very low status (West 1846/1865:267).[11] Nonchiefly men did virtually all horticulture, deep-sea fishing, and canoe-making. Men crafted all weapons. In addition, men were supposed to carry water and collect firewood, two activities associated in most of the anthropological literature with women. Chiefly men sometimes made sinnet rope (Wilkes 1852:1:4), went deep-sea fishing, did inlaid work on weapons (Erskine 1853/1967:149), and upon occasion even did agricultural work (Mariner 1827:1:325–326).

There were activities that were not gender-specific. Some coconut-fiber rope-making (Neill 1955:127), house construction, and lagoon fishing involved both women and men, whether organized at the request of chiefs or among the nonchiefly people. Child care also was assumed by both men and women.

Barbering was done by men and women, although most barbers were supposed to have been women (Gifford 1929:148). Chiefly women could barber chiefly men. Barbering implied a breach of the *tapu* on touching the head of anyone superior in rank. It is thus likely that it was done by those who were immune from the *tapus:* people who were higher in rank, such as relatives on one's sister's side, or people who were *matāpules,* since they were mostly of foreign origin.

Warfare was not a full-time occupation before the late eighteenth century. It does seem to have been predominantly a concern of men. But women were not excluded from the battlefield. They could take revenge on behalf of a slain husband, brother, etc., and were admired for doing so (Mariner 1827:1:239). Women accompanied most war parties to other islands, ostensibly to guard the war canoes during the fighting, but

> During the battle, several of the . . . women came to the scene of action, that they might be near their husbands to assist them if wounded. (Ibid.:166)

One invasion force from the Vava'u island group consisted of five thousand men and one thousand women (Thomson 1904:338).

Kinship Connections and the Division of Labor

The division of labor by relationship revolves around the *fahu,* the claims to labor and products defined by the higher rank of sisters. *Fahu* encompassed the relationship of a sister to her brother, her relationship to his children, and her children's relationship to their mother's brother and his children. In her role as sister and father's sister, a woman exercised prerogatives that included a privileged access to the valuables and men's products in her brother's household. She could claim usufruct lands associated with her brother. These prerogatives were enjoyed by a woman's children as well, vis-à-vis their maternal uncle and their cousins.

The *fahu* for chiefly people was extended to include lineages, and this entailed tributary relations. If one were a father's sister, *mehikitanga,* either metaphorically—as in the case of interlineage connections—or collaterally—as within one kindred—the claims were substantial. One could claim not only the production of "brothers" and "brothers' children," but also the production over which the "brothers" and "brothers' children" had claims. It is uncertain whether *tu'a* people's father's sisters or sister's children could *request* production of the maternal uncle's people, but it is clear that they could claim the valuables and men's goods of those to whom they were *fahu.* Even after the *fahu* was banned (1929), in the 1930's a nonchiefly woman could harvest food from her brother's plots without previously informing him of her intentions (Beaglehole and Beaglehole 1941:75). The goods could not be denied her, nor was it necessary to obtain even nominal approval for the exercise of these prerogatives—even though the practice was illegal.

Seniority as a ranking principle also influenced the division of labor and labor claims in general. Older siblings, male and female, could call on younger ones to perform appropriate tasks. Within a household, there could be a domino effect, especially along gender lines. Since seniority might contradict ranking of brothers and sisters, the situation across gender lines was more complex. Since sisters outranked brothers, it was clearer that an older sister would be more apt to be heard in her demands than, say, an older brother requesting a younger sister to do something.

Marriages were arranged through the *fahu* prerogatives and the relationships set up by marriage also influenced the division of labor. Indeed, the institution of generalized exchange among the topmost chiefly groups can be seen as an exercise of the *fahu* prerogatives of the father's sister.[12] The relationship of siblings-in-law of the same gender involved consistent one-way labor claims. A man called his wife's brother *matāpule* or attendant (Burrows 1970:56). The term embodied the relationship of the two groups: a man's wife's natal group provided goods and services to her marital group. The wife's brother was lower ranking than his sister's husband, because his sister was higher ranking. Correlatively, a woman was higher-ranking than her brother's wife or wives.

A woman had access to the labor of her brother's wife or wives; she could claim goods made by them or request production of them. If a brother's wife was not cooperative, the husband's sister could cause her deliveries to be difficult (Collocott 1928:130). A woman also could claim the "living wealth" of her brother's wife or wives: she had the right to adopt her brother's children (Gifford 1929:26; Collocott 1928:18). Adoption is perhaps an inadequate term (Carroll, ed. 1970). Since the children were in a sense identified with their father's sister, she could reclaim their identity from the children's father, since she outranked him. In other words, the father's sister indirectly controlled the wealth production—in terms of goods as well as fertility and continuity—of her own natal group. Again, the unity of production and reproduction in the kin setting is underscored. Through the *fahu*, a woman could reclaim the valuables—including children—which otherwise might have been lost to her after marriage. The sister's children also had, through their mother, important claims to men's and women's products made by the people of their mother's natal group.

In myth, the husband's sister was sometimes an ominous character. One story has the sister of the groom attempt to feed her new sister-in-law the chiefly portion of meat, even though the bride is not relatively chiefly to her husband's sister. Instead of pork liver, however, the meat was human liver (Collocott 1928:24). There are other stories of a husband's sisters trying to kill their brother's wife (ibid.:25). Since residence was patrilocal, the husband's unmarried sisters were likely to live in the same locality. But at least for *tu'a* people it was thought unwise to marry far from one's birthplace, since it would remove one's children from their mother's brother and the goods they could claim. So, although a woman had to defer to her husband's sister, she also could claim goods from her brother and her natal kin group.

Rank and Gender in Class Formation

The division of labor by rank, which tended toward class formation, was counteracted by the division of labor by gender. As a consequence, the chiefly estate—even the highest chiefly ranks—never ceased to be engaged in the production of necessary items. Chiefly women produced valuables, which were crucial in the validation of the maker's rank, in the reproduction of the chiefly group as a whole, and in the reproduction of Tongan society as kin-based. Both chiefly and nonchiefly women produced mats and *tapa* of various types for distribution in life crisis ceremonies, and as compensation for those who performed services for the donor. The products were valuables, wealth objects, but in many cases they also were used in everyday life. Most of these *koloa,* or valuables, were functional and in fact were used by those who made or received them.

Chiefly men were removed more easily than women from productive activities. Men's work, *ngāue,* was considered nonchiefly. One of the markers of high rank for men was the cessation of work, or minimal involvement in the higher forms of men's work. For chiefly women, though, there was a contradiction. While women's activities were productive and thus, in a sense, nonchiefly, the products were chiefly. To make these objects demonstrated women's status—even the highest-ranking chiefly women's—as the sole creators of socially recognized wealth. Women's production was intrinsically of greater value than men's "work" and thus was not only necessary but also chiefly.

Women's work was more profoundly involved than men's in the replication of production, distribution, and consumption ordered along kinship lines, that is, with expectations of material returns for goods presented, either directly or indirectly. For chiefly women to be engaged in production questioned neither their rank nor the estate stratification. At the same time, the necessity of the highest-ranking women to be so engaged underscored the kin-based nature of that stratification and, thus, a fundamental similarity of Tongans, from paramount chief to *tu'a.* As chiefly and nonchiefly people, women engaged differentially in production, but all had a direct involvement. Women of all ranks created and distributed the goods which embodied and ensured the cohesion of the stratified kin structure.

So long as chiefly women remained involved in the creation of valuables in a direct way, rather than solely through nonchiefly women, subsistence production—in the larger sense of the continuity of production for use—could not become class organized. The chiefs expected lower-ranking chiefly people, *matāpules, mu'as,* and *tu'as* to provide goods and services that ensured the continuity of the chiefly retinues; but in return, there were customary expectations of material reciprocity as well as fertility assurances. For the chiefly group as a whole to become a politically dominant class, a major change had to occur. Either the validation of chiefly title had to become divorced from the demonstration of chiefly connections to the rest of the population, or social authority had to become associated with something other than chiefly title. The kinship idiom could remain as a formal or rhetorical device, but its substance had to be redefined, at least between chiefly and nonchiefly estates.

Women's involvement as the sole creators of socially valued products effectively prevented the emergence of class relations. This ambivalence of women's work being simultaneously chiefly and nonchiefly—paralleling reproductive and productive aspects of the items—anticipates a later reduction in the status of women when productive activity became divorced from rank. In the postcontact period, the reproduction of the highest social group became possible without the demonstration of rank through the creation and exchange of wealth objects. As rank became estranged from social authority, the makers of the items that validated rank (women) and the people who orchestrated the status changes for chiefly people (chiefly women as father's sisters) were no longer essential to the reproduction of the preeminent position of chiefs. Ironically, the pivotal importance of women in the reproduction of kin-based rather than class relations contributed to the degradation of women's authority as classes and state institutions emerged.

6. Exchange and Value

Queen Salote *(quoted in Bain 1967:77)*   *. . . our history is written, not in books, but in our mats.*

AT THE time of contact, the value of an object in Tonga still embodied the status of the maker(s). The predominant difference in the value of objects stemmed from the gender of the makers. *Koloa*, or valuables, made by women, were chiefly relative to *ngāue*, or work, made by men. Why was women's labor considered more valuable?

The tendency is to seek rationalist explanations (e.g., Harris 1974; cf. Diener, Rubkin, and Nonini 1978). But the reasons cannot be found in women's relative involvement in subsistence production. Men's products largely provisioned the society. Women's products contributed other aspects of subsistence: clothing, flooring, bedding, carrying devices, storage containers, as well as food delicacies. In Tonga, food was, in a sense, assumed—except during chiefly succession disputes, when provisions could become scarce. Although it was categorically inferior to women's products, food was acknowledged as the foundation of the society in rituals such as the *'inasi*, the first fruits ceremonial. The claims of kinship were expressed in the distribution of food; to sell or barter food with another Tongan, or a visitor, was to deny one's shared humanity.

The higher value of women's labor cannot be explained by differential control over women's and men's labor. Women's labor was claimed by a range of kin, both women and men. While women were not independent or in full control of their products, since control varied with rank and kin roles, neither were their products controlled by men or any other single group. This also was the case for men's products.

Utilitarian considerations also are not great indications of value:

Malinowski (1961) noted for the Trobriand region that the prized *kula* valuables—armshells and necklaces—frequently were unwearable even as ornaments because of their age or inappropriate size. Similarly, while mats were used in everyday life in Tonga, the finest ones were used only on ceremonial occasions. Some baskets were made solely for presentation as gifts—they might be completely useless as containers. Certain forms of decorated and plain colored bark cloth were used only during life crisis rites, such as marriages, births, funerals, and so on. Weiner (1979) makes a case for objects which have some durability becoming important markers of status, but she points out that the connection is not a necessary one: the highly valued banana leaf bundles in the Trobriand Islands wear out and are replaced regularly.

Structuralist explanations would imply that there is no reason other than the particular, timeless symbolic code for why women's labor was more valuable. But while the symbolic system and the categorization scheme in Tonga differed markedly from our own, they were constituted out of people's engagement in making a world. The explanation lies in how value is constituted in societies unlike our own, societies where producers substantially control their conditions of life, including the means of making a living.

The value of items in a commodity situation—where most goods are produced to exchange in a market—derives from the labor time embedded in the object; this labor time includes the cost not only of maintaining the worker, but also of socializing him or her, training, and otherwise ensuring that production can continue (Marx 1881/ 1967: vol. 1). But where distribution is ordered not through markets but through kin and quasi-kin (e.g., rank) relations, value is determined differently. Where the maker retains control over the production process—including the acquisition of raw materials, tools, and the making and distribution of goods—labor is not alienated. This was predominantly the case in precontact Tonga. Value, therefore, was not determined by the same factors as in commodity production. Where labor is not alienated, value rests not only in the amount of socially determined labor embodied in the object, but also in the social personhood of the maker. Labor is not abstracted or divorced from the person; value can then derive from the status of the person as a creator.

Spheres of Exchange

The division of labor by rank and gender set up separate and unequal spheres of exchange. The sphere that derived from the division of labor by rank defined objects as chiefly (*'eiki*) or nonchiefly (*tu'a* in this case). The sphere created by the division of labor by gender comprised items considered as valuables (*koloa*) or work (*ngāue*). These two spheres were not isomorphic: because they crosscut each other, the intersections allowed for items to be exchanged across boundaries. The contradictory factors, then, structured the articulation of the spheres. Within each sphere—as within each estate in the kinship structure—products were internally graded. Some wealth objects were more chiefly than others; some work items were more or less chiefly than others. The internal ranking depended on the maker of the item, the type of item, and other influences analyzed below.

Women's and men's products could be exchanged, but only through the mediation of the other sphere, of chiefly and nonchiefly goods. For instance, within the "work" sphere, special yams were "chiefly"; they could be exchanged in certain circumstances for less "chiefly" women's products, but only because each was in some manner, chiefly. The women's products remained more valuable, however. At the same time, things made by women of the chiefly estate were exchangeable only for other such goods.

It is unclear whether *any* valuables or wealth objects were considered to be nonchiefly: it is highly unlikely that any were. It is doubtful whether any items considered to be *ngāue* were "chiefly," beyond the work sphere.

The reproduction of Tongan society depended on the production and exchange of valuables made by women and, because of the prerogatives of women as father's sisters through the *fahu*, controlled by them (Collocott 1923b:223; Neill 1955:141; Mariner 1827:1:320). Women could give valuables to men, in return for sexual favors, for example (Alpers 1970:289). Men also had access to wealth through the *fahu*: they could claim valuables, as could their sisters, from their mother's brother. Thus, to acquire wealth objects, even the highest-ranking chiefly men required reproduction of *fahu* rights: the acknowledgement of a sister's higher rank was requisite to acquisition of wealth, as well as of title.

During life crisis ceremonies such as marriages, births, and funerals, *koloa* were distributed: the bulk of the wealth went to the father's sister and her children. According to Goldman, the *koloa/ngāue* spheres of exchange were not mutually transferable (1970: 301). Unlike the situation in Samoa, he argues, where the transfer of valuables for food was complicated but complementary, in Tonga the spheres were mutually exclusive. The introduction of mitigating or crosscutting spheres of chiefly/nonchiefly goods refines this interpretation. Taken in isolation, women's and men's goods would not be mutually exchangeable: no amount of work products could be exchanged or presented for any amount of valuables. But it seems that the valuables made by nonchiefly women, especially *tu'a* women, were exchangeable—by both chiefly women and men—for the "chiefly" sort of men's products and for services by nonchiefly people—*matāpules, mu'as,* and *tu'as.* This rewarding of services, including sexual liaisons, with *koloa* underscores the value of manual, personal, and reproductive labor. At the same time, there is a presumption that food was readily obtainable and, thus, not very valuable.

Women's role in production involved the making of valuables, including children. As bearers of children for the husband's chiefly "house" or nonchiefly local kindred, women symbolized group continuity. "Work," done by men, ensured the women's well-being. This seems to imply that women accepted food in return for valuables, such as children; like foreigners and strangers, they would thus mix the spheres of exchange, to the advantage, in this case, of the husband's kin. Chiefly lineages could be viewed as exchanging women for women—balanced in kind, though not in numbers or in rank. *If* one assumes the patrilineage to be the basis of kinship and, symbolically, a masculine sphere, then male-male exchange would be formally balanced—women for women—while male-female exchange would be unequal—food for children. In such a scheme, women would receive less than they would give, getting work products for valuables. But this view of the kin system ignores the influence of both sibling and chiefly/nonchiefly ranking.

The father's sister transcended marriage-based affiliation. Before, during, and after marriage she had similar rights in her natal kindred or, at times for chiefly groups, patrilineage. Through the *fahu,* a woman had access to the valuables she had created and those of her natal group, as created by her mother's brother's people and her own brother's wives. The father's sister could claim the children of her brother, the "valuables" created by her brother's wife. Were it not for this critical right to adopt, the sister's marriage into another lineage would entail the exchange of productivity—a valuable-maker, a woman—for products—food, marriage gifts, birth gifts, and so on.

These spheres of exchange had meaning primarily for chiefly people. Marriage alliances were not as politically charged for nonchiefly people. Lineage affiliation—as much as it was effective—became increasingly tenuous for nonchiefly people, since chiefly groups often sought to dissociate themselves from local kindreds. In addition, nonchiefly people did not entirely control the distribution of their labor and products, although they would rebel against an oppressive chief (Gifford 1929:182). Whether women gave children for food was academic for the nonchiefly kindreds: everyone gave to the chiefs, rebelled, or faced punishment for infringement of the chiefly *tapus* (Goldman 1970:303). The exercise of material *fahu* rights was at times a risk for nonchiefly people. The transfer of goods might transgress chiefly prerogatives. To limit possible chiefly interference, nonchiefly people tended to marry locally, or within the same chiefly district (Beaglehole and Beaglehole 1941:78). Goods transferred through the *fahu* would remain in one district. This arrangement supports the view that local kin groups were kindreds, rather than patrilineal segments.

Within Tonga, there were customary exchanges of foodstuffs between coastal and inland kindreds. *Tu'a* people who lived in inland areas within one chiefly district exchanged specialized *ngāue* food products for fish and other goods associated with people who lived on the coast. The chiefly districts, as is typical of Polynesia, approximated a "pie slice," to use Sahlins' phrase, of the resource areas of a larger island, or sometimes an entire island.

Exchange between chiefs and nonchiefly producers formed another sphere of exchange. The nonperformance of "work" was a mark of rank for men. Chiefly women produced only valuables; they also had some of the productive capacity of lower-ranking women at their disposal. Chiefly women controlled the disposition of the goods they produced, subject to the claims of higher-ranking female chiefs and relatives. They also indirectly controlled the productive capacity and reproductive capacity of their natal kindred or lineage— through the right to adopt, the authority to arrange nieces' and nephews' marriages, and the capability of cursing their brothers' wives and rendering them sterile. In addition, chiefly women received goods associated with men—*ngāue*—in their own right as high-ranking people, rather than through their husbands. Nonchiefly women also could claim men's goods through the *fahu*, that is, as sisters, and thus were not dependent upon husbands to provide men's work.

Exchanges of *koloa* probably involved both chiefly and nonchiefly Tongans. Mariner (1827:2:97) implies that the exchange of valuables was controlled by chiefly people. In the context it is unclear whether he means chiefly women, or chiefly people in general. *Koloa* could be given by chiefly people to nonchiefly people. Such valuables were presented within *tu'a* ranks during life crisis ceremonies, such as the recognition of a midwife's success, wedding rites, and so on.

With regard to inter-island exchange, in particular, long-distance trade, mats and *tapa* were exchanged for local valuables, e.g., red feathers from Fiji, fine mats from Samoa. Women went with men on these long-distance and inter-island trading expeditions (Mariner 1827:1:260). What women did is not entirely clear. The trips to Fiji sometimes involved warfare prior to the establishment of exchange relations; voyages to Samoa and other islands were more peaceable. It is likely that women bartered women's products while men bartered theirs (Anderson in Beaglehole, ed. 1969:3:863). People on voyages, Anderson commented in 1777,

> always carry a considerable quantity of Cloath, matts &c and provisions. . . . The number of people, amongst which are always several women, being at least four times more than is sufficient to Navigate the Boat. (Anderson in Beaglehole, ed. 1969:3:939)

Exchanges on voyages among the three Tongan island groups—Tongatapu, Ha'apai, and Vava'u—took a more or less kin-ordered form, gifts rather than barter. Sometimes voyages provided an opportunity to marry in another island. It is probable that non-Tongan exchange was sponsored by chiefly people, since it is unlikely that anyone else could present the number of valuables and supply the amount of food consumed during construction to the builder of the large, sea-going vessels. Trade in Tongan history is not well documented, but it seems that *tu'a* people could barter *ngāue* and *koloa* as well, perhaps by leave of the chiefs, more likely when chiefs were physically absent.

Exchange value, however, was never dissociated from use-value in the precontact situation. The products made by nonchiefly people for presentation to chiefly people could have been destined by the chiefly people for trade in Fiji or Samoa, but so far as the producers were concerned, production was not for exchange.[1] Rather, the production was for discharge of obligations to higher-ranking people, for the prestige and reciprocal expectations inherent in presenting a gift, or for direct consumption. The producers could reasonably expect to receive recompense in the form of chiefly largesse, food, valuables, and so on. In addition, the chiefly people who sponsored the trading trips were seeking exotica to underscore or display their own continuity as chiefly persons, a pattern of consumption which marked their status. The exchange was, as Sahlins has pointed out in another Polynesian context (1972:83), one of use-values, rather than commodities. The production of *koloa* and the production or nonproduction of *ngāue* simultaneously demonstrated and validated one's social status.

The exchange between chiefly and nonchiefly people, whether or not the goods were destined to be traded for exotic prestige items, was not commodity exchange.[2] Donations or tribute, depending on power relations, are a form of distribution which can become commodity exchange. Trade based on and oriented toward production for use can become commodity exchange when the purpose of trade becomes accumulation and reinvestment, rather than consumption or display.

Nonchiefly producers gave goods and services to the chiefs in exchange for material returns, affirming customary use-rights, or fertility-assurance. The chiefs exchanged prestige goods for other wealth items, which were used to help replicate chiefliness. The purpose of the production of mats and *tapa* for the chiefs was not necessarily for trade, but for prestige, as a marker of the pseudo-dependency of the *tu'as* on the chiefs (for use-rights to land and other resources) and of the chiefs' own high status. The *tu'as*, however, as much as possible presented such goods to the chiefs *as gifts*, for in that way, they received prestige and incurred the chiefs' obligation to be generous in return (Mariner 1827:2:133). The extraction of goods and labor service from the underlying population was, at times, sufficiently severe to be termed tribute—and to spark rebellion. The redress was always to restore chieftaincy, that is, to underscore the kin-based reciprocal obligations of chiefly and nonchiefly people.

Value of Labor and Products

The constitution of value as embodied in objects has long been a focus of inquiry in political economy. Marx discussed how value—as distinct from price—is constituted in commodities in a capitalist economy (1881/1967:1:Ch. 1). His conceptualization requires modification for understanding of value in either communal or tribute-based modes of production. Tongan society, stratified, but still kin-based, provides a setting for examining value in precapitalist social formations. The later influx of merchant capital relations, commodity trade, and, eventually, capitalist relations of production highlights certain historical changes in the constitution of value.

The basic difference in value, as mentioned above, was according to the gender of the maker(s). Further distinctions were made within each of the women's and men's spheres. Women's goods, types of mats, *tapa* or bark cloth, the decorated bark cloth known as *ngatu*, baskets, and so on were internally graded as more or less valuable. Similarly, men's goods or *ngāue* were internally ranked, depending on factors explored below. In addition, both women's and men's goods were categorized and evaluated according to the importance of the occasions for which their presentation or consumption was suitable. Certain mats and foods were appropriate for particular events. Within the sphere of *ngāue* or men's products, the same term could be used to describe a pig or a *kava* root suitable to a certain type of occasion (Beaglehole and Beaglehole 1941 : 57−58).

Still another dimension of relative value concerned the rank of the person who had requested the production, who claimed it, or who was presented with the object upon completion. Thus, a mat made by a *tu'a* woman at the request of a paramount female chief would have greater value than one made at the request of a lower-ranking chief. Locality influenced value in a parallel manner. Certain regions or islands were associated with high-ranking female chiefs. In the early twentieth century, the influence of locality upon value was noted by one observer:

> Even if a mat obtained from Tungua [the Ha'apai island residence of the Tamaha] should prove to be of not much account as a mat yet it derives value from its origin in the island of the Tamaha. (Collocott 1928 : 141; see also 1923a : 178−179)

The partial association of value with the persons requesting production and with regions associated with high-ranking people is symptomatic of increasing stratification. That is, value was at least somewhat dissociated from the producer, although it was not associated solely with the object itself.

The labor time needed to complete an article also was an important consideration within each of the *koloa* and *ngāue* spheres. But labor intensity was significant only within each sphere; it was not important across the spheres. It appears that the status of the maker(s) was more important. *Tapa,* made collectively, was highly valued. But mats, made individually or with exchange labor, seem to have been more "chiefly" than bark cloth. One fine mat could take a woman up to four years to plait; such mats not only were functional, they also embodied local history and cultural continuity. Fine mats were critical for the validation of any change in personal status, whether the person involved was chiefly or nonchiefly.

Durable products were more highly valued than ephemeral goods,

Figure 7. Vava'u women plaiting a mat. Photo by the author.

again within the separate spheres of women's and men's products. Durables acquired value from the entire social context, not only from the amount of labor embodied in them. In other words, *whose* labor was involved was far more important than *how much* labor was involved. Quantity was not as important as quality. Quality in the precontact situation was not abstracted from the personhood of the creator. The creator's status, the object's prospective use and history had precedence over aesthetic considerations.

The age of an item indicated its social experience: who had initiated the object, who had presented it to whom, on which occasions, and so on. The more "experienced" an item, the higher its value. Aesthetic aspects of an object—skill in execution especially—were appreciated, but the item's historical dimensions were far more important. Mats, *tapa,* and *ngatu* (decorated bark cloth) increased in value, whether or not they remained functional or ever were functional, the more they were used publicly to mark the changing statuses of people who held them for a time (cf. Beaglehole and Beaglehole 1941; Malinowski 1961).

In this context, Queen Salote told a British official in the 1960's:

> Each line of kings [*sic:* chiefs, the *ha'a*] had its own ceremonial mats which were carefully preserved from generation to generation. In fact, our history is written, not in books, but in our mats. I have in my possession a number of historic *ta'ovala* [a type of fine mat], including those from the sacred Tui Tonga line. . . . The *ta'ovala* I wore when I met Queen Elizabeth on Her Majesty's arrival in Tonga was six hundred years old. Worshipped in the 13th century as a symbol of the ancient gods, the mat belonged to the chiefly family of Malupo on the island of 'Uiha. (Quoted in Bain 1967:77)

Labor was not abstracted from the person. While it is possible to discern relative value according to the labor involved in the production within each of the spheres of exchange, a labor theory of value is insufficient to determine an item's overall value in the kinship context. Labor, the transformative action of a person, was conceptualized by the Tongans as such. But the action was not embodied in the object, as where labor is abstracted from the actor. Instead, the actor was in many senses embodied in the creation.

Equally important was the social universe into which the item was born. The fertility reference is not accidental: children were conceptualized as being brought into being by the mother's labor: they were her *koloa. Koloa* were valuable because they were the creations of women; *ngāue* were less valued because they were men's products. The quality of the labor embodied in each sort of product was indistinguishable from the persons engaged in the production. Labor was not an undifferentiated concept. The differentiation was linked to intensity, skill, tediousness, and so on. But the differentiation was, first and foremost, according to the status of the creators and, secondarily, according to the event or person who occasioned the production.

Alongside gender, other dimensions of the social self entered into the evaluation of an object, whether the item was gathered (not associated with women only), grown, constructed, or manufactured. Appropriation from the natural environment—itself a transformation no matter how close to gathering or hunting the activity appears— within each sphere was less valued than more dramatic transformations of "natural" goods. Rare natural items were valued, but even more so if they were humanly transformed. In Tonga, smaller, carved whale teeth were more esteemed than larger, uncarved ones (Mariner 1827 : 1 : 250). If value derived mostly from the social personhood of the maker, gatherer, or grower, the dimensions of value were as multifaceted as the determination of any person's overall status.

A person's status was a melange of considerations of estate, rank, gender, kin relationship in a given context, and life experiences as expressed in various socially validated changes throughout life. In addition, a person's status was embedded in the social nexus in another way: status was related to the number and quality or statuses of those people who had claims to one's production or labor, whether the labor involved was productive or reproductive. In other words, one's kin group's status was another determinant of personal status, as was the rank of the chiefly persons with whom one was associated as a chiefly, *matāpule, mu'a,* or *tu'a* person.

The value of the objects one produced followed from this nexus of kin associations. In the first place, the value of a handmade or garnered item, or horticultural product, was associated with the estate of the maker. Anything made by a chiefly person—usually indicating a chiefly woman—was more valuable than anything made by a nonchiefly person. The differences between the spheres of *ngāue* and *koloa* reflect the lesser involvement of chiefly men in what we would consider productive labor, and the concomitant involvement of chiefly women in socially necessary production.

Within the rubric of things gathered or grown, e.g., fishing and horticulture, rank and gender considerations determined the relative value. For example, shellfish, gathered by women, were more highly valued than fish, gathered by men, although both women and men did lagoon fishing. Turtles, being associated with women, were more valuable than other deep-sea creatures gathered by men. Still within what we would consider the food realm, transformed items and exotic or unusual specimens were more highly valued than raw or ordinary items. In this way, "chiefly" food dishes prepared by *tu'a* women outranked the baked foods prepared by men. But by the same token, prepared foods which were made by *tu'a* men outranked raw foods gathered or harvested by *tu'a* men. To merit presentation to the sacred chief in the first fruits ceremonies, the special type of early-ripening yam had to be "dressed"—wrapped as people were wrapped in *tapa* for special occasions—in specially prepared pandanus leaf strips.[3]

The highest value would be accorded a finely plaited mat (*ngafi ngafi* or *kie*), several generations old, made by an elderly Tamaha— the highest-ranking Tongan chief. With regard to valuables or *koloa* made by nonchiefly women, additional value would be accorded an item made at the behest of a paramount chief. Value of nonchiefly-made products also would be enhanced if they came from a region associated with a paramount chief, especially a female chief.

One can discern a potential separation of the value of the producer from the value of an item in the precontact situation. The possibility of such a split is apparent with regard to nonchiefly women's products. On the one hand, certain of their products were destined for chiefly people and thus were no longer considered the embodiment of their total social personhood, only their nonchiefliness. In other words, these women's status as sisters, wives, and so on was subsumed as far as production for chiefly people was concerned. Their status was reduced to their nonchiefly estate and to their gender. Yet, at the same time, nonchiefly women produced valuables for local consumption and distribution. This aspect of their labor remained tied to their multifaceted social selves and reflected their particular relations with others of similar rank and estate. The process of alienation is perceptible, even in the absence of real commodity production, although it remained incomplete. On the one hand, the *tu'a* women produced "chiefly" goods, wealth, valuables— as did chiefly women. On the other hand, the value of these goods did not derive from their own status the way both chiefly women's goods and men's goods in general did. The production of valuables by nonchiefly women came closer to alienated labor than any other production in the precontact society: value rested more in the labor time needed to make the object and in the status of those for whom the object was destined than in the creators as social persons. Within Tonga, nonchiefly women's products were used in chiefly consumption, as payments for various services by *matāpules* and other nonchiefly people, as gifts and tokens of largesse, and to mark significant life transitions. Even where these *koloa* became part of long-distance trade, the goods received in exchange were utilized in similar ways, for similar ends, with the added aura of being imported.

Women's products validated the relationships among people which were questionable during critical changes in life status, whether these involved the life cycle or the assumption of chiefly titles. From birth through death, the presentation of women's goods marked the personal transcendence of the individual or couple around whom the occasion and crisis centered. In addition, the products reaffirmed and wrapped—at times literally, as at marriage and at death—each participant in a nexus of mutual responsibility to those who had wrapped them, who had made the transcendence possible. The chiefly estate could not reaffirm connections and changes through time within itself, except through chiefly women's engagement in creating such "binding cloths." Without chiefly women's involvement, chiefly people could not make claims upon nonchiefly people as the embodiment of fertility and continuity, prosperity and *value*. If all chiefly people were removed completely from production, the chiefly estate's dependency in all these arenas upon nonchiefly groups—the sole remaining creators of value—would be unwrapped, revealed.

Value and State Formation: A Crisis of Reproduction

For class relations to emerge, women's labor had to become constrained or deprived of the integrative functions it traditionally had provided. Women's products were simultaneously subsistence necessities and crucial markers of social reproduction: local or kin group history, personal growth and maturation, relations among kindreds and chiefly houses, and so on. Either nonchiefly women, particularly the *tu'as*, would have to be suppressed as producers of wealth, or the entire sphere of valuables had to be redefined in a way abstracted from the status of the women who made them. One resolution to the problem of wealth creation can be seen in Incaic Peru, where certain types of textiles became wealth objects independent of the maker, while other types could only be produced by women of particular classes. The sumptuary privileges detailed in archaic law codes provide another way in which the relationship of social personhood to valuables can be mediated in class formative situations: the production of wealth objects is restricted to certain statuses, and the use of the objects so created is restricted to certain categories of consumers.

For classes to emerge out of this kinship nexus, chiefly women would have to limit their cognatic claims, for the sake of lineage continuity and regular succession. That is, for chiefly women, either the roles of sister and paternal aunt had to become secondary to those of wife and mother—or the roles had to be fused, as with the sister-wives of Hawaii. Otherwise, the chiefly group would continue to fragment and reconstitute itself over time as *chiefly*, but not as a class removed from production. The recourse available to rival claimants to title—cognatically substantiated rank, validated through wealth objects provided through the *fahu*—had to be limited, if not eliminated. Cognatic claims served the interests of local, nonchiefly kindreds in their insistence on material balance in chiefly/nonchiefly exchange.

To justify their existence as a nonproducing group, state-associated classes must deny local autonomy or prevent it, since their ostensible coordination and redistributive functions would otherwise be revealed as superfluous. In Tonga, for instance, the customary exchanges of foodstuffs between coastal and inland kindreds needed no chiefly sanctions; collective work groups in fishing were ordered through kin connections as well. In other state formative situations, the denial of local autonomy, the coordination provided through custom, often involves undermining the capacity of local kin groups to reproduce themselves without the intervention of the state. This may be through the regulation of marriages, food storage, or crop specialization, or through conscript labor demands on adult and nubile men or women.

In Tonga, the continuity of both chiefly and nonchiefly groups was concretized in the products made by *all* women. This, coupled with the call chiefly people had on nonchiefly women's production, signified the incompleteness of attempts by chiefly groups to control local reproduction. At the same time, the chiefs' capacity and need to appropriate nonchiefly women's products indicates that *value-creation remained outside the control of chiefs*. Put another way, *value-creation remained intrinsically chiefly, but only because of women's role in social reproduction.*

The struggle for control over local reproduction, then, came to focus on women, particularly women in their "chiefly" roles—sisters and paternal aunts. Here the coincidence of chiefliness and womanhood was especially resistant to chiefly people's—including chiefly women's—claims to exclusive value-creation and control of cultural prosperity and social continuity. As sisters and paternal aunts, and as creators of valuables, women continuously created bilateral and cognatic integration across kin groups. They thereby prevented the emergence of immutably ranked lineages that could be fused with social power; class formation was constrained. As wives and mothers, women reproduced, in a narrower sense, descent groups which could become permanently ranked, were it not for the reintegration and leveling effects of sisters' and fathers' sisters' prerogatives through the *fahu*. The father's sister had call on the production and controlled the accumulation of wealth: she, or people on whom she had call, distributed valuables at those moments which marked the continuation of mutual, kin-based responsibilities—regardless of patrilineal bias. The attempts to inject foreigners in place of *fahu* relatives during the life crisis rites of chiefly people constituted one attack on kin-based forms of stratification.

Apart from the insertion of non-kin-related foreigners, there were other challenges to the re-creation of kinship society. Chiefly women were not engaged in the same way as nonchiefly women in the production of valuables; chiefly women created the design stamps and led the production. The tendency for the stamped varieties of bark cloth to become more highly valued than the plain sorts (today, the plain varieties are rarely made) also indicates class formative tensions: something becomes valuable because it belongs immutably to a particular chiefly house. The assertion of immutable ownership, regardless of future exchanges, signals an attempt to accumulate on a permanent basis. It also anticipates codification, the recording of history by the owner and thus assertion of creating it. The use of stamps implicitly denies the role of the makers—as a group—as the creators of wealth: the production process is subordinated to the ownership of the object. When Queen Salote informed the British official that "our history . . . is written in our mats," part of the message was an assertion, that Tongan history was made by the chiefly houses.

Chiefly women's involvement in the production process was somewhat attenuated, but they remained engaged. Class formation would be served by their estrangement from production. For this to happen, valuables would have to be acquired in a way apart from chiefly involvement—as where wealth objects become commodities—or Tongan valuables could be replaced by other forms of wealth. Alternatively, chiefly women might remain productive, in a situation where wealth-creation was made their exclusive province, like certain types of weaving in early Greek states. The locus of value might become dissociated from the producer and vested instead in the controller of the finished product or in the object itself, i.e., the labor embodied in the object rather than in the producer. To some extent, each of these possibilities was attempted, or can be discerned in the tensions which characterized the making of wealth in the precontact society.

No consistent pattern had emerged by the time of European contact in the mid-seventeenth century. One of the major reasons for this inconsistency lay in the strategic importance of valuables—irrespective in this case of the rank of the producer—in the assurance of cultural continuity. This continuity included *all* Tongans' kinship connections, intergenerational, intragenerational, marital, natal, within and between estates and ranks. It was impossible to remove chiefly women from *koloa* production precisely because valuables embodied reproduction, in the sense of cultural, that is, kin-based, continuity. The problem for the chiefly estate remained how to keep the idiom of kinship connection while divesting it of the responsibilities incumbent upon such connections. The creation of value and the exchange of valuables reiterated on a continual basis the content of being kin, not merely the formalities.

7. Gender Relations at Contact

Will Mariner
(1827:2:143–144)
[Infidelity] must be with the connivance of their female attendants and servants, who always attend them [female chiefs] abroad, not as spies over their conduct, but as companions. . .

TONGAN conceptions of gender—what was thought to constitute differences between the sexes—were as conflict-ridden as their concepts of authority, rank, and kinship. There were marked tensions between women and men, and these tensions paralleled other dynamics related to stratification. Tongan society before contact was enmeshed in the struggles of class formation; in this unstable situation, gender relations became increasingly charged and, in some contexts, hierarchical. At contact, gender, rank, kinship, and age factors continued to determine personal status and social authority. But there was a growing split between expressed etiquette and everyday actions both within the chiefly stratum and between chiefly and nonchiefly people.

Violence against women provides one gauge of the intensity of this conflict. At contact, it was said to be rare. The arenas in which it occurred point to the influence of class formation on sexual objectification and on control over sexual activity.

Another gauge of gender hierarchy is the social and political involvement of women. As Karen Sacks has pointed out for a range of African societies (1979), in Tonga, class formative tensions were expressed in the relative authority of sisters vis-à-vis wives. In both arenas, there were tendencies toward gender hierarchy and resistance against it. Resistance in such a case means reproduction of ambiguous gender relations. What can be said of Tongan society at contact is that gender had not become disassociated from other aspects of personal status and authority. Therefore, gender hierarchy did not exist.

Attitudes

Attitudes of men toward women are difficult to assess. Most of the evidence comes from early travelers, whose accounts include few interviews with women. Our information, then, derives mostly from interviews with men, and chiefly rather than nonchiefly men. The few women interviewed were chiefly. According to Mariner, Tongan men considered women to be weaker than men:

> [As] they [women] are the weaker of the two [genders], it is thought unmanly not to show them attention and kind regard; they [women] are therefore not subjected to hard labor, or any very menial work. (Mariner 1827 : 2 : 95)

The chiefly men whom Mariner interviewed considered the division of labor by gender as due to women's relative weakness, regardless of the importance attached to women's products or the control women exercised over their distribution. Similarly,

> At meals, strangers and foreigners are always shown a preference, and females are helped before men of the same rank, because they are the weaker sex, and require attention. (Ibid. : 134)

> Strangers and females generally obtain somewhat more than is due their rank. (Ibid. : 232)

Chiefly men presented "kind regard" as the reason for such preferential treatment. Such sentiments cloaked in etiquette what were in fact rights of higher-ranking female kin. They avoided admitting their lower rank and, thus, obligation to sisters.[1] Mariner knew that two Tongans could never have "the same rank."

Early European travelers noted that Tongans seemed to assign hard work and menial tasks to men, even as they commented upon how little anyone worked. One of Cook's officers, ship's doctor William Anderson, commented in 1777:

> The province allotted to the men is as might be expected far more laborious and extensive than that of the women. . . . we find them [women] eased of the laborious employments which their natural delicacy of frame requires, but treated with that respect to which they are often more justly entitled than their lordly masters, and have even a great sway in the management of affairs. (Anderson in Beaglehole, ed. 1969 : 3 : 932–933)

One of women's responsibilities, reef fishing during the day cannot be considered a light task (Neill 1955:138). It involved diving for shellfish and other marine creatures in deep tidal pools. Anderson noted:

> They have also great numbers of pretty small seines that they use to catch fish with in the holes on the reefs when the tide ebbs, besides the barb'd gigs which they strike some with[2] [in lagoon fishing] . . . and it is the only thing that can be reckon'd laborious where we find the women are sometimes engag'd, and where they handle the paddle as dextrously as the men.[3] (Ibid.:940)

Cook remarked on his confusion about authority and deference behaviors—particularly where certain men prostrated themselves to certain women (Cook in Beaglehole, ed. 1969:3:170, 136).[4]

Chiefly men's rather chivalrous attitudes toward all women—coupled with the opposite in actions toward lower-ranking women—can be seen throughout the early accounts. That chivalry is not to be confused with protectiveness can be seen in one incident. When women were supposed to be evacuated from one region during a period of warfare, one chief protested to a higher-ranking chief:

> If our women are to be sent away, send away also the guns, the powder, and all our spears, our clubs, our bows and arrows, and every weapon of defense. With the departure of the women our wish to live departs also, for then we shall have nothing left worth protecting, and, having no motive to defend ourselves, it matters little if we die. (Mariner 1827:2:29)

At the same time, captive women could be raped during times of warfare.

There are few hints in the literature about how women viewed Tongan men, or how they viewed their own strengths and weaknesses. Most of the recorded comments from chiefly women concern their attitudes toward European men and customs. From actual events, however, it is clear that women and men sometimes disagreed about women's political involvement. Warfare was seen by both women and men as a thing of men, and yet, even in this realm, gender, rank, and kin connections have to be considered as a seamless web of influence. For example, when a sister of the female paramount chief of Vava'u urged her sister's male advisors and subordinate chiefs to go to war, she broke into the assembly (most likely at the instigation of the paramount, her sister), brandishing a war club and spear, and said,

> . . . if the men are turned women, the women shall turn men, and revenge the death of their murdered chief. (Mariner 1827 : 2 : 136)

Her words shamed the advisors and convinced them to support the paramount and go to war against the sisters' nephew. During the warfare on Vava'u, one of the nephew's wives defected. He asked his aunt to return the woman, saying "It was a war between men, and not women." She refused his request (ibid.: 185).

Another female paramount chief insisted that a male relative of hers—an up-and-coming paramount chief himself—publicly perform the ritual prostration toward those of higher rank, placing her foot on his head. He seemed upset about it, but she told the Europeans present that he "was bound to pay her these marks of respect, because it was from her he derived his dignity" (Labilliardière 1800 : 353).

Age added to both chiefly and nonchiefly women's authority. Older women and men were accorded great respect, regardless of rank differences (Mariner 1827 : 2 : 134). Older chiefly women kept genealogies and sometimes acted as advisors to male and female paramount chiefs (ibid.: 10–11). Probably referring to nonchiefly women, Anderson noted:

> When they cease to bear children they appear to gain instead of lose respect and though they then appear to have some weight in the management of the younger sort it seems ultimately to be left to the decision of the men, who though absolute exercise their power in a very gently [sic] manner except in a few cases. (Anderson in Beaglehole, ed. 1969 : 3 : 945)

It is unclear whether the men he mentioned also were older; nowhere is it specified on what basis he claimed that their power was "absolute." Cook owed the retrieval of an adze—taken by a man—to a delegation of four nonchiefly women, headed by an older woman (Cook in Beaglehole, ed. 1969 : 3 : 443). Assertiveness was characteristic of chiefly women's demeanor, and both chiefly and nonchiefly women were active in public arenas.

Control over Sexuality

Sexuality in kinship societies generally has been approached with regard to the control of women's fecundity, relative autonomy in sexual liaisons, marriage arrangements, and so on. To understand the sexuality of Tongan young people at contact, we must consider sexual relations in the context of kinship and rank. Just as marriages even for the lowest-ranking people were not totally a matter of personal preference, there were constraints on the allocation of sexual favors. Kin, above all the father's sister, greatly influenced the selection of marriage partners. Similarly, older and higher-ranking male and female relatives had certain rights in unmarried young people, including the temporary allocation of those young people's sexuality (Cook in Beaglehole, ed. 1969: 3: 444).

One example is the "village child," discussed previously. A village (at contact a kindred, since settlement was dispersed) could send a lovely young unmarried woman to a male chief until she conceived. The subsequent child, the "village child," was revered along with its mother, for the chiefly connection. One can safely assume that this brought favors from the chief to the kindred as a whole.[5]

The willingness or unwillingness of the young women is not known. It is possible that fathers and paternal aunts had priority in these matters over mothers and maternal relatives. Early travelers, when approached by unmarried women to have intercourse in return for nails, cloth, or other valuables, interpreted this action as prostitution. The above situations indicate that the young women may have been acting according to the wishes of higher-ranking relatives.

Unmarried women could act on their own as well. Certainly there were precedents for receiving valuables for sexual favors. It was customary, for instance, for a woman to give a mat to the first man with whom she had intercourse (Collocott 1923b:228). Mariner commented that unmarried women "may do as they please, without any shame or disgrace until marriage" (quoted in Somerville 1936:369). He probably was referring to nonchiefly women, since the higher the rank, the more closely a young woman was watched. Gifford reported that a chief's daughter who was seduced might be beaten (1929:184). But if some of the young women were not acting on their own, we need to consider whether partial control of sexuality by older relatives was focused exclusively on women.

There were in the precontact period young men known as *mana'ai*, those who have *mana*, who were said to be handsome. Their function is somewhat obscure. In one context, Collocott supposes them to have attracted young women as concubines for chiefly men;

but he also says they were supposed to find a husband for the daughter of the sacred paramount male chief, that is, for the future Tu'i Tonga Fefine (1928 : 46–47). These men were supposed to woo people from other chiefly districts, or from areas not associated with the chief to whom they were attached. In another place, Collocott and John Havea mention an occasion when a Tu'i Tonga Fefine sent one of her attendants to find one of the *mana'ai* (1922 : 57). He was baking bread, which implies that he was nonchiefly. Collocott says these men had no real social status, meaning *mana'ai* was not a rank, but that their families forwarded their interests (1923b : 228). Young, good-looking men were a means for nonchiefly families to form advantageous connections and to accumulate mats and rolls of *tapa*.

The existence of such a group of wooers, whether for male or female chiefs, indicates a limit on chiefly people's capacity to commandeer the sexuality of lower-ranking people. For male chiefs, concubines had to be attracted, rather than compelled. It is conceivable that chiefly people could command low-ranking people within their own areas, but needed indirect, sexually alluring methods of attaining men or women from other chiefs' areas. The "use" of such young men by their kin groups to acquire valuables is analogous to the temporary alliances of unmarried nonchiefly women with male chiefs and, after contact, with wealth-laden Europeans.

In general, Tongans' attitudes at contact toward sexuality varied dramatically from both European ones and twentieth-century Tongan mores. As Anderson observed, in 1773:

> Both men and women seem to have little knowledge of what we call delicacy in Amours; they rather seem to think it unnatural to suppress an appetite originally implanted in them for perhaps the same purposes as hunger or thirst, and consequently make it often a topic of public conversation, or what is more indecent in our judgement, have been seen to cool the ardour of their mutual inclinations before the eyes of many spectators. (Anderson in Beaglehole, ed. 1969 : 3 : 945)

Sexual activity was not considered either shameful or private, where the parties were unmarried. Brothers and sisters avoided sexual joking in one another's presence, but sexual joking was commonplace for both women and men, in mixed company.

Marriage

Most Tongans were monogamous. The term for "spouse," *oanna,* was not gender-distinguished: there were no terms for "husband" or "wife" (Vason 1810:142). Symbolically, a married couple was identified as a set of partners. The conjugal unit was not the basis of production, however. Husbands and wives were not dependent upon each other in an economic sense.

Chiefly men generally were polygynous. Usually, they had several wives, the number depending upon rank and prominence. Eight wives were considered numerous. These women were supplemented by a range of concubines, who acted as attendants for the wives. Anderson commented:

> Monogamy is the mode of men & women living together, and though the superior sort have commonly several women it does not appear that Polygamy is allow'd to any but their king [sic] . . . (Anderson in Beaglehole, ed. 1969:3:945)

In fact, the high-ranking chiefs all had primary and secondary wives, as well as concubines. Marriages were viewed as binding, although divorce was rather uncomplicated. Of the expectation of permanency in marriage, the ship's doctor continued:

> It seems however of less consequence that the marriage should be rigidly binding where the free intercourse between the sexes amongst the younger sort is not at all reckon'd criminal but rather encouraged. (Ibid.)

Women entered their husbands' lineage upon marriage. This, of course, had a reality only for chiefly people, since for lower-ranking people, lineage affiliation was unimportant or unrecognized; they had cognatic kindreds, the *kāinga.* The new wife usually adopted her husband's people's deities (Gifford 1929:318), although, as we have seen, as a sister she remained critically important in her natal kin group.

Officially married wives of a high-ranking chief, particularly the primary wife, could bring with them one or more secondary wives, *fokonofo,* from their cognatic kindred. The term denoted the relationship between superior and inferior co-wives. The term used for a husband's relationship to his concubines was *sinifu* (Beaglehole, ed. 1969:3:170n; Gifford 1929:190). Co-wives often were younger sisters of the primary wife, or women from her mother's brother's side, people to whom she was *fahu*.

The relationship of co-wives is supposed to have been harmonious. Considering the importance of ranking and seniority with regard to authority, this should come as no surprise. The primary wife chose the secondary wives and concubines with whom she would live and to whose labor she had claims. Captain James Wilson, the commander of the *Duff*, the first missionary ship to land at Tonga, attributed the absence of "domestic broils" in polygynous households to the husband's authority:

[This] may, in a great degree, be owing to the absolute power each man has over his own family, every woman being so much at her husband's disposal, as renders her liable to be discarded on the smallest displeasure. (J. Wilson 1799/1968:276)

The reality appears to be that co-wives were close relatives and divorce relatively simple for a wife to precipitate. One female chief, sister to the high chief of Vava'u, compared the virtues and problems of European monogamy with those of Tongan polygyny. She was fifteen years old at the time, and was speaking with the captain of a visiting ship:

She thought the custom of having only one wife a very good one, provided the husband loved her; if not, it was a very bad one, because he would tyrannize over her the more; whereas, if his attention was divided between five and six wives and he did not behave kindly towards them, it would be very easy to deceive him. (Mariner 1827:2:49)[6]

The solidarity of co-wives can be seen in another incident as well. A secondary wife had gone to visit her father on another island. When another canoe was to visit the island, her husband sent her a bale of *ngatu* (decorated bark cloth) and several strings of beads, as well as his *'ofa*, "love unceasing"; the primary wife sent the same greeting, along with three fine Samoan mats. A gift of fine mats was comparable to the husband's present and unnecessary if the primary wife did not feel as she said (Mariner 1827:2:51). The term *'ofa* did not connote romantic love: it conveyed a combination of "friendship, mercy, and humanity" (ibid.:130). Desire or yearning was indicated by *manaco* or *monucka* (ibid.:lxxviii; J. Wilson 1799/1968:247).

People of chiefly and *matāpule* rank often were betrothed at an

Figure 8. Tongan women dancing for female chiefs. Engraved by George
Cooke. From Labilliardière 1800.

early age, alliances being arranged by their paternal aunts. Mariner
estimated that a third of the married women—and obviously men as
well—had been so betrothed (Mariner 1827:2:51). He discussed the
prevalence of marriage in the Islands circa 1810:

> . . . about two thirds of the women [old enough to be marriage-
> able] are married, and of this number full one half remain with
> their husbands till death separates them; that is to say, full one
> third of the female population remain married till either them-
> selves or their husbands die: the remaining two thirds are mar-
> ried and are soon divorced, and are married again perhaps three,
> four, or five times in their lives, with the exception of a few who,
> from whim or some accidental cause, are never married. This
> calculation is made with due reference to women living on the

plantations, who are almost all married to the *tooas,* who till the ground and remain constantly so; the unmarried women, therefore, live principally at the mooa, or place where the chiefs, matabooles &c. dwell, and are attendants upon them or their wives. (Ibid.)

Chiefly retinues, then, were composed of married and unmarried *matāpules,* and unmarried young people of all ranks. At any time, there would be a number of divorced people who had not yet remarried.

As a wife, a woman was supposed to defer to her husband's arrangements, no matter how high her personal rank, or whether she outranked her husband (Mariner 1827:2:95). The common pattern among chiefly people of mother's brother's daughter/father's sister's son connections reinforced the lines of marital authority: the husband was *fahu* to the wife. This stands in contrast to the parallelism indicated in the term *oanna* for either spouse. Perhaps the parallelism was more the case for nonchiefly people, especially the *tu'as,* while authority was more of an issue where rank considerations were more prominent, as within the chiefly estate.

In any case, a wife could never be denied the respect due her personal rank. If a woman married a man higher in rank, she received additional respect from others on that account. This was not accorded a man who married a higher-ranking woman. But where a man married up, his higher-ranking wife had access through the *fahu* to the lands of her natal kin, and to the men's and women's goods of her brothers and their wives. Mariner noted that a man who married up "has the advantage of her larger property" (1827:2:96).

Adultery

Married women were expected to be faithful (Neill 1955:59). A married man who was unfaithful frequently faced serious consequences, including abandonment. Adultery for nonchiefly people was most apt to involve two married people, or a married man and an unmarried woman, since unmarried men were supposed to respect married women (Mariner 1827:2:141). The term *hia* was used to describe the wrong-doing implicit in murder; the same term was used to refer to adultery with the wife of someone of equivalent or superior rank (Gifford 1929:183). If a man was adulterous with the wife of a chief, Collocott claims that his own kin might kill him to avoid the husband taking vengeance on the kindred as a whole (1923b:227). This also could be seen as the kindred claiming the right to determine punishment, as opposed to chiefs making such a determination. In adultery and other aspects of sexuality, chiefly and nonchiefly people had opposed interests. Corporate responsibility for illicit sexual liaisons underscored how much personal status remained embedded in kinship connections. While collective identity appears to emphasize the power of chiefs—punishing an entire kindred for an individual's offense—it in fact shows the solidarity of the kindred in limiting the chiefs' ability to single out members for repression.

Chiefly punishments appear to have been carried out only when the chief was present. If the chief did not directly oversee the punishment, it might not occur. William Anderson recorded one such event, involving adultery with a high-ranking woman:

> . . . a party of indians [*sic*] had got into the ring where our people traded, struck one of their own people with a club . . . when one of our men interposed and sav'd him from being killd. The man died soon afterward. We were informed that he had been discovered in a situation rather indelicate with a woman who was Taboo'd. We however understood that she was no[t] otherwise Taboo'd than by belonging to another person [i.e., married] & rather superior in life to her Amoroso . . . they told us she would only be slightly beat. (Anderson in Beaglehole, ed. 1969:3:962)

The people who beat the man were the local chief and his attendants (Samwell in Beaglehole, ed. 1969:3:1310).

Evidence concerning chiefly women's infidelity is contradictory. In contrast to the statements made above, Collocott claimed that "Great ladies had many lovers" and that they could bear children to these lovers (1923b:225). Some authors have assumed that this refers only to the highest-ranking female chief, the Tamaha. At least after the scuttling of generalized exchange among the top three chiefly lines, she reputedly "could have no recognized descendants" (Cook in Beaglehole, ed. 1969:3:136). This might explain the absence of marriage, or at least nonrestrictive marriages, in her case.

There are indications, however, that while married chiefly women were supposed to be faithful, they also had lovers. The secondary wife who visited her natal kin in the incident mentioned above was attended in her voyage by her own kin. She may have been "watched," but by sympathetic eyes. Correlatively, it was a general principle in Tonga that "All children of a female noble are, without exception, noble [chiefly]" (Mariner 1827:2:89). In other words, not all of her children might have the same father, or even chiefly fathers. The wife (Funagi) of a high chief ('Ulukālala I) at the time of Cook's first visit was reputed to have been that chief's father's mistress while she was still married to her first husband (ibid.: 10). Infidelity on the part of chiefly women was one means of political engagement apart from their roles as sisters and mothers.

Mariner believed that an affair involving a high-ranking married woman necessarily depended upon the collusion of her attendants, who accompanied her "as companions, it not being thought decorous, particularly for the wife of a chief, to walk out by herself" (Mariner 1827: 2: 143–144).

The evidence about punishments for married women, particularly chiefly women, is scarce and contradictory as well. In some contrast to the case where the woman was "only slightly beat," Mariner commented upon the relative severity of punishments for adulterous chiefly women:

> For the wives of chiefs . . . death might be the speedy reward of infidelity. As to those of lower rank, they might at least expect a severe beating and the offender himself come off as badly, if not worse (ibid.: 144).

Another early European visitor, Captain Wilson of the missionary ship *Duff*, said,

> Unchastity among females of rank, and especially after marriage, we have heard is punished with severity; however, we have not as yet known an instance. (J. Wilson 1799/1968: 276)

Why he and the missionaries had not "known an instance" might be attributed to the collusion Mariner suspected. This cooperation was well recognized among Tongans:

> As to considerable faults, such as a woman's infidelity to her husband, it would remain as much a secret with any of her own sex, (if they accidentally knew it) as it possibly could with herself! (Mariner 1827: 2: 140)

For concubines, adultery was more risky. If an adulterous concubine was discovered, all of her fellow concubines were blamed and all were punished (Collocott and Havea 1922: 120).

With regard to adulterous husbands, Mariner claimed that most married men were "tolerably true." Any affair was kept secret from the wife to avoid insulting her, because "it is unnecessary to excite her jealousy, and make her perhaps unhappy" (Mariner 1827: 2: 147).

The woman who was having an affair with a married man did not associate with his wife for the duration. Afterward, even if the wife knew, the relations between the women were not strained. It was considered bad form for a wife to vent any jealousy, either toward the husband or his paramour (ibid.).

Divorce

Both chiefly and nonchiefly people could divorce and remarry (Labilliardière 1800:376), but divorce was at the discretion of the husband. However, Tongan wives were not locked into unhappy or brutal marriages until their husbands relented:

> When a man divorces his wife, which is attended with no other ceremony than just telling her she may go [note that this implies the divorce may be in her interest], she becomes the perfect mistress of her own conduct, and may marry again, which is often done in a few days afterwards, without the least disparagement to her character. (Mariner 1827:2:145)

The immediacy of remarriage indicates that adultery may have been a frequent cause of divorce. Since divorce would depend upon knowledge of a wife's affair, it seems plausible that wives who wanted a divorce may have arranged discovery of their liaison.

Children of an age to require parental care went with their mother (Mariner 1827:2:148). It is not clear, however, what age or stage of maturity this implied. Neither is it mentioned whether or not older children remained with the father. Mariner emphasized that there were no contests over custody.

Child support also was not an issue. Marriage was not an economic necessity for women, whether or not they had children. *Fahu* prerogatives gave women, as sisters, subsistence rights. They could appropriate their brothers' foodstuffs and valuables to support themselves in a separate household if desired.

First marriages usually were arranged. But apart from the strategic marriages characteristic of the higher ranks, people tended to choose subsequent spouses for personal reasons. One reason that women—particularly lower-ranking women—may have opted for marriage is that married women were free from the advances of unmarried men, especially young chiefly men (Mariner 1827:2:147).

Divorced and widowed women were not reproached for having sexual liaisons as they wished (Mariner 1827:2:146). If a divorced woman chose to remain single,

. . . she may admit a lover occasionally, remain at his house without being considered his wife, having no particular charge of his domestic concerns, and may leave him when she pleases, without the least reproach or the least secrecy. (Ibid.: 144)

Such women were not, however, "fair game" for any man:

Great presents are by no means certain methods of gaining her [unmarried, divorced or widowed woman's] favors, and consequently they are more frequently made afterwards than before. Gross prostitution is not known among them. (Ibid.: 146)

Moreover, it was considered shameful for a woman to change lovers often.

Widowhood

The word for "single women" meant either never married women or widows, without distinction (Mariner 1827:2:lxxxv). Widows still capable of child-bearing were expected to remarry, although they were not forced to do so. At the same time, widows could remain single and admit lovers, since marriage was unnecessary for women's subsistence. Like divorcees, widows could acquire provisions and men's labor through the exercise of their rights as sisters and father's sisters. Conduct of affairs was open; in the one reported case, it is clear that the co-wives of a deceased paramount chief enjoyed this absence of restrictions:

Mafi Habe . . . did not, after the king [*sic:* Finau 'Ulukālala] died, marry another, or admit a lover; although one chief . . . who was considered the handsomest, and one of the most agreeable men in all the Tongan islands, became passionately in love with her. (Ibid.: 144)

She lived with her father for some months after her husband died, and Mariner comments:

. . . she might have married again, without any impropriety, two months afterwards [i.e., after the death of her husband], or allowed an amour without any reproach. (Ibid.)

Widows whose husbands were slain in battle or executed normally were allowed to claim the body for burial (Mariner 1827:1:238).

The widow of one man executed for conspiracy against a paramount chief armed herself and tried to rally widows of other conspirators to avenge themselves on the wives of the paramount chief and his subordinates (ibid.: 239). The gender parallelism is worthy of note: as their husbands sought to assassinate the paramount chief, so the wives would assassinate his wives and those of his subordinate male chiefs. The reaction to this widow's attempt also is notable: the paramount male chief viewed her with approval, saying that she was brave, and that her effort was "convincing proof that her affection was great . . . and genuine" (ibid.). Nevertheless, it was not seen as a threat: no other widows joined her.

Human sacrifice was associated with the life crises of the highest-ranking male chiefs—there is no mention of high-ranking women becoming seriously ill or dying—and this sacrifice included women, men, and children. At the end of the eighteenth century, when a Tu'i Kanokupolu was dying, one of his lower-ranking sons was strangled to appease the father's personal gods, "that his father might recover" (J. Wilson 1799/1968: 238). Fijian men and the boy's eldest sister—people who would not be *tapu'd* by the killing—performed the strangulation (ibid.: 239–240).

When this administrative paramount died, two of his wives were slated for strangulation and burial with him in the same tomb. The funeral and the strangulations were presided over by the Tu'i Tonga Fefine, the female sacred paramount, borne on a litter carried by four men, and accompanied by her brother, the Tu'i Tonga, alongside on foot. They were followed by the two wives, one composed ("indifferent" in the account) and the other weeping (J. Wilson 1799/1968: 240).

The practice of widow sacrifice or suicide was not customary for any but the highest-ranking male chiefs (Tu'i Tonga, Tu'i Ha'a Takalaua, and Tu'i Kanokupolu). In addition, on the death of the sacred male paramount, a male *matāpule* or attendant might be buried with him (Gifford 1929: 79). In some cases, this was seen as suicide; in others, as sacrifice.

The first missionaries incorrectly assumed the primary wife of the Tu'i Kanokupolu was to be strangled (J. Wilson 1799/1968: 236). Mariner said that the primary wife of the Tu'i Tonga, the Moheofo, was so strangled (1827: 1: 273n; 2: 127), but the situation is murky, since her younger sisters/co-wives shared her title. The practice was halted by the Tu'i Kanokupolu during Mariner's residence in the early 1800's. The widow in question was the Tu'i Kanokupolu's paternal aunt, so it seems unlikely that he could have stopped her suicide against her wishes.

The strangulation of the primary wife, the Moheofo, is not analogous in any direct sense with the sacred rulership pacts found in Homeric Greece. In Tonga, the parallel authority figure was the sister, not the wife. The reason might lie in the Moheofo's particular fecundity. Orderly succession to the male sacred paramount title was sought through limiting the number of children she bore. The sexual latitude available to widows in general would create succession problems: if the mother of the next Tu'i Tonga were to have many children, the contention for title would be disastrous. In this light, both stopping the practice, and the rumors that the primary widow of the administrative high chief might be slain, signal a shift in effective power relations from the sacred paramount to the administrative paramount. The fact that the Tu'i Kanokupolu called for its cessation appears less a humanitarian deed than an assertion that the sacred paramount title had become ineffectual.

Mariner heard that the widows of another Tongan paramount chief had strangled themselves from grief, but he questioned the accuracy of the report:

> . . . it is an undoubted fact, that suicide is exceedingly rare among them [the Tongans]. (Mariner 1827 : 1 : 283n)

Tongans who witnessed Fijian chiefly women having themselves strangled upon the death of their chiefly husband told Mariner this practice was "unnecessary and useless" (ibid. : 273).

Violence against Women

Most sources agree that Tongan women enjoyed high status relative to European women of the time, and were relatively immune from everyday violence. Travelers described household dynamics as tranquil and marital relations as affectionate. Yet extramarital intercourse could result in wife-beating, and premarital intercourse for chiefly women also could incur a beating. Periodic or chronic wife-abuse was exceedingly rare and, at least in some cases, resulted in capital punishment. Mariner mentions a man who

> used to beat his wife unmercifully. He formerly had a wife who, in times of scarcity, he killed and ate. (Mariner 1827 : 2 : 39)

Mariner, probably acting in the foreigner's role as enforcer of Tongan mores on behalf of the local chief, had clubbed the man on several occasions when he was found to have beaten his wife. The man also was reputed to have killed some of his own children. When Mariner mortally wounded the man, it was with the tacit approval of his Tongan companions (ibid.: 2 : 38–39). The connection between wife-beating and cannibalism is significant: a husband who beat a wife—at least beat her "unmercifully"—obviously was considered abhorrent, inhuman. Such a man surely was also a cannibal!

Tongans, with the exception of certain warriors during times of warfare, were not cannibals. Cannibalism was considered to be an appalling, Fijian practice, not Tongan. In the incidents described, only men were accused of eating human flesh. Men who did practice ritual cannibalism on slain enemies were shunned and treated with disgust by women in their local areas, who reviled them with, "Away! You are a man-eater!" (Mariner 1827 : 1 : 173).

Rape

Rape was known, but was supposedly rare (Mariner 1827 : 2 : 147). Tongan concepts of rape differ from our own, however. In precontact Tonga, intercourse where one party—generally a woman—is unwilling was considered a crime only in certain circumstances. If the woman was married, rape by any man was punishable by severe beating, public shaming, or death (ibid.: 1 : 231). If the woman was unmarried and chiefly, the man would be killed and his entire kindred endangered. The incident of the eleventh Tu'i Tonga, who in legend raped his virgin sister, has been mentioned. The action would be considered criminal not only because she was unwilling, but because he was lower ranking than she. As Mariner explained it, rape was a matter of indifference, "provided it be not upon a married woman, or one to whom respect is due, on the score of superior rank, from the perpetrator" (ibid.: 2 : 101).

If a man raped the daughter of a chief—herself a chief—and the culprit knew that the chief knew or would find out, he would inform his family. All his relatives would go to the grandson of the woman's father (her brother's son), making the most of the privileged familiarity of grandchildren to grandparents, and ask him to intercede. The man might be forgiven but, more important, his kindred would be forgiven. Even if the rapist was forgiven, at the first opportunity—infraction of a chiefly prerogative in the chief's presence, for instance—he would be killed (Gifford 1929 : 184).

In times of peace, rape appears to have been most often committed by young chiefly men; the victims usually were unmarried, nonchiefly women. As in other aspects of Tongan society, rank and maturity considerations (such as married status) contributed to the definition of offenses and the punishments meted. Although the term was used, rape was not considered to be a crime if the victim was unmarried and nonchiefly. Such actions were condoned by chiefly people, but not encouraged. At a *fono* or assembly called by a chief, during the marriage festivities of one Tu'i Tonga, a respected older *matāpule* man exhorted "the young men to respect, in all cases, the wives of their neighbors, and never take liberties even with an unmarried woman against her free consent" (Mariner 1827 : 1 : 124).

The problem was what constituted "free consent." In sexual politics, the relative strength of the chiefly group vis-à-vis the nonchiefly people was reflected in the incidence of forced intercourse:

> With respect to the wives of the lower ranks in society [i.e., the *tu'as*], they are oftener to be met with alone, and on such occasions sometimes consent to the solicitations of chiefs whom they might happen to meet, not . . . from any abandoned principle, or want of affection to their husbands, but from a fear of incurring the resentment of their superiors. (Mariner 1827 : 2 : 144–145; see also 2 : 143)

In war, women might be killed or raped, made prisoners of war, or distributed as booty. Male prisoners of war, called *popula* or slaves, usually were tortured and killed (Farmer 1855 : 140). Rape during warfare carried with it no subsequent stigma for the woman. Mariner wrote in this regard:

> When a woman is taken prisoner [in war], she generally has to submit; but this is a thing of course, and considered neither an outrage nor dishonor. (1827 : 2 : 147)

Chiefly women were not raped as a rule, but were kept as hostages (ibid. : 1 : 216). Even *tu'a* women might be spared if they were married. However, if a high chief was the target of an assassination attempt, every effort was made to kill the entire chiefly retinue—including all co-wives, concubines, and children—in order to devastate the whole group (ibid. : 2 : 82; 1 : 97).

Tonga at contact was not a violent society. Rape and wife-beating were known, as were clubbings and war-related fatalities, but they were rare. Violence was differentiated by gender, but sexuality outside of marriage precipitated violence against both women and men.

Were Tongan Women Subordinate?

The social encouragement of sexual liaisons has been viewed by Ortner as one indication of male dominance in an "aristocratic" society (Ortner 1981; cf. Goldman 1970). She does not identify it with class formation, but sees it as a variation on an aboriginal patriarchy. Ortner considers women subordinate in all societies where gender and age are primary determinants of the division of labor (1981; 1974).

Ortner argues that in Tonga, with increasing stratification, women's status rose, even though their political authority remained less than men's. She attributes this status rise to the encapsulation of gender within the so-called prestige system. Because Tonga was stratified, women had greater mobility and higher status, since the division of labor by gender and age was subordinate to the ranking system. She proceeds to characterize one of the ranking principles as sibling seniority, and then confines her discussion to the ranking of brothers (Ortner 1981). Sisters, as in Goldman, are analytically defused of their political involvement. Moreover, the importance of the sister role is seen as that of holding familial honor. This was the case, but it did not subsume the sisters' social and political engagement. The analysis ignores sisters' responsibility for marital arrangements and their critical role in succession to title. Instead, women are portrayed, as is typical in structural-symbolic analyses, as those who are exchanged. Sexuality and conjugal relations thereby appear as control over women, which was not the case.

The social encouragement of sexual relations between certain ranks is typical of estate-type stratification, since kin links to lower-ranking people help muster support in succession disputes.[7] Ortner identifies high-ranking men/low-ranking women as the permissible/encouraged pole of sexual connections and low-ranking men/high-ranking women as the impermissible pole. There is validity to this, given the evidence from early accounts.

However, Ortner insists that high-ranking women's sexuality was closely guarded by their male kin—fathers and brothers especially, as in Lévi-Strauss (1969)—and she takes at face value statements that chiefly wives were to be faithful. Hypergyny, upward marriage of women, was present, but infidelity, divorce, and marriages between people of similar rank also were commonplace. She describes an idealized arrangement for limiting legitimate succession to male chiefly titles, which, as shown in Chapter 4, was never realized. Ortner relates what some of the male chiefs may have wanted to exist, but the historical evidence contradicts this ideology. The de facto arrangements were that young people (chiefly and nonchiefly) gathered around chiefly compounds and spent a great deal of time together. Unmarried chiefly women were closely guarded by their older female relatives—both maternal and paternal—but married women enjoyed ample room for sexual and other politicking in both sister and wife roles.

The function of encouraging the sexual activity of lower-ranking chiefly men, she argues, was to expand the chiefly people's links with nonchiefly people as chiefliness melded into nonchiefliness. While this was one outcome—the higher ranks of chiefs remained aloof—the political consequences are not appreciated by Ortner. Such liaisons sometimes were voluntary, and chiefly people did not consider the less consensual forms to be rape—but the term was used by nonchiefly people. The result of sexual liaisons between chiefly men and nonchiefly women was not mobility for the nonchiefly women—they never became chiefly—but an increase in status for their children. This contrasted markedly from the usual derivation of rank from the mother.

Nevertheless, Ortner argues that motherhood was not an important source of social prestige for women. The data contradict her on this point, particularly for the women caught between the estates. Bearing many children was thought to make a woman less desirable (Collocott 1928:131). But both chiefly and nonchiefly women received status accrual through maternity. Motherhood did not necessarily entail childbearing: adoption and fosterage accomplished similar status ends (cf. Carroll, ed. 1970). For chiefly women, the status increase was a marker of further maturation as an adult. For nonchiefly women who bore children to chiefly men, the status meant an identification of their sexual potential with the chiefly estate: their children were "half-chiefs," perhaps *mu'a* in rank, which was higher than the mother's *tu'a* status. The point here is that the association of children's rank with that of the mother was challenged by the exigencies of reproducing (in the sense of continuity) a chiefly estate: For high-ranking chiefly people to dissociate from lower-ranking kin, and still retain kin claims to nonchiefly people, their own lower-ranking relatives had to be linked with nonchiefly people. But chiefliness in such a situation was asserted to derive from either parent, not the mother alone. The implicit association of gender hierarchy with stratification is clear. The assertion was that abstract chiefliness superseded kin-based determinations of rank, at least vis-à-vis nonchiefly women. Maternity thus became a status conduit for nonchiefly women, but only by denying women's customary embodiment of children's rank.

Tensions toward increasing stratification emphasized wifely and motherly roles at the expense of the sister role. Far from auguring an increase in women's status, stratification tended to heighten the less authoritative roles of women. The less authoritative roles carried status benefits, but none which combined social authority with exalted status, as the sister role did.

The potential for gender hierarchy lay particularly in the wifely role. In that role, political involvement usually had a sexual aspect and, at least for chiefly people, husbands had more authority than wives (see Sacks 1979). However, at the time of contact, the wifely role was not central for women.

Gender relations at contact were mediated by rank and kin considerations. They were most tense between estates: the relations of chiefly men and nonchiefly women showed the most tendency toward gender hierarchy. But there were tensions within the chiefly estate as well. Tongan men—at least the chiefly men with whom the early European writers had most contact—considered women to be weaker and, thus, deserving of indulgence. Older chiefs' attendants harangued young chiefly men about the rape of nonchiefly women, but did nothing worse than publicly humiliate the rapists. But the fact that gender concepts were embedded in an overarching kinship structure and a division of labor that included the chiefly estate in direct production prevented the emergence of gender hierarchy.

As one might suspect, the greatest gender conflict occurred in the arena where tendencies toward alienation of labor were pronounced. Nonchiefly women made valuables, which chiefly men tried to appropriate when women became war captives. The countervailing tendencies in this case came through chiefly women's claims—as sisters—to the labor and products of lower-ranking women and their own lower-ranking male kin. At the time of contact, in gender relations as in rank and kinship, the division of labor paralleled authority patterns. Within the chiefly estate and between chiefly and nonchiefly orders, gender relations were ambiguous and fractious.

PART THREE

Conversion, Commodities, and State Formation

Bullets do not respect chiefs.
—Tongan chief (quoted in
West 1846/1865 : 266)

8. Early Contact

Willem Cornelis
Schouten, *1616*
(quoted in Dalrymple,
ed. 1770/1967:58)

. . . they do not understand selling or buying, but
sometimes we gave them things and they us.

James Cook, *1773*
(quoted in Beaglehole,
ed. 1969:2:245)

. . . we were welcomed ashore by acclamations from an
immense crowd of Men and Women not one of which
had so much as a stick in their hands [without
weapons], they crowded so thick round the boats with
Cloth, Matting & to exchange for Nails . . .

THE PERIOD following contact involved Tongans in dramatic social upheaval. Several concomitant processes together resulted in the creation and imposition of state structures, drawing all the chiefdoms into a monarchy with judiciary and legislative institutions and systematic taxation. The precontact tensions toward class formation crystallized into definitive class relations, which were bolstered by, and in turn reinforced, the emerging centralized state.

Class relations, which are requisite to state formation and dependent upon it for continuity, were catalyzed through the same processes: the introduction and extension of Christian ideology, redefinitions of the purpose and consequences of warfare, redefinitions of use-rights and labor claims, the imposition of an uncustomary division of labor, and the creation of a sphere of commodity production. Wesleyan Methodist missionaries provided an ideology of immutable hierarchy (both religious and secular), an impetus for continuous commodity production, and a consistent supply of European weaponry. Why certain Tongan chiefs encouraged these foreigners, why they were allowed to become advisors and eventually government officials, can be understood only with reference to the ongoing political and economic tensions in Tonga. Each of the processes affected women and men differently. In the dialectic of class and state formation, women found their social authority and personal autonomy more restricted than men's. Out of the ambiguous and tense gender relations prior to significant contact, women became subordinate.

Explorers and Early Travelers

The period of early contact, roughly between 1616 and 1810, was one of sporadic visits by European exploration and trading vessels. The explorers and merchants who landed in the Tongan Islands during this period were Willem Cornelis Schouten and Jacob LeMaire in 1616, Abel Janszoon Tasman in 1643, Samuel Wallis in 1767, James Cook in 1773–1774 and 1777, Morella in 1781, the Comte de La Pérouse in 1787, Edward Edwards in 1791, and Jacques Julien Houtou de Labilliardière in 1793. By the end of the eighteenth century, not all visitors left with their ships: a number of European men were temporarily incorporated into Tongan society. These resident foreigners included ships' officers, sailors, the first missionaries, and, after 1800, several escaped convicts from New South Wales and Botany Bay. The convicts were treated as all other foreigners were treated. They were brutal to Tongan women, however, and, over time, the Tongans executed all of them (Vason 1810:81). The missionary ship *Duff* in 1797—at the onset of one war of succession—and the *Port-au-Prince* in 1806 brought "early travelers" who lived in the Islands for four years each and later wrote memoirs of their stay (George Vason and Will Mariner). More regular contact, including cargo ships and, later, whalers, began after 1810.

Europeans and white people in general came to be known as *papālangis*; the term dates from Tasman's voyage in 1643, and may refer to the cloth borne by the ships as sails and as cargo. The people may have been named for their valuables.[1] The intermittent visits saw the introduction of non-gift exchange. Tongans acquired European weapons through appropriation and barter, and iron implements through barter and sexual favors. The new weaponry increased fatalities in the interchiefly warfare and led to consolidation of settlements around newly constructed fortresses. This early period of sporadic contact and uncertain supplies of European goods heightened tensions among the various chiefly factions, as expressed in intensified warfare, but the purpose of warfare remained unchanged.

Truck and Barter

The earliest landing by Europeans was by Schouten and LeMaire in 1616. They touched the two northernmost Tongan outliers, Tafahi and Niuatoputapu. John Cawte Beaglehole says that they bartered for provisions—coconuts, yams, bananas, and pigs (1934/1966:132). Yet Schouten's account presents the exchanges as mutual gift-giving (Dalrymple, ed. 1770/1967:58).

When Tasman landed at Tongatapu and Eua in 1643, he reported barter for "hogs, yams, coconuts and fowl" (Beaglehole 1934/1966: 152–153). Both women and men brought items ranging from "some unknown vegetables" to "a garment made of rind [i.e. bark cloth or *tapa*]" (Dalrymple, ed. 1770/1967:77–79). The Dutch merchant bartered nails, iron tools, copper wire, sailcloth, satin, beads, and mirrors for foodstuffs. The groups which boarded Tasman's ships to barter were mixed—young and old, men and women "with all kinds of provisions" (ibid.:77). He noted that "they had not a single weapon about them" (ibid.:75).

Initially, Tongans heaped foods and valuables upon Europeans for their goods (Rickman 1781/1966:116). Tasman reported that a delegation from the ships in one day got forty pigs, seventy "fowls," and "vegetables in abundance, for a few nails, a little sailcloth, &c" (Dalrymple, ed. 1770/1967:79). Cook, reporting on his own arrival a century later, wrote:

> They seemed to be more desirous to give than receive; for many who could not get near the boats, threw into them . . . whole bales of cloth, and then retired, without either asking, or waiting to get anything in return. (1777:2:192)

His account cites both generosity and hard bargaining. In 1793, Labilliardière noted that in spite of fixed prices for provisions, lower-ranking people still haggled with Europeans for long periods of time (1800:341). James Wilson remarked upon landing at Tongatapu in 1798 that "their demands were so high that but little was purchased" (1799/1968:97). He added,

> Besides iron, our cloth and small blue and green beads were in high . . . estimation among them; and some of them even desired us to bring such on our next visit. . . . But it may be observed that *they are so scrupulous in dealing that they . . . generally stand for the full value of every thing.* (Ibid.:283; italics added)

He was evidently quite annoyed at their insistence:

> . . . the canoes again surrounded us to trade, demanding for half a
> dozen cocoa-nuts what would purchase a hundred at Otaheite
> [Tahiti]. (Ibid.: 100)

The direct involvement of women, even of high-ranking women, in
this trade is well documented (e.g., Cook 1777:2:223; Anderson in
Beaglehole, ed. 1969:2:863). The ships received regular visits from
female chiefs:

> . . . a woman of rank paid us a visit; she was attended by many
> chiefs, and a vast number of females . . . After her came four
> stout fellows carrying a bundle of cloth . . . this was presented to
> the captain, who gave her in return such things as fully satisfied
> her . . . (J. Wilson 1799/1968:108)

In this time period, male chiefs usually came with foodstuffs or
Tongan weapons to barter; female chiefs almost always brought decorated and plain bark cloth or finely plaited mats. This was in keeping with the gender division of labor, and can be taken as indirect
evidence for what women did on long-distance voyages to other island groups: they traded women's wealth for foreign valuables, while
men traded their products.

Visiting Europeans sometimes were stripped—literally—of their
possessions (Labilliardière 1800:346; Rickman 1781/1966:121, 127;
C. Horne 1904:29). Several observers, including chiefly Tongans, attributed this to the lack of manners or self-restraint on the part of
the lower-ranking people, especially the *tu'as*. Although some items
were recovered by chiefs, in other cases the chiefs could not, or would
not, retrieve stolen objects (Labilliardière 1800:339). A number of
incidents make it clear that chiefly people also availed themselves of
similar opportunities and accepted some of the loot as gifts (Cook in
Beaglehole, ed. 1969:3:100; Labilliardière 1800:341; J. Wilson 1799/
1968). Being "light-fingered" was not considered a crime in Tongan
society, unless the object were *tapu*'d (Mariner 1827:2:101). It was a
mark of dexterity and cleverness and, so, viewed with amusement,
as long as the victim was a foreigner and not a regular trading partner
or kinsperson.

When one Tongan took an adze from one of Cook's ships, he was
shot and wounded seriously. Cook then tried to regain the adze by
negotiating with an older woman,

. . . Who had always a great deal to say to me from my first landing, but upon this occasion she gave her tongue free liberty . . .
all I could learn from her arguments was that it was mean in me
to insist on the return of so trifling an article, but when she
found out I was determined She and three or four more Women
went away and soon after the Adze was brought to me, but I saw
her no more . . . (Cook in Beaglehole, ed. 1969 : 2 : 443)

Cook had deeply offended the woman's sensibilities as a trade partner. To have avenged a loss by wounding another and still insist on
the return of a mere trade item, and to insert a trade partner as an
intermediary in such a task was too much. The episode also shows
the sway of female relatives, particularly older women, in relations
with Europeans.

Tongans sometimes looted European ships. The "Friendly Islanders" of Captain Cook sacked the *Port-au-Prince* in 1806, killing
nearly everyone on board. The regrets expressed later centered on
Tongans' erstwhile ignorance of European trade: the chief had not
known that money might be useful, thinking instead that it was a
chit in some game, and thus allowed the cash to be destroyed (Mariner 1827 : 1 : 214). Later, they took two U.S. ships, the *Duke of Port-
land* and the *Union*, and two whalers at Vava'u (Dillon 1829 : 1 : 274).
There were several other conspiracies against visitors, including
Cook, but these were abandoned for lack of agreement about purpose
or tactics. Tongans' plunder and sometime slaughter of Europeans
can be placed in the context of European reactions to theft, namely,
shootings and severe whippings, which the Tongan chiefs found
excessive (Labilliardière 1800 : 361). One officer cut a Tongan man's
arm to the bone with an ax for stealing an iron tool (Rickman 1781/
1966 : 121).[2]

Why was there such a willingness to barter and, often at the same
time, such plotting to appropriate the European goods? The simultaneity was due in part to interchiefly squabbles. Ships landed only
where ports were deep; chiefs in those regions benefited greatly from
the trade. At the same time, the provisioning of the ships put a drain
on local resources. The foreigners also were strangers, not linked in
any reliable manner to the local people. Exchanges, therefore, were
balanced, but the potential for enmity was present so long as there
were no kin or fictive kin connections. At the same time, strangers
were useful to chiefs, since they were free from the *tapus* and sources
of information about other visitors, especially traders: individual
chiefs tried to attract and keep Europeans. Interchiefly rivalries over

two deserting sailors sparked a three-day skirmish between the crew of J. S. C. Dumont d'Urville's *Astrolabe* and the local people (Dillon 1829:1:266).

Great pains were taken by certain chiefs to prevent the travelers from landing at other points in the islands. Cook was told that the area he planned to visit had no decent harbor (1784:1:401). According to one of his now-royal descendants, one chief deliberately misled Cook into avoiding one of the best harbors in the islands, because "he saw in the white man a threat to his own influence in Vava'u and Ha'apai" (Bain 1967:124).

The issue among the chiefs was, in part, control over the Europeans and their valuables; there was a concern for the retention of prestige in a situation where European goods might become available to anyone with produce or women's wealth, or sexual willingness.

Higher-status Europeans, ships' captains and officers, sought alliances with local chiefs which were not kin-based, but exchange-based. Lower-status foreigners, such as the sailors, were in many respects safer: they controlled fewer of the desirable goods and they contracted quasi-kin ties with local women and their families. Those who controlled the disposition of most of the goods were unwilling to establish durable links, that is, kinship ties, with the chiefly groups. Since the European officers remained "outsiders," they also remained vulnerable to attack by Tongans. For a foreigner to be under the protection of a chief was insufficient: the assurance of safety could be withdrawn, since it was only based on barter. The Europeans' unwitting mistake was to refuse to acknowledge the equivalent or superior status of their hosts—thus failing to establish any definite status for themselves. A man without social status was human only in the abstract: he could be bilked or killed, even as male war captives were killed.

In the eighteenth century, most of the visitors were English. They sought goods that would be useful in the Asian trade as well as provisions for the next leg of the voyage. Colored feathers acquired in Tonga were traded in other Polynesian islands. Cook mentioned that Eua, an island near Tongatapu, was an excellent source of brilliantly colored feathers. No single commodity was sought: anything that had potential as a trade item was desired. Tongans were correct in their assessment of Europeans' lack of discretion. This apparent aimlessness of acquisition—Tongans were unaware of the trade in India and China—did not encourage commodity production in the Islands. The European visits were irregular and the possibilities for outright seizure not precluded.

Trade relations in this period did not alter Tongan spheres of exchange significantly. Indigenous notions of the relative value of objects and the integrity of men's and women's goods remained unchallenged. Tongans set the terms of barter and simply would not accept certain items as returns for their presentations of food, mats, or other goods. They did not trade their wealth for items of lesser value, in terms of their own spheres of exchange.

Tongans would accept European valuables in exchange for less valuable goods, such as foodstuffs and men's goods in general. This was to their advantage and merely exposed the Europeans' ignorance of value. Use-value remained the primary consideration behind every transaction: the goods acquired by the Tongans would not be used to augment further production of trade objects. Monetary value or the possibilities of a profitable second transaction were not effective lures:

> For articles of iron they will venture any thing. . . . Among other things, the cook's axe was stolen . . . the captain gave the cook ten new guineas to purchase another axe from the natives; but his endeavors . . . were in vain, they only laughed at him for his offer. (J. Wilson 1799/1968:283)

The Europeans appeared to have no effective spheres of exchange, that is, no idea of the value of things. Tongans were amused by the Europeans' lack of discernment in barter, as this rather condescending journal entry shows:

> [the sailors bartering for curiosities] went even so far as to become the ridicule of the Natives by offering pieces of sticks, stones and what not to exchange, one waggish Boy took a piece of human excrement on the end of a stick and hild [sic] it out to every one of our people. (Cook in Beaglehole, ed. 1969:2:225)

The trade between Europeans and Tongans in this era appears on an equal footing. But freezing this period in time leads to an illusion of subsequent "supply and demand" notions of equality.[3] The "voyages of discovery," with the exception of Tasman's, were not explicitly commercial ventures. But the voyages were sponsored to facilitate subsequent mercantile activities. From 1643 to 1800, before regular South Pacific trade routes were activated, trading was so sporadic and the acceptability of cheap "valuables" offered by Europeans so unpredictable, that the give-and-take seems fairly balanced. Tongans, however, had no way of knowing that the purpose of the early voyages was to investigate sources of materials and products which could be used in East Asian trade and to locate adequate harbors, land suitable for European settlement, and, later, whaling areas. If one considers the longer perspective, as Sahlins does not in his discussion of European trade with indigenous peoples (1976), the "equality of trade" argument is untenable.

Europeans did tailor the commodities they brought to indigenous wants, but the critical point is whether the indigenous people could withdraw from the trade, *refuse* to trade. Another critical element is the nature of the objects traded. The provisions, mats, bark cloth, and so on *were not commodities* at this point. The objects the Europeans brought were, that is, the items were used not only in exchange, but in a particular type of exchange. Commodities form a moment in an accumulation process: they are exchanged in order to actualize the value of the labor embedded in them, to acquire additional capital for reinvestment. The provisions and other items Tongans made were used in a very different type of exchange: a useful good (in the broad sense of reproductive, not the narrow sense of utilitarian) was presented for another item whose destiny was to be consumed without reinvestment in expanded production. In later times, the same items would be traded as commodities with the Europeans. The difference lies not in what items were traded, but in *how they were produced.* In later times, Tongans making the items lost control over the disposition of their products. The goods were traded by an emerging landed gentry for the receipt of goods both to bolster their own position *and* to expand the production of trade items. In the sense that the European trade introduced commodities into a use-directed economy and was used by chiefly people to further their interests, it could—and later did—transform Tongan labor relations.

Tongans and the Europeans who reached Tongan shores during this early period were similar in terms of relative power. Tongans recognized the greater destructiveness of European muskets and cannons, and chiefly people eagerly sought these weapons. But the Europeans did not always recognize or sufficiently appreciate the sophistication of Tongan strategic and tactical capabilities in warfare. Visitors were ignorant of Tongan customs with regard to exchange partners, spheres of exchange, and authority patterns. Their ignorance made the potential for destruction more balanced than a mere comparison of technologies might indicate.

Sexual Contact

Certain of the early travelers considered that prostitution existed in Tonga (Cook 1784:1:401); others disagreed, citing the general sexual exploration of young nonchiefly women prior to marriage (Mariner 1827:2:146). One of the major justifications presented by the first missionaries for their activities in Polynesia was the "depravity" or "degradation" of the women. Missionaries blamed the women's moral weakness, their climate-induced indolence, or chattel-like subordination to men.

In 1643 Tasman, the first European to visit Tongatapu, described the women's behavior when they boarded the ship for the first time:

> Other women felt the sailors shamelessly in the trouser-front, and indicated clearly: that they wanted to have intercourse. The [Tongan] men incited the sailors to such a transgression. (Quoted in Sharp 1968:45)

The Tongan men were urging the foreign men, not the Tongan women.

Lower-ranking, unmarried women often would sleep with Europeans in return for iron items and cloth or clothing, that is, for valuables.[4] A sailor named Samwell commented:

> We found no great Difficulty in getting the Girls on board, for the Charms of a Hatchet, a Shirt or a long nail they could no more withstand than we could theirs which were far from being despicable. (Samwell in Beaglehole, ed. 1969:3:1075)

There is no evidence of coercion in the young women's activities, with the solitary exception of one war captive. Mariner wrote of the landing of the *Port-au-Prince* in 1806:

> Only one woman came on board and she was one of the lower order [*tu'a*], who was in a manner obliged to come by order of a native, to whom she belonged as a prisoner of war, and who had been requested by one of the officers of the ship to send a female on board. (Mariner 1827:2:211)

There were lower-ranking young women who avoided sexual intercourse with the visitors. It is likely that they had veto power if their relatives suggested such liaisons:

There were many women who either from their connections
[higher rank], natural timidity, or absolute aversion to such pro-
miscuous engagements are not to be pregnable on any terms, independent of those who are understood to be married. (Anderson
in Beaglehole, ed. 1969:3:945)

In contrast to the other accounts, Mariner claimed that Tongan
women did not associate much with foreigners. He attributed this to
a mixture of "patriotism," knowledge of the way women were treated
elsewhere, and their "natural reserve" (1827:2:211). He probably was
referring to women of higher rank, whether chiefly or nonchiefly
(*matāpule* in this case). He might have added their view of the ex-
cesses and abuses of some of the few resident Europeans (Vason
1810:90).

Sexual liaisons were occasions for bargaining. A woman, or those
male or female relatives speaking on her behalf, would propose an
appropriate return gift for the European in question to present to her
(Labilliardière 1800:333). Samwell commented:

During our stay here we had a constant Intercourse with the
Women both on board the Ships and on Shore, & the price was
a Shirt or a Hatchet for the Night; they were brought to us &
the Bargain made by their Fathers, Brothers [This is unlikely,
given the avoidance of sexual talk between sisters and brothers]
or some Friend or Relation (Samwell in Beaglehole, ed. 1969:
3:1044).

As Captain Wilson reported in 1797:

Female chastity is not much esteemed among the lower orders, it
being a common practice with the chiefs, in our visits to them,
to offer some of their females to sleep with us; the practices of
our abandoned countrymen making them believe this is a favour
we could not well do without. Our first refusal seemed to excite
surprise, but has generally prevented a second temptation from
the same person. (J. Wilson 1799/1968:275–276)

When an older woman brought a young woman to Cook, the
younger woman "wanted a shirt or a nail." The older woman explained that he could have her and then present the gift later, an offer
which signified a closer relationship between Cook and herself, but

Figure 9. Early contact: French sailor and Tongan pleasures. From Labilliardière 1800.

. . . this not suteing me niether the old Lady began first to argue with me and when that fail'd she abus'd me. (Cook in Beaglehole, ed. 1969:2:444)

It is plausible that such an initial agreement would have been necessary to avoid accusations of theft or a return gift that was not valuable in Tongan terms.

A woman generally selected one sailor and would not sleep with another until the affair was terminated. During Cook's extended visits, several women chose to accompany their lovers to other Tongan islands before deciding to take their leave. As the rather appreciative Samwell wrote:

They [the accompanying women] made shift before they left us of
getting most of our Linnen from us, especially from those who
were not rich in Hatchets. They are of a very amorous complex-
ion & highly deserving of what they got. (Samwell in Beaglehole,
ed. 1969 : 1044)

As discussed previously, young people's sexuality was not entirely
under their own control. Older and higher-ranking women and men
had some disposition of their younger, lower-ranking relatives' sexual favors. It was traditional to follow such a bestowal of potential
fecundity (by either women or men) with gifts of some value, particularly mats and cloth. Older and higher-ranking relatives, including
chiefly people in the region, would benefit materially from the adventures of their lower-ranking kin. The sailors provided one means
for unmarried, nonchiefly women to acquire highly desirable iron
tools and exotic cloth that they would not otherwise have been able
to obtain. They would present the goods to higher-ranking relatives
and thereby gain prestige not generally accorded women of their age
and status. Their subsequent use-rights and expectations of respectable marriage were not affected by premarital sexual adventures.

Imagery: Tongans in European Eyes

Mutual appearances help us understand the quality of early Euro-
pean/Tongan relations. The issue has been investigated in other
parts of the world, usually with reference to the emergence of racist
attitudes (e.g., Lips 1966; McNickle 1973).[5] Typically, the peoples
encountered in voyages of discovery are at first presented as radically
different, but civilized people; only when colonial settlement, mercantile expansion, or ideological conversion becomes the focus of attention do the images shift to those of savages. The changing image
of Tongans to Europeans paralleled the focus of capitalist expansion for the particular country at the time, and the focus of state-
associated religious ideology at the time. Coming from areas heavily
influenced by the Reformation, the early Dutch explorers presented
the Tongans as barbarians. Their image of the women was as unattrac-
tive and immodest. Later voyagers were from countries influenced
by the Enlightenment, and presented the Tongans as civilized. Still
later, English Protestant missionaries, whose explicit goal was to
bring Christian civilization to the heathen world, painted a depraved
image of the Tongans.

The Tongans saw the Europeans as bearers of useful valuables and
were willing to incorporate them in various ways into a Tongan uni-

verse. The existence on board a ship of a hoard of valuables that was not being shared left the Europeans open to attack, but where barter was generous and reprisals for theft minimal, threats of attack were blunted. Europeans were identified with their wealth objects, the *papālangi* or cloth-men. Surely it must have been odd for *men* to come bearing women's wealth, white and red linen and woolen cloth. In this early period there was at least one case of mistaken gender identity. One adolescent was aghast when she found out the cabin boy was not a female: she had been affectionate and close to this person of her own age prior to his becoming too familiar for her taste and chiefly rank.

On the appearance of the people, Europeans were at first rather complimentary, with the notable exception of the stern Schouten and LeMaire. In 1616 Schouten described the men from the Tongan outliers of Cocos and Traitors' Islands (Niuatoputapu and Tafahi) as "valiant and large in stature . . . strong and of good make of body and limbs" (quoted in Dalrymple, ed. 1770/1967 : 57). The women, he continued, were

> very deformed, as well in face as body, and little, their hair cut short [i.e., he is referring to married women] . . . they have long breasts . . . which in some hang down to their belly like leather sacks; they are very immodest, exposing the use of their bodies in the presence of all men, even of their king [*sic*] himself, only under a mat. (Ibid.: 58)

LeMaire seconded Schouten's opinion:

> The women were ugly, their breasts hanging down to their belly . . . transgressing the bounds of decency every moment. (Ibid.: 57n)

In all probability, the Dutch explorers were allowed to see only older, married, lower-ranking women during their brief stopover, that is, women who would be unavailable for sexual liaisons. The Dutch obviously were offended and intrigued by the women's clothing. The contrast between the men's and the women's stature might indicate that the men were higher ranking, since, as in many other Polynesian societies, chiefly people were fed an impressive amount to demonstrate literally how weighty they were socially.

Tasman, twenty-seven years later, described the inhabitants of Nomuka, another Tongan outlier (which he named Rotterdam Island): ". . . the women were pretty much of the same stature and as stout limbed as the men" (Dalrymple, ed. 1770/1967 : 81). In his description of the women of Tongatapu (1643), Tasman presents information that corroborates the earlier account, but in a more congenial tone:

> . . . the women from the waist to the knees wear a covering of matted leaves, but all the other parts of the body are naked, and their hair shorter than that of the men . . . in every respect their behavior was very courteous and friendly. (Ibid. : 179)

Other European visitors mention the hair styles of the *tu'a* and married women, but the English and French explorers thought the women attractive, to say the least: "The countenances of the women are in general very pleasing, and highly animated" (Labilliardière 1800 : 383). A sailor on Cook's voyage noted that women's hair styles were differentiated by rank:

> The lower Class [*sic*] of young women have their Hair cut short, while those of the Agee ['*eiki*, chiefly] order wear it long & flowing. (Samwell in Beaglehole, ed. 1969 : 3 : 1042)

Other accounts also remark upon differences in behavior, privileges, duties, dress, and diet both between chiefly and nonchiefly estates and within the ranks of chiefly people (Vason 1810 : 108–109; Cook 1777 : 2 : 218; 1784 : 1 : 388).

Women and men dressed similarly, compared with the dress of European women and men at the time. Both women and men wore ornamental bead necklaces, amulets and bracelets; they wore decorated or plain *tapa* in what appeared to the Europeans to be a similar fashion, but women also wore decorated aprons (Cook in Beaglehole, ed. 1969 : 2 : 267, 272). Lower-ranking people wore fewer garments than chiefly people. The subtle differentiation of women and men in dress was lost on visitors from countries with dramatic gender distinctions in dress.

The early travelers were quick to discern behaviors that reflected differences in rank, since these seemed to parallel their own stratified societies. Cook observed in the 1770's:

> The principal Women who have at all times an Air of consequence and dignity in whatever they do, never perform among them [dancers in an evening celebration] . . . (Cook in Beaglehole, ed. : 3 : 111; cf. Labilliardière 1800 : 351–352)

Mariner elaborated in the early 1800's:

> . . . as to the women, they are universally humane. A few, indeed,
> of the principal wives of the chiefs are proud and haughty, and
> consequently tyrannical; but, considering the women generally,
> they are exceedingly benevolent . . . quarrels among the women
> are very rare. (1827:2:140)

Most of the Europeans commented on the relative health of the
population:

> The natives . . . are in general tall and well made, for which they
> are principally indebted, no doubt, to the abundance and good
> quality of their food. The fine shape of these people is not de-
> graded by excessive toil. (Labilliardière 1800:382–383)

The most negative comments about the overall way of life were written by Schouten and LeMaire with reference to nearby Horn Island
(1616). According to LeMaire,

> . . . they are without religion, as brute beasts, and have no knowl-
> edge of merchandise, living like people of the first world [i.e., the
> earliest time], without labouring, having for foods the fruits of
> the trees and fish quite raw. (Quoted in Dalrymple, ed. 1770/
> 1967:57n)

Schouten echoed LeMaire: ". . . they neither sow nor reap, nor do
any handy work" (ibid.:58). While Schouten appeared ambivalent
about their standard of living, LeMaire was unequivocal:

> This people live miserably in little huts along the shore, about
> twenty-five feet in circumference, and twelve or less in height
> . . . no furniture but some dry grass [probably plaited mats] to
> sleep on . . . the king [sic] himself has nothing else in his hut.
> (Ibid.:56n)

A century and a quarter later, during the Enlightenment, all visitors
except most of the missionaries were laudatory in their evaluations
of the people's health, diet, and manner of living. Mariner, the young
ship's clerk whose life was spared when the Tongans pillaged and
seized the *Port-au-Prince*, praised the Tongan way of life repeatedly,
from the absence of poverty to the respect accorded women and older

Femme des Isles des Amis.

Figure 10. Tongan woman, wearing *tapa* and decorative apron *(sisi)*, as seen by a French visitor, 1790's. Engraved by J. Laroque.

Homme de l'Isle des Amis.

Figure 11. Tongan man, wearing *tapa* and decorative apron *(sisi)*, as seen by a French visitor, 1790's. Engraved by Labrousse.

people, and the absence of hunger except in times of natural disaster or occasionally following periods of warfare (1827:2:173). Cook commented, "No one wants the common necessities of life" (1777: 2:223). Most of the accounts pay particular attention to the orderliness with which gardens were cultivated and the bounty which they yielded with relatively little effort, compared with the lot of European peasants (Cook in Beaglehole, ed. 1969:3:127; Gifford 1929:8).

The high status of women impressed the early travelers, whether they saw it positively or not. Cook noted with surprise that chiefly women

> tip of their Cup of the liquor made of the [*kava*] root, in their turn with the men without the least ceremony, nay, I have even seen the men so genteel as to help the Ladies first. (Cook in Beaglehole, ed. 1969:2:268)

Serving women first is better explained by their higher rank than by masculine courtesy. The order of drinking reflected relative rank in the drinking circle. All the authors note that women ate with the men, not separately as in most of Eastern Polynesia. William Anderson added that the women "have even a great sway in the management of [economic and political] affairs" (Anderson in Beaglehole, ed. 1969:3:933).

But most visitors were confused by the ranking system. Both Cook and Labilliardière thought the Tongan system appeared feudal (Labilliardière 1800:380). Several were aware that certain women outranked the male sacred high chief, although the accounts disagree about the cause, seniority or (correctly) sisterly status. One traveler falsely attributed the exalted rank of the Tamaha (daughter of the female sacred high chief) to the rank of her Fijian father. The fact of sisters' higher rank was difficult for the observers to absorb. When the sacred paramount (Tu'i Tonga) attempted to explain his relationship to the Tamaha and her mother (his sister) and why he had to prostrate himself in their presence, he told Anderson that

> when his father was alive the sister of this father . . . reign'd jointly with him at Tonga[tapu]. (Anderson in Beaglehole, ed. 1969:3:954)

Tine, the Tu'i Tonga Fefine, explained the intricacies to Labilliardière; she seemed to take pleasure in forcing a male paramount chief (who tried to avoid her) to prostrate himself (Labilliardière 1800: 375–376).

For Enlightenment era travelers Tongans appeared as sometimes civilized, sometimes savage; the accounts all contain an ambivalent admiration for their customs and way of life. The travelers appreciated the orderly conduct of everyday life, the coupling of industriousness with ample leisure, of amorousness with marital fidelity. They were shocked by entertainments such as female boxers, the seemingly capricious power of chiefs, the sacrifice of finger joints and, occasionally, of lower-ranking people at times of serious illness and death. Several observers—particularly Cook and Mariner—expressed concern that contact with Europeans already had had deleterious consequences for the Pacific peoples, and would continue to have such an effect. Their attitudes would conflict with those of the resident missionaries and merchants who followed.

Weapons and Warfare

Firearms, obtained through barter and plunder prior to the 1820's, intensified existing chiefly succession disputes. In theory, the new weaponry—especially muskets and cannons—allowed permanent conquest of other islands. The significance of the weaponry was that it did not result, before the adoption of Christian ideology by one chiefly faction, in conquest or class formation. The limitations of chiefly authority were not dissolved merely by technological change. The new technology of destruction made the warfare more deadly, but it did not alter the purposes of indigenous warfare.

Tongan men customarily fought on the side of the chief in whose district they were living at the time rival chiefly factions decided upon warfare. Since there was a great deal of visiting in the precontact period, it was likely that both men and women would have relatives in enemy areas. The likelihood of enemy relatives would be heightened for chiefly people, due to marital alliances and the frequency of succession disputes among collateral kin. As a result, defections, particularly of wives, were frequent.

Male prisoners generally were tortured or killed, rather than used for work by their captors. The slaughter of most adult men on the European ships the Tongans captured was in keeping with customary warfare. The killing of male prisoners remained the case during the early contact period, regardless of the utility of foodstuffs (men's work) in the European trade. Female captives, if they were unmarried or of low status, could be raped, but sexual liaisons or secondary marriages were not as a rule the consequence of captivity. Female prisoners of war usually were held by their captors until ransomed with women's wealth by relatives. Some female captives married into the captor's kindred; an English woman who was captured in one of the Tongan ship raids became a respectable Tongan wife (Dillon 1829:1:274). The presence of a female captive did not remove other women of the captor's household from production. Children usually were spared.

The wars of succession that followed the introduction of the new weaponry (the last years of the eighteenth century and the first few years of the nineteenth) transformed settlements from the dispersed hamlets noted by Cook, to more concentrated dwellings clustered within easy walking distance of strategically located fortresses (Cook 1777:1:214; Mariner 1827:1:87). The destructiveness of the new arms spurred the construction of earthen enclosures. Originally built for offensive use of the new weapons, the fortresses quickly became used more to withstand cannon and musket attacks (Mariner 1827:1:94–95; Wilkes 1852:2:8). The fortresses became refuges for the surrounding populations, and sieges became possible.

Tongan chiefs refused to use cannon fire against footsoldiers, for it was considered cowardly simply to mow down the enemy (Mariner 1827:1:165). There also were reservations about the use of firearms against Tongans. The European arms were unpredictable (Labilliardière 1800:342). Guns also reduced the prestigious man-to-man combat that kept fatalities relatively low and vanity high. Getting to the heart of the succession warfare, one contender commented, "bullets do not respect chiefs" (quoted in West 1848/1865:266). Whatever their ambivalence about the weaponry, the chiefs included resident Europeans as advisors.

During this early civil war period, an incident took place which reveals the transformation of methods and results of warfare following the introduction of European weaponry. The incident bares the constraints on chiefly authority as well as the potential for women's status to decline should class relations emerge. The war in question is taken as a crisis demonstrating the extent to which fundamental authority still rested with the kindreds, in spite of the assertions of chiefly power.

The paramount chief of Vava'u, who was the father's sister of Finau 'Ulukālala I, was at war with her nephew over his murder of the previous paramount chief of Vava'u, another of her nephews. When one of Finau's wives defected, the father's sister refused to return her to him (Mariner 1827:1:186–187). In response to her refusal, he planned to ambush several women from the enemy group as they reef-fished. A group of chiefly and nonchiefly men were sent to attack them: Finau ordered them to kill the women. In the ambush of thirty women, twelve escaped, including the defected (chiefly) wife of Finau's son. Five women were killed and thirteen were captured (ibid.: 187).

The thirteen captives were not killed,

> partly from motives of humanity, and partly from those of profit (as they [the captors] could employ them in making gnatoo [*ngatu* or decorated bark cloth] &c.). (Ibid.: 188)

Upon arrival at the chief's compound, conflicts arose among several of the women's relatives and their captors. The relatives claimed the women:

> according to the old Tongan custom, which decrees, that all persons shall be in the service of their older and superior relations, if those relations think proper to employ them. (Ibid.)

The captors claimed the women "on the right of conquest." Finau was called upon to settle the disputes, which he at first declined to do, since

> . . . they had no right to bring the prisoners there to create disturbances, but should have despatched them according to his orders. (Ibid.)

He finally declared that the best way to settle the problem would be to cut each woman in half. Faced with this alternative, the disputing parties negotiated their differences, some women going to their relatives, others to their captors.

Succession: Kinship or Conquest?

The episode described above highlights problems of transition from a kinship basis of social authority to one based primarily on power and allegiance. Questions arise: if paramount chiefs were decisive and powerful, why did Finau not punish the captors for their disobedience and their effrontery in bringing disputes over the spared captives to him? Why did the chief want the women killed in the first place? Why did the captors spare the women? The disputes raise the question of labor claims in conditions of intensified warfare: what were the tensions within customary claims that could lead to claims through conquest?

One of the key issues is the tension between kin-based and power-based claims on people. The war was between a female chief and her brother's son—the chief who installed her upon the death of another of her brother's sons and who was implicated in the murder of his brother. The incident exemplifies the quandary which confronted chiefs whose authority derived from kin ties, in a situation where control became possible regardless of reciprocal claims inherent in kin-based authority.

Evidently, the ability of even a strong paramount chief such as Finau 'Ulukālala I to command people in his group was limited. In his presence, the captives might have been killed: apart from executions of killers or insane people, all executions were carried out in the presence of the chief. In his absence, the captives were spared. The captors clearly did not fear chiefly opprobrium, since they brought their arguments over the allocation of the captives to his attention. There were chiefly men in the war party, and this may have blunted his power. But since there were chiefly women in the captive group, why did he want them slain? His wife had defected; she had not been slain, so vengeance is unlikely.

The chief could have been asserting control over the war party: raiding groups were fairly autonomous, and Finau may have been testing the men's willingness to side with him. He may also have been asserting his right to allocate the captives, through the denial of allocation. He may have anticipated the disputes which might arise and have wanted to avoid them. Whatever the motivation, each shows an attempt, on the one hand, to avoid exposing a lack of authority and, on the other hand, to further his authority. Still, why would he want to avoid disputes, when in all likelihood he would be asked to arbitrate?

The captors argued conquest as their claim on the women's labor, while relatives rested their case on customary labor claims exercised by older, higher-ranking kin. The chief's claims on the labor of the men who became temporary warriors rested on kin ties, as well as current residence, since most residents were related through marriage, descent, fosterage, or adoption to the chiefs. To allow the captives to live, the chief would have to choose between labor claims on a non-kin basis (conquest) and kin ties. To decide in favor of non-kin claims would be a dangerous precedent.

Finau was expanding his control over Vava'u and Ha'apai through conquest, using, in part, firearms from the European trade and plunder. But he was justifying the expansion on traditional grounds: he was the brother of the late chief of Vava'u. To side with the captors would be to deny kinship rank as the primary basis of claims in other people's labor—and thus to deny the basis on which all

Tongan chiefs justified their call on other people, especially the lower-ranking producers.

If, on the other hand, he sided with the higher-ranking kin against the captors, he would by implication deny the legitimacy of his own claims to tribute from Vava'u. For he was lower ranking than his father's sister, the paramount chief of Vava'u, and thus would have no right to her people's products. Indeed, he would owe her tribute. To install himself on the basis of secular power rather than kinship demanded military domination. But if he abandoned chiefly kin ties, he had no monopoly over the European trade or sources of weaponry: others might overthrow him.

Either choice was untenable. The success of his succession bid depended upon a combination of contradictory claims—kinship and conquest. Given the consequences of either choice, and given his incapacity to keep the women for himself (his own wife deserted him—it would not help his reputation), it is not surprising that he told the disputing parties to cut the women in half. Preservation of ambiguity was better than dealing with the consequences of dismantling the basis of chiefly authority and signaling an all-out power struggle.

Captors and Labor Claims: Kinship or Slavery?

For the captors, the incident points to the potential of slavery emerging, even as the results underscore the customary ends of warfare during this period. By and large, men's work fed the society: men's products were bartered for iron implements useful in improving productivity. But during these wars of succession, male captives still were tortured or executed, rather than being set to work farming for their captors to acquire more firearms or iron implements, or making war clubs to help in the capture of more prisoners.[6] But without additional men to wield the weapons, the production of more war clubs would be unreasonable. Participation in warfare still depended on kin ties and residency.

Women, however, produced the socially recognized markers of status. Stored in the rafters for later presentation during ceremonies that validated life status changes, or presentation to chiefly people, the wealth increased the donor's prestige. Female captives provided, in addition to labor to make these valuables, *a source of wealth apart from the captor's kin:*[7] his wife, his mother's brothers and their wives, and other lower ranking relatives. A captor could present *koloa* on social occasions regardless of his capacity to call on the labor of female relatives. The potential was created for wealth to be-

come disassociated from kinship connections and kin-based responsibilities. If conquest became grounds for keeping captives permanently, *domestic slavery in women would result*. The temporary
bondage until ransom in valuables would become servitude.

The wars of the late eighteenth and early nineteenth centuries increased the numbers of captive women. One of the missionaries-
gone-native, Vason, mentioned his part in violating a sanctuary (he
was a foreigner and not subject to the *tapus*) and helping to capture
women who had taken refuge there. The women were turned over to
their captors (1810:173). Female captives continued to be ransomed
by their own relatives or to become ordinary members of the kindreds of their captors. In either case, they brought wealth to the
captor.

It is not mentioned whether the captor's higher-ranking relatives
had claims to a captive's products through *fahu* rights. The degree of
disruption to the kin structure would hinge on this information.
Other influences can be traced. A captor of *tu'a* rank could only
board a limited number of captives, since he produced most of the
food they and other members of the household consumed. For captors who exercised claims to other men's labor, the number of captives could be larger. At no time in this period was the number of
female captives sizable. But the frequency of warfare and the shift in
the scale of warfare that accompanied the advent of European trade
could have resulted in slavery akin to that in pre-colonial West Africa or the Northwest Coast of North America. By the time of the
missionaries, small-scale chattel slavery was reported (J. Wilson
1799/1968:256–257).[8]

Warfare in Transition

Warfare was changing, but the use of captive labor remained in accordance with customary valuation of that labor: women's products
were intrinsically more valuable. The insertion of more efficient
technology of destruction heightened existing tensions within the
chiefly stratum, between kin-based authority and conquest-based
power. During this early contact period, however, the goal of warfare
remained succession to chiefly title, that is, the exercise of kin-
based claims to lower-ranking people's labor and products. There was
no means to resolve the kinship authority/non-kin power dilemma.

So long as warfare remained in the idiom of chiefly succession
(and chieftainship dependent primarily upon kinship rank), there
were implicit limitations placed on what happened to the defeated.
During the war, enemies could be killed with impunity; the men

and women in the immediate retinues of chiefs were special targets for ambush, massacre, or capture. But when defeat was acknowledged, no further killing ensued. The losers acknowledged the title acquisition of the victorious chief or went into temporary exile—arable islands were reserved for this special purpose. Defeated chiefs frequently retained their titles and positions in their home areas. There was, in short, no challenge to the use-rights of the nonchiefly population.

The defeated side owed wealth objects and chiefly foodstuffs to the victors, but the amounts were comparable to previous levels of non-chiefly donations. Conquest in the early contact period arranged distinct lines of superiority and inferiority among the chiefly factions, with nonchiefly prestations following the ranking. There was no intensification of production expected, only a redirection of the "chiefly portion" of whatever production was ongoing (Mariner 1827 : 1 : 136). Chiefs sometimes were displaced, but never from their home areas; nonchiefly people might change their attachment to chiefs, but they were never dispossessed.

The increased intensity of warfare during the last years of the eighteenth century and the first years of the nineteenth paled in comparison with the later civil wars in Tonga. In the middle years of the nineteenth century, the wars of Christian conversion and political unification drew all the Islands into a centralized state, with a former chief and his retainers becoming the king and nobility. What had been warfare over a limited share of certain products—mats, *tapa, ngatu,* yams and other chiefly foods—became contests for control over land allocation and increasing surplus extraction. The donation of the "chiefly portion" became the capacity to extract labor and products regardless of return. What was produced and in what amounts no longer would be determined by the local people.

The "holy wars" were wars of permanent conquest and were recognized as such by all the participants. Conquest involved more than a redirection of tribute or gifts. Defeated opponents of the new regime saw lands confiscated, labor intensified, and consistent taxation imposed. The former chief and Christian king reassigned the appropriated lands to his chiefly and nonchiefly supporters. In addition, the defeated chiefly and nonchiefly people were forced to renounce their "heathenism" and commence training for Christian conversion.

9. Missionaries: The Crusade for Christian Civilization

Captain James Wilson
(quoted in Griffin
1822:143)

A people . . . whose manners were but a few degrees above the state of the brutes, and in many things below them . . . such a people were not easily or speedily to be civilized and brought under the influence of the rational, orderly, and ennobling influence of Christianity.

CHRISTIAN missionary activity in Tonga was supported by some chiefly groups, tolerated by others, and actively opposed by many. The theocratic and patriarchal ideology appealed to those chiefly factions who, with their supporters, attempted to cut themselves off from kin-associated obligations. Following an aborted attempt at the turn of the century, Wesleyan Methodist proselytizing began in earnest in the 1820's. Conversion sparked or aggravated warfare among various chiefly factions. With missionary backing, warfare shifted from traditional concerns with chiefly succession to efforts to impose or oppose a centralized government. In the course of the nineteenth century, converted Christian chiefs and their retainers would conquer the Islands and be invested as the royalty and nobility of a Tongan kingdom.

Christian proselytizing included forced conversion and the transformation of certain Tongan products into commodities. Both imposed conversion and commoditization eroded women's—particularly nonchiefly women's—sources of autonomy and authority. The creation of a sphere of commodity production will be discussed in the next chapter. The concern here is with the Christian conversion process, its relationship to the development of state institutions in Tonga, and the impact of Christianity on gender relations.

Arrivals and Alliances

Missionaries arrived in Tonga in 1797, sponsored by the London Missionary Society (LMS). The party consisted of nine men, both ministers and artisans, and they landed at Tongatapu, the main island. The evangelicals were befriended by Mumui, a paramount chief.[1] The missionaries avoided any attachment to him, for fear that his impending death would cause disturbances in which they, or their property, might be imperiled (J. Wilson 1799/1968: 103). One of the white residents on the islands told them of this possibility and despite their dislike of the man, they heeded his warning. The missionaries made use of two other white residents as interpreters and liaisons with the various paramount chiefs of Tongatapu. They decided to attach themselves to Finau Tukuaho, the Tu'i Kanokupolu, and to remain with Mumui "only . . . if they could do no better" (ibid.).

The Tu'i Kanokupolu offered them his protection, a house plot, and a section of land for their use. They elected to stay with him because he was considered the most powerful chief in the Islands (J. Wilson 1799/1968: 104). They planned to split into smaller groups for proselytizing as soon as they were acclimatized. When Finau died, the missionaries became embroiled in the succession disputes discussed in the previous chapter.

They did not understand Tongan warfare. A group of Tongans fleeing to temporary exile after the defeat of their chief invited the missionaries to accompany them. They refused to go, saying they had no quarrel with the enemy chiefs. Soon after, the missionaries were attacked and three were killed. The others escaped.

From the outset, the missionaries had been accused of threatening Tongan independence. Mariner claimed, according to a chief who was involved, that one of the British residents initiated the accusation. The missionaries had revealed him to his chiefly patron as an escaped convict. According to Finau 'Ulukālala, the missionaries were angry because of his attempt to pilfer an iron cooking pot and because they suspected him of stealing half their pigs. After being unmasked as a criminal in his home country, the man was reviled by the Tongans. In retaliation, he told local chiefly people that the missionaries were

> sent out by the king of England to bring pestilence upon the
> people of Tonga, and that they accordingly shut themselves up in
> this house, to perform witchcraft . . . which was the cause of the

pestilence which then raged (there was an epidemic disease at the time, which was very fatal among the chiefs, two or three dying every day) . . . (Mariner 1827 : 1 : 73)

Missionaries never allowed Tongans to attend their ceremonies, while Tongans invited the missionaries to theirs. For this reason, and the epidemic, the chiefs took the man seriously. The convict went on:

> . . . by and by you will all be cut off, and the king of England will take possession of your islands: for although you have the remedy in your power, you will not make use of it. (Ibid.)

The succession wars followed soon after this incident and the missionaries were attacked. Those who escaped were sheltered on other islands, and the following year all but one left on a passing merchantman for Port Jackson, New South Wales. The one who remained was George Vason, who had "fallen away" from missionary life. He would return to England two years later, having repented his lapse and abandoned his Tongan wives.

Work and the Word: Commerce and Conversion Struggles

From these inauspicious beginnings, certain basic features would be played out in subsequent missionary efforts. First, the missionaries were concerned not only with conversion, but also with the development of commerce, cash-cropping, and occupational specialization. The LMS *Duff* brought tropical products such as cochineal and plants such as cacao and tobacco[2] to Tonga for the express purpose of introducing profitable commercial crops (Love, in J. Wilson 1799/ 1968: xci). These crops, it was hoped, would generate funds to help make the mission self-sufficient. The evangelicals wrote that they wanted to introduce sheep as a "great advantage" to the Tongans,

> not only by supplying their deficiency of food, from which many of them suffer at present [This contradicts all other accounts of the time], but by leading them into habits of industry, to which they are strangers; for though they are more industrious than most of their neighbours scattered about this sea, far the greater part of their time is spent in idleness. (J. Wilson 1799/1968: 280)

The missionaries, then, considered the people to be simultaneously lazy and half-starved. This blatant contradiction can be found in many Western authors' accounts of peoples slated for colonization, including some anthropologists', as discussed by Sahlins (1972 : Ch. 1).

The mercantile aspects were not a sideline, but of a piece with the proselytizing efforts. The Secretary of the London Missionary Society, on behalf of the directors, instructed Captain Wilson of the *Duff* to compare the Marquesas and Tonga with regard to the

> safety of our women, probability of introducing our improvements, supply of provisions, the products of the islands in sugar, cotton, sandalwood, etc. (Love, quoted in Griffin 1822 : 125)

Those elected to go on the mission ship were chosen not only for their Christian commitment, but also for their "useful arts" (Love, in J. Wilson 1799/1968 : xciv), as smiths, carpenters, and the like. Besides four ministers and a surgeon, the party included:

> twenty-five Missionaries or settlers . . . having been for the most part engaged in business or mercantile employments, highly necessary to impart the principles and habits of civilization to the South Sea Islanders . . . (Griffin 1822 : 107).

The nine assigned to Tonga were unmarried men. The six women on the voyage were not signers of the Missionary Covenant, because they were defined as wives, not missionaries in their own right.

The *Duff* missionaries' conversion strategy included a top-down approach: attach missionaries to powerful chiefs, convert the chiefs, and help the chiefs consolidate their control over other groups. From the outset, the missionaries ignored all other forms of authority in favor of power and protection. They ignored considerations of high rank, kindness, wisdom, respect, and so on. For instance, they knew that many women were high ranking, but they did not treat female chiefs as they treated similarly ranked male chiefs. When the Tu'i Tonga Fefine, the next Tu'i Kanokupolu (her nephew), and Finau 'Ulukālala all sent roasted hogs to the missionaries during the mortuary rites for the dead Tu'i Kanokupolu (her brother), the missionaries sent a packet of iron tools to the future Tu'i Kanokupolu (Tukuaho) and nothing to his father's sister or the other chief (J. Wilson 1799/1968 : 241).

Although the initial proselytizing was aimed at the more powerful of the various paramount chiefs, the more far-reaching changes the missionaries sought were directed at lower-ranking and especially nonchiefly people. But the latter goal was secondary to cementing political alliances with strategic chiefs. The missionaries offered their services as advisors, as did all resident Europeans.

The advisory role fit with Tongan custom, since, as foreigners, the Europeans were incorporated into Tongan ranks as *matāpules*. They were aliens who had skills which were at the disposal of the chiefs who allotted them land for use. The missionaries had artisan skills and knowledge of English and *papālangi* ways. From the Tongan point of view, missionaries were a variation on the castaway and stranded whites among them (Ralston 1978). As foreigners, they were immune from the usual *tapus* on touching chiefly people; missionaries were used as barbers (J. Wilson 1799/1968:233). Other foreigners were used occasionally as executioners[3] and more often as warriors. As *matāpules*, they were compensated for artisanal skills. When the future Tu'i Kanokupolu visited the missionaries with a request for grinding one iron tool into several, he brought "two pieces of cloth," that is, a typical gift of *tapa* to a *matāpule* (ibid.:246).

Uneasy Alliances: Missionaries and Other Europeans

European men resident in the Islands in the late eighteenth century arrived there through a variety of circumstances. At nine, the LMS missionaries outnumbered all the others on Tongatapu. Most of the rest were sailors who had jumped ship. Of these, three were released or escaped convicts from the prison colonies at Botany Bay and New South Wales. One of the convicts had been a debtor; the others had committed violent crimes. (John Singleton and Will Mariner would not arrive until 1806, when the LMS missionaries were gone.) Another resident was a boy, son of a Hawaiian woman and a Scottish man, who had been adopted by the widow of the Tu'i Tonga, the Moheofo, when Tongans captured a passing ship (Mariner 1827: 2:78n). Some of the men tried to start new lives upon their arrival; their success depended on establishing kin links with their hosts and adopting Tongan ways of behaving.

The released and escaped convicts who antagonized the *Duff* evangelists met different fates. One was turned over to the captain when the *Duff* returned to Tongatapu; he was returned to Port Jackson. Two others were executed shortly after they had alienated their chiefly patrons—one had raped the chief's daughter (Vason 1810: 90). Others left the Islands on passing ships, while the adopted boy remained with his new kin, as did several other stranded or voluntary exiles.

One mission history describes Tongatapu as being "overrun by released convicts . . . who incensed the people against the missionaries" (C. Horne 1904:27). The missionary journals mention only three. But the presence of other Europeans augured both a potential loss of privileged access to the chiefs, and the horror of "losing control" in a land where no one had to work hard to live comfortably. The latter fear was not without foundation. One of the missionaries, Vason, "went native" to the shock and dismay of his fellows (Vason 1810; B. Thomson 1904:136). In a later account of the tribulations of the LMS missionaries, Vason is said to have "deserted them and become unfaithful to his Christian profession, joining the natives in a life of immorality" (C. Horne 1904:27). In his own account, Vason concurred[4] and made suggestions for future missions, such as sending only married men (Vason 1810:70, 114).

The missionaries were contemptuous of other white residents, but there was always a strain of opportunism in their mutual relations. Several of the residents robbed and tried to cheat the missionaries of property, at times by force (J. Wilson 1799/1968:255). At least two of the residents urged the chiefs to "attack and plunder" the mission compounds. The missionaries knew these men were attached to the same chiefly sponsors and protectors as they were, so they carefully timed their complaints against the men, whom they considered liars and thieves. One of the men who most annoyed the missionaries was once married to the daughter of the head navigator (a *matāpule*) for the future Tu'i Kanokupolu, Tukuaho. This man, Ambler by name, "beat one of the women he lived with inhumanly, who ran away, and the friends of the other carried her off" (ibid.: 232). Yet in the next sentence the missionary said, "he rendered us considerable service by instructing us in the language." The missionaries used even "the most wicked looking fellows" as interpreters and go-betweens (Griffin 1822:129).

Other European residents warned the LMS missionaries continuously that the chiefs were going to steal their property, even as they themselves were taking what they could. The missionaries believed the warnings, though, because

> . . . there is not a man on the island but who would tell us upon inquiry, that they are 'matde monucka,' that is to say, "dying in love" [an interesting mistranslation[5]] for our things. (J. Wilson 1799/1968:247)

Missionaries hoarded goods, while other *papālangis* tried to ingratiate themselves to chiefly people in Tongan fashion, by sharing goods—including goods from the mission compound. The other residents married locally, as did the renegade missionary, and many took advantage of the discrepancies between European and Tongan sexual mores. They profited from trade whenever possible and offered services to local chiefly people. They were by no means a unified group, although some banded together in the face of the missionaries' threat to their new prestige. Many were secretive about their origins; all seemed afraid that the class differences between themselves and the missionaries might be revealed to the chiefs. Quarrels within the settler group were frequent and the bickering among the *papālangis* sometimes exasperated their chiefly patrons to the point of warning all the foreigners to shape up.

Both groups of Europeans were tolerated because they helped the chiefs to deal with visiting ships (J. Wilson, 1799/1968:254–255). They also posed no threat, since they were so internally divided (Erskine 1853/ 1967:151–152). Chiefs competed politely with each other for missionaries, not only because they had desirable goods and skills, but also because they brought the promise of additional goods to their patrons. The chiefs were aware that the *Duff* would return and that other ships were likely to follow, bearing more useful goods for the missionaries (J. Wilson 1799/1968:247). The chiefs, then, played the missionaries off against the other Europeans: chiefs would accept goods stolen from missionaries and then decry the perfidy of the settler-thief when the missionaries complained.

The experiences of the LMS missionaries set several precedents for later missionary efforts (beginning in 1822). Later missionaries would echo the top-down approach and the currying of favor with powerful, rather than other prominent Tongans. They also would use resident Europeans when it was in their interests to do so, and they would mistrust and speak ill of the others in the interim. Later missionaries also would identify their task as not only conversion, but "civilization": cash-cropping, specialized division of labor, social authority restricted to men, increased productivity, encouragement of commodity exchange, and the forging of institutions of state.

There were two other consequences of the first missionary attempt. First, the failure of the LMS party in Tonga meant that there were only minor disagreements when the Wesleyan Methodists wished to attempt a mission in Tonga twenty-five years later. The two groups divided the Pacific with little squabbling over religious turf (Russell 1845:262). Second, the Tongans were regarded as vicious and dangerous, following the exodus of the LMS: "savagery and duplicity were the leading characteristics of the people of Tonga" (C. Horne 1904:27). The later view contrasts markedly with the first reports of the LMS missionaries.

A profound decentralization followed the wars of the late eighteenth and early nineteenth centuries. The Wesleyan Methodist missionaries encountered a fragmented political scene when they arrived in the 1820's. This fragmentation would not necessarily have led to the emergence of a powerful paramount chief, since the wars were conducted for traditional reasons, namely, claiming through superior kinship part of the ongoing production of lower-ranking kin.

Christianity subordinated kinship considerations to allegiance to a sacred authority. Evangelical sects, such as the Wesleyan Methodists, also justified the use of force to accomplish salvation through conversion. The Wesleyan Methodists who came to Tonga also were English, and brought with them a model for the reorganization of authority. Their model was based on the landed gentry and monarchical structure of preindustrial England.

The first Wesleyan Methodist missionary, Rev. Walter Lawry, arrived in 1822 and immediately explained his religious purpose to a gathering of seven chiefs, to whom he gave twenty chisels and two axes (Morrell 1946:105). He was well received, but after three months, a *matāpule* spoke menacingly of Christian activities at the chiefly *kava* circle. Since *matāpules* spoke publicly only on behalf of the chiefs to whom they were attached, the comments show the chiefs' continuing mistrust of the foreigners:

> . . . the white people were come as spies, and would be followed by others from England who would take away the Island Tongatapu from them . . . these people are always praying to their *Atuas* [gods] as the other [LMS] missionaries were, and what was the consequence of their praying? Why, the wars broke out, and all the old Chiefs were killed. (Lawry, quoted in Morrell 1946:105)

Lawry was well aware that missionaries were seen as "harbingers of soldiers who would come to kill them and seize their land." He was not surprised that "they consequently treated me with suspicion" (Lawry, quoted in Bain 1967:31). Lawry did not remain long in Tonga, but upon his return to England (for personal reasons) he arranged to have other missionaries replace him.

In the interim, proselytizing was conducted with some success by Langhi, a Tongan missionary. Formerly an interpreter for a merchant ship's captain, he had traversed the Southern Pacific. Langhi married and converted to Christianity in Tahiti, which already was Christianized. In 1825 he left Tahiti for Tonga, accompanied by one of his wives [!], an Otaheitan woman, and two missionary natives [Tahitian] . . . he succeeded in converting his chief, the great Thubow [Tubou,[6] in line to be Tu'i Kanokupolu] and all his subjects in Nogoluffa [Nuku'alofa]. (Dillon 1829:1:271)

By the time the Wesleyan Methodist party arrived in 1826, they found a mission station already in operation, as well as a chapel

. . . with three or four hundred persons desirous to receive their instructions; a state of things resulting almost [!] entirely from the exertions of a converted pagan. (Russell 1845:262)

This first band was reinforced by the arrival of others two years later. Some of the chiefs on Tongatapu attributed the (slow) inroads that the new religion was making to the neglect of Tongan ways. The last Tu'i Ha'a Takalaua had died in 1799. A Tu'i Kanokupolu had not been invested since the death of the last one in 1820. The man who would be Tu'i Tonga was alive, but he had not been invested; he lived in Vava'u, where his mother had been exiled after her unsuccessful bid for the Tu'i Kanokupolu title. An opposition was forming around the issue of Christianity, but the stakes would be higher than chiefly succession.

Holy Wars: Conquest and Consolidation

The Wesleyan Methodists who arrived in 1826 attached themselves to the paramount chief of Ha'apai, Tāufa'āhau, who was the son of Tukuaho, the *Duff* missionaries' patron. He also was heir apparent of the as yet uninvested Tu'i Kanokupolu. In time Tāufa'āhau would become the first Tongan king, George I. The alliance between the missionaries and this powerful heathen chief alienated the Tu'i Tonga, the Tu'i Tonga Fefine, and many other chiefly groups on Tongatapu and Vava'u, the other major island groups. Christian missionaries had a considerable role in the later reinforcement of the Tu'i Kanokupolu position and its conversion into kingship.

The political disputes in the islands from 1810 to 1826 centered on various paramount chiefly factions vying for redirection of existing tribute. Following 1826, the focus shifted to the unification of administrative control in the hands of an individual (Erskine 1853/1967:127). The French Catholic (Marist) priests alleged in the mid-1800's that "Tāufa understood quickly the advantage he could draw from the Protestant religion" (Hervier 1902:131; my translation).[7]

Tāufa'āhau did not convert until 1831, but he kept the missionaries at hand. Prior to his adoption of Methodism, Tāufa'āhau had convinced his kin not to allow one of their women to marry the Tu'i Tonga. The refusal implicitly defied the rank superiority of the male sacred paramount.

Tāufa'āhau manipulated both customary and European means of consolidating administrative power. As patron of the missionaries, he was in a position to ensure that Christianity was not widely accepted until its utility in his consolidation efforts was demonstrated (Wright and Fry 1936:251; Gifford 1929:192).

The Christian mission presented Tāufa'āhau with the prospect of unifying the Islands politically as a return, on a "civilized" and Christian level, to the sacred chieftainship of the past. The missionaries ignored both the traditional constraints on the sacred paramount, seen in contention for title and popular unrest, and the parallel authority exercised by his sister, the Tu'i Tonga Fefine. Aspects of traditional chieftainship were selected: the resulting ideology was both elite and patriarchal.

Christianity had tremendous potential as a challenge to customary authority based at least in principle upon sacred rank: it provided a sacred alternative, based on immutable hierarchy, without succession troubles from the sister's side. In the missionaries, Tāufa'āhau perceived a means to extricate power from customary constraints. Before his conversion, he had boasted to them:

> . . . I am the only Chief on the Island [Ha'apai in 1828]. . . .
> When I turn they will all turn . . . (Morrell 1946:108)

The Tongan chiefs on Tongatapu who opposed the political machinations of the Ha'apai paramount united to support the would-be Tu'i Kanokupolu, a younger brother of the LMS missionaries' chiefly patron. On the proviso that he renounce his recent Christian conversion and help stop the spread of the religion, the chiefs of Tongatapu installed him with the paramount title (Erskine 1853/1967:127). For a time he did renounce Christianity, but Tāufa'āhau, his paternal nephew, convinced him to return in 1830. The action split his following into fellow converts and chiefs who felt betrayed (Wilkes 1852:2:10). Shortly after this extension of Tāufa'āhau's influence into Tongatapu, he converted. On the occasion of his baptism in 1831, he adopted the name George (after the king of England) and his followers became Christian *en masse*.

The traditional chiefs, from that time on, simultaneously opposed Christianity and political centralization. The Tu'i Kanokupolu was based in a district of Tongatapu, while George remained based in Ha'apai. But they joined forces to depose the traditional chiefs of Tongatapu and unite the two groups politically. The conquest of Tongatapu took more than twenty years of intermittent, violent struggle. In Tonga, state formation involved conflict between kinship and an emerging civil sphere on a number of levels, including open warfare.

Following some intricate manipulation of the kinship system, George was selected to succeed the deceased paramount of Vava'u (West 1846/1865 : 154, 160–161). As a result, the people of Vava'u were not forcibly incorporated into the kingdom. To this day they retain a sense that they are not "subjects" of the state, and continue to exercise a semi-autonomy which periodically erupts as a political crisis.[8]

By 1833, George and his allied chiefs and *matāpules* controlled most of Vava'u, all of Ha'apai, and part of Tongatapu. The missionaries backed these efforts fully. They considered the centralization of power a mark of civilization and supported the person most likely to establish a political order. They also found conversion immeasurably assisted by conquest. The alliance was not without tensions, however. In 1833, after being invested as paramount chief of Vava'u, George Tāufa'āhau also abducted for himself the primary wife of the Tu'i Tonga (Collocott 1923a : 184; Lātūkefu 1977), a move which signaled his willingness to challenge the symbolic authority of the sacred male paramount. The elopement was not condoned by the missionaries, who expelled him from the church, but a year later he married the woman in a Christian ceremony and was readmitted (Lātūkefu 1977 : 129).

Firearms were made available to all the chiefs through plunder, which continued until 1830, and trade in coconut oil (Erskine 1853/1967 : 157; Sterndale 1874 : 2–3). The Christian chiefs had an additional source of supply, namely, the missionaries (Wright and Fry 1936 : 251; Gifford 1929 : 192). The Wesleyan Methodists fomented hostilities, fanned existing flareups, and provided arms for the Christians (Morrell 1960 : 52).

In 1837 one of the traditional chiefs and his people forced the Christians to abandon the recently reopened mission station at Hihifo on Tongatapu, the district associated with the Tu'i Ha'a Takalaua group. The traditionals killed four people in the process. The Tu'i Kanokupolu, Josiah Tubou, called in George, who called on Rev. John Thomas in Vava'u for consultation about reprisals. In the following weeks,

. . . Thomas preached on texts which told of the clash between Jehovah's chosen people and the Heathen opposition. (Cummins 1977a:33)

One Sunday the traditional faction raided Christian garden plots while the Christians were in church. The next day the Christians stormed the traditionals' fortress at Ngele'ia, burned it, killed twenty people, and took everyone else prisoner (Cummins 1977a:34). The difference in scale and type of warfare is marked, even though both sides had firearms: The Christians retaliated for raids on yam gardens with wholesale conquest (Wilkes 1852:2:4).

A week later, after another raid on gardens during church services, Christian forces attacked and destroyed the fortress at Hihifo. The Christians killed three hundred women, men, and children (Cummins 1977a:34). The slaughter was not in accordance with Tongan custom. The inspiration might have been drawn from the chorus repeated throughout Rev. Thomas' text the day before:

. . . and Joshua smote them with the edge of the sword, and utterly destroyed all the souls that were therein, he let none remain. (Ibid.:34–35)

Some of the missionaries considered warfare a suitable means to advance Christian progress in the Islands. The minister wrote to his family after this massacre of "heathens":

. . . we hope to get more places to preach at than we have ever had . . . King George is conquerer but he gives all praise to the Lord. . . . I am sure that you will rejoice that God is so good to us. (Thomas, quoted in ibid.:38)

In a letter which shocked his London superiors, he added:

. . . the good effects of this successful war with the heathen and their gods, by our Christian kings and their people, will be felt in all the islands . . . having been conquered by Vava'u and Ha'apai Christians, thousands [on Tongatapu] will turn unto God . . . (Ibid.)

In spite of the disaster, the other traditional chiefs of Tongatapu remained in armed opposition.

At this point (1840), a visiting U.S. ship, sent in search of whaling sites in the Western Pacific, stopped at Tongatapu. The captain, Charles Wilkes, was asked to negotiate peace terms between the traditionals and the Christians. Of his initial encounter with George, Wilkes wrote:

> We . . . found him . . . building and fortifying a town [on Tongatapu], and his forces daily arriving from Vavao and Hapai. Indeed his whole conduct did not leave us any room to doubt what his inclinations were, and that the missionaries and he were mutually serving each others cause. (1852:2:7)

With misgivings, Wilkes agreed to mediate.

The liaison between the traditionals and the Christians was the Tamaha (Wilkes 1852:2:7–8). She was the daughter of a "heathen" chief and married to a Christian chief. She was a Christian, but her natal kin remained traditionals. As Tamaha and related to both sides, she could be assured of safe passage. She carried proposals from the traditional chiefs:

> . . . they desired peace, and to be left in the quiet enjoyment of their land and their gods, and did not wish to interfere or have anything to do with the new religion. (Ibid.:9)

Wilkes took exception to the images the Christians gave him of the "heathens":

> The heathen are represented by the Christian party and missionaries as a set of cruel savages, great liars, treacherous, and evil-disposed; and this character seems to be given to them only because they will not listen to the preaching; and it is alleged they must therefore be treated with severity, and compelled to yield. . . . I must here record, that in all that met our observations, the impression was, that the heathen were well-disposed and kind, and were desirous to put an end to the difficulties. (Wilkes 1852:2:13)

When he discovered that the Christian party was not negotiating in good faith, he gave up the attempt. He thought that George and the missionaries would fight until they forced the "heathens" to become Christian or "to extermination, which the number of their warriors made them believe they had the power to effect" (ibid.:9).

Shortly thereafter, a British naval officer was asked by the Methodist missionaries to send terms to the recalcitrant traditionals at the fortress of Pea on Tongatapu (Morrell 1960: 52). When they refused to surrender, he and his armed forces attacked the fortress (Hervier 1902: 132; Wilkes 1852:2:24). They were soundly defeated, the officer killed in the fighting. Following this "heathen" victory, there was a lull in the fighting. The lull indicates that the purpose of the traditionals was self-determination and a continuance of chieftainship, rather than conquest. They were not challenging the other chiefs' religion, but defending their right to remain non-Christian. The pragmatism of their move is open to question, given the necessity to defend custom with bullets and the intention of the opposition to use conquest as a vehicle for conversion. Nevertheless, several of the chiefs expressed their willingness to die rather than become traitors to their own ancestors (Wilkes 1852:2:10).

The relative quiet ended in 1842 with the arrival of French Catholic priests at Tongatapu. They may have been invited by the opposition chiefs (Morrell 1960:310). In any case, they were adopted immediately by the opposition. Previously a Marist priest had landed at Vava'u (in 1837), but the Methodist missionary there had advised George to send him away, which he did (Hervier 1902:133). Allied with the "heathen" chiefs of Tongatapu, the priests began to vie with the Methodists for both pagan and Christian souls. They represented, both to the chiefs who sponsored them and to the English missionaries and Christian chiefs, the potential for French intervention (Erskine 1853/1967:134). The traditional chiefs sought to ensure their autonomy through the introduction of another type of Christianity and with it, international politics.

In the face of possible French intervention, George could rely on the cooperation of almost all of the English people in the Islands—settlers, traders, and missionaries (Hervier 1902:135). When the Tu'i Kanokupolu died in 1845, George assumed the title of King. He asserted control over all the Islands. From this time on, the English considered him king of Tonga, irrespective of the entrenched opposition on Tongatapu.

The Wesleyan Methodist missionaries accused the "Romish" priests of attempting to "question and invalidate the hereditary and titular power of king George" (West 1846/1865:54). Because the Catholics were associated with the "heathens" in opposing George's transformation of kinship into kingship, both Catholics and traditionals were called "Devils" and warfare resumed. George viewed the Catholics as a threat to his newly acquired position. He met the missionaries' concern that the Marist priests might find French support with a written request for protection by the British (1847), should the French attempt to annex Tonga (Morrell 1960: 311–312; Erskine 1853/1967: 133).

The successor to the Tu'i Tonga became the focal point of the opposition: the priests portrayed him as a sacred king, an image drawn from preindustrial France, comparable to the Wesleyans' Tongan fantasy (Hervier 1902: 129–130; Morrell 1946: 110). Based at Pea, the Marists succeeded in converting many of the traditional chiefs, including Fieota, the sister of the Tu'i Kanokupolu and the primary wife of the Tu'i Tonga (Hervier 1902: 136). She brought her retinue with her, including the chief of Pea, Ata, and his lower-ranking kin. In 1848 the Tu'i Tonga effectively became Catholic (ibid.: 139–140). These conversions should be seen as a strategy for the traditional chiefs to remain independent of George's expanding rule. If the previous wars were fought because they were heathens, then they were now Christian.

In 1851 George decided to take control from two traditional chiefs who led the opposition on Tongatapu. He moved the court to Nuku'alofa on Tongatapu (it has remained the capital) from Lifuka in Ha'apai. By dint of thinly veiled threats, he ensured that the Tu'i Tonga group would remain neutral in the fighting (Morrell 1960: 313). George explained to a French bishop, who expressed concern about another religious war:

> The object of the present war is to subject the rebels to the Government . . . it appears evil in my eyes that your converts in general have joined the heathens in opposing my rule. (Quoted in letter of Rev. Amos, June 1, 1852, quoted in Morrell 1960: 313)

One traditional stronghold negotiated peace terms and agreed to become Christian, that is, Methodist. The fortress at Pea, where the French priests lived, held out for months of siege in vain hopes that the French government would intercede, as they had in Tahiti. Finally, they surrendered. Many were arrested and many more went into exile, to Ha'apai and Vava'u (Hervier 1902: 141). The priests were exiled, until the consolidation of state control and threats from the French government resulted in a royal declaration of freedom of religion—as long as it was Christian. Groups associated with the former Tu'i Tonga and Tu'i Tonga Fefine remain Catholic to the present day.

Opposition to the government faction was the reason for George's final war against the Catholics and heathens. He was correct in his assurances to the bishop that the war was not religious in the strictest sense. The fusion of political centralization goals with Methodism would be challenged in the future, and George's more fundamental commitment to political control would be obvious.

The justification of the initial holy wars—that conversion by any means and death to the intransigent were preferable to a life without salvation—rang increasingly hollow to those who opposed the chiefs and retainers who became the nobility. Conversion was the beginning, not the end. The missionaries saw Christianity as a way of life, including centralized political control, commodity production and exchange, non-kin-based authority, and patriarchal familial relations.

In the late nineteenth century the association of devilry with opposition to the state took another form. This time, the "Devils" were those Wesleyan Methodists who opposed the creation of a state church, the so-called Free Church of Tonga. This internecine Methodist war in 1885 reflected both chiefly rivalries and opposition to the control exercised by the Wesleyan Methodist Mission in Australia and New Zealand over the lucrative Tongan mission (see Korn 1978; Morrell 1946). Both churches continued, and eventually the rift was mended. New rifts would occur, reflecting the changing interests within the nobility and popular discontent (B. Thomson 1902: 162).

Opposition did not disappear. In the 1890's the powerful and controversial minister-advisor to George I, Shirley Baker, was attacked in an assassination attempt (Rutherford 1971). It failed, and of the twelve men involved, five were pardoned, one was sentenced to penal servitude (hard labor on royal plantations), and six were shot (Ruhen 1966: 116). There followed a general repression of the kindreds of those who were arrested and of all who refused to join the state church (Rutherford 1977). When a visitor in the early 1960's was eagerly escorted to view the graves of those shot, he was told by his guide,

A man can be a great rogue and earn less punishment, and these were not rogues. They were good men. (Ibid.: 113)

The visitor tried to find out why the graves, over seventy years old and in a fairly remote area, were so well tended. People seemed reluctant to explain. One man said simply, "We think a lot about these men" (ibid.: 116).

The Domestication of Women: Gender and Conversion

The imposition of Western standards of appropriate conduct and arenas of work on Tongan women, coupled with Christian emphasis on husbands' authority and wifely duty, met with intense resistance. The degree of resistance can be gauged by the severity of punishments for infractions. The missionaries attempted to alter traditional sources of women's authority through social pressure, religious instruction, and legal compulsion.

The campaign sought to redefine Tongan concepts of gender and to reduce Tongan women's political and economic authority. The variable success of the missionary efforts depended upon concomitant and intertwined political and economic processes: the shift to production of cash crops for taxes and export, restriction of use-rights to land, and the development of civil and domestic spheres. The effects of tax-rents, cash-cropping, and changing land tenure will be discussed in Chapters 10 and 11. At present the concern is pressure on women to adopt to mid-nineteenth-century middle-class English standards of behavior. The circumstances which made substantial conformity necessary were shaped by emerging commodity production and state intervention.

The missionaries were fully aware of the high status of women in Tonga. One of the *Duff* evangelists commented:

> The respect paid to this old lady, and to many of her sex in Tongataboo, distinguishes them from the servile condition to which females are subjected in other savage states or tribes. Here they possess the highest degrees of rank, and support it with a dignity and firmness equal to the men. (J. Wilson 1799/1968: 108–109)

At the same time they were aware of the differences between Tongan and their own sexual mores. The Tu'i Tonga Fefine boarded the *Duff* and was given "an elegant English dress" by the captain. The missionaries reported that

> . . . she admits no fixed husband as companion, but cohabits with those of the chiefs whom she pleases to select, and has several children. (Ibid.: 271)

Before the missionaries were ensconced in the Islands, there is some acceptance in their writings about the differences, while they stress that such behavior would have to change once the people were Christian. In the covenant signed by the LMS missionaries, the section on marriage is explicitly patriarchal: the wife was to be "loving, faithful, and obedient" (J. Wilson 1799/1968:419). Marriage was to endure, regardless of later Catholic accusations that the Wesleyans promoted frivolity through divorce laws (Hervier 1902:129). During this early period, the other missionaries tried to convince their "fallen away" companion, Vason, to shun his Tongan wife, who was a "heathen," since they were not married in the eyes of God (only according to Tongan ceremony). He refused to "desert" her, so the missionaries decided that they should at least formalize the vows. She was agreeable, until the nature of Christian marriage was explained:

> . . . it was a solemn engagement for life, to be faithful to her husband, and that nothing but death could release her from the bond. When she understood this, she would not consent. (Vason 1810:126)

The missionaries then persuaded Vason to leave his wife; he did and then took up with the divorced daughter of one of the chiefs until he asked the chief to send for his wife again. She consented to return and the chief provided them with a house and land (ibid.:128).

Christian monogamy was an endless source of amusement for Tongan women during the early period. Three young chiefly women who visited Labilliardière on board asked a number of questions about French marriages. When they were told that the great men of France and even the kings of Europe had only one wife each, they laughed. Labilliardière concluded that this information "gave them no very high idea of their [the kings'] power" (1800:367). The young sister of one paramount chief visited the captain of an American ship in the early 1800's. Of monogamy she reasoned:

> . . . either the white men must make very kind and good tempered husbands, or else the white women must have very little spirit, for them to live so long together without parting. (Mariner 1827:2:49)

The Wesleyan Methodists who followed in the 1820's did not move to change divorce proceedings, which customarily had been at the instigation of the husband. But certain aspects of customary divorce were systematically distorted. Traditionally, a wife who left a cruel husband was not returned by her kin or friends. A wife who deserted her husband and took up with another man was not forced to abandon her lover. In other words, women had de facto means of effecting a divorce, irrespective of the official method. In the earliest edicts issued by the future king (early 1840's), there were constraints placed on informal divorces:

> Should a man leave his wife and refuse to return, she shall claim his plantations, and whatever property he may have possessed: and in case a woman forsake her husband, she shall be brought back to him, and should she decline to remain, it shall not be lawful for her to marry so long as he lives. (Russell 1845 : 401)

As early as 1850, the government sought to make divorce a civil concern. But even partial enforcement was impossible before 1875, when the first civil courts were established.

Before the missionaries, widows had been expected—but not compelled—to remarry if they could still bear children, especially if they were childless. Choice of the second spouse was open to the widow, but both sororate and levirate arrangements were recognized. If they remained single, they could cohabit with their lovers or merely sleep occasionally with men. The Wesleyan Methodists, through the implementation of land use laws and the restriction of use-rights, sought to enforce widow chastity.

The missionaries directed a great deal of energy toward the control of female sexuality, for both unmarried and married women. The sexual code affected nonchiefly unmarried women most severely. The first of these regulations—again, prior to the creation of a vehicle for enforcement—was framed in the 1830's by the missionaries working with George before he was king. They sought (with resounding lack of success) to restrict Tongan women's relations with sailors, in all likelihood as much out of concern for public health as for public mores. The missionaries recognized the complicity of kin in such liaisons:

> Should a person living on shore entice a seaman to leave his vessel, he shall pay a fine of eight dollars; and should any one know of such a desertion or seducement, and not give notice, he shall also be fined. (Russell 1845 : 401)

Following this protective legislation, the missionaries became more overt in their attempts to impose Victorian middle-class standards of behavior on women in general, and unmarried women in particular.

Women found adulterous or guilty of "fornicating" faced prison sentences, stiff fines, or labor service on royal plantations (Erskine 1853/1967:130). They were not condemned by their communities— in fact, the "jailbirds" were a source of appreciative local pride— but the women still had to work for the king for a specified time. The battle continued throughout the nineteenth century and well into the twentieth. At the turn of this century, one young married woman, who often was arraigned on morals charges, explained her predicament to the British administrator:

> She was born into the world, she said, to enjoy herself, and as the capacity for enjoyment wanes when one is old and ugly, pleasures must all be crowded into the fleeting hours of youth. (B. Thomson 1904:147)

The missionaries also tried to rework Tongan women's appearances to be more suited to Victorian middle-class standards. In at least one instance, this campaign undercut the war against female sexual exploration. Before the arrival of the missionaries, nonchiefly women's hair was cut when they were around the age of twenty. From then on, they were called *fefine motu'a* or "old woman." The haircut symbolized maturity and worked at the same time as an inducement to marry, since a woman feigning youth would be ridiculed by her age-mates. The Wesleyan Methodists thought short hair was mannish and insisted that all women wear their hair long, as chiefly women did, regardless of age (Cumming 1882:35). By the turn of the century, one British administrator commented wryly:

> By a mockery of fate, a laxer moral tone allows a girl to prolong her independence to the limit set by time to her attractions, and she finds life so amusing that she defers marriage until the last possible bridegroom has left her for a younger generation. (Ibid.:373–374)

The missionaries' rigidity and lack of attention to the rationale of Tongan customs created such inconsistencies. Given the ministers' efforts to force married women to conform to their notions of wifely duty, one can understand why young women would want to defer marriage.

One of the first missionary assaults on Tongan sexuality concerned women's breasts: defining female breasts as enticing and shameful, the Wesleyan Methodists insisted that they be covered (Wilkes 1852:2:16). So women added a flap of *tapa* to their wraps.

Their care in the matter did not indicate an adoption of the missionaries' attitudes. As late as the 1870's, a visitor remarked:

> The women, however, evidently have little idea of shame in the matter, and often the cloth is put on so loosely that it affords no cover at all. (Mosley 1879:287)

Missionaries attributed adultery in part to Tongan husbands' philandering. They held wives responsible for creating the conditions leading to philandering. The solution, then, was framed in terms of wifely behavior. Sexual availability was made a wifely duty, according to the Wesleyans, even where custom disallowed it. Traditionally after childbirth, a new mother was secluded for a month, cared for by women from both her kindred and her husband's. Until the baby was weaned, the mother was supposed to refrain from sexual intercourse. This was intended to prevent another conception and the premature weaning implied by another baby. The missionaries forbade the seclusion and the abstinence. By the early 1900's, Tongans had complained to a British colonial officer that the higher rate of infant mortality was due to premature weaning. Tongans explained that there was no adequate substitute for mother's milk until the child could eat solid foods (B. Thomson 1904:375–376).

Infanticide in such a situation would be possible, but it appears to have been rare. There were laws on the subject, however, so there must have been some cases. Abortion appears to have been practiced, even though children born outside marriage were not condemned and did not detract from the mother's marital prospects. Inadvertently, the missionaries may have encouraged abortion through their virulent condemnation of "illegitimate" children and their mothers. A contributing factor may have been the introduction of steel blades in the late nineteenth century. The administrative officer blamed the declining birth rate at the time on "the increased skill of women in the forbidden forms of surgery" (B. Thomson 1904:374). It is not known whether his statement was based on rumor, criminal cases, or projection.

In general, wives were harangued as sinful and subject to public sanction if they did not comply with missionary notions of marital duty. Women were urged to take up domestic tasks, work considered feminine in the Victorian middle class—sewing, cooking, housekeeping, and child care. Sewing, certain housekeeping tasks, and infant care were sufficiently related to Tongan practices as to be unobjectionable. Married women were not isolated from their kin and the tasks did not devolve onto a solitary wife's shoulders. Older children continued to be associated with peers or the same-sex parent; child care remained a matter of shared responsibility, with men involved less than previously. Cooking and other tasks were *ngāue,* men's work, and demeaning to women. Women often refused to take up such low-status tasks: even today, cooking responsibilities can spark arguments between spouses.[9]

Missionaries thought one reason for Tongan wives' unwillingness to be obedient was the authority they exercised as sisters. Marriage was not an institution women needed for economic security. Missionaries set about making marriage essential for women's economic well-being.

The Wesleyan Methodists actively discouraged the exercise of sisters' rights, because of the influence it had in keeping married women independent of their husbands and because it violated the sacredness of private property. Sisters and their children could simply take goods and food through the *fahu,* undercutting the missionaries' attempts to instill the virtues of accumulation through hard work. *Fahu* rights were one of the "heathen customs" forbidden in the mid-nineteenth century, missionary-drafted law codes, but the ban was not implemented until the late 1920's. The prerogatives of the father's sister role were judged correctly to be inimical to "proper" inheritance, that is, through patrilineal primogeniture. The political implications of the legal impositions will be discussed more fully in the next chapter.

Missionaries placed particular pressure for conformity on women. Always attentive to the risks of alienating their chiefly, later noble sponsors, the Wesleyan Methodist missionaries focused special attention on nonchiefly women. The state-associated church attacked the customary division of labor by gender, the involvement of women in socially vital production, the authority of women in their various kin roles, and women's control of their sexual and reproductive lives. The campaign was conducted in the name of uplifting the moral and social status of the Tongan woman. Progress was measured against Victorian middle-class English standards, even into the twentieth century. The relative success or failure of the missionaries' push reflects in part the capacity of chiefly and nonchiefly women to alter, blunt, avoid, or adapt the impositions to suit their own ends. The framework for women's changing options was the development of state structures to bolster the new class relations, and the imposition of commodity production for a capitalist market.

Christianity and State Formation

Christianity provided a rationale for class relations and civil authority. Disputes among the various chiefly and nonchiefly groups, already heightened through the introduction of European armaments, became focused on one chiefly faction's attempt to consolidate political control over all of Tonga. The Wesleyan Methodist missionaries brought an ideology that justified the abandonment of kinship ranking as a basis for social authority. The Christian tenets drew upon existing tendencies toward gender hierarchy in Tongan culture and used those aspects that could be made to fit with Christian patriarchy. From the outset, missionaries saw their task as the civilization of Tonga. To them, civilization entailed the forging of institutions of state and the creation of a landed gentry and a diligent peasantry, as well as the implementation of gender and kin roles appropriate to a Christian people involved in farming and commerce.

After the conquest of the Islands, the church provided a vehicle for promoting loyalty or obedience to the central administration. Non-kin-based authority was encouraged through church attendance and tithing, and pressures were brought to bear at a local level through mission regulations. Repression was common in areas under Wesleyan Methodist influence. Public floggings, broken teeth, branding on the shoulders, and forced labor on mission plantations and buildings were punishments meted out by the church to both male and female offenders (Monfat 1893:204).

The Wesleyan Methodist church appeared to mediate between the civil administration and the kin communities, while its ultimate loyalty rested with the state. Everyone was equal before God and all Tongans were subject to divine law, even though some were more subject to civil law than others. Certain kin roles were vested with new or increased authority through the ministers' invectives first and, later, legal intervention. The role of the church with regard to kinship was to split the loyalties of the kindred: husbands were granted far more authority over wives than ever had been customary; the sister's role was downgraded, effectively reducing the sources of social authority for women.

As a mediating institution, the church intervened in social reproduction where the state could not at the time. Still in their kindreds, local people could be drawn into choirs, collection rivalries, Bible groups, and so on. By doing so, people were sure not to incur the displeasure of the local landed nobility. In addition to this reinforcement of time spent apart from kin-related activities, church activities reinforced new social relations. Mission collections involved commodity production; positively sanctioned pleasures and social events were directed to the praise of an all-powerful male deity. People used the church in different ways and at times made their involvement with it analogous to traditional pursuits (Korn 1978). But the analogy was a formal one: a woman could use the church collections to build prestige, as wealth accumulation for presentation to chiefly people had been prestigious in the past. But the church could not be called upon to reciprocate, and the wealth presented— money—did not share the same meaning as traditional *koloa*, valuables, made by women.

As is typical of all state-associated religions, the role of the Wesleyan Methodist Church was dependent upon the continuation of class relations. The mission depended upon and bolstered the emerging class relations. Missionaries supplied firearms, assisted in drafting legal and criminal codes, facilitated tax and rent collection, and created new tensions within the potentially rebellious kindreds through pressure on kin roles and responsibilities. The church provided a cross-class institution with an appearance of autonomy from the state-associated classes. The activities it sponsored were social at the same time as the tenets upheld the righteousness of private accumulation of wealth. Because church ceremonies were social, they paralleled and sometimes replaced customary social gatherings and life crisis rites. Rituals and practices that had been kin-controlled were challenged by the penetration of the indirectly state-sponsored ideology. The mission, then, helped both to produce and to reproduce the emerging state and class society. Christian ideology could not have been imposed without the sponsorship of a dominant class; the dominant class in turn drew its rationale for rule from the same ideology. The success of the mutual relationship rested on the involvement of both the emerging nobility and the missionaries in developing ways of extracting goods and services without incurring rebellion. This process involved both state formation—the making of a "native kingdom"—and fostering commodity production and trade.

10. A Native Kingdom: Creating Class and Gender Stratification

Alfred P. Maudslay   *The present system of imprisonment [is] creating crimi-*
(1878/1930:220)   *nals by the hundred.*

THE MISSIONARIES sought to create a civilization in the image of a romanticized eighteenth-century England. The prescription called for a landed gentry, a yeoman peasantry, chaste maidens and dutiful wives, hard-working and authoritative husbands and fathers, a king bound by constitutional constraints, a nobility enlightened by adherence to Christianity, and, of course, a powerful clergy. But Tongan society was not a *tabula rasa:* it had its own history, its own political dynamic, and—like any stratified society—an assortment of views of the past. The set of institutions and political struggles that emerged as "the Tongan state" can be understood as a result of the relative power of the direct producers and their kin-defined communities, the emerging nobility and landed class, the traditional chiefs and their supporters, the missionaries and commercial agents. These political struggles did not take place in a vacuum. The shifting interests of Britain, France, and, later, Germany also were played out in the Islands.

Regardless of successful conquest and an ideological justification for rule, class relations in Tonga could not survive without a range of mediating institutions to buttress the new stratification. This set of mediating structures included both church and state. During the holy wars of the 1830's, 1840's, and early 1850's, King George I and his faction worked with the missionaries to devise law codes suitable to the Christian civilization they were imposing. The defeat of the Catholic and traditional forces in 1852 did not eliminate opposition to the nascent state, it merely changed the ground rules.

The Constitution of 1862 regulated the relations of the king and the new nobility, but the 1875 version—drafted primarily by Rev.

Shirley Baker—strengthened the monarchy at the expense of the nobles (Im Thurn 1905 : 57). From 1875 on, the king attempted to eliminate all sources of opposition through a variety of means, but mostly through the legal-judicial structure. The consequences were not what any party had envisioned.

In the course of the nineteenth century, the emerging civil authorities attempted to crystallize both class relations and gender hierarchy. The class relations that emerged were by no means stable. They were legislated through land and inheritance laws and backed by the threat of force. But the continued prominence of several dispossessed or marginalized traditional chiefs, supported by popular discontent with the regime, ensured that opposition to class relations continued.

The relative success of legislating women's subordination depended upon the vicissitudes of civil penetration at the community level. The political authority of women in the civil sphere certainly was blunted, and producing women found their use-rights to resources severely curtailed. The degree to which Tongan women are subordinated today, on the local level, is an aspect of the relative strength of the remaining kin sphere of production. Where the traditional division of labor by gender, rank, age, and kin connection is most circumscribed or embedded in class relations, women's authority and autonomy suffer the most. In the dominant political economy, the armature exists for subordination, but resistance still is marked.

The creation of legal structures out of kin-defined customary practices signals a struggle between kin communities and the civil authorities (Diamond 1951; 1974 : Ch. 8). The reworking of custom to the benefit of class stratification also is part and parcel of state formation. Codification involves a notorious rigidity absent from practices in kinship societies; the reduction of ambiguity usually affects women and men differentially (Rapp 1978a; 1978b). Typically, there is an attempt to mute antagonism to the changes by using customary forms with revised content.

In the Tongan case, the coalescence of state institutions involved an overhaul of chiefly-nonchiefly relations and of the customs that helped to re-create that form of stratification. The emerging state-associated elite used aspects of custom to rationalize their actions, which, in practice, were opposed to custom. Sweeping negations of customary land tenure arrangements, kinship rights, women's social authority, labor claims, and definitions of both crimes and punishments have characterized the last 150 years. Typically, the denial of custom was phrased in the idiom of tradition or the idiom of kinship. But resistance to the redefinitions reflected the degree to which people were not mystified by rhetoric.

Restriction of Use-Rights

After the holy wars, the imposition of novel land tenure laws profoundly altered people's use-rights to soil. For the direct producers, changes in land laws were relatively slow. The tendency from code to code was to restrict the hereditary possession that local kindreds had exercised. The codes also sought to limit the power of the chiefs, while they rewarded those who supported the king. Mostly chiefs, these supporters were transformed into a state-associated nobility and a landed gentry. The new arrangements helped to consolidate a class structure and subsume the prior stratification by estate or order.

Traditionally, a victorious chief either would maintain the defeated chiefs in their positions, once they accepted the superiority of the victor, or would reassign the titles to others in the defeated chiefs' kindreds. The defeated chiefs might go into exile temporarily, but they were not permanently dispossessed from their home areas. At stake had been the relationship of one chiefly group—associated with a particular area—to another.

During the 1830's and 1840's, Tāufa'āhau/George I would grant chiefly title to one of the defeated chiefs' sympathetic relatives, even a potential successor, if the relative was a Christian. More typically, he compelled the defeated to convert and reallocated the title to someone outside the defeated group, who had shown particular loyalty to the Christian faction. A captain from the United States noted the new practice when he visited the area controlled by Tāufa'āhau in 1840:

> The titles consist of the name of the district over which the chief rules, and of which they receive the revenues, with 'tui', a word synonymous with lord [by that time] before it. . . . there are others who have distinct titles, as Lavaka, the king of Bea [Pea, the "heathen" stronghold in Tongatapu], one of the bitterest opponents of the Christians . . . and Ata, Takafauna, and Vaca, the great chief of Houma. The latter was deposed a short time since, yet still retains his title among the heathens. (Wilkes 1852:2:10)

The king and his supporters sought to solidify their position by appropriating the land base and labor claims of the opposition. After the "holy wars," the king rewarded the chiefs and six *matāpules* who had supported the Wesleyan Methodists with titles and the use of lands associated with those positions (Marcus 1977b).

In 1850, the king claimed all land by right of conquest (Maude 1971 : 109–110). The continuing threat of conquered but hostile kindreds, coupled with the absence of a judicial structure, slowed implementation of drastic land tenure revisions. The codes of 1857 and 1862 asserted that all land was owned by the state, in the name of the king, and only the state could alienate land. Lands were divided into three types of holdings: Crown, royal (land allotted to the king's patrilineal kin), and hereditary estates. In form, the division approximated the customary association of chiefly kindreds with particular regions, with the exception that the lands of Tāufa'āhau and his kin were now considered royal and state lands.

The 1862 code also banned in-kind donations to chiefs and labor service (Im Thurn 1905 : 58). At the same time, the code created tax-rents to be paid to the Crown, some of which would be siphoned off by the hereditary chiefs (ibid.). Usufruct rights could be inherited, but they were contingent upon patrilineal primogeniture and loyalty to the king. In content, then, the laws anticipated a class of estate-holders who received both tribute and labor service, by reason of their connection to the Crown.

The 1862 laws relating to land tenure appeared to codify custom. In precontact Tonga, use-rights had been granted indefinitely to elderly representatives of local cognatic kindreds, the *'ulumotu'a* (cf. Maude 1971 : 108). In practice, the kindreds held the soil, while chiefs came and went. Individuals would receive use-plots through their connections to these local kindreds. In dealing with the chief, the *'ulumotu'a*, by reason of age and extensive kin network, often would act as a spokesman for the kindred.

Under the 1862 code, land was to be allotted to the people who needed it, according to their needs, under conditions reminiscent of those prior to centralization. In addition, the ban on labor service or continuous material support for chiefs curbed the potential power of traditional chiefs, while it won popular support for the new regime. The "Konisitutone" provided that:

> . . . the chiefs shall allot portions of land to the people as they may need, which shall be their farm, and as long as the people pay their tribute and their rent [i.e., tax-rents] to the chief, it shall not be lawful for any chief to dispossess them . . . (West 1846/1865 : 434)

Figure 12. Edward Winslow Gifford's map of Tongatapu, 1929. From Gifford 1929:173. Reproduced by permission of Bishop Museum Press.

There was no direct reference to gender in this section of the constitution, with regard to either the chiefs or the producers. The implication was that land would be allotted to men primarily, since men did most of the agricultural labor. The new laws did refine custom in particular ways. For instance, taxation in the form of rent was introduced in place of labor service or donations to the chief. Chiefly exactions had been sporadic and in accordance with what people already were producing; taxation was systematic and the form was determined by the state. Gender bias in land holding was incipient in the constitution. While the statement above implies that women could be allotted land, the constitution held *men* sixteen years old and older responsible for paying tax-rents for their hereditary estates or use-allotments (Im Thurn 1905 : 58). Both chiefly and nonchiefly men were to pay tax-rents to the government; the king was responsible for paying "Governors, . . . magistrates, and policemen, and all Government officials" (ibid.).

By 1875, a system of courts and police had been established throughout the Islands. Missionary-merchant-state connections supplied all three groups with steady sources of revenue and labor. The stability of the ruling coalition depended on the cooperation between the monarch and the landed gentry. George I considered his rule sufficiently entrenched to revise the land laws. The 1875 code subjected all Tongans—chiefly and nonchiefly—to arbitrary dispossession. The assertion of state determination of succession and loyalty were implemented (Im Thurn 1905 : 14).

The laws represented a balance of power between the estate-holders and the state in the person of the king. The laws limited the customary control over land and behavior exercised by nonchiefly kindreds. The 1875 code gave the estate-holders and other state-associated agents the right to allot land directly in the form of leases to male heads of households (Maude 1971 : 110). This undercut the position of the '*ulumotu'a*, the spokesmen of the kindreds. Legally, use-rights no longer were obtained through one's membership in a loosely structured kindred. Instead, chronology (sixteen years and up), gender, and marital status (husband) determined eligibility. Widows found their continued use-rights challenged; married and divorced women were refused official access.

The 1875 code strengthened the role of the hereditary estate-holders. Estate-holders could declare lands uncultivated and then lease them to foreigners, paying the usual state-regulated tax-rents. Abuses under the new system made access to land extremely tenuous for small producers. Popular protest against the expropriation was widespread and brought British intervention. Reforms in 1891 made all leases to foreigners regulated by the state, in the name of the king; the state would receive a 10 percent royalty on each lease (Tukuaho and Thomson 1891:61). To avoid the situation where estate-holders would simply not distribute land to commoners, the reforms made all men sixteen years and above responsible directly to the government for their allotments (*'api*). The size of the allotment was set at 8 1/4 acres for the tax-plot, with a small lot allocated in a village, for use as a house site (W. Horne 1929:312). The code also prohibited commoners from accumulation of use-property or petty landlordism: no person was allowed to hold two tax allotments (Tukuaho and Thomson 1891:63). The class of landlords thus was limited by statute to the *nōpeles* and the few *matāpules* who had been elevated by George I.

The reforms limited the capacity of estate-holders to become full-fledged rentiers tied to foreign agricultural enterprises; they certainly met with fierce resistance by the estate-holders. By 1915, another compromise was reached: the state granted the allotments, but the estate-holder was consulted (W. Horne 1929:111). Regardless of government assertions, over time the estate-holders have regained effective control over allotments (see Marcus 1977b).

Today, they are responsible for carrying out the census—determining how many men are eligible for allotments—and for registering the use-plots. To become eligible for an allotment, a man has to be a registered taxpayer. In addition to age and taxpayer status, the applicants must show readiness to cultivate the plot; generally this is interpreted as planting coconut trees for commercial copra production (Allen 1921:116). In addition, registration is in the hands of the estate-holder. Since there are more men sixteen years old and above than there are use-plots available (i.e., not already leased), applicants frequently must provide additional money, labor service, or produce to the estate-holder in return for his approving the registration of their allotment (Maude 1971:114–115). Some men do not bother to apply for their allotments. Instead, they borrow land from relatives and friends. Men who have registered allotments may encounter trouble getting credit for commercial production: leased land cannot be used as collateral, and the town site is technically granted from governmental or estate-holder lands. Often, an allotment-holder will illegally sublet his parcel while he migrates overseas to earn the cash for a truck or other capital improvements. Thus, an intricate system of informal subleasing has arisen, particularly of cash-cropping land (ibid.:119), but in the face of growing land shortages, this is now extending to subsistence-cropping land.

Many small farmers are forced to become tenants on hereditary estates, without holding official allotments. The rents involved are hefty, equivalent in some places to the average annual cash income. In this situation, groups of relatives or neighbors contribute to rent a bush parcel, and subdivide it informally to meet subsistence-cropping needs. In one case, twenty-three cognatically related households from an urban neighborhood, with an average annual cash income of $450, chipped in to meet the fairly standard annual rent, $300 Tongan. On top of the rental, however, each member of the group had to provide a large basket (*kato*) of each new crop to the landlord: in other words, "first fruits" were demanded and received. Had the producers been able to sell the "first fruit" crops in the marketplace, each would have received at least $50. In terms of consumption, one basket of yams would last a family of six about two weeks. The landlord in this case sold the "first fruits" in the Nuku'alofa market, grossing at least $1,150.

In this exploitative situation, popular resistance can be seen in circumventing legal avenues to land use, and in emphasizing kin-based avenues. Nevertheless, because land cannot be sold and because from 1900 to the 1970's there was little long-term leasing to outsiders, the rate of landlessness in Tonga (60 percent of all eligible men hold no land) is still less than that in other Pacific islands (Government of Tonga 1973). Still, the rate of landlessness is increasing, due to the hereditary estate-holders' manipulation of allotment registration, and population increase.

Women's access to land is now through husbands or along such informal lines (Ledyard 1956:202). The laws on widow tenancy have placed more pressure on them to remarry than was the case prior to contact. The restriction of women's use-rights has been reinforced by additional legal constraints, which have limited their capacity to call on nonmarital relationships for access to subsistence resources.

Stratification, Old and New

The estate structure continued in a modified form (nobles and commoners), and to this day has served to obscure the existence of hereditary estate-holder, state functionary, mercantile, and producing classes. The nobility, *nōpele*, emerged from those chiefs who had been allotted estates and their legitimate patrilineal descendants; the dispossessed chiefs were not included in the nobility, nor were collateral descendants of the estate-holders (Marcus 1977b). Contrary to customary practice, all children of a female "noble" were not automatically noble.

The estate-holders as a class included the *nōpeles* and certain *matāpules* and their patrilineal descendants. The estate structure obscured the composition of this landlord class. Some of the hereditary estate-holders were not noble (Tukuaho and Thomson 1891 : 61).

The new land tenure system was presented as if it were based on custom: all land in Tonga is said to have been vested in the Tu'i Tonga, the sacred paramount chief. George I, the Christian king, was presented as such a sacred paramount. His allotment of lands to those chiefs and *matāpules* who had worked closely with him during the conquest was presented as a variation on the sometime reassignment of titles after a succession dispute. District chiefs had been assigned by a paramount. But the analogies were false. One difference was that lands were not *vested* in the king as a steward (Sahlins 1972); he claimed to own all of Tonga. Another difference was that the lands he allotted to his retinue were heritable, subject to his approval of the heir, and the estate-holders were not necessarily people customarily associated with the lands (Maude 1971 : 111). A number of the opposition chiefs were dispossessed or had their traditional regions reduced in size (Im Thurn 1905 : 14). In addition, the inheritance of estate-holding became more restrictive. The codes regulated the pathways to succession, reducing the number of collateral claims. Patrilineal primogeniture became primary. Succession disputes were brought under the jurisdiction of the courts, another extension of the state as arbiter of custom (Marcus 1977a).

What had been a chiefly order was transformed into an aristocracy and a landlord class. The association of a chiefly kindred with an area became state ownership and private landholding. The estate-holder did not have to be especially concerned about local prosperity, under threat ultimately of popular support for a contender; the state protected his position. The estate-holder acted as a landlord, whose relationship to the state and the king gave him access to revenues. In return, the state extracted taxes in the form of ground rents for each allotment. The estate-holder could keep whatever he could extract as rent beyond the tax-rents for the state. In short, the land tenure structure fit the description provided by Marx of use-rights in an "Asiatic" or tribute-based mode of production (Marx 1858/1964; 1881/1974; Amin 1976).

The commoners as an estate came to include the traditional *tu'a*, *matāpule*, and *mu'a* ranks, as well as many of the chiefly people who opposed centralization. Today, the nobility includes only the royal family and those chiefly people selected by the state to hold hereditary lands. The class structure crosscuts these orders. Producers can be of chiefly, *matāpule*, *mu'a*, or *tu'a* rank, although these categories are no longer recognized officially. The producing class includes small farmers, fishermen, and artisans; women and men of this class also carry on petty marketing, and some are wage laborers. There are commoners who are nonproductive in the strictest sense: a small but growing group of shopkeepers and an assortment of *matāpules* and other commoners who are employed by the state as bureaucrats and other functionaries. The landholding class also is state-associated; some of these are *matāpules*, although most are nobles. The estate structure before contact has been altered to meet the needs of the new class arrangements. Enough of an overlap exists to leave room for claims that it is continuous with tradition. But in strategic areas, there is departure from customary stratification: that departure has involved increasing insecurity for the producing class.

Custom versus Law

During the centralization wars, the Christian faction invoked custom to justify unprecedented and restrictive regulations. The extension of power relations had a double edge: one side was conquest, the other side, redefinition of custom. The new order was phrased in terms of chiefly *tapus*, that is, the reservation of items for chiefly use or future consumption. The traditional forces rejected assertions that the new form of *tapu* was in keeping with Tongan custom:

> The heathen . . . complained that their temples were desecrated, their customs broken in upon, and their pleasures destroyed by the Christian party, who endeavored to interdict their comforts, and *force laws upon them in the shape of taboos through their king.* . . . The heathen now said that they could no longer endure these acts, and were determined to resist. (Wilkes 1852:2:6; emphasis added)

The traditionals did not challenge the right of chiefly people—in this case, Tāufa'āhau (later George I)—to *tapu*. They objected to the use of *tapu* to prevent the exercise of customary rights.[1]

Crime and Punishment

In regions where George and his retainers had consolidated control, one custom no longer was used to deny another. In the conquered areas, changes were more direct. The 1850 law code, drafted by George I with missionary advice, was only partially implemented, and only in Vava'u and Ha'apai. At the time the only vehicle for enforcement was the customary one—the rather immediate use of *matāpule* retainers, since law courts were not instituted until the 1870's. The significance of the 1850 code lies in its anticipation of future state intervention. The interdictions were almost uniformly against customary practices and punishments specified forced labor. For instance, the code forbade dancing,

> as well as all Heathen Customs; and if any are found practising such they shall be tried and on being proven guilty, work one month, and in the case of repetition, two months. (Quoted in Rutherford 1971 : 60)

The punishments proposed were innovative, taken from the missionaries' knowledge of penal servitude under contemporary British law, coupled with the growing use of war captives as slaves by right of conquest. In Tonga previously, transgressors of chiefly prerogatives had been pardoned, thrashed, or, on occasion, killed; but never had they been expected to perform labor service as atonement. The effects of such labor-based punishments were noted by Rev. Thomas West, writing in the 1840's. It seems that in 1847, the Wesleyan Methodist mission station at Neiafu (Vava'u) was burnt twice. The first torching was recognized generally as an attempted assassination of the missionary and his wife. The arsonist was caught and was to have been killed, but the missionary "interceded" and had the chief commute his sentence to "penal servitude for life" (West 1846/1865 : 195–196). Forced labor was not customary and the effect of the sentence can be taken as evidence. The arsonist

> died two years afterward very suddenly . . . the probability being that he had taken poison rather than continue any longer in a state of criminal servitude as a *tamaoieiki,* or slave. (Ibid.: 197)

The term was not the same as the one used for war captive, *popula.* The new term robbed the prisoner of his adulthood; he was the "chief's boy," someone who was a social child, used for adult tasks. The inability to transcend his crime and condemnation for eternity to social nonexistence were intolerable conditions.

This form of unfree labor became an important force in the production of goods for the European trade from the 1860's on. The crucial role of penal servitude in commodity production is discussed in the next chapter. The concern here is with the range of activities that came to be defined as criminal. Like most edicts in emerging states, the early code asserted state control over life and death, rights to use resources, reproductive choice and sexual practices, and consumption patterns. As in many precapitalist states, at first the state was identified with the person of the ruler. Attempted suicide was punished by forced labor for the monarch. Reproduction of kinship, through marriages, adoption, funerals, and so on, was subject to civil regulation; law mimicked or undercut custom. Also typical of state formation as a process, there was an assertion of the right to intervene in custom and social institutions long before there were attempts to effect such intervention.

Legislating Morality

The code presented in 1857, five years after the defeat of the Catholic and "heathen" forces on Tongatapu, included a number of laws on morality. The 1857 provisions regarding sexuality and biological reproduction foreshadowed broader restrictions of women's authority. For example, abortion was defined as attempted manslaughter. Anyone found guilty of attempting to induce abortion had to "work for the king for twelve months" (St. Julian 1857:71).

Parity for women and men existed in some of the laws, notably those concerning sexual liaisons: any man or woman convicted as a "fornicator" had to work for two months, and if a repeat offender, three months (ibid.:71). "Bundling" brought three weeks' labor. One form of sexual liaison, *taga*, was known traditionally: a man would creep into a house at night—usually by prearrangement—to have intercourse with a woman. The code gives indirect evidence that *taga* was usually prearranged. The law held the man accountable; the punishment was two weeks' work for either the act itself or "making signs."[2] The punishment for adultery, for either a man or a woman, was a penalty in pigs and yams, to be paid to the spouse (St. Julian 1857:71). The punishment for rape involved the same fine as for adultery, but to be paid to the victim; the perpetrator also had to work at forced labor for three months (ibid.:72).

From 1862 on, cash fines were imposed for "fornication," adultery, and other sexual offenses. Nonpayment of fines was cause for internment at hard labor for various periods of time. Subsequent codes (1875, 1891, 1894, 1900, 1903, 1907, 1919, 1929, 1967) refined the definitions of the crimes and, in general, stiffened the penalties. The later laws sometimes specified different punishments for men and women. Cash fines usually were comparable. Women would have a more difficult time obtaining cash than men, however, since wage labor was defined as *ngāue*, men's work (Shumway 1971).

By 1894, an adulterous wife had to pay up to $60 (240 shillings), or to prepare for the Minister of Police a mat or piece of *ngatu* of comparable worth (Government of Tonga 1907:92). For fornication, a woman had to pay $25 or make a "task of native manufacture" worth not more than $25 for the Minister of Police. By that time, "hard labor" for pregnant women was commuted to the making of "native manufactures" for the state (ibid.). None of the law codes—including the 1967 one—have considered forced intercourse in marriage as rape (Government of Tonga 1907:379; 1967:231). There is no evidence as to whether or not marital rape was recognized in the precontact situation, but the protections for runaway wives were far more plentiful in the earlier period.

Marriage and Divorce: Creating the Family

The 1857 code referred obliquely to customary practices. For instance, polygamy was banned; it was defined as either multiple husbands or multiple wives. Penalties paralleled those for adultery (St. Julian 1857:71). Early writers reported that some forms of adultery—desertion included—constituted socially acceptable means of divorce and remarriage. The law gave priority to the first marriage and held the subsequent one to be adultery, thus limiting women's access to divorce. Under the new laws, anyone who abandoned a spouse could incur forced labor until he or she returned to the marriage (ibid.:70). Since divorce had been at the discretion of the husband, the statute should be seen as directed primarily at wives. After courts were instituted in 1875, divorce became costly as well. Court costs, to be paid in cash, were prohibitive to all but the chiefly. Even after the divorce reforms introduced by the British after the Protectorate was set up (1900), court fees made it virtually impossible for nonchiefly women to get divorced legally, since their access to cash was even more restricted than was men's. The restriction of divorce and the strengthening of husbands' authority meant far less control over their sexuality for women. Today the fees for divorce are relatively low, but informal divorces are still commonplace.

A law banning the manufacture of *tapa*, in effect from 1875 to 1880, undercut a major source of women's social authority, namely, the making and distribution of wealth objects. The impact of the *tapa* law is examined in the next chapter. It suffices to say here that missionaries convinced the king that making bark cloth was uncivilized. Restricting women's customary involvement in production and social reproduction dovetailed with the laws on sexual conduct and contributed to a growing dependency of women upon men and, specifically, upon husbands and fathers.

The state claimed the right to determine appropriate marriages. The laws on incest show a pattern of codifying customs that emphasized patrilineality, while subverting customs that supported cognatic ties. The state banned marriage with a range of relatives, not all of whom had been considered *tapu* traditionally. For instance, there was a ban on one of the preferred marriage patterns in the pre-contact society, namely, mother's brother's daughter/father's sister's son (W. Horne 1929:272; Government of Tonga 1907:386–387). The law was exceedingly unpopular, and in all likelihood impossible to implement, but it was not repealed until 1935. Also in contrast to prior practice, the state prohibited a divorced person from marrying his former wife's sister, or her former husband's brother, during the lifetime of the ex-spouse (Government of Tonga 1907:386–387; 1967:266). In the 1890's, the penalty for incest—including sexual relations with relatives traditionally preferred as sexual or marital partners—was hard labor for life (Tukuaho and Thomson 1891:36). From 1919 to the present, the penalty has been the same as for rape, but, if consensual, applied to both parties (Government of Tonga 1967:164).

Many of the early laws made continued use-rights of women in various kin roles contingent upon their sexual conduct. Most of these laws remain on the books. The growing dependency of wives upon husbands has left women particularly vulnerable, and laws have linked wives' relative security to their sexuality. As late as the 1930's, for instance, a deserted wife could expect court-ordered subsistence payments from her husband only if she remained faithful to him *in absentia* (W. Horne 1929:289). Widows continue to be affected. A widow has been allowed to retain use-rights to her husband's land and house site only if she remains chaste (Tukuaho and Thomson 1891:63; Government of Tonga 1967:662). Any widow proven to have "fornicated," or remarried, forfeits her use-rights, even if she has small children to support (Neill 1955:148). If the husband dies intestate, the widow may retain only the town site, the crops in the fields, poultry, pigs, and *tapa;* the courts decide the allocation of the tax-allotment and other property (Government of Tonga 1967:259). Similarly, if a man dies without sons or grandsons, his unmarried daughters can use his land only as long as they are not found to have "fornicated" (ibid.:623).

Producing people's response to these regulations has included rather impressive noncompliance. It is said that prosecutions of widows are rare these days (Maude 1971:112). Extra-legal—that is, customary—divorces and remarriages were commonplace in the 1940's

(Elkin 1948 : 359 – 360), and de facto divorces occur today when husbands who migrate abroad cease sending money to their wives. Children of customary marriages are still considered legitimate by the community, but they cannot legally inherit property.[3] For producers, who have by law only a life-interest in agricultural plots, inheritance of property is less important. The inheritance laws are circumscribed through gifts during the lifetime. In this way, cognatic claims survive, even those of sisters and father's sisters.

In precontact Tonga, wives were expected to defer to husbands, but they were not dependent upon husbands. In political matters today, women are considered their husbands' wards. From the creation of Parliament in 1862, voting has been restricted to male taxpayers twenty-one years and older (Shephard 1945 : 161). Sway in official politics is not possible for most nonchiefly men, either: there are seven representatives for "the people" in Parliament, compared with seven representatives for only thirty-three estate-holders (Crane 1979 : 74). The nine Cabinet ministers, selected by the king, also sit in Parliament, giving the nobility and the monarch effective control. All women are effectively disenfranchised, a situation which is not in keeping with the precontact political situation.

The legal structure also has restricted the kind of work women may do, the degree of advancement they can attain, and the remuneration they can expect relative to men (W. Horne 1929 : 87). Wage scales discriminate against women in all types of employment, including state jobs (ibid. : 327). When they can find wage labor, women are confined to agricultural processing, clerical, and lower-level teaching pursuits. Today, these legal and informal restrictions continue. In addition, a married woman's income is considered legally to be part of her husband's income (Government of Tonga 1967 : 930).

Alone, the legal constraints outlined above could not impose dependency of wives upon husbands. The changing division of labor by gender contributed heavily to women's declining economic position, as seen in the next chapter. But even as women became economically dependent upon *men,* the prerogatives of women as sisters and father's sisters would have prevented *wifely* dependency. Sisters could rely upon brothers because of the sisters' higher rank. Unfortunately, at the same time as these laws were being promulgated, the rights of sisters and sisters' children also were being attacked.

Restriction of Fahu *Claims: From Sisters to Wives*

Tongan women had exercised less authority as wives than as sisters and paternal aunts. From the outset, the emerging state attacked women's authority as sisters. The 1857 code sought to limit the influence of the *fahu* and, concomitantly, to strengthen the role of the nuclear family as a social unit. The code consistently stressed the centrality of the conjugal pair, and especially the authority and responsibility of husbands, over any collateral kin connections. For example, it was forbidden for anyone to "interfere to stop a wedding" (St. Julian 1857:70). This may have been framed in part because of resistance to the imposition of church marriages in conquered areas, but it also eliminated the right of the father's sister to arrange or veto marriages for her brothers' children. The law "freed" young people from the authority of the paternal aunt, while it subjected them to the less flexible constraints of the mission and the state. Another statute called upon men to

> work and prepare food for their wives and children. If they voyage it is their duty to leave food. (Ibid.)

Previously, women and children could appropriate food and other goods from brothers and mother's brothers. Legally, in the form of what appears to be protection, collateral claims were being severed.

Another attack on the rights of sisters and father's sisters focused on redistribution. Again, the nuclear family was granted legal precedence over the kindred. The 1857 code banned several forms of exchange associated with production for use, especially redistribution of gifts on special occasions. The missionaries correctly perceived the flow of goods as a barrier to accumulation. The marital unit was supposed to industriously set about accumulating wealth, and limit consumption to spouses and their children. The statute read:

> . . . as it is improper and impoverishing (to adhere to) the forms adopted at our [customary] weddings, whatsoever the relations feel inclined to present to the parties that are to be married it is their own, not to be distributed again. (St. Julian 1857:70)

Later statutes specifically banned redistribution at funerals and marriages (Government of Tonga 1907:75, 90). Both of these laws limited the rights of father's sisters (see Marcus 1977a). Previously, especially among lower-ranking chiefly and nonchiefly people, the father's sister distributed the deceased person's goods and conserved a healthy share for herself.

Laws governing succession to estate-holders and nobility also have truncated the claims of cognatic kin, particularly sisters. In the aboriginal society, sisters and sisters' children had substantial claims to title and to the labor of the brothers' side of the kindred. Indeed, there is some evidence that among chiefly people, children had claims to the lands of their maternal uncle (Gifford 1929:175). In Niue at the turn of the century, customary practice held that

> A grown-up son inherits his father's house and land, but the daughters seem to have claims upon their mother's brother. (B. Thomson 1904:136)

Beginning in the 1860's, succession rules redefined these rights: most of the regulations remain in effect today. The succession regulations have limited the size and created the patrilineal composition of the estate-holding class.

One of the first restrictions involved adopted children. Adoption of her brother's children had been one of the options available to a woman. It enabled her to keep active use-rights and authority in her natal kin group, regardless of her marital status or fecundity. Adoption was commonplace in the precontact society, and also was used to expand kin networks both laterally and vertically. The 1875 law code ruled that

> . . . no adopted children shall succeed to estate or title, or to anything; only the children of blood relations and by marriage. (Im Thurn 1905:55)

Although technically a brother's or sister's child could inherit, the adoption restriction made it difficult for them to do so if legally defined closer relatives existed. For example, a woman lost the right to pass use-rights to her brother's children on a par with, or even in preference to, her own children or those of her husband by a former wife. In practice, considering the pattern of adoption in Tongan society, the restrictions on adoption truncated cognatic claims in favor of lineal ones. The change not only eliminated one of the major means by which women kept control over reproduction, it also made barrenness an unprecedented issue.

Legally, no Tongan woman could inherit a position unless her father left no male issue, sons or grandsons. No man claiming relationship through a woman (e.g., a sister's son) could inherit, if any other male relatives existed. For instance, a deceased man's grandson by his youngest son had priority over his eldest son's daughter or his eldest daughter's son (W. Horne 1929:324). If there were no male heirs, a granddaughter by a deceased son had priority over a man's own daughter (ibid.). A woman could inherit a title to an hereditary estate only if she was the firstborn of a sonless male line (ibid.: 322). Even in that case, if her father had a brother, she had to wait until her paternal uncle's death. In other words, the sister, father's sister, and sister's sons, who exercised claims to goods and title in the precontact society, lost virtually all claims.

Compounding the effect of redistribution laws and succession regulations, the state has banned all exercise of *fahu* prerogatives (W. Horne 1929: 700). Leaving aside for the moment the impact of commodity production, the *fahu* ban has done more than any other force in fostering dependency of wives upon husbands. Legally, a woman can no longer rely upon the provisions supplied by her brother or call upon the labor of her brothers and their wives; her children cannot avail themselves of his goods (Neill 1955: 19). Resistance to this ban is pronounced in local practice. For instance, if a woman is an adult unmarried mother or a divorcee, her brothers will generally provide for her and her children, although it may become a matter of considerable contention if she continues to have children. The customary rights persist, but because they are illegal, *fahu* rights no longer can be assumed. As one man explained, "A husband now considers it more important to provide for his wife's needs than for his married sister." But the same man added,

> . . . it is *fakatonga* [customary] for me to respect and protect them [my sisters]. . . . My father's sister . . . is almost as important to me as my mother. She was consulted about the name my parents chose for me, and will also have a say in who I marry. (Quoted in Crane 1978: 10)

With *fahu*-based claims made illegal, the structural autonomy of wives vis-à-vis husbands has been eliminated, at least where the law has been enforced. For noblewomen, the ban has another implication: a sister or father's sister can no longer act as regent for minor heirs to title and lands. The state now claims the right to appoint a regent. For all Tongan women, the sister's control over inheritance, over the fertility of her brother's wife, over the marriages of her brother's children has been subverted first by church ceremonies and, later, by state regulations.

State Crisis and British Intervention

Throughout most of the nineteenth century, Great Britain was content to have Tonga remain a neutral "native kingdom" (St. Julian 1857:14; Condliffe 1930). The prominence of the Wesleyan Methodists in the Islands was assumed to be sufficient to ensure sympathy with British interests. Some British agents viewed with considerable ambivalence the influence of the missionaries on the conduct of Tongan affairs (St. Julian 1857:13). In fact, the missionaries' interests in promoting their proselytizing and constructing Christian civilization were not identical with British geopolitical interests (Maudslay 1878/1930:218, 233).

In the 1860's and 1870's, the Methodist mission developed close ties with a major German commercial firm, engaged in copra export. The merchants, Godeffroy and Son, worked with the mission to build both parties' revenues; the traders also provided loans to the king (Sterndale 1874:2). The merchant connection led to the introduction of Bolivian silver coinage and to a treaty of friendship with Germany in 1876. Alarmed by both the currency change and the provisions of the treaty, British officials intervened in 1878. Great Britain enforced Tonga's neutrality by appropriating the coaling station Tonga had ceded to Germany as part of the treaty (B. Thomson 1902: 153). They intervened again in 1891, citing the unhealthy influence of the mission on the king and further irregularities in government finance; at that point, the British insisted that Tongans accept British advice in drafting a new law code (Tukuaho and Thomson 1891).

The emerging state institutions depended upon the existence of class relations, as a source of revenue (the producers) and of staff (nonproducers). The state existed primarily to support the maintenance of a nonproducing class, the royalty and its coalition of landed retainers, merchants, and functionaries. From 1875 on, the king and his staff acted solely on behalf of the royal coterie—rather than on behalf of stabilizing class relations in general. The illusion of the state as mediating class relations disappeared: a constitutional crisis led to British intervention. George I died in 1893, and by the turn of the century the fragility of his coalition of nobles, merchants, and missionaries became evident.

The next king, George I's grandson, George Tubou II, set off a series of debates about constitutional reform regarding land leases and succession. Leases were, in theory, regulated by the state and issued in the name of the king. In practice, a number of the king's relatives and other nobles had not properly assigned use-plots to the commoners who had legal rights to them (Im Thurn 1905:13). They either retained the lands for cultivation with penal or wage labor, or leased the lands to foreign agricultural concerns. The 1891 changes in land-tax laws made men responsible for paying the cash tax whether or not they had an allotment. The state also claimed the right to allocate allotments directly, bypassing the estate-holders. In the process, the king and his advisors alienated a significant number of the *nōpele* estate-holders (Fusitu'a and Rutherford 1977). The land reform was not successful:

> . . . after some lands had been properly assigned, further assignment has been suspended: and there are many persons as yet without their land. (Im Thurn 1905 : 13)

In addition, the land that was allotted to producers could not be used at will. To increase revenues for himself and the nobles, the king issued an "almost perpetual" ban on commoners using coconuts (ibid.: 12). Since sale of copra provided the major source of cash income for peasants, and since taxes were to be paid in cash, the ban increased the number of defaults on taxes. Default was punishable by sale of the violator's possessions or hard labor (Tukuaho and Thomson 1891 : 30). In addition, the premier appointed by George Tubou II, Sateki, prosecuted defaulters with enthusiasm. He also alienated the traders by ordering goods through his friend, Rev. Shirley Baker—then in Auckland after a British investigation of his mercantile activities as head of the Tongan mission—rather than through Tongan merchant houses (Fusitu'a and Rutherford 1977 : 177–178).

Another irregularity concerned state finances. Revenues obtained from land-taxes, which were to go to pay bureaucrats and police as well as to provide for the king, appeared to be siphoned into the king's private account (Im Thurn 1905 : 12). There was no expenditure for road-building, well-drilling, or other local projects. The combined hardships created by these practices sparked a level of popular protest serious enough to alarm Parliament.

A contributing factor to the crisis within the elite concerned the king's marriage. Tungi, the high-ranking chief who had worked to repeal the *tapa* law, was the grandfather of a woman, 'Ofa, whom the king was supposed to marry. The king rejected 'Ofa in favor of a woman of lower rank (B. Thomson 1902 : 159; Seddon 1900 : 21). The proposal enraged a number of chiefs and nobles, led by Tungi and Fatafehi, the Minister of Lands and a chief in the Tu'i Tonga line (Im Thurn 1905 : 3). Tungi was next in line for succession to the kingship if George Tubou II had no offspring.

Several high-ranking chiefs urged the king to reconsider—'Ofa was high ranking, in the Tu'i Ha'a Takalaua line—but he insisted on marrying a woman whose rank was not impressive. Marriage to a lower-ranking woman attacked the customary association of high office with high rank, derived from one's mother. Children of the king's marriage would not have particularly exalted rank. The Minister of Lands, who owed his own position to his mother's rank, was appalled. The king dispossessed Tungi of his hereditary estate, "reducing him to poverty" (B. Thomson 1902:164).

The crisis the king precipitated concerned the relationship of kinship to class. Succession to the kingship was to be through patrilineal primogeniture; the problem was that the king was asserting that mother's rank had nothing to do with succession to high office. The king's marriage asserted that class status and legal inheritance overrode rank considerations, and statescraft overshadowed a core tenet in Tongan culture, namely, that one's rank derived from one's mother. In protest, 'Ofa and her sympathizers joined the Church of England (B. Thomson 1902:162). They also courted British officials (Maudslay 1878/1930:229–230). The British offered advice to the king; when he refused it, the British High Commissioner for the Western Pacific issued an ultimatum to the Parliament and the king:

> . . . the real choice before them all as Tongans was between, on the one hand, frank acceptance of the guidance which the British Government was offering, or, on the other hand, immediate loss of their King and, eventually, of their independence. (Im Thurn 1905:9)

The king was not pleased with the arrangement, although Tonga successfully avoided colonial annexation (Seddon 1900:14). The British consul presented the treaty establishing the Protectorate to the king along with several thinly veiled threats:

> The King expressed himself very anxious to hear late news of the war in South Africa. . . . [I tried] to impress the King with the benefits to be derived from the protection of Great Britain. . . . the Boers were beaten, and in their hearts bitterly regretted that they had ever broken their agreement with the British. (Ibid.:26)

Tonga became a British Protectorate in 1900. Even the opposition chiefs were not contented with the new status. When Tungi was visited by British officials shortly after the Protectorate agreement was signed, his suspicion showed in the interview. He made many inquiries about New Zealand, and particularly about the Maoris under the British flag. . . . It was explained to him that so satisfied were most of the independent native races that but a short time ago fought against us that Sikhs, Ghoorkas, Maoris and others had volunteered by the thousands for the war in the Transvaal. . . . [He] inquired as to the longevity, health, etc., of the Maoris and the hygienic measures adopted for them. (Seddon 1900:52–53)

Tungi refused to allow the officer's militarism to detract from more significant issues, such as indigenous depopulation and land loss. The imposition of the Protectorate limited the powers of the monarch and stemmed what could have been serious social unrest. The constitutional reforms of the early 1900's stabilized the government and separated the "emoluments" of the king from the State Treasury. Tax-allotments again were granted to Tongan men of sixteen years and above, but the government reserved the right to contract leases with outsiders (Colonial Office 1909:12). The reforms did not stop leases to foreign agricultural firms, for up to ninety-nine years (Shephard 1945:162). In 1932, a colonial report presented somewhat contradictory information:

Only land not needed by the natives may be leased to white [*sic*] companies, who have established large coco-nut plantations. (Yonge 1932:247)

The question of need remains a matter of political struggle.

Threatening full-scale colonization, the British blunted both the tendency toward autocracy and the widespread protests that proposed a return to less stratified conditions. The Tongan government in the twentieth century would parallel more closely that of other constitutional monarchies in a capitalist setting. In 1954, Tonga returned to independence, and the last vestiges of political dependency were removed in 1971.

The emergence of technically defined state institutions in the nineteenth century was fostered by the missionaries and the chiefly faction that had conquered the Islands. The subsequent dynamics revolved around the issues of the relative power of the monarch, the political position of the new nobility and estate-holding class, and the influence of the missionary-advisors. The legal structure drew selectively on custom, English common law and precedent, and political exigencies. The penetration of civil structures has had a detrimental effect on commoners' and women's economic and political authority. But law can constitute only an armature for subordination. Conditions must be created for the civil order to become part of everyday life. The development of commodity production for a capitalist market provided the requisite conditions.

11. Changing Production: Commodities, Tribute, and Forced Labor

Charles St. Julian
(1857:7)

. . . it is by foreign commerce, foreign capital and foreign enterprise, that the resources of the islands must be developed . . .

Constance Gordon Cumming (1882:1:20)

The teachers [missionaries] in these isles . . . by every means in their power encourage the adoption of European cloth . . .

CLASS RELATIONS and state structures could not have developed without fundamental changes in the labor claims and the relations that ordered the making, distribution, and consumption of necessary goods. What had been a society engaged solely in production for use, where items traded were then consumed, became oriented in part toward production for exchange. The latter involved the making of goods for the purpose of accumulation for further investment. The production-for-use orientation continued, but even this sphere was altered: part of the "use" production included taxes in kind, which then were sold by the king, the nobility, and the missionaries to support themselves, to expand their investments, and to expand the functions of the state that protected their interests.

After the early stage of contact, Tonga became a regular stopping place for ships bound for China and the East Indies. Resident Europeans, particularly the Wesleyan Methodists, operated as merchants as well. The missionaries considered commerce to be a hallmark of civilization, so they stimulated the transformation of use-goods into goods for market. In close cooperation with both the Christian chiefs and, later, major shipping companies such as Godeffroy and Son, the missionaries conducted a brisk trade in coconut oil and, later, copra. In return, they sold or distributed firearms and, in the second half of the 1800's, textiles and clothing. The profits helped some of the ministers build modest fortunes and facilitated the expansion of the mission throughout Tonga and to other islands.

The consistent acquisition of the goods to be traded depended upon the formation of class relations and state structures. The state tax-rent system, which the missionaries helped to design and implement, was one means of channeling agricultural products to the international market. Tax-rents in turn depended on the creation of a landed gentry, on the one hand, and landless tenants, on the other hand. The other major means of extraction was the institution of penal servitude. The definition of crimes and punishments allowed a system of forced labor to emerge, where prisoners would work on state or royal lands, producing goods for the trade, or on so-called public works, building roads and other infrastructure for commerce and governance. Together, forced labor and tax-rent collection constituted the first consistent surplus extraction in the islands.

The surplus generated was then used to obtain goods which helped to support the continuity of class relations and the state. In the early nineteenth century, firearms presented a means of ensuring compliance with labor demands. After consolidation of political control, the imposition of other commodities, such as textiles, and material support for missionary activities presented another, more subtle means of undermining production for use. Reproduction of the local kindreds became contingent upon the provision of items for exchange, as defined without recourse by the groups that demanded the products.

Commodity production remained confined primarily to an international market until the twentieth century. A national market did not really exist: most peasants oriented their agricultural endeavors to subsistence crops, with cash or rent crops as a supplement. Until the late nineteenth century, cash was useful to tenants only in the payment of tithes to the church, tax-rents, and legal fines and costs. Other items were obtained by barter. In the twentieth century, in-kind barter exchanges for food and other necessities have been transformed for the most part into cash-mediated sales. By the end of the nineteenth century, wage labor supplied a part-time income for many peasants. Since the 1940's dependency on wages has increased steadily, and now includes urban and international labor migration for men.

The Tongan economy came to be dominated by capitalist production, but the involvement of the state in fostering capitalist enterprises entailed the use of a precapitalist form of production and extraction, namely, a tribute-based mode of production. To this day in Tonga, the state claims the land, permanent alienation of land is not allowed, and taxes are identical to rents. In theory, although not in practice on hereditary estates, the tenants pay tribute in goods, cash, or labor to the state in return for retaining their use-rights to soil and to house sites. The imposition of this type of political economy served the needs of the merchants in obtaining a consistent source of commodities. The differences are legion between the labor service and tribute, on the one hand, and precontact use-rights and kin-based labor claims, on the other. The transformation from kinship to class and chieftainship to state involved increasing insecurity for nonchiefly people. Political struggles spurred and were spurred by changes in production from use-directed to market-oriented. The role of the missionaries in commodity production cannot be divorced from their role in the development of centralized authority, since the weaponry used by the Christian faction was acquired through the missionaries and Christian dominance of trade with Europe. After conquest and consolidation, the missionaries and the new nobility forged links with a growing number of foreign and, later, Tongan merchants and commercial establishments on the Islands. Throughout the nineteenth century, the political and economic changes took place under the threat of annexation by Great Britain, France, or Germany. The ambivalent alliances of missionaries, merchants, and nobility are important in understanding the changes in Tongan politics with the penetration of capitalist relations.

Extraction: Skewing Indigenous Exchange

The destruction of Tongans' trade with Fijians for sandalwood following commercialization of that item anticipated the impact of commodity production on spheres of exchange within Tongan society. Sandalwood was scarce in Tonga and could not be transplanted, although some chiefly people had attempted its cultivation before contact (Mariner 1827 : 2 : 268). To acquire the wood, which was used to scent the coconut oil worn by chiefly people, Tongan expeditions both fought and traded with Fijians (ibid. : 67). For use of their sandalwood, Tongans presented Fijians with whales' teeth (chiefly men's items, *ngāue*), *ngatu* (decorated bark cloth), mats, and the type of mats used for sails.

When Tongans began to obtain European trade items, they included nails as gifts to the Fijians. But by 1800, Europeans began to conduct their own sandalwood expeditions. Some Tongans tried to join in the new form of trade. At least one partnership was set up between a European sandalwood shipper and a group of Tongan men. The Tongans cut wood and in return received trade items from the merchant-captain. But on one island, when the islanders refused to cooperate, the crew massacred them (Erskine 1853/1967 : 144–145).

More typical was an absence of "partnership." The whites offered the Fijians more of both worlds: greater repression if the wood was not provided and more trade goods than the Tongans could give. This inflation undercut Tongan expeditions for wood, which was still destined for consumption. By 1806, Tongans had to give Fijians axes or chisels, plus the traditional whales' teeth:

> Whales teeth are exceedingly scarce and other [Tongan] articles are too bulky for ready exportation [in the quantities then required]. (Mariner 1827 : 1 : 167)

The virtual absence of sandalwood in Tonga meant that Europeans and Americans did not overrun the Islands in the early 1800's.[1] Poor whaling conditions in Tongan waters worked to Tongans' favor in the subsequent period (1820–1850) of commodity extraction. Unlike most of Polynesia, Tonga was not a stopping point for the whalers, so the people were spared the ravages of the whaling officers and their crews.

Women's Products and the Gender Division of Labor

Labor demands on nonchiefly people intensified with production for exchange in the market sense, but the goods they produced were not theirs to sell. International trade was dominated by the missionaries and the Christian chiefs who supported the mission. The separate and differentially valued spheres of Tongan production—women's and men's, chiefly and nonchiefly—did not survive the transformation of certain Tongan items into commodities for the Euro-American market.

In the course of the nineteenth century, women's products were demeaned in a number of ways. Increased labor demands drew workers away from traditional subsistence and resulted in changes in the division of labor by gender—especially in the household. This shift might have been temporary, were it not for the pressures placed by the missionaries and the nobility to sanctify the new division of labor, by deeming it more in keeping with divine law. In addition, European commodities such as textiles made everyday uses of women's products, particularly *tapa* in various forms, redundant. The changes in the division of labor by gender, coupled with the import substitution, skewed authority relations in the household and helped to create dependency of women upon men.

Coconut Oil and Copra: Declining Value of Women's Labor

Tongans produced coconut oil before contact, on a small scale and for domestic consumption. Smokeless and odorless, the oil lit Tongan homes at night (Griffin 1822 : 186n; Neill 1955 : 133). Its primary use was as a skin salve, applied after bathing and for special occasions. Some of the oil was scented with sandalwood and reserved for chiefly use. Nonchiefly women had primary responsibility for its production. Like other products made by women, coconut oil was a valuable.

Chiefly people used the oil daily for skin protection and to make the hair glisten (Anderson in Beaglehole, ed. 1969 : 1309). One early traveler incorrectly assumed the *tu'as* had no access to it, although he might have been referring to the sandalwood-scented variety (ibid. : 932). But, like other women's products, flower-scented oil was used even by *tu'a* people when attending chiefly-sponsored dances and feasts, or relatives' marriages, births, and funerals (Mariner 1827 : 1 : 381). The evening dances held to mark special occasions— such as the arrival of foreign visitors—called for nonchiefly women dancers, whose hair dripped with the oil (J. Wilson 1799/1968 : 249).

Extraction of the oil was labor intensive (J. Wilson 1799/1968 : 379). If contemporary practice is an indication, men collected the coconuts, hulled and split them. The coconut meat was grated into a trough and allowed to sit in the sun for several days until the oil separated (Labilliardière 1800 : 363).[2] The oil was then poured off and the residue fed to pigs. The oil was blended with herbs, flowers, and, solely for chiefly people in the Tongan case, sandalwood. The mixture was then stirred daily and allowed to absorb the scent for three weeks to a month. It was then stored in large seed pods for personal use, or large sections of bamboo for transport (ibid.). It took sixty to seventy coconuts to yield one gallon; one tree bore approximately ninety nuts a year (West 1846/1865 : 164, 142).

Before whale oil replaced it, following the expansion of the Euro-American whaling industry in the 1820's, coconut oil fueled lamps in Europe. Then as now, coconut oil was used in cosmetics and soaps. After the period of intermittent trade and plunder, rival chiefs obtained firearms through the sale of coconut oil. Missionaries provided additional arms to those whom they favored, and handled negotiations with shipping agents and European traders.

As a commodity, coconut oil was not used locally; for the Euro-American trade, the oil could not be scented. Also, the traders wanted vastly more oil than had been needed when the oil was made for domestic use. Coconut oil production for use continued, but in addition to the commodity production.[3] In other words, scented oil had to be made after the trade oil.

There is little mention of chiefly-ordered intensification of women's production of the oil. At the time (1815–1830), the chiefs were unable to make onerous demands upon nonchiefly women, outside of the more stratified areas under Tāufa'āhau's control and missionary influence. During this period, coconut oil was an important commodity, but existing labor relations did not allow for consistently large supplies from Tonga.

The Pacific whaling industry burgeoned from 1820 to 1850, and for most of that period demand for coconut oil waned (Grattan 1961: 86). As the whales became scarce, coconut oil again became a major commodity. By this time, the mid-1840's, centralized political control was more firmly ensconced in Ha'apai and Vava'u. Labor demands for the areas controlled by George I and his retainers could be more predictably enforced. Such extractions could not be done in the parts of Tongatapu that had not been brought into the nascent kingdom. A visitor to Tongatapu in 1852, before the final defeat of the "heathen" and Catholic factions, noted:

> There is but little trade going on . . . cocoa-nut oil and arrow-root, being the same as in the Samoan islands, but in smaller quantities. (Erskine 1853/1967:316)

After the conquest, George I imposed a tax in coconut oil on men; revenues were to go to the mission (Morrell 1960:316). In other words, men were to be responsible for presenting women's products to the church. In the precontact period, men had presented their own agricultural goods at the *'inasi* or first fruits ceremony for the sacred paramount.

Missionaries demanded proof of Christian conversion through material contributions. For example, the missionaries would trade Bibles to men for coconut oil (West 1846/1865:215). This implied both that men could acquire oil from the women who made it, and that men, rather than the producers, controlled the product's disposition. In addition, men were presented as primary recipients of the Word. Mission stations augmented their sources of oil by tithing and donation contests.[4] They encouraged the continuance of competitive giving that had characterized the *'inasi* prestations. Indeed, the Wesleyan Methodist church capitalized on the abolition of the *'inasi*, by timing the annual church contributions campaign to coincide with the former harvest ceremonial period. A decade after the conquest of the Islands, Rev. Thomas West could report:

. . . the natives now derive from it a large revenue of wealth, by the manufacture and exportation of cocoa-nut oil. Nothing of this kind was done, of any importance, before the year 1846. At that time the Missionaries adopted various measures calculated to encourage the manufacture of the article, and to facilitate its sale to resident foreign traders. They also explained the duty incumbent upon professed converts . . . of personally contributing to the support and extension of missionary agencies . . . native churches now meet the total expenses of the missionaries, Native ministers, and religious institutions amongst them. The islands have also been brought thereby into much closer, and more frequent, intercourse with the Australasian colonies of Great Britain. (Ibid.: 141–142)

The mission station above collected 130 gallons the first year. One consequence of the intensified coconut oil production was the growth of trading companies. The alliances forged between the missionaries and other resident Europeans remained uneasy, but in this case profitable. Rev. Walter Lawry noted that, even in 1850, coconut oil production was increasing, although he worried about the habits of commerce Tongans learned from the traders:

Many tuns [of coconut oil] per year are being shipped off, for which they get calico and cutlery. Here is incipient commerce. They are certainly not merely keen, but greedy, traders. This arises partly from a desire to have our wares, partly from their ignorance of the relative value of their articles and ours, and partly from the foolish, and worse than foolish, things which they have picked up from foreign traffickers. (Lawry 1852:70)

A British official reported in 1857 that "cocoanut oil may be considered the staple product of this region" (St. Julian 1857:25). By 1865, West noted with evident satisfaction:

Already several residents, who, in by-gone days, landed on the shores of these islands, destitute wanderers, have, through the assistance of the Missionaries, and by the development of this branch of commerce [coconut oil export], realized a handsome competency, and have risen, deservedly, into positions of influence and importance among the people. (1840/1865:142)

The "wicked looking fellows" of the early mission period had been transformed from renegades into "destitute wanderers" and thence into upstanding businessmen, all through the ministrations of merchants' capital. Their role in less savory means of gaining influence, such as usury, was ignored. After centralization, missionaries claimed to be civilizing both Tongans and the local Europeans, by promoting commodity production, on the one hand, and mercantile establishments, on the other. For all the rags-to-riches verbiage, the mission dealt most extensively with a large German commercial firm based in Hamburg, Godeffroy and Son.

The intensification of coconut oil production might have continued if a hydraulic coconut oil press had not been developed in Europe. Godeffroy's installed presses in Bremen and Hamburg in the late 1860's (Sterndale 1874:6). The impact of this technological change on Tongan social relations was profound. Tax-rents, tithes, and donations shifted from coconut oil to the dried coconut kernel, copra. The new process reduced the availability of an important by-product for Tongans: the residue from the hydraulic operation was sold in Europe as cattle feed, instead of fattening Tongan pigs. With the development of commercial production of nitroglycerine, which at the time used coconut oil in the preparation, the demand for copra increased again. Through missionary cooperation and a series of loans to King George I, by 1870 Godeffroy virtually monopolized the copra trade. By 1874 production of coconut oil had declined dramatically; Godeffroy's Tongan copra exports had increased from 700 tons in 1870 to 1,400 tons the following year (ibid.:2).

"Cutting" copra also was known aboriginally, as a stage in coconut oil production. It was considered to be men's work, *ngāue*. Men gathered, hulled, and split the coconuts, which were then sun-dried and shipped. While copra was not a valuable, it could be exchanged for the same kind of commodities (primarily textiles by the 1870's) received previously for the women's product.

As long as women remained engaged in coconut oil extraction for the new government and the missions, there was no confusion of spheres: valuables were received for valuables (*koloa*). Intensified copra extraction, while reducing the labor demands on nonchiefly women for commodity production, increased demands on their labor for subsistence and maintenance tasks. Labor demands on nonchiefly men increased, taking them away from what had become domestic work, which women then had to assume. In such an imposed, contingency situation, a temporary adoption of men's work would not be demeaning to women.

But Christian missionaries insisted that women as wives do the cooking and other "womanly" chores even when the men were available. In addition, demands for copra (or for money from the sale of copra) accelerated: tax-rents in kind or in cash, repayment of credit extended by European traders, social pressure to contribute as much as feasible to the mission, and so on. To meet the pressures, women would help with copra production at peak periods.

Nonchiefly women, then, were disadvantaged in several ways by the change to commodity production. Until 1850, their product was used to obtain the armaments used by the Christian faction to consolidate control over the Islands. The labor service demands were made possible by the new ideology of Christian civilization, with its emphasis on commerce and class hierarchy, and backed by the threat of violent reprisal. The commodities received, firearms, facilitated the expansion and consolidation of centralized political authority. The makers controlled neither the disposition of their product nor the objects received in return. The only feature that remained intact was the receipt of valuables (firearms and cloth) for valuables (coconut oil).

With the shift from coconut oil to copra, two additional disadvantages accrued to women. Disruption of the customary spheres (valuables for valuables, men's products for men's products) implicitly demeaned the value of women's products: European valuables were received for a men's product. In addition, the pressures on men's labor time meant that women assumed men's domestic tasks; missionary pressure, which had the force of law, encouraged a permanent redefinition of the household division of labor by gender. At the same time, women were drawn into doing some of men's productive tasks, but as an auxiliary force and, therefore, without authority to determine the disposition of the product.

Coffee and Koloa: *Changing Definitions of Wealth*

Coffee was introduced to the Islands in 1852. King George I had twenty thousand bushes planted during the 1860's. For a time, a white resident operated a five-hundred-acre coffee plantation, on land leased before the 1875 constitution restricted leasing agricultural land to foreigners (Morrell 1960:317). The crop never was a major export; its significance for commodity production lies in how it was introduced.

Coffee was *koloa*, a valuable, and thus a women's product. That this term should be applied to an agricultural product which is not greatly transformed for consumption was not in keeping with customary determinations of value. The definition of *koloa* was changing, as was the definition of women's work.

West reported an incident that reveals the disjuncture and relative power between traditional and commercial concepts of *koloa*. A few coffee beans were presented to one *tu'a* woman by her "wise lord." She grew them and then tried to barter half a dozen beans at a mission station twenty miles away (West 1846/1865 : 134–135).

A number of changes are evident in the example. First, women were directly involved in cultivation. Previously, their primary role in agriculture had been to transform crops into "chiefly" consumables. The missionaries encouraged the adoption of such pursuits as appropriate for peasant women (B. Thomson 1904 : 373). Second, the chief who gave the woman the beans was considered a lord (and a wise one) by the missionaries: they not only envisioned a class structure on the English model, but saw commercial cropping introduced from the top as an indication of wisdom. The mission station as trading post indicates the deep involvement of the missionaries in the encouragement of commodity production. Third, the woman traveled twenty miles to barter a few beans. For her, quantity was less important than the fact that they were *koloa*, intrinsically valuable. She had incorporated the new item as much as possible into the customary product ranking.

But the crop was intended for export, and the subordination of indigenous determination of product ranking to the expansion of commodity production is clear. Six beans were not enough for barter, regardless of their being a woman's product and regardless of the arduousness of the trip to the trading post. The crop was introduced by the foreigners and intended for sale to them. By the 1860's this was grounds for defining an object as *koloa*. As West put it, "Whatever the white man likes and pays attention to, must be 'koloa lahi', great riches" (1846/1865 : 134). The expansion of commodity production stressed exchange value, not use-value. Certain women's products for indigenous use remained *koloa*, but another definition—from the sphere of commodity exchange—encapsulated the customary one. *Koloa* in the new sense was determined by the destiny of the product and its merits in the international market; the personhood of the makers of the item was irrelevant.

Tapa *and Cotton: Replacement of Women's Products*

Missionaries, in most cases with the cooperation of the king, placed pressure on Tongans to substitute European goods for indigenous goods. Women's economic position already was jeopardized because of the switch from oil to copra, the use of their labor as supplemental to men's, and the definition of commodities as *koloa*. It declined further with import substitution.

European traders and their Tongan allies sought to undermine the production of indigenous bark cloth. The missionaries concurred, since they did not think the various types of *tapa* demonstrated progress in Christian civilization (Cumming 1882:1:20). They also saw dress as a means to increase industriousness, and thus, the production of commodities. They believed that stimulating demand for clothing and books among the elite as prestige items would cause the nobles to encourage lower-ranking people to produce more, to adopt similar clothing patterns, and so on. Rev. Walter Lawry, visiting the areas under George I's control in 1850, reported with some pride:

> They will begin to imitate those [Europeans in this case] who are above them. This, indeed, they have begun to do: the chief men and [missionary lay] teachers wear an upper linen garment, in addition to their usual dress; the females often do the same. This will spread, and require them to get cocoa-nut oil, and the like; as they have already begun to do. . . .
> . . . Two new wants are creeping in among them, namely, books and clothes; to obtain these, they will have to put forth their energies and make cocoa-nut oil, which they can, if they please, produce to a very large amount. (Lawry 1852:70, 250)

In addition, the missionaries insisted that people who attended church dress in European garb; since church attendance was necessary to stay in the good graces of the secular powers, the pressure was fairly effective. But in the evening people would change into their customary garments (Maudslay 1930:223–224). The king urged the people to dress *faka-papālangi*, or European-style (Scarr 1967:92). These efforts culminated in a law banning *tapa*, issued as part of the Constitution of 1875. Passed with the tacit approval of the king, but in his absence, it made wearing *tapa* in any form illegal. Manufacture of the cloth was limited to one day a week (Cumming 1882:1:32).

Missionaries were deeply involved in drafting this set of sumptuary laws, as they were involved in the formulation of previous codes. The laws were extremely unpopular, but the fines for disobedience were stiff (Maudslay 1878/1930:224):

> A woman who is found without a pinafore, even in her own house, is fined $2. Should she venture beyond her threshold minus this garment, she is liable to a fine of $3. (Cumming 1882:1:20)[5]

The fines were not directed solely at women: a man without a shirt was fined $10. The alternative to paying the fine was forced labor on royal or state lands. A visiting British administrator was shocked that during 1877 alone, almost 90 percent of the people were fined or imprisoned, that is, at forced labor, for breaking the sumptuary laws (Morrell 1960: 318).

The law banning *tapa* may have been framed to stimulate cotton textile sales, in which the mission had an interest (Cumming 1882: 1:31). A British consul considered Rev. Shirley Baker responsible and accused him of receiving a commission on cotton fabric sold through Godeffroy and Son's merchant house (Rutherford 1971).[6] Other sources claim that George I wanted to show that Tongans were civilized in the European sense, in order to avoid annexation (Scarr 1967). Certain missionaries opposed the law—they believed it threatened mission coffers, since money might be spent on clothing instead of the mission—but resident traders encouraged the law (Rutherford 1971: 60–61). The ban certainly stimulated sales, as one older Tongan lamented to the British official:

> We Tongans have now but one ambition—to get black clothes and wooden houses. . . . People are obliged to neglect their planting and their ordinary work. . . . The women do nothing, now that *masi*-making [*tapa*-making] is forbidden. To get money for the missionary collections is the great object of everybody. The women's object is to vie with their friends and neighbours in showy European dress. (Quoted in Morrell 1960: 318–319)

When the king returned to the Islands, he expressed anger at the *tapa* law (Cumming 1882: 1: 32). But the ban remained on the books until popular protest—taken up in Parliament by the representatives of the people—led to its repeal in 1880 (ibid.: 1: 33n).[7] Older Tongans feared irreparable damage, since wearing *tapa* implied a lack of prosperity.

The legal stimulation of demand for cotton textiles affected women in several ways. Even after the *tapa* ban was lifted, people had to wear European clothing to church; the new clothing became more prestigious for daily use as well. This undercut *tapa* as an everyday subsistence necessity. *Tapa* and *ngatu*, the decorated variety, continued to be important in ceremonial, even state-associated occasions, but household members no longer relied on women's labor groups for clothing (Mander 1954: 368). With the replacement of *tapa* by cotton fabric, women's work groups convened less often.

The commoditization of cloth made households dependent upon

Figure 13. Tongan woman wearing *ngatu*, preparing for dance performance, centenary of Catholic education celebrations, Nuku'alofa, 1986. Photo by the author.

foreign sources for a subsistence item. Cotton textiles and clothing had to be purchased with cash or other goods. Given the market for copra, and its status as a men's good, men had greater access to the foreign commodities. Later, when cash replaced barter, men had greater access to cash, since wage labor was pronounced by the missionaries to be *ngāue*, men's work. Women either depended upon men for clothing, or transformed the textiles purchased by men into clothing for household members. Thus, not only were valuable women's products, *ngatu* and other types of *tapa*, replaced by a commodity for everyday purposes, but women's access to the new commodity was mediated through men, rather than established by virtue of their own rank and status (cf. Etienne 1980).

Certain uses of noncommodity cloth have continued to this day. *Tapa* (especially *ngatu*) and mats still are necessary to validate certain life changes. But the nature of the ceremonies and their role in social reproduction have changed. Civil and church rituals for marking life status changes began to parallel or replace customary ceremonies during the second half of the nineteenth century. Concurrently, occasions for which women's products were essential, and controlled by women, declined. On the one hand, then, a valuable women's product was replaced as a subsistence necessity by one more readily available to men. On the other hand, the remaining ceremonies of social reproduction for which women's products were valued have become increasingly circumscribed by civil-religious structures.

Some have argued that as long as goods remain important in the marking of life status changes, the products and their makers have not lost status (Weiner 1976). The Tongan case contradicts this formulation. Traditional ceremonies persist in form, but they no longer control the social determination of status changes. As occasions for ceremonial exchanges have become encapsulated or marginalized by state and mission rituals, Tongan women have lost authority in the only realm where their labor still is publicly visible, irreplaceable, and recognized as valuable.

Labor Relations and Exchange

Commodity production did not characterize the entire Tongan economy in the nineteenth century. Even today, a sphere of production for use exists, although subsistence now demands a cash income as well. Commodity production was a necessary component of class and state formation in the Tongan case, but the growth of commercial agriculture and foreign trade did not result automatically in a cash economy, a labor market, or the transformation of most goods and services into commodities. For the merchants, mission, and Tongan nobility, capital accumulation occurred through the export of goods acquired through a variety of means and the sale of other commodities to the general populace. Often, the sales were stimulated through the legal structure. Where cash did change hands, it remained in a sphere associated with the *papālangis* and their Tongan allies.

Unfree Labor Forms

Wage labor was not important in Tonga before the twentieth century, even though the sphere of commodity production expanded greatly. Religious, civil, and commercial institutions created alternative sources of labor in the nineteenth century, including penal servitude, debt bondage, and labor service in tenancy. Debt bondage and pawning eventually were outlawed in the late nineteenth century, but penal servitude and tenant labor service continued.

The Constitution of 1862 freed "chiefs and all people from enforced labour and any form of slavery" (Im Thurn 1905:58). At the same time, a range of earlier vice laws were retained or revised, which called for "hard labor" as a form of punishment. The morals laws and the 1875 sumptuary laws created a steady supply of laborers. Some offenders were incarcerated at night, but in the 1870's the numbers were so large that most prisoners were free to live at home, as long as they showed up for forced labor every morning. One visitor in 1878 was shocked at the numbers of prisoners (Maudslay 1878/1930:220). Another questioned the severity of the punishments, but noted:

> . . . all Tongan criminals labour for the good of their brethren, eminently to the improvement of the isle [Tongatapu]. (Cumming 1882:1:16)

Hard labor was defined as work for the government. In practice prisoners worked as agricultural laborers on royal, state, and noble estates, as well as on the copra and banana plantations rented by Europeans.

Hard labor was not restricted to men. While many women convicts were set to work making wealth objects for government officials and nobles (Erskine 1853/1967:136), others were assigned what was considered men's work. One of the main roads in the port town of Neiafu, in Vava'u, was constructed of coral rubble, extracted and

laid by hand by convicted adulteresses (Fonua and Fonua 1981:18).
One woman in her late seventies told me that her grandmother as a
young woman had been so sentenced. She recalled her grandmother
telling her, bitterly, that their hands bled constantly from the sharp
coral. Her grandmother told her that even at the time people thought
the punishment was cruel. Although the road was given an official
name, no one remembers it: local people call the street Hala Lupe,
"The Road of the Doves," after the sad songs sung by the prisoners as
they worked.

Debt bondage had a slightly different history. There were tendencies toward chattel slavery in the early 1800's, but debt slavery
emerged after the consolidation of political control. One example of
the collaboration of church, state, and commerce in creating the
source of cheap labor can illustrate. From the 1860's until the British
imposition of Protectorate status at the turn of the century, the mission and the government sold copra through the Godeffroy and Son
merchant house, and both received loans from it (Scarr 1967:88).

One common practice became a scandal. Godeffroy and Son would
advance cash to the mission in return for future copra:

> Mr. Baker or his agent [missionaries] . . . sits in the church, . . .
> sounds a conch shell and summons the people to attend. . . . He
> offers them money for the missionary collection, to be paid for in
> copra at the rate of 25 lbs for a shilling. . . . If they do not borrow
> what he thinks is enough, he tells them to take more. (Gordon,
> quoted in Morrell 1960:319)

People would be apt to take more, for Baker was a close advisor to
the king. Merchants, missionaries, and the government all used debt
to acquire commodities:

> Baker—with the full support, even encouragement, of his Mission
> superiors in Sydney—had employed a mode of collection which
> forced the people into debt with Godeffroys. (Scarr 1967:94)

During the mission's fiftieth anniversary celebration in 1876, Godeffroy's sent agents to the villages the day before the competitive mission collection and advanced funds in return for promissory notes
(Maudslay 1878/1930:225). Mission donations were prestigious and
a way of keeping in the good graces of the local elite—in a formal
sense, they resembled the *'inasi* or first fruits offerings of the past—
and people promised more than they could deliver. The mission re-

ceived over £15,000, but the firm had trouble collecting the whole of the promised copra (Scarr 1967 : 88).

In large part because of the cordial mission–German merchant–government alliance, in 1876 the king granted Germany a coaling station at one of the finest harbors in Vava'u (B. Thomson 1902 : 172). Disturbed by the growing influence of Germany in the Islands, in 1878 the British mounted an official investigation into the doings of Rev. Shirley Baker, the head of the Tongan mission. Baker's collusion never was established solidly, but there was a great deal of indirect evidence (Maudslay 1878/1930 : 241). In any case, close cooperation between church, state, and commercial firms had not begun with him and continued in other forms after the investigation. Recovery of debts was one arena of government cooperation with the firm.

According to one visitor in 1878, the state was enforcing a system of debt bondage:

> . . . under the new laws [the debtors] were brought into court and distress warrants issued, if they could not pay, and *they were sold up or had to give their labor to the Germans until the debt was liquidated.* (Maudslay 1878/1930 : 227; emphasis added)

Debt servitude encompassed pawning as well: the debtor could send a relative to work off his debts. Legal codes drafted under British supervision ended the debt bondage to foreign companies (Morrell 1960 : 321). The 1891 code held that the courts would not assist any European who had extended credit to any Tongan in recovering the debt (Tukuaho and Thomson 1891 : 41).

Wage Labor

As long as labor could be acquired in sufficient quantity to produce the commodities for trade, there was no further need to restructure labor relations. The role of resistance also cannot be underestimated. Direct producers correctly assessed the role of wage labor in capital accumulation and, consequently, avoided any involvement in wage labor. Rev. West noted:

> The natives always look with suspicion upon any schemes involving the large employment of labour, from an idea that their individual effort, devoted to the same production of what is wanted, on their own personal account, will yield a better return than mere wages they might receive from an employer. *They look on him as*

one trying to enrich himself at their expense. (West 1846/1865 : 145; emphasis added)

Missionaries unwittingly dispelled any notion of aboriginal scarcity of resources in their explanations for the reluctance of Tongans to seek paid employment:

> . . . so abundant are the natural resources, from which [Tongans'] wants are supplied, that they feel very independent, in regard to wages obtained for time and manual labour. They will, most cheerfully, barter and sell, to foreigners, the produce of their own labour; but they have a great aversion to work for wages or hire. (Ibid.: 144–145)

The solution proposed by the mission was to create the need for commodities. A change in people's attitudes toward wage work, Rev. West noted:

> will be accelerated by the pressure of newly felt, and increasing necessities, arising from an extended intercourse with foreigners. (Ibid.: 146)

The mission collaborated with both merchants and the Tongan government to institutionalize the scarcity, making employment necessary.

Tongans' success in resisting involvement in wage labor throughout most of the past 150 years can be attributed in part to the availability of subsistence plots, albeit through tenancy. The government's policy of not allowing permanent transfer of land to non-Tongans limited foreign investment to trading houses or lease of Tongan estates. The absence of private property in land limited the amount of capital investment in agriculture, compared with other Pacific islands (Colonial Office 1909). Merchants could lend money for estate-holders to purchase coffee bushes or banana trees,[8] but the production process remained out of the control of the financier (cf. Roseberry 1978b). Until the late nineteenth century, Tongan land policy created increased demands for labor service by the new nobility, lease-holders, and the state. The demands did not foster wage labor. As long as labor service could be provided through debt payment, penal servitude, tithing, or tenancy arrangements, wage labor was unnecessary.

Money Uses

Tongans learned of money in the late 1700's. They knew Europeans considered it a form of wealth, but were unconvinced of its utility and suspicious of its effects on Europeans' generosity (Cook 1777). In the early 1800's, when Mariner wanted to purchase passage back to England on a passing European vessel, he received some of the cash from a woman in Ha'apai for some beads he had acquired. The rest was supplied by his adoptive mother, a chiefly woman. The money in question was part of the plunder of the *Port-au-Prince*, the ship on which Mariner had arrived (Mariner 1827:2:77n, 78n). Although Tongans at the time did not consider money wealth, women stored it, since they were responsible for indigenous wealth objects. Mothers especially were repositories of money and, to this day, children ask mothers for financial assistance for major purchases.[9]

Throughout the nineteenth century, money remained what Karl Polanyi termed "special purpose" (1957/1968:264–266). Money was not a universal medium of exchange, particularly in the remaining kin-defined sphere of production, exchange and consumption. Cash was used for some transactions with merchants and missionaries, who also acted as money-lenders. Some access to cash was necessary for everyone. Direct producers needed money for donations to the mission and for payments to the state: fines (the alternative was forced labor) and, from 1880 on, tax-rents.

For merchants, missionaries, royalty, and the estate-holders, capital accumulation did not demand an internal cash economy. Accumulation required only a steady supply of coconut oil, copra or bananas, and insertion in an international capitalist market. Throughout the nineteenth century, the internal distribution system remained non-capitalist. Kin connections governed local distribution of indigenous subsistence goods. The commodity sphere was restricted to imported and exported items. Exchange relations with outsiders, like those between rural communities and townspeople, were conducted through barter. In the 1850's one ship's captain remarked:

> The pig-market this morning turned out an utter failure. The excuse made by the authorities was the shortness of the warning, but Mr. O'Brien thought [Tongans] showed very little knowledge of barter or inclination to part with their stock. One old woman, for instance, having set her heart upon an iron pot . . . refused to receive any other article for her *one* pig; and similar demands . . . were made by others. As we have no stock of iron

pots . . . we were obliged to content ourselves with a supply of
vegetables, principally yams, . . . sent off to me by the king.
(Erskine 1854/1967 : 124)

Direct producers resisted the transformation of barter into a cash
market. Certain transactions had to be in cash—mission donations
after 1860, taxes after 1879—but most European items were obtained from merchants through the barter of copra or bananas.

Taxation

In 1853, as thanks for missionary aid in the wars of conquest, King
George I gave twenty gallons of coconut oil to the mission. He announced that from then on every man would give four gallons a year
to the mission (Morrell 1960 : 316). This edict is the first indication
of any systematic taxation. The land laws, implemented between
1852 and 1862, imposed an annual tax-rent upon every Tongan man
sixteen years old or over, payable in coconut oil. The revenues received belonged in theory to the state; in practice, they became the
king's emoluments until the British-drafted reforms of the 1890's (Im
Thurn 1905 : 12).

The codes of 1862 and 1872 increased the amount of coconut oil
extracted as tax-rents from four gallons to sixteen (ibid. : 58). The
codes specified that the taxes could not be paid in cash without incurring a fine (Sterndale 1874 : 2). Tax evasion was defined as sedition
in the 1862 Constitution. In such cases, taxes were due in cash,
along with a cash fine.

> In case of default in paying taxes the effects of the defaulters
> shall be sold by auction, and the amount shall be doubled. (Im
> Thurn 1905 : 59)

The change to cash tax-rents appears related to the merchant-
mission-government connection. According to a former employee, in
1878 the Godeffroy company made an agreement with Rev. Shirley
Baker, head of the Tongan mission, to enlist him in getting the government to impose taxes in cash rather than in produce (Hanslip, in
Maudslay 1878/1930 : 240). In return, Baker would receive a commission on every ton of copra sold to the firm (ibid. : 241). Previously, the
firm had fronted money to the mission, which then had extended
loans to local people in time for the annual mission collections. The
loans were to be repaid in copra to Godeffroy and Son. The scheme

netted the mission hard currency, but the firm had to enlist the newly installed courts to collect on the promissory notes. Cash tax-rents would eliminate the need for lawsuits. Taxes were paid in cash from 1880 on.

The courts and local nobles prosecuted those who defaulted on their taxes. In 1878, a British official with the Western Pacific High Command asked one Tongan estate-holder if he had collected tax-rents from the tenants on his island. He replied,

> There is but little outstanding, as the debtors have been sold up without mercy. The movable property of the people is sold by auction to pay the taxes. (Jiosaia Sipu, quoted in Im Thurn 1905 : 15)

In the late nineteenth century, an increase in Tongan nobles and other estate-holders leasing lands to Europeans created a degree of landlessness, in spite of depopulation (Cumming 1882 : 1 : 34). The state received 10 percent of the rent from every lease to foreigners (Im Thurn 1905 : 13). The leases were granted in the name of the king, so the state retained claims to own the land (Tukuaho and Thomson 1891 : 61). In theory the lands leased were not under cultivation. But customary agricultural methods included fallow periods, and considerable land was leased that was part of the agricultural cycle (cf. Bodley 1982). An undetermined number of tenants were dispossessed. The shrinking tax base led to a revision of the land-tax in 1891. Under British advice, the tax-rents were increased by 30 percent and the tax expanded to include a head-tax:

> Every male Tongan subject . . . shall pay the Land-tax whether he holds an allotment or not. (Tukuaho and Thomson 1891 : 66)

The conversion of the land-tax into a partial head-tax provided the first official stimulus for Tongans to participate in petty commerce or wage labor.

New Necessities, New Commodities: The Twentieth Century

In the nineteenth century, consistent consumption of commodities by the direct producers had to be legislated or contrived through debt relations. With the gradual increase in cash-cropping, on the one hand, and landlessness and wage labor, on the other, commodities have become necessities without legal compulsion. Wage labor has slowly grown in importance: as late as the 1920's the number of people involved in wage labor was "negligible" (Colonial Office 1927: 11); during the Depression, people simply turned to subsistence pursuits again. In 1945 a report pointed out that there were "few European lease-holds" and that "labour is scarce and expensive" (Shephard 1945:162). The expansion of a labor market followed World War II.

The increasing need for cash is tied directly to two factors: diminishing access to land and inaccessibility of credit for those who are not commercial farmers or regular employees. Increasing landlessness is usually attributed to population increase, but patterns of leasing and registration of allotments by the government, the royalty, and the nobility explain land scarcity more fully. By 1973, only 40 percent of the land—in government, royal, or noble hands—had been apportioned to Tongans in bush or town allotments; approximately 16 percent was leased to churches, foreigners, or large farmers; 18 percent was held by the government, and 27 percent was held in undivided noble and royal estates (Government of Tonga 1973). At that time, 60 percent of all eligible men did not officially hold any land (Crane 1978:19). The situation has worsened over the past decade, spurring international labor migration on a mass scale.

Credit also fosters involvement in wage labor and other commodity markets. Small-scale cultivators who have official allotments cannot qualify for bank loans, since there is no collateral except crops in the field. Improving the quality of subsistence crops or cash crops is extremely difficult for the small growers. Renovating a house, or purchasing capital improvements, such as a truck, usually demands that someone in the family seek a job overseas.

Today, in other words, maintaining a household is virtually impossible without periodic injections of sizable amounts of cash. Small farmers, with or without allotments, are forced periodically to migrate abroad in search of wage work. Migration has become commonplace over the past decade; in 1979, 10,000 Tongans lived overseas; today the number is estimated at 40,000 (Crane 1979:52). Of the sixty-five households in a survey I conducted in late 1986, over 90 percent reported a close family member working overseas for a specific home or capital improvement in Tonga.

The location of available jobs has reshaped the settlement pattern. What had been a fairly even distribution of population among the three island groups, Tongatapu, Ha'apai, and Vava'u, at the turn of the century shifted by 1944 to 60 percent of the population living on the main island. In the immediate postwar period, migration for work or for post-primary education, viewed as prerequisite to employment, accelerated the movement of people from the countryside to the towns, and especially from the outer islands to the capital. By 1976, approximately 70 percent of the population lived on Tongatapu (Crane 1979:69). The capital city more than quadrupled in population from 1939 to 1979, due primarily to in-migration (ibid.:51), and the rate of growth has not diminished. The government is now the largest employer in the islands; there is little industry, and the mercantile establishments do not offer many jobs.

Within the limited wage labor sector in Tonga, the missionary-inspired gender division of labor favors male employment; pay scales are much lower for women than for men. Young women have been able to work as domestics since the 1920's (Colonial Office 1927:11). In recent years, educated young women with family connections have garnered work as clerks and secretaries in the major towns. Unlike those in many Third World countries, Tongan working women generally are not fired when they marry or have children, although in some cases they return to a lower position after maternity leave. Similarly educated and situated young men land jobs as lower-level bureaucrats and functionaries and can remain in civil service for their careers.

Unemployment or inadequate employment is a growing problem, particularly for those who cannot afford to remain in school, who fail their school-leaving exams, or whose families are not well connected. The children of subsistence farmers are the most seriously affected: their families have the lowest income and thus have trouble paying the post-primary school fees, and although large families are useful in agricultural production, the younger children and the daughters cannot look forward to readily accessible land.

Women unable to find employment have sought to earn cash through marketing activities and craft production. In the past decade, tourism has stimulated craft production, particularly of women's goods. In some cases the cash generated is pooled for community efforts (Small 1985), but in my survey of craftswomen in Vava'u—most of whom were married to subsistence farmers—such income was most often used by the producer's family or bilateral kindred alone. The income from petty marketing fulfills many day-to-day cash needs—sometimes even paying school fees—but it is not sufficient for such major expenditures as a motor vehicle, installation of indoor plumbing, or construction materials for a home.

In the survey I conducted, more than two-thirds of those who were working overseas were men. As a rule, young women migrate overseas only if they will be living with close relatives. Married women will migrate with their husbands or, if the marriage is long-term and stable, alone. Overseas, women tend to work in factories, domestic service, or child care. Unmarried and married men may seek office or construction work in Tongan towns, but more frequently they must migrate outside Tonga for agricultural, factory, or construction work in New Zealand, the western United States, or Australia. Some of the cash received through migrant labor is sent to help support relatives in rural and urban areas; some is channeled directly or redistributed within Tonga to relatives without adequate access to land. Cash remittances from overseas Tongans are vital to the national economy. They currently are the only corrective for the overwhelmingly negative balance of payments, outweighing the value of copra exports, the largest single export category (Crane 1979:38–39).

The focus on commercial cropping has created a need for imported foodstuffs, primarily flour, sugar, and tinned meat (Neill 1955:139; Lappé and Collins 1977). Other commodities have replaced indigenous products: kerosene or benzene for lamps and cooking, matches, and cotton textiles and clothing (cf. Bodley 1982). The other force creating the need for imported items is land scarcity.[10] Lands still are held by the state and allotted to nobles and other state-associated officials. But since the later nineteenth century, many estate-holders have become engaged in commercial agriculture themselves, or have leased arable lands to foreign companies (Yonge 1932:247). Sixty percent of the population remains on the land, involved in agriculture (Maude 1971:112). The state retains an interest in commercial agriculture: it has regulated the quality of copra since 1929, and has acted as the sole purchasing agent for copra and bananas from 1935 on (W. Horne 1929:553; Shephard 1945:162; Baker 1977). For small-scale tenants, the need for cash-cropping has reduced the capacity to satisfy dietary needs, except in Vava'u. There, the major cash crop, vanilla, coexists with subsistence crops: the vine grows up a small tree, whose leaves are used in everyday cooking. The advantage of coconuts is that they can be used for cash or consumption needs. But as one European resident commented:

> When you have no money, 50 acres of coconuts is enough for 50 families and will support them well. If you sell the copra it isn't enough for one family. (Ruhen 1966:169)

Bananas grown for export, because they are perishable and more susceptible to disease, cannot double in time of need as a subsistence crop (Shephard 1945:162). The food situation is not as serious as in some parts of the Pacific, because most Tongans engage in some subsistence production and reserve the right to fish in lagoons. In fact, allotment-holders still are required by law to plant half the 8¼ acres in well-spaced coconuts and the other in sufficient food crops to support their "dependents" (ibid.; cf. Deere 1979). There still is a law permitting the gathering of coconuts for food and drink along the roadside if the traveler is in need (Government of Tonga 1967:392). In fact, one of the mottoes on Tongan coins, "Food for All," is still the reality today. There are increasing health problems related to diet, but hunger is not one of them.[11]

As late as the 1950's, Tongans were reluctant to engage in more cash-directed labor than was necessary. Men would sell split coconuts to local shopkeepers, who would sun-dry the nuts, bag and ship the copra, or sell the bagged copra to another trader. People understood that they could get higher prices if they dried it themselves, "but the incentive of the higher price for extra work does not make a universal appeal to the villagers" (Neill 1955:134).

The creation of an internal market for food took almost a hundred years (cf. Polanyi 1957/1968:255).

> The Veitongo villagers were shocked beyond measure that anyone should even think of selling food. Food was provided by nature and it seemed against the dispositions of God that it should not be as free as flowers. (Ruhen 1966:49)

Until the 1950's it was unusual to find food for sale, rather than for barter. In the 1960's flowers were still free, although the coconut fronds needed for house construction in the traditional style no longer could be gathered without payment (ibid.:13). Towns today have marketplaces where indigenous foodstuffs are sold. Women typically are the vendors. Coconut oil is being made in its scented form again, but for sale this time: the sellers are clustered in one part of the Nuku'alofa market (ibid.:40–50). Cash is now used to purchase all European items and many Tongan commodities as well. Barter still exists, but most marketplace transactions are in cash.

Art and History as Commodities

The expansion of the commodity sphere in the twentieth century has again redefined women's products. After the repeal of the *tapa* law in 1879, women resumed the fabrication of the cloth for exchange on special occasions. Production for use of several types of the cloth, as well as of mats and other valuables, has persisted to this day. The use of fine mats, *ngatu* or decorated *tapa*, and other custom-

Figure 14. Tongan woman painting *ngatu,* Tongatapu. Photo by the author.

ary valuables was until recently associated with social reproduction: the goods helped to mark the changes in status of people throughout their lives.[12]

But women's goods no longer validated all life status changes. Missionaries insisted on church ceremonies to validate marriage; later, the state also created a civil ceremony for the same purpose. Similarly, the state came to regulate funerary ceremonies, birth registries, and succession to title. Tongan ceremonies paralleled these religious and civil rituals, but they no longer were sufficient to establish the status changes. In other words, social reproduction had come to privilege civil and religious spheres over the kin-determined one. Women have remained pivotal in kin rituals, but kin rituals no longer reproduce the totality of social relations. Women's wealth no longer comprises the wealth of the society. A British report from early in the twentieth century revealed the meaning of women's products, viewed from the perspective of the dominant concern with commodity production:

> . . . the manufacture of [bark cloth and mats] being confined to women whose manifold labours in connection therewith do not, unfortunately, add to the national wealth. (Colonial Office 1909 : 7)

One result of the confinement of women's products to a ritual sphere—and the encapsulation of that ritual sphere in overarching class relations—has been the abandonment of a number of production techniques aimed at everyday usage. Fieldworkers in the late 1930's documented the loss of two methods for making *tapa* more durable (Beaglehole and Beaglehole 1941 : 67). Other visitors commented on the changing quality of bark cloth:

> Cotton prints, except on ceremonial occasions, have usurped the place of tapa and in this change the craftsmanship of tapa-making has suffered. (Neill 1955 : 144)

Another visitor was shown a "very old Tongan mat." It was

> a garment almost as fine and as soft as silk made with needles fashioned of fishbones. This has long been a lost art. (Luke 1945 : 2)

After Tonga was made a British Protectorate (1900), missionary influence was reduced and the government was buttressed through the introduction of standard British colonial administrative procedures. The attention of the nobility turned to the appropriation of Tongan history. Mats and *tapa* again became fashionable, as heirlooms and markers—but not embodiments—of status. Queen Salote reintroduced the wearing of traditional Tongan dress by all state officials. She also sought to preserve the early techniques of mat-making, *tapa* and *ngatu* manufacture. The queen founded the Langa Fonua, a women's organization which trains women in the earlier skills (Bain 1967). The attempt at preservation underscores the irrelevancy of the valuables in validating status changes after class relations and state regulation of succession emerged. The nobles compete with one another for ancient and finely wrought valuables, but the meaning has changed. Techniques had not been passed on, because they no longer were essential for production and reproduction.

As is the case with many items deprived of subsistence functions and restricted to a prestigious sphere that no longer has substance to its symbolic value, some forms of *tapa* and *ngatu* have become elite goods. They are considered works of art. In the past twenty years, *ngatu* has become collectible in the international "primitive art" market. What had been an integral part of Tongan women's identity—women as valuable-makers and -keepers for their households and kin—has been redefined fundamentally. Most producing-class women continue to make *ngatu* or mats for marriages, funerals, or other occasions of life transition. But these occasions, crucial to kinship relations as they are, no longer mark the reproduction of *all* social relations, because kinship exists within a class context.

At contact *tapa* was one expression of a woman *as a kinswoman* working in a group, for herself, if she was chiefly, or at times for chiefs as redistributors of goods and embodiments of community prosperity, if she was nonchiefly. *Tapa* and *ngatu* were valuable because they were made by women. The value of a particular piece derived from the rank of the maker(s) more than from any quality of the object itself (Collocott 1928:141). Woman's labor was socially necessary, socially organized, and socially valued. As *ngatu* and historical pieces of *tapa* have acquired a limited art market, the focus has shifted from the creator as a social actor to the creation itself.

Production no longer is done by all Tongan women. Making *ngatu* has become a specialization; specialists are evaluated by the quality of their products, rather than the reverse. Tongan and foreign buyers exhibit Tongan "cultural heritage" and endangered or forgotten art forms. But the creation of the product has become in most instances divisible both from the maker and from other aspects of the maker than her labor. The maker has become an expert, dependent upon the qualities of her product and its value as a commodity.

The indigenous and international art markets have different foci.

For the indigenous market, plain *tapa* and fine mats are sought, as well as the decorated variety of bark cloth. For the international market, *ngatu* and finely woven, decorated mats and baskets are preferred. For both, historical pieces have a higher value. Some mats and *tapa* are heirlooms and cannot be purchased; when the first king dispossessed opposing chiefly families, many of their valuables came into the possession of the king's supporters. An occasional piece may be purchased, but for the most part the historical pieces are worn or exhibited on ceremonial occasions.

The international market defines the goods as "primitive art," a designation few Tongans find tolerable. The categories of value echo Euro-American schemes: painting and sculpture outrank the so-called decorative arts. Certain forms of basketry and plaited mats including colored feathers have only recently joined the stamped and dyed *ngatu* as art forms, acceptable to a limited number of Western collectors.

Production in this setting no longer is solely for local consumption. Production is partly for use still (kin-associated exchanges) and partly for exchange. Commodity production of mats and *ngatu* has been organized cooperatively in various localities by Catholic and other religious personnel, expressly to support church activities and community development (Small 1985). In Vava'u and elsewhere, a few cooperatives have been organized by women themselves (at times with male woodcarver members), for special community projects, or—more often—to increase their percentage of the sale price of baskets, mats, or *ngatu*. Women in the state-associated classes do not engage in production of these valuables, except as an accomplishment. It is considered charming if a young noblewoman takes up such activities, showing her care for the preservation of tradition. In contrast to the setting at contact, production of *ngatu* has become a recreation, rather than a continuous creation of objects that embody local history. No one could deny that mats and *tapa* remain important in Tonga today. Many of the occasions on which they are presented are formally similar to precontact status change ceremonies. But the nature of their meaning has changed from precontact times. The makers no longer have the same connection to their labor and their products, and the products no longer have the same role in reproducing Tongan society as a whole.

Commodity Production and Social Reproduction

Merchant capital describes a way of accumulating wealth through wholesale and retail operations. Ideally, goods are obtained at low

cost and shipped for sale at a profit. The profit is applied to expand or
further control the market for the commodities. As a rule, the market has been outside the supply area, to cloak better the value and
derivation of the goods and to protect the merchant's access to them.
Sandalwood, *bêche-de-mer*, coconut oil, copra, and bananas from
the Pacific islands were sold in East Asia, Europe, and the British
colonies in Australia and New Zealand.

Where supplies are consistent, merchants can remain disengaged
from orchestrating production. In a situation of reliable supply, merchants are only indirectly responsible for reproducing conditions for
continuous commodity production. The relationship of merchant
capital to societies with a communal mode of production—those
organized through kin or quasi-kin connections, oriented toward
use-goods—focuses on fostering a commodity sphere. This may be
either encouraged or imposed, either alongside or in place of production for use. Generally, where the commodity sphere coexists with a
sphere of production for use, the commodity sphere is dominant. In
other words, where it can be enforced, the priority becomes production for exchange. The extraction of sandalwood with indigenous labor is a case in point: many of the merchants obtained supplies from
local "contractors"—the maintenance of the work force was not the
concern of the merchant. In some cases the workers were deserted or
killed after the ships were loaded.

At contact, Tongans fabricated goods and provided services for use,
including as "use" gift exchange and barter with others who produced for use. To transform customary labor claims into ones which
would create items for market exchange required the development of
classes and institutions that would protect both class relations and
the extraction of commodities. The goods received through trade—
weaponry in particular—facilitated the conquest needed for political consolidation. The rationale was supplied to a receptive chiefly
faction by Christian missionaries.

The collusion of missionaries, merchants, and an emerging ruling
class provided the catalyst for commodity production. The reproduction of Tongan society in such a situation became a political crisis
(Thompson 1975; Gailey 1985b). Reproducing the conditions for further commodity production implicitly denied the full reproduction
of conditions requisite to production for use. For commodity production to continue, production for use had to be subordinated to production for exchange.

In Tonga, the conditions needed for commodity production included the political domination of the direct producers, the creation
of tenant farmers and artisans. The labor relations involved in com-

modity production were exploitative, whether in the form of providing tax-rents to a nonproducing elite, serving a prison sentence at hard labor, repaying credit, or working for wages. The maintenance of the producers depended upon labor and goods provided, as did continued use-rights to resources. The institutional apparatus that backed these exploitative relations invoked coercion—at first military and later judicial—if the goods or services were not supplied.

The mechanisms for extracting goods for export distorted customary labor claims, while the king, the nobility, and the missionaries invoked the idiom of kinship to justify the extraction. Communal production has continued on the local level, but as one part of a larger political economy. Overarching these relations are those which siphon goods and labor from the kin communities to the state in the form of tax-rents, in exchange for use-rights to the soil.

In Tonga, articulation of three modes of production can be detected, with a capitalist one dominating. Social reproduction not only involved the continuity of tribute extraction and—as a resistant residuum—communal production, but also a commodity sphere. The capitalist mode of production encapsulated both tributary and communal production, since the tribute extracted, in goods or labor, was destined for a capitalist market (cf. Van Binsbergen and Geschiere, eds. 1985). Only part of the tribute amassed was consumed directly or traded for other, often luxury goods for consumption by the elite. Most of the tribute was marketed for accumulation and investment at home or abroad. The capitalist sphere determined what would be extracted through the tribute relations.

Over time, capitalist relations—in the form of wage labor, floating-price cash markets, and a growing dependency on commodities for subsistence—expanded at the expense of the communal and tribute-extracting modes of production. At present, social reproduction entails the re-creation of all forms of production, although the communal one is now marginalized both politically and economically. It also remains the one arena in which Tongan women have significant authority. The tendency over the past 150 years has been for the kin-based arena to become a "domestic" sphere, as opposed to the "public" sphere of commercial and state activities. The process has not been consensual, and the role of the emerging state in fostering capital penetration has been pivotal.

12. Dialectics of Class and State Formation

Tongan woman, *1986*　*What is culture? Pālangis [papālangis] don't know. The nobles don't know—how can they know? They don't do anything! Only we [hard-working people] know. Fetokoni'aki, helping one another, that's culture. Pounding tapa and making mats, that's hard work and that's culture, too. Giving and sharing food and koloa with your kāinga [kindred], your neighbors, your fāmili, that's culture. Brothers and sisters, father's sisters and brother's children, passing things from generation to generation, that's culture. The rest is nonsense.*

IN RETROSPECT, state institutions in Tonga appear inescapable, capital penetration inexorable, Christian ideology causative, gender hierarchy perennial, and opposition muted or nonexistent. But hindsight can create optical illusions. If state formation is analyzed as a process, rather than an event or a brief period, the picture changes. The profound transformations in Tongan social, political, economic, and cultural relations in the past two centuries are given a background.

Class formation, not simply particular European imperial interests, becomes a central dynamic. The problem explored for Tonga has been how prestations to chiefly people can change from reciprocal obligations in a concrete, material sense, to one-way tribute, with an ideology of reciprocity. In other proto-state contexts, higher-ranking lineages or resident alien kin-organized peoples can act the role of the chiefly estate in Tonga. The dynamics of class formation always involve the emergence of exploitation, the extraction of goods or labor without equivalent compensation over time.

Class formative dynamics in Tonga long predate European contact. In other words, like other kin societies, Tongans *have a history.* To deny the continuous creation and reproduction of their society prior to European intervention is to privilege imperial expansion over internal contradiction (cf. Wolf 1982). Tongan's tension-filled relations shaped to a significant degree the quality of capital penetration in the nineteenth century. Colonialism in the sense of capital penetration was crucial but, in this case, indirect, operating through the transition from kin-defined stratification to class relations. Everyday life, the order provided by customary activity, has become politicized as a form of resistance: the defense of use-oriented production, communal property, and kin-defined use-rights.

Communal production has been subordinated to commodity production and class-defined use-rights, but it has not disappeared. Now marginal, the persistence of cognatic labor claims and sharing characteristic of the precontact society constrains the degree to which class relations and the taxation, judiciary, and other governmental structures order everyday life. The Tongan state is not a total state: the uniqueness of Tonga as a political economy and as a culture derives from the struggles of at least the past four hundred years. The struggles are ongoing; currently the society shows a tense and unequal coexistence of use-production through kin relations, tribute production through tax-rent demands, and commodity production through both free and unfree labor.

Contradictions in Stratified Kinship

Tongan society prior to capital penetration was not egalitarian in the reductive sense. Local kindreds were ranked, and stratification by estate or order existed. However, the presence of orders did not mean the existence of classes. Both nonchiefly and chiefly kindreds had hereditary rights to the soil and other subsistence resources. In addition, not all chiefly people were nonproductive: many chiefly men and all chiefly women were engaged in subsistence manufactures of some sort. The highest-ranking males were nonproducing, at least for most of their lives; depending on the political dynamics of the time, they either were supported by donations from local kindreds or, at peak periods of power, extracted tribute in products and labor service. While nonproduction was a marker of high status for men, the making of valuables was a marker of high status for women. Since wealth items also were subsistence goods and essential for the reproduction of labor claims, chiefly women always were involved in socially necessary production. Labor claims were established through relative rank, since superior rank gave one claims to lower-

ranking people's labor or products. But rank had to be validated socially, through the presentation and distribution of valuables. All
people were embedded in a range of relationships, some of which
gave them claims, while others involved claims to their labor or
products.

Struggles began long before contact between those whose authority derived from kin considerations and those who sought to dissociate themselves from such kin constraints. But as long as chiefs who
sought power based their claims to others' labor or products on their
own cognatic kin connections, a centralized polity could not develop.

It is likely that most of Tonga was politically centralized and perhaps also class stratified during its hegemonic phase over Samoa and
parts of Fiji, ending in the twelfth century. Classes, if they existed,
certainly were not stable: the period ended with three successive assassinations of the sacred male paramount chief. The situation underscores another aspect of the thesis presented here: class relations
may emerge temporarily, but they cannot endure without the support and mediation provided by institutions to cloak their essen-
tially exploitative nature. Products and labor cannot be extracted re-
liably by a ruler or a lord: there must be taxation or conscription of a
sort (in Tonga, tax-rents and penal servitude). The earlier era also indicates another dynamic of state formation coming out of kinship
relations: conquest abroad, far from showing domestic power, frequently is the only means of avoiding rebellion at home.

Within the chiefly estate, there were contradictions between cognatic kin claims and patrilineal tendencies, as well as between rank
as the justification for social authority and the need to gain widespread support for acquisition of chiefly title. In addition, there were
tensions between chiefly men and women over the political involvement of women as sisters and paternal aunts. Rivalries within the
chiefly order both reflected and constituted the inconsistencies
within the principles of ranking: seniority, genealogical connections
through males, and sororal superiority. As long as collateral and cognatic claims—by brothers and sisters—remained key in determining succession to chiefly title, and as long as chiefly women's products were both similar to nonchiefly women's goods and needed to
demonstrate high status, the chiefly estate could not become a
chiefly class. Cognatic claims made it impossible for anyone to become a titled chief without reinforcing *all* the principles of ranking
and establishing a reputation for generosity and skill in promoting
local prosperity. The vagaries of succession reproduced chiefliness as
justifying superior labor claims through kinship, but not rulership.

Between nonchiefly and chiefly orders, there were contradictions between the hereditary use-rights of local, nonchiefly kindreds and the stewardship role of titled chiefs. Assertions of political control over goods and labor were effective only in the chief's presence. Assertions of tribute extraction were limited by the necessity of ensuring local prosperity and the donors' expectations of return goods. The chiefs claimed they received tribute; lower-ranking people claimed they presented gifts to the chief. Both, in other words, claimed control over the timing and the sort of goods and labor provided. Since there were no instances—only threats—of nonchiefly dispossession, and since chiefs did, in fact, give things to every person who presented goods, and did sponsor feasts and ceremonials that involved redistribution, nonchiefly people's claims appeared better grounded than the chiefs'. Exceptions—cases of chiefs who did extract goods and services, regardless of return—were met with assassination or a popular rebellion that installed someone who acted more in keeping with chiefliness.

The Tongan case, like other class formative situations, indicates that sexuality is an arena where tensions for and against class relations are evident: the more heightened the tensions, the more charged the sexual relations. In stratified but kin-ordered societies, pronounced social emphasis on sexual activity, whether positively or negatively valued, can both embody and deflect political tensions. Tendencies toward class formation could be seen most vividly in the relations of chiefly people to nonchiefly women, in terms of both production and control over reproduction in the sexual sense. Wealth produced by nonchiefly women derived some of its value from the social status of the person who had initiated the production, showing a degree of alienation of labor. The politics of control over reproduction were played out both within and between the estates. Unmarried, nonchiefly women were vulnerable to the sexual advances of chiefly men, while unmarried chiefly women were supposed to be virginal.

A potential certainly existed for gender hierarchy. In the chiefly kindreds, which were more patrilineal toward the top than among the lower ranks, women were more constrained in their sources of social authority. Since rank was inherited theoretically through the mother, the sexuality of higher-ranking chiefly women was more closely watched, by both other women and men, than that of chiefly men or nonchiefly women. The point here is that chiefly women's sexuality was not controlled by chiefly men. The other major contradiction in gender relations concerned the simultaneous roles of women as wives and sisters, and men as husbands and brothers. As wives, women exercised less authority than husbands; as sisters they exercised more authority than brothers. As long as the sister/brother relationship remained vital in determining labor claims and access to products, women could not become subordinate to men.

Coexisting Modes of Production:
Kin-Communal, "Asiatic," and Capitalist

Capitalist colonization as a historical process has forcibly drawn kinship-ordered and precapitalist class-based societies into a larger process of accumulation and economic expansion. The question of the degree to which the previous forms of political economy survive, and why, has sparked a heated debate among scholars concerned with development, decolonization, and revolutionary change (Laclau 1971; Banaji 1972; 1977; Cardoso 1975; Hindess and Hirst 1975; Mintz 1977; inter alia). The question of how radically different, even opposed modes of production are made to articulate has been posed in the abstract (Althusser 1969; Poulantzas 1975). Rarely has articulation been investigated historically (Kahn 1980). It seems that mercantile activities can provide one linkage (Patterson 1985).

Merchants rarely become involved in arranging production, as long as sufficient supplies of commodities are available. However, this neutrality comes about only where class relations already exist, as in West African kingdoms during the early transatlantic slave trade. Where stable class relations do not exist, as in Tonga at contact, there is no stable supply of goods. Merchant capital does not arise spontaneously in societies in which the organization of production, distribution, and consumption is along kinship or quasi-kinship lines. Although mercantile activities can appear to be transformative, they are so only within a larger process of class and state formation. Merchants require the existence of a class society and state structures for their entrée and to enforce the conditions needed to ensure a source of commodities. If these do not exist, merchants try to foster them.

Still, in the Tongan case, as in many others, mercantile relations were not directly state-sponsored; therefore, conquest by capitalist countries was not an immediate threat. In such a setting, traders could not rely on their home country to impose class relations. The situation was more nebulous. Traders could use private armies or trickery, as with "blackbirding" in the South Pacific sandalwood trade and debt peonage through extension of trade goods on credit. In Tonga, traders worked to encourage class stratification, by cooperating with and supplying certain factions of high-ranking people.

Class relations are essential for commodity production to emerge as a dominant sphere. State institutions are needed to buttress class relations. In the stratified kin situation of Tonga at contact, pressures for and against class formation were ongoing but inconclusive. The catalyst for class and state formation was provided by representatives from capitalist societies, namely, the missionaries and merchants. In the Tongan case, merchant capital cannot be considered transformative without the concomitant influences of the emergent state and the stimulus to commerce provided by the Wesleyan Methodist mission.

Tribute Extraction and Capital Penetration

In a tribute-based mode of production, the kin groups are encapsulated in an overarching tax-rent and labor service structure. Reproduction of kin relations becomes contingent upon fulfilling material and labor obligations to the dominant, state-associated class. The state claims the land and the rulers allot holdings to officials in return for a steady supply of goods and an assurance of military support if necessary. The formulation offered by Marx can be seen in many precapitalist state societies: production for use persists, but tribute and labor service demands reduce the capacity of the kin groups to determine production (Marx 1852/1972; cf. Krader 1975; Amin 1976). A commodity sphere may emerge, dominated by the state-associated class or classes, using tribute for foreign trade or the imposition of an internal market (Marx 1881/1967: 1: 334).

To some extent, this form of precapitalist state emerged in nineteenth-century Tonga, but in conjunction with commodity production for a capitalist market. In tribute-based social formations, conflict between kin communities and civil institutions may render kin relations ineffectual in assuring use-rights or subsistence goods. Communities may be politically dispersed or marginalized; changes in tax-rents may virtually dissolve the kin community as one based on production for use and shared resources. Kin forms may persist, but the content of kinship—security of livelihood through hereditary use-rights, reciprocal and diffuse labor claims—can be narrowed. Indeed, the definition of who is effectively kin becomes politically charged. Commodity production may dominate all production, rents replace taxation, and lands effectively become privately owned. In Tonga, all of these aspects can be identified.

Chiefly and nonchiefly orders could be drawn into a precapitalist form of class relations—tribute, slavery, or forced labor—with greater ease than into typically capitalist relations, private property owners and wage laborers. Middle-class English evangelists consciously attempted to construct a landed gentry, tenant farmer, and independent artisan class structure, backed by a constitutional monarchy as a form of state. The Tongan faction that favored political centralization had its own agenda, combining selective features of customary chieftainship and land tenure with the militarism and immutable hierarchy of the evangelists' Christian ideology. Even though precapitalist class relations were easier to effect than capitalist ones would have been, the transition was bloody from the kin-based stratification to indigenous tribute-extraction through a land-holding, state-associated class. Nonchiefly and chiefly groups that opposed the regime and were dispossessed nevertheless sought to retain the use-rights and labor claims associated with kinship and kin-like forms.

Land tenure arrangements seem to preserve certain customary forms, such as use-plots and the association of a high-ranking person with a given area, but the nature of use-rights has been altered fundamentally. Only male producers as heads of household can obtain use-rights from the state and from estate-holders, in return for taxes, labor service, or rents. In former times, access to land was determined by hereditary association with the land, through membership in cognatic kindreds. Estate-holding families now form a state-associated class, whose association with the land no longer is customary, but derives from subordination to the Crown, patrilineal succession, and provision of tax-rents to the state.

Tonga is not a precapitalist state society, however, but a capitalist society with precapitalist means of extracting goods and services for both the state and the market. The state asserts ownership of the land and in theory controls the access of officials to land. But the state allows estate-holders to lease lands for use to Tongans residing in the area (and some foreigners), in return for rent. Part of the rent goes to the state as taxes (tax-rents). The identity of rent and taxes characteristic of the tribute-paying mode of production is clear. The identity is obvious on the royal and state lands, but on the hereditary estates of *nōpeles* and *matāpules* there is a split. Rent is in part accumulation and in part tax-rent; the split is between private accumulation and civil revenues. The dynamic is reminiscent of prerevolutionary China: peasants paid taxes as rent when the state was strong; when the officials were effectively landlords, they paid both rent and taxes.

Rent emerges alongside taxes on the local level, with state-associated land-holders the recipients of the accumulated wealth. Taxation both preceded and included rent: the role of the state thus far has been to simultaneously foster capital accumulation and secure the political and economic dominance of the landholding class. In this juxtaposition of state tax-rent extraction and additional rent extraction by state-associated classes lies a dynamic which feeds into the dominant capitalist sphere in Tonga. The tribute structure has acted as a midwife to capital penetration. The capacity to lease lands on a long-term basis can be seen as another conduit for effective alienation of resources and a form of private property through leasehold. The tribute-extracting state has been necessary for capital accumulation, but the expansion of the capitalist sphere is necessarily destructive of the fusion of tax with rent and the continuation of landholding rather than ownership.

Merchant Capital and Commodity Production

Commodity production can exist in the absence of capitalism. The Aztec *pochtecas* exchanged goods on behalf of the ruling class, but the transactions of commodities between the Aztec and neighboring Mesoamerican states did not result in capital accumulation (Chapman 1957; Leacock 1972:55–56). Correlatively, the same product can exist in some contexts as a commodity and in others retain its use-value. Coconut oil had such a dual existence in Tonga during the nineteenth century. Textiles in the Incaic state were exchanged for other commodities or services rendered, presented as gifts to seal alliances, and made for domestic consumption; even elite women made textiles destined for gift exchange, direct use, and trade (Murra 1962; Silverblatt 1978). In the Tongan case, however, commodity production was linked from the outset to a capitalist market. In Tonga, consistent production aimed at marketing presupposed laborers or peasants and politically dominant people removed from direct labor, who would compel commercial or tribute production if the laborers gave too much priority to subsistence work. Commodity production in this case also required a social division of labor which included means of ensuring both specified products (coconut oil or copra) and reliable quantities (taxation, forced labor, or tithes). Through missionaries and other European traders, merchant capital helped to transform existing kin-based relations of production. But merchants, missionaries, or chiefs alone could not have imposed such a configuration. Merchants determined only the particular type of goods that were marketable and the amounts needed; they intervened in state and mission affairs through public and private loans and, only later, through leases for commercial agricultural land.

Commercial ventures rested on the development of systematic surplus extraction. To effect this required means of repression—in this case, a foreign commodity, firearms. The weapons were vehicles for political centralization by the faction surrounding the future king. But firearms, while necessary for systematic extraction of products and labor, were not sufficient. The other element was a novel rationale for conquest, one which denied the primacy of kinship as an organizing metaphor for society. The missions provided the rationale of civil society and government under God-given law. The state and the state-associated nobles and missionaries then could implement tax-rent and penal systems, which in turn ensured labor to make goods to be sold to commercial firms.

Class relations and a state structure were essential for the merchant houses to ensure a steady flow of commodities. The nature of those class relations was of little concern to the merchants, as long as they were stable enough to provide commercial crops. The commodities that underwrote the merchants' accumulation were provided through a combination of corvée, taxation in kind and in cash, and mission donations, as well as through debt payments and government compulsion. Some of the products were made as tribute. Those who extracted the goods treated them as commodities; only in the later nineteenth century did direct producers begin to cut copra and make other goods for commodity exchange. Each of these methods of surplus generation and extraction was backed, at first openly and later implicitly, by munitions and penal restrictions.

To maintain the labor force, both capital accumulation and tribute extraction depended on the survival in some form of kin community and production for use. The emerging state institutions and commercial enterprises could not alone maintain the workers needed for commodity production or tax-rent extraction. Kin-based labor relations and use-rights could not be completely eliminated, because they were necessary for social reproduction. Complete disruption of the customary relations would create chaos in production—some type of subsistence sphere was needed, if only to minimize the costs of obtaining the desired commodities.

The continuation of certain communal practices—such as borrowing or sub-letting land based on need, subsistence cropping, labor exchange, and redistribution of goods—limited as well as ensured capital penetration in the Islands. The slow growth of wage labor during the twentieth century shows the priority given by the state-associated classes to mercantile forms of capital over industrial capital. At the same time, the landholding classes have little direct control over the labor process, excepting penal labor.

On the one hand, the legal and economic structures have altered the nature of kinship relations: conjugal households have a far more prominent role in production, distribution, and consumption than was the case in the precontact society. On the other hand, the tribute system and the needs of mercantile capital have ensured for the peasantry a degree of communal control over production and distribution. This partial control has created the basis for alternative views of Tongan society and culture, and the continuation even of illegal forms of sharing, such as the *fahu*.

Articulation

Articulation among the three modes of production has been provided through the state. The state has acted on behalf of capital accumulation and the position of the dominant class, but the institutions of state—taxation, legal-judicial, executive—obscure this partisan stance to some extent. In theory, everyone is taxed, everyone is expected to be loyal, everyone is subject to the rule of law.

Reproduction of the present political economy is an ongoing crisis. The reproduction of tribute extraction is opposed to the reproduction of communal property and labor relations, and yet dependent upon a partial continuance of kinship forms. Reproduction of commodity production is contingent upon the tax-rent tribute structure, and yet expansion of commoditization is inimical to the reproduction of the property and labor relations intrinsic to a tribute-based state. Each mode of production is partially reproduced, but reproduction of the capitalist one is at the expense of the other two.

The primacy of capital accumulation—rather than use-production or tribute—was established at the beginning of the twentieth century, with the British constitutional reforms. The tributary mode of production has persisted mainly because there is no impetus to transform commercial cropping to large-scale agribusiness. Banana production can be mechanized—the Castle and Cooke and United Fruit assembly lines in Central America are examples—but there is little room for extensive cultivation in Tonga, given the necessity for some land remaining for subsistence pursuits to keep wages at a sub-reproduction level. Petty commodity production has emerged alongside the tributary structure—peasants produce copra, bananas, or vanilla for tax-rent and other cash needs—but most commercial cropping is conducted through labor service and tax-rent demands on tenants by estate-holders. The prevailing form of capital accumulation remains mercantile relations, but there is some semi-industrial use of hereditary and leased estates.

Estate-holders are involved in commercial production, using the tax-rent structure as one means of ensuring a labor supply. They control access to use-plots and therefore can demand labor service in return for registering an allotment. Some use wage labor periodically: they purchase one commodity, labor power, to produce another commodity, copra, bananas, or vanilla. The estate-holders then own the end-product. Estate-holders control, but do not own all the means of production: they remain only hereditary possessors of the land. The estate-holder may use the crops above and beyond the land-tax for his own accumulation. But the capacity to expand in the agricultural sphere is limited by the precapitalist land tenure arrangements. A few tenants are commercial farmers, in which case the tax-rent extraction is compounded by other forms of exploitation. For instance, in Vava'u, one entrepreneur leased parcels to grow pineapples for export and for sale in the main island. Using distant, less prosperous relatives as a wage labor force, the firm netted $30,000 Tongan in the third year of operation. The man chafed at the restriction on private ownership of land: if he had his own land, he explained, he could find laborers easily enough because of the land shortage. In some cases, the grower can lease additional land to expand production, but more frequently, the accumulated capital is invested in other ventures: shipping, processing, finance. In the future, as the commodity sphere grows, it is likely that land will become effectively alienable. The landed gentry will lose their primacy, either being transformed into classic landlords or replaced by commercial investors. Politically, there will be pressure to open state offices to more (wealthy) non-nobles, a sort of bourgeois reform found in a number of other places. The pressures can already be seen. For instance, an underground newspaper, founded by a former civil servant, regularly publishes exposés of governmental corruption or ineptitude, fueled by leaks from most of the government ministries. There is talk among the nobles of bringing the man up on subversion charges, but the paper flourishes. It is very widely read in both urban and rural areas. In 1986 a suit was brought by a non-noble lawyer, quietly backed by a number of merchants and civil servants, against Parliament for gross mismanagement of funds. Popularly the suit was seen as an attack on the nobility. The high court took the case under advisement: that it was not simply dismissed indicates the threat to the political order posed by the new class.

There is a potential alliance between the monarchy and this petty capitalist class, comprised primarily of college-educated commoners who float between civil service and business. On the political front, the members of this mercantile and professional class are pressing for increasing participation in top-level governmental policy planning. Their interests are also served by the widespread discontent, expressed privately by entrepreneurs and small farmers alike, with the nobles' penchant for restricting access to their lands.

The agricultural sector, then, shows both the coexistence and the disjunctures of the three modes of production with greatest clarity. Production for use, tribute production, and commodity production are conducted, often using the same labor supply, under different legal constraints. The state, through land tenure and labor laws, provides the coordination requisite to accumulation and reproduction of the existing class structure.

Apart from the state, churches constitute the major mediating institutions in the society. The sectarian differences reflect and embody political factions (Korn 1978). As with the state, the message is acceptance of class relations and the existence of some form of civil society. Pressures for reform often emanate from the various sects, but none stresses fundamental social change. Sectarianism reflects class fractions, tensions within classes; the major churches have cross-class congregations, providing the illusion of community (cf. Gramsci 1971).

But alongside the religious institutions lies the corpus of proverbs, legends, myths, and lore altered to meet the changing circumstances, but as a commentary on civil society. The source of the cultural renewal is necessarily those who remain engaged in direct production, in the Tongan case, the tenant/artisan/petty-marketing sector. Since their production is oriented toward reproduction—at least partially for use—they constitute a critical voice, whether or not they are explicitly critical. Their aim is not the aim of the nonproductive classes. The manifest content of the stories and proverbs, rituals, and ceremonies generally is nonpolitical; their existence is profoundly political. The most marginalized—but still necessary—mode of production thus also underlies the most revolutionary activity, albeit behavior of the direct producers appears to be accommodating to existing circumstances.

The coexistence and continuing accommodation of contradictory modes of production—communal, tribute-extracting, and capitalist—underscore the incompleteness of state formation in Tonga. The production-for-use sphere continues; kin and quasi-kin relations still organize a significant portion of social labor. Moreover, the persistence of the kin-based use sphere shelters producing people from the assertions of culture determination by state-associated classes.

The entrenched character of economic, political, and ideological resistance is testimony to continuing efforts by Tongans to arrest the growth of exploitative relations.

Kinship and the State

State formation opposes the reproduction of kinship groups as self-determining bodies. Some of the processes associated with the dissolution of the kin community[1] in the tribute-based mode of production are evident in the Tongan case. Limiting the power of the kindreds to determine production and social reproduction has been accomplished through state and capital penetration (cf. Geschiere 1982).

Local kindreds have changed in structure, due to economic and legal constraints. But they have retained some hereditary claims to the land, regardless of inheritance laws. Legally, the kindred no longer holds land: only heads of households are allotted use-plots. Extralegally, people acquire use-rights through borrowing and informal subletting of lands belonging to cognatic kin.

The strength of the kindred can be seen in the spontaneous creation of new, kin-based structures such as the *fāmili*, to meet pressures placed on the traditional kindred without dissolving the latter institution. The *fāmili* is not the nuclear family touted by the missionaries: instead, it is a kin and quasi-kin grouping of households that share exchange labor and other forms of mutual aid (Korn 1974). In other words, the *fāmili* discharges some of the functions associated with the traditional kindred, which no longer can operate in the same manner.

The creation of new forms to perform customary functions can be seen as a response to the state's efforts to appropriate customary forms to perform new functions (cf. Diamond 1951). The state appropriates the notion of a use-plot, but changes the terms necessary for access to use-rights. The kin community, faced with official and church disapproval of kindred-based redistribution and labor sharing, creates an unassailable institution—even called the family—to preserve those leveling mechanisms and sources of social security. The state outlaws customary claims, such as the *fahu*; the kin community, operating through innovative forms, protects or at least refuses to condemn the new criminals. The state and the church create a form of marriage which is restrictive of women's autonomy; local communities recognize informal divorces and remarriages.

The commodity sphere has eroded the kin community partially:

goods taken from nonchiefly people were traded for munitions which facilitated further control over production. Money has come to mediate most spheres of exchange, including status change rituals. In other words, the proliferation of commodities now includes some production apart from use or tax-rent needs. Labor exchange still is along community and kin lines, and much sharing of goods and services continues. But peddling or part-time wage labor now supplements most producers' incomes.

Over the past 150 years, the kindreds have forfeited substantial control of labor and products. Taxes are in cash; rents for those on non-state lands are in cash, in kind, and in service. But nonchiefly producers have not lost complete control, since the sector of full-time wage laborers is small and mostly state-associated.

The process of capital penetration into the kin communities continues, but it has been erratic. During the Depression of the 1930's, commodity production in Tonga virtually ceased: production for use and kin-mediated exchanges burgeoned. The irregularity of capital penetration reflects both the tribute-related land tenure system and resistance by local kindreds and *fāmilis* to the transformation of production and property relations. The degree to which women's labor remains highly valued and the degree to which women retain considerable authority depends upon the persistence of this kin-based, production-for-use sphere.

Gender and State Formation

In state formation, both women and men are threatened with the loss of their capacity *as kin* to reproduce Tongan culture. The relations of women and men reflect and embody society-wide kin-civil conflict. As social inequality outside of limited contexts and mutual negotiation developed, all customary contexts of authority were challenged, not only those between estates or ranks. Women's customary sources of social authority and prestige have been under attack from a number of different directions. The roles and situations in which women enjoyed relative autonomy and were accorded respect and social recognition have been undermined in legal, religious or ideological, economic, and social spheres. Yet here, too, resistance has been steadfast, if not immediately apparent.

For classes and political institutions to emerge, people's identity and autonomy had to be constrained. Women have been the focus of civil and religious assaults, both of which have had economic as well as political consequences. The reasons for this onslaught can be found in the customary gender division of labor. Women's labor, more than men's, ensured the continuity of Tongan society *as a kin-defined culture, not simply as a population.* Women's products, over which they had control—subject to the same claims of superior kinship as men—helped to reproduce the ambiguities and tensions intrinsic to stratified kin relations.

Women bear children, but Tongan women's involvement in social production and reproduction was far more extensive than their birthing functions (cf. Meillassoux 1972; 1979; Rey 1979). The valuables they made included children metaphorically, but all of women's work was socially necessary. Women's wealth established social personhood and enabled a lifelong process of socially documented status transcendence for every person. Women and their goods validated the continuous creation of Tongan society in its various constituencies—chiefly, nonchiefly, married, unmarried, *matāpule, 'eiki, mu'a, tu'a,* elders, youths, women, men, children—and through the life cycle—birth, marriage, parenthood, death. They marked the socially recognized passage of titles and names throughout life and from generation to generation.

Both men and women performed productive labor and socialization, but women's labor was more valuable in the broader context of social reproduction, and was acknowledged as such. Women's labor and products, and the relations among people expressed in women's kin roles, reproduced the contradictions within kinship that limited social stratification. State formation out of a kin-defined society must involve the curtailment of local kin groups' autonomy. In Tonga, therefore, women's labor and products, and those kin roles most closely associated with the reproduction of ambiguity of social authority, had to be devalued. For Tongan women, the pivotal kin role was that of the father's sister, who controlled the rituals of life passages and prevented lineal chiefly succession from becoming institutionalized. As class and state structures emerged, Tongan society lost the ambiguity of kin-constituted authority in chieftainship and acquired instead the force-backed clarity of rulership.

Revisions of sexual conduct drew upon existing tensions in the society at contact, but skewed them in favor of a pronounced double standard (cf. Leacock 1981). For women, use-rights to land and other resources were made contingent upon fulfillment of sexual proscriptions. For nonchiefly women, the revision of marriage has made divorce much more difficult, at the same time as marriage of some form has become an economic necessity. The constraint on premarital sexual relations has not, of course, eliminated the practice. But, at least during the nineteenth century, the criminalization of sexual experimentation created a ready supply of forced laborers, almost uniquely nonchiefly. Today, the culture still condones premarital liaisons, while the legal and religious institutions condemn them. Children born outside of official marriages are still incorporated into the mother's cognatic kindred, but they no longer have equivalent rights to those of children born to a married couple. The upshot is ambivalence on the part of the young people and the injection of sexual conquest into what had for the most part been mutual attraction.

For women of the *nōpele* order, what had been restraint or discretion for chiefly women became a demand for fidelity and chastity. With the banning of polygyny, noblewomen have lost a supportive cohort of resident kinswomen. Noblewomen are under legal and familial pressure to produce male heirs, since daughters have fewer legal claims than sons to title and lands. Women of this order no longer can act as regents for minor successors: their role has become reproductive in the biological sense. The assertion by chiefly men that succession was a men's concern—an assertion contradicted by the political dynamics in the society at contact—has become a reality for most high-ranking women.

The women who became *nōpele* colluded in the transition. Chiefly women had considered estate and rank before gender, as had chiefly men. As nobles, these women's authority within their estate is less than their ancestresses' authority was within the chiefly order. But their class position affords them privileges apart from their declining status as women. Traditional chiefly women face different circumstances. Like traditional chiefly men, they still are accorded respect and unofficial authority by local nonchiefly people, but they do not have the security and revenues that class dominance provides for noblewomen. Some *matāpule* women have increased social status, as wives of state functionaries; a few have more social authority, as wives and only children of the few *matāpule* estate-holders.

Nonchiefly women who were not retainers of the chiefly faction that became the landholding class have fared the worst. As kindreds have become increasingly fragmented through economic, jural, and religious pressures, these women have experienced the erosion of customary supports. The contradiction between Christian and civil changes, on the one hand, and economic demands and kin-defined responsibilities, on the other, has created tensions within marriages, among siblings, between parents and children, and within the community as a whole. The male-important ideology promoted in the churches, schools, and law courts has made resistance on customary grounds difficult for women.

One side of the traditionally ambiguous status of women has been demeaned, namely, the sister's authority over her brother and his children. At the same time, aspects of Tongan women's traditional status which approximated Western gender roles have been emphasized. The institutions which most promote Western standards— civil marriage, church marriage, public and private schools, hospitals for birthing, undertakers for burials—directly oppose the very life-transition rites over which women exercised control. Civil-religious institutions, mandated by law, threaten to replace the very functions in which women's social authority was most pronounced: status determination, succession, and inheritance.

Accompanying these civil and religious challenges has been the devaluation of women's labor in an economic sense. Wealth no longer is uniquely women's creation. Many goods made by women now are commodities and thus subject to the market fluctuations of worth. *Koloa* as a category now includes any valuable item, whether or not it was made by a Tongan woman. The sphere in which traditional valuables still are priceless and necessary no longer reproduces the entire society. In addition, commodities have replaced everyday necessities which had been made by women. Because of legal and informal discrimination against women in hiring and pay, women have been forced to seek alternatives. These have included joining cooperatives producing craft items, becoming small-scale peddlers, or relying on men for needed cash income.

The jural restrictions on sisters' claims to brothers' goods has shifted partial dependency on men into dependency of wives upon husbands, a situation unknown in the society at contact. The banning of the *fahu* attacked not only sisters' rights, but also a range of claims to goods and labor by cognatic kin: men and women had a call on their mother's brother's goods and perhaps even use-rights to his lands. The *fahu* ban thus weakened women's social authority and the integrity of the cognatic kindred at the same time. The *fahu* restrictions aggravated an existing inequality: wives deferred to husbands. In the new context, the countervailing relationships of sisters to brothers and paternal aunts to nieces and nephews cannot be used openly.

Nonchiefly men's authority has waned, due to changing use-rights, restriction of cognatic labor claims, and the need in many cases for seasonal or periodic wage labor. But the role of husband has increased in social authority: land use is determined according to male heads of household, and the conjugal unit has assumed a greater role in production and politics. The customary authority of husbands has been augmented by the constraint placed on alternative sources of men's goods for women. Tongan wives are not, of course, completely dependent, since most have developed supplementary income sources and since the outlawed claims are still practiced. But the structure of dependency exists and they are more dependent than at contact. The split between practice and law challenges the solidarity of the kin community, particularly when tensions are embedded in close relations.

Non-elite Tongan women have not become restricted to reproductive labor, that is, maintenance work in the household and childbearing and -rearing. Most women remain productive. What has changed is the value of their labor and their authority in what has become a civil sphere. Their work is socially necessary, but their authority is restricted to a kin-defined realm. In addition to their productive labor, in the wake of men's increasing urban and international labor migration, women have had to assume more housekeeping and child care responsibilities than in the past. Even in the domestic sphere, they control less than when there was no public-domestic split (see Lamphere 1974).

Class relations and gender hierarchy emerged as part and parcel of state formation as a process. The removal of an elite class from direct participation in subsistence production, coupled with the creation of institutional backing to defend and justify this removal, signaled the development of exploitation. For local kindreds to be subordinated to the continuation of nascent class-based property and labor relations, the kin-defined institutions most heavily involved in ensuring social reproduction had to be suppressed. In Tonga, the gender division of labor and the prominent role of the father's sister had primacy in the continuous creation of kin-based labor claims and use-rights to resources. The subordination of the kinship sphere— including production for use—to the reproduction of class relations and commodity production reduced the value of women's productive labor and restricted the sources of women's social authority. For all women, social authority has become contingent upon class position. Elite women, removed from direct production, have a solely reproductive role. Producing women, while barred from official political participation, retain informal sources of authority along kin lines and by virtue of their involvement in production. State formation as a process asserts that women's role is primarily that of childbearing and reproductive work. How much that is a reality depends upon how closely women are tied to the state. For non-elite Tongan women, the assertions of the state and the constraints of economic necessity have had deleterious consequences for their status. Defense of the production-for-use sphere and cognatic kin relations also has supported women's authority, at least within the producing classes. Gender hierarchy coalesced with class stratification, but resistance against class relations has buoyed women's status to some extent.

The Tongan case shows that exploitation and inequality are not synonymous. The absence of systematic exploitation in the society at contact involved structures that pitted one form of inequality against another. Class stratification and gender hierarchy emerged when inequalities were made consistent. The reduction of ambiguity in the kinship structure, and its subordination to class-based claims to resources and labor, involved repression on an unprecedented scale. Kinship and gender, the core dimensions of the communal division of labor, were the arenas of struggle. The emergence of state institutions marked the onset of new forms of stratification, but not the end of opposition. Subsistence priorities keep flexible use-rights, widespread sharing, and cognatic labor claims alive. Resistance to gender and class stratification depends on the continued reproduction of the kin communities, a reproduction only partially in producing people's control. Gender hierarchy emerged with class and state formation. The beleaguered producing communities embody the memory and vision of a different reality.

Appendix
Sources and Methods

RESEARCH INTO the precontact dynamics of kinship societies that are not known archaeologically is still in the formative stages (see Rigby 1983). All too often, it has been assumed that since standard historical methods cannot be applied (as there are no written records or survivors), the peoples involved "have no history" until the arrival of the civilizations that record and, thus, invent history (e.g., Wolf 1982). Research into state formation and gender hierarchy as interrelated developments is a concern that bridges the disciplines of archaeology, ethnology, political economy, history, and political science. To get at the dynamics in Tonga that eventuated in surplus extraction, it was necessary to delve into the prestate and preclass period. To unravel both the emergence of state institutions and the tensions associated with class formation, two periods of Tongan history are most important: the two hundred years prior to European contact and the two hundred years following contact. The first period, roughly 1450–1650, was characterized by stratified and tension-fraught kinship relations; the extent and strength of the authority of chiefs fluctuated.

The second period begins with the arrival on the Islands of various representatives of Western and capitalist institutions. Especially from the late 1700's on, the various processes identified with capitalist colonization were used by a number of opposed chiefly and nonchiefly groups in ways that militated for and against political centralization and class formation. Gender-associated relations of production and reproduction figured prominently in these class formative tensions. Relations between women and men shifted dramatically from the late eighteenth to the mid-twentieth centuries, precisely the period during which the class and state structures evident today first emerged.

Sources

For Tonga, written materials are abundant—both primary and secondary sources—if somewhat Eurocentric and difficult of access. Wherever feasible, I have used only texts from the period in question to evaluate the political and economic dynamics. Occasionally, I have used a few well-researched histories of the Pacific islands (Williamson 1924; Ward 1948; Wood 1945; Morrell 1960; Oliver 1961;

Grattan 1961; 1963; Scarr 1967; Couper 1968; Burrows 1970; Crocombe 1973; Rutherford 1977; Forman 1978). Data culled from such disparate, sometimes internally inconsistent sources have been weighed against each other, and against the different circumstances of later, ethnographic studies.

The precontact period is, of course, the most difficult to document. Various chiefly people's accounts of Island affairs are given in the early travelers' and European residents' writings. The chiefs represented different political factions, so the information reflects their particular interests. I have used their interpretations as chiefly perspectives, not reality. Later ethnographic work (beginning in 1915) has involved efforts at genealogical reconstruction of chiefly lineages and kindreds; oftentimes these are contradictory, for solid political reasons (Hocart 1915; Collocott 1923a; 1923b; 1928; 1929; n.d.; Gifford 1929; Ve'ehala and Tupou Posesi Fanua 1977; Marcus 1980). Legal codes, dating from the mid-nineteenth century, provide indirect evidence of dynamics within the chiefly stratum and between chiefly and nonchiefly strata. The conflict between customary expectations and legal obligation becomes evidence for custom prior to the creation of legal codes (Tukuaho and Thomson 1891; Im Thurn 1905; Government of Tonga 1907; 1967; W. Horne 1929).

Things become easier for the period just after European contact, as written records exist. Captains and other officers of Dutch, French, and British ships left logs and diaries (Schouten and Lemaire in Dalrymple, ed. 1770/1967; Tasman in A. Sharp 1968; Cook 1777; 1784; Labilliardière 1800). John Cawte Beaglehole has compiled all the diaries left from Cook's several voyages, including a lively journal kept by a literate sailor (Cook, Anderson, and Samwell in Beaglehole, ed. 1969).

From the early nineteenth century there are, in addition, narratives collected some years later from shipwrecked sailors. The best-regarded of these is William Mariner's account of 1806–1810, recorded in 1817 and reissued in 1827, but there are others by men who jumped ship in the Islands. The captain of the first missionary vessel left an account (J. Wilson 1799/1968). One of the London Missionary Society evangelists, who "went native," left a rather ambivalent journal of his four years in the Islands (Vason 1810). Other perspectives are provided by Wesleyan Methodist missionary journals, beginning in the late 1820's (Orange 1840; Russell 1845; West 1846/1865; Lawry 1852; Gill 1876; C. Horne 1904; Blacket 1914; Moulton 1921; L. Baker and Baker 1951). Perspectives from Roman Catholic missionaries can be gleaned from journals kept by the French Marist fathers who proselytized in the 1850's and again after religious freedom was allowed in the later nineteenth century (Hervier 1902; Monfat 1893; Malia and Blanc 1934; Tremblay 1954).

Throughout the nineteenth century, visiting ships kept logs which sometimes revealed substantive information about Tongan affairs. These accounts reflect the concerns of merchants and, for military vessels, the interests of the sponsoring country. French, British, and American captains provided differing views of the holy wars and the civil-kin conflict of the centralization period (Dillon 1829; Dumont d'Urville 1834; Fanning 1838; Wilkes 1852; Erskine 1853/1967; Mosley 1879; Edwards and Hamilton 1915).

For the period just prior to and during the Protectorate, the Foreign and Commonwealth Office libraries in London house a myriad of Tongan and British governmental records. In addition to official reports, law codes, and legal records, these documents include less formal memos and notes. They are supplemented by the reminiscences of various colonial administrators active in the Islands (St. Julian 1857; Maudslay 1878/1930; Cumming 1882; Kelly 1885; Reeves 1898; Seddon 1900; B. Thomson 1902; 1904; Im Thurn 1905; Dalton 1919; Bain 1954; 1967). Political historians have supplied collected writings of a number of these colonial officers and prominent private citizens who figured in Tongan politics (Strauss 1963; Scarr 1967; Rutherford 1971; 1977; Davidson 1975; Cummins 1977a; 1977b; Shutz 1977).

The various European materials reveal another important factor: there was no "conspiracy" or consistent coalition among traders, missionaries, colonial advisors, and any of the chiefly groups. Their mutual hostility and mistrust fairly bristle in their writings about one another (Wright and Fry 1936; Ralston 1978). Nevertheless they did share common assumptions about maleness and femaleness, appropriate spheres of activity and authority for women and men, and a belief that progress inevitably was associated with civilization on the Western model (see Diamond 1974: Ch. 1; see also Melville 1846/1964: Ch. 27). Often they shared commercial interests, regardless of their differences. The ethnocentrism of the Europeans' shared values, such as a commitment to "progress" and "civilization," was echoed by many chiefly people. Most chiefly people agreed with the Europeans that the nonchiefly people were inferior both in a moral and in a civilizational sense. Where Tongan chiefly groups differed from the Europeans was with regard to what constituted "civilization."

Missionary interpretations of chiefly and nonchiefly gender relations reveal as much—if not more—about Victorian middle-class morality and class ideology as they do about Tongan chiefly or nonchiefly values. Missionary journals in general exhibit marked dissensions between the proselytizing groups, even among those of the same sect. Parallel observations on the part of early travelers, missionaries, and colonial administrators or advisors at times indicate more about the aliens' shared traditions—or hegemonic structures in the "home country"—, their common lens, than any "fact" about Tongan life. In addition, histories as told by chiefly persons—above all, those who eventually became part of the nobility—were adopted by missionaries and colonial advisors as recorded Tonga history.

The evaluation of texts thus embroils the researcher in political intrigue. For example, the chiefly group which most consistently opposed the consolidation of state institutions also was the group associated with the later and less successful (French) Roman Catholic mission. Catholic Tongan histories thus present, in part, interpretations of nineteenth-century events by this chiefly group and, in part, the changing interests of the French state in the Islands.

To ground statements about tendencies and trends in the formation of classes and state institutions, and changes in the status of women in the twentieth century, I have relied on ethnographic work done on Tongans and related Polynesian peoples, and my own field data, collected in 1986. I have used the same approach of contextualizing the authors, the regions and people with whom they were associated, and the time period to evaluate the data and arguments.

Oral histories, collected by anthropologists from several chiefly people, present views of Tonga prior to contact consonant with the conflicting and changing interests of each of those chiefly groups. The relative emphasis given to matrilateral or patrilateral kinship connections does not necessarily indicate either matrilineal or patrilineal descent. Disputes with regard to which form of descent or mode of succession was more proper or predominant are impossible to resolve in favor of only one form. What is clear is that only one form became the legal form, and that many chiefly genealogies have been revised to meet the new needs. This point becomes important in analyzing more recent ethnographic research. Often, most informants who cooperate with an anthropologist represent one kindred or one particular chiefly group (e.g., Korn 1974; Marcus 1977a; 1980). Tongan kinship is presented in accordance with the viewpoint of that group. The results, one should note, are not thereby wrong; they are reflective, rather, of the claims of that faction at the time.

Notes

Introduction

1. *Subsistence* as used here refers to production needed for the maintenance of a way of life, not simply survival. Marx's term *production for use* is better, since use covers both utilitarian goods and the goods needed to ensure the reproduction of necessary social relations. Put another way, survival, except in the harshest environments or during natural calamities, is assumed in a kinship society, since resources are shared (Sahlins 1972). For peasants, survival becomes a political question (Wolf 1966). Famines in state societies are either directly caused by extraction despite local needs, or indirectly caused by disruption of production. The latter instances often involve monocrop agriculture, which invites periodic infestations by pests (the Biblical "plague of locusts"). Such disasters appear to be natural, but are of political origin.

2. These societies have been called "primitive," at times in a derogatory manner—stressing a supposed "backwardness." Some scholars have used the term *primitive* appreciatively, to call attention to the depth of human history that has been spent in non-exploitative relations (Diamond 1974). While the latter use is appropriate, I prefer the term *kinship* because it avoids any possible implication of inferiority. On the positive side, it draws attention to the way in which relations of work, maintenance, distribution, consumption, and re-creation are conceived. The term *kinship societies* is used here to indicate a communal mode of production.

3. Social reproduction is explored in depth in Part Two, which considers different aspects of kinship in the precontact period. It refers to the re-creation of an entire set of social relations, including a division of labor, means of socialization and preparation for production, means of recruiting or creating future group members, maintenance of nonproducing members, beliefs and customary behaviors, and so on. The concept includes, but is not restricted to, reproduction in the biological sense.

4. Gender hierarchy is based on how sex differences are seen to shape the social identities of women and men. The term *gender hierarchy* is used instead of patriarchy, since the latter term implies control by the father. While this was the case in many early state societies and persists in some peasant societies, more pervasive is an association of social authority with maleness, whatever that means in cultural terms. The term also describes contemporary Western capitalist societies, where patterns of conduct considered to be "male" also are identified with success or power, even as most men and women have little power.

5. *Socially necessary production* refers to the appropriation or making of those goods required to reproduce the society as constituted. This definition is refined in Chapter 6, on exchange and value.

6. *Chiefly* and *nonchiefly* are used throughout in preference to "noble" and "commoner." The latter terms refer to strata which exist in present-day Tonga, but the complexities of precontact ranking and stratification make their use for that period a distortion (see Gailey 1981; 1985b; Urbanowicz 1979).

7. Primary sources are those recorded by eyewitnesses; secondary sources are those which analyze prior accounts. The use here is in keeping with historiography, where travelers' accounts, missionary and traders' journals, colonial administrators' diaries and communications, and recordings of nonliterate people's accounts, as well as those of field researchers, would be considered as primary.

8. Class formation in previously kin-organized societies in the face of colonial pressure or, now more often, capital penetration, has been noted throughout the world (Cabral 1969; N. Sharp 1976; Poewe 1978; Bell and Ditton 1980; Van Binsbergen and Geschiere, eds. 1985).

1. The Subordination of Women

1. See, among others, Coquery-Vidrovich 1975; Krader 1975; Claessen and Skalník, eds. 1978; 1981; Seaton and Claessen, eds. 1979.

2. See Linton 1971; Van Allen 1972; Reiter, ed. 1975; Rohrlich-Leavitt, Sykes, and Weatherford 1975; Sacks 1976; 1979; Leacock and Nash 1977; Silverblatt 1978; Etienne and Leacock 1980; Gailey 1981; 1984a.

The distinction between institutional and attitudinal sexism derives from the literature on racism. Briefly, attitudinal prejudice can be corrected through changes in socialization processes; in this society, schooling, religious beliefs, mass media, and household influences would be pivotal. More fundamental discrimination is evident in social institutions, rooted ultimately in the normal functioning of the political economy. Changes in attitudes could be brought about with relative ease, compared with the eradication of institutional discrimination. For example, affirmative action in this country resulted in at least a few black people gaining access to middle-management positions in banks. However, institutional racism persists in the practices of said banks (regardless of the bank officer's color or promotion schedule) in red-lining—the denial of mortgages to prospective homeowners in low-income areas. Attitudinal sexism has been altered somewhat through the efforts of the women's movement, but institutional sexism can be seen in occupational segregation by sex and the necessity for women to conform to male standards of behavior in professions.

3. I have discussed the range of this set of arguments elsewhere (Gailey 1987). They include "man the hunter," "male supremacist complex," and sociobiology explanations of female subordination (Ardrey 1966; 1976; Laughlin 1968; Washburn and Lancaster 1968; Tiger 1969; 1971; E. Wilson 1975; 1978; Divale and Harris 1976; Harris 1977). Among the many voices critical of the biological determinist arguments prior to and including sociobiology are Mead (1928/1973), Linton (1971), Oakley (1972), Leibowitz

(1975), Leakey and Lewin (1977), Friedl (1978), Montagu (1980), Leacock (1981), Benderly (1982), and Kreniske (1984).

4. Research on West African societies was conducted by Rey (1973; 1979), Meillassoux (1975; 1979), and Terray (1979b), among others. Godelier (1980) has based his related thesis on class formation on these works and field research in Papua New Guinea.

All assume that women do not control the products they create. This results perhaps because each anthropologist focuses exclusively on *food* production. But even in this narrow realm one wonders if they have noted the complexities of claims to other's labor and products. Etienne's (1980) work on the Baule of the Ivory Coast documents such networks of claims with regard to food and nonfood subsistence production.

5. Many features of the so-called lineage mode of production in West Africa derive from the societies' historical position on the fringes of emerging state societies. On the margins, they were subject to periodic slave raids, or partial incorporation into taxation-conscription systems. In either situation, the conditions for making kin relations more rigid would be created. In addition, the later pressures of colonial penetration and current capital penetration have doubtless had an impact on the regulation of kinship connections and attention focused on control of products and circulation. It is quite possible that the claims in a married woman's natal group and those in her husband's group have undergone profound changes through the processes of class and state formation in the colonial and neocolonial periods; ethnohistorical research of the sort done by Van Allen (1972) is needed.

6. This point has been made by a number of scholars. See, for example, Bunzel 1938; Diamond 1951; Radin 1971; Leacock 1978; 1979; Etienne and Leacock 1980; Poewe 1980.

7. The impact of capital penetration and colonization on women's authority is traced in Etienne and Leacock 1980 and Leacock 1981.

8. Considerations of life experience do not as a rule dissolve gender stratification in this country. The association of women with a domestic sphere (even if they are employed) and men with a public realm is true regardless of age. Older people, because of discrimination, are "privatized," and both women and men lose status when they are not employed. But the salary and wage discrimination against women transcends their experience: while women must work in most cases, they remain linked to domestic responsibilities; this association includes a moral judgment (women should be home) that serves to justify lower wages.

9. See Diamond 1951; V. Muller 1977; Silverblatt 1978; Sacks 1979; Gailey 1980; 1981.

2. State Formation

1. In Great Britain, the inability of functionalism to explain the "sudden" ferment of nationalist movements throughout the collapsing empire spawned another attempt to resuscitate equilibrium models of society. The

Manchester School anticipated systems theory in the injection of conflict into earlier equilibrium models (see, e.g., Gluckman 1963; cf. van Teeffelen 1978). Later, as the British economy faltered within and unrest grew, equilibrium models were abandoned in favor of more historical, particularly Marxist, approaches. For the relationship between archaeology in the United States and different phases of capital accumulation, see Thomas Patterson (1985).

2. Lowie's attack on Morgan constituted an attack on the radical tradition in Europe and the United States. It also may have helped push anthropologists sympathetic to Marxism toward a defense of linear evolutionism, a problem evident in most of these works from the 1930's through the Soviet revelations about Stalin.

3. The articles edited by Claessen and Skalník (1978; 1981) and Seaton and Claessen (1979) are examples of the range of this scholarship in anthropology. Other representative works include, inter alia, Leacock 1972; Diamond 1974; Coquery-Vidrovich 1975; Krader 1975; Meillassoux 1975; Godelier 1977; 1980; Terray 1979a; and Van Binsbergen and Geschiere, eds. 1985.

4. Feminist works in the Marxist tradition that are explicitly concerned with state origins and gender hierarchy include V. Muller 1977; 1985; Rapp 1978a; Sacks 1979; most of the articles in Etienne and Leacock, eds. 1980; Gailey 1980; 1981; Leacock 1983; and Silverblatt 1987.

5. Skalník (1981) follows Engels' emphasis on commoditization a bit too narrowly; commodity exchange is a minor development in many tribute-based social formations.

6. Examples include Meillassoux 1975; Poewe 1978; Rey 1979; Terray 1979b; and Gailey 1980.

7. Both Krader (1975) and Skalník (1981) err in their characterization of surplus extraction in the tribute-paying or tax-rent mode of production. Both claim that surplus value is extracted through the emerging class relations. This is impossible in the absence of fully alienated labor. In the case of peasantries, in the "Asiatic" mode they remain hereditary possessors of the means of production, assertions of sovereign ownership aside. Their alienation is partial. The rudimentary existence of commodity exchange in tribute-based social formations does not allow for surplus value to be expressed. Thus, what *is* extracted is *surplus product* (in the form of tax-rents in kind or in cash) or *surplus labor* (in the case of labor service).

8. Sahlins discusses state bias in the description of economic organization among kinship peoples (1972 : Ch. 1). Diamond has reevaluated the notion of progress inherent in most anthropologists' writings on the state (1974). Sacks (1976) points to the detrimental effect of bias in favor of the state on research into women's status.

9. Bateson's work on Bali and Wallace's work on cognitive mapping both point to the unshared or partially shared meanings in class-ordered societies (Bateson 1970; 1972; Wallace 1965). The critique of Geertz and Sahlins implicit in Bateson's and Wallace's works was suggested to me by Betty Potash.

Redfield's work on peasant societies also shows the discrepancies between the elite conceptualizations of the social universe and the peasantry's.

10. The relationship of peasants to revolutionary movements has been discussed by many scholars. See, for example, Wolf 1969; 1982; Krader 1975; V. Muller 1979; and Scott 1985.

11. The only oblique reference to a potentially central role for resistance movements by a peasantry is in Willey and Shimkin (1973 : 491), but the systems approach minimizes popular involvement.

3. Authority and Ambiguity

1. Goldman, in his conceptualization of the "status lineage," recognizes the ambiguities in Tongan ranking, but he privatizes sisters' high rank and thereby minimizes the political involvement of chiefly women (1970:291). His distinction of ranking by seniority and sibling gender is careful, but he associates each with a different realm, public for the former and domestic for the latter. In the light of the prerogatives of chiefly sisters vis-à-vis their natal kindreds or lineages, this is not fruitful.

2. Tongan kinship has been examined by a number of anthropologists in the twentieth century, among them Gifford (1929); E. Beaglehole and P. Beaglehole (1941); Aoyagi (1966); Goldman (1970); Kaeppler (1971); Korn (1974); Urbanowicz (1979); Marcus (1980); Ortner (1981).

3. Polynesian kinship, particularly the relationship of descent to rank, has been discussed by many anthropologists, e.g., Sahlins (1958; 1963); Kirchhoff (1959); Firth (1968); Goldman (1970).

4. I have used spellings of Tongan words prevalent in the literature. Controversies over Tongan spelling often reflect other, more substantive political positions. For instance, I have not adopted the Wesleyan Methodist spellings. Urbanowicz (1979) discusses the politics of Tongan spelling. The meanings of the various terms and the derivations of the meanings also are debated. I have indicated which sources I used for the phrases and terms in the text.

5. Recent research into local kin groups in contemporary Tonga has been conducted by Aoyagi (1966), Kaeppler (1971), and Korn (1974). Korn discusses the *fāmili* and *kāinga* as overlapping bilateral kin networks beyond the household which involve different types of mutual aid. The work is extremely useful. The possibility that the *fāmili* (from the English word) is a recent form which has assumed functions formerly fulfilled by the *kāinga*—which has weakened since contact and Westernization—warrants further investigation. The kindred in general has been under pressure from a variety of sources, especially with regard to the *fahu*. (These pressures are discussed in Chapters 10 and 11.) The invention of new cultural forms to meet traditional demands—and the adaptation of older forms to meet new needs—is well documented for other areas experiencing fundamental socioeconomic change, such as state formation or colonization. See, in particular, Diamond

1951; 1974; Leacock 1954; Van Allen 1972; V. Muller 1977; Rapp 1978a; 1978b; and Silverblatt 1978; 1980.

6. The political redefinitions of the *tapu*—and of custom in general—has parallels in most state formative situations. In Hawaii, the chiefs' manipulations of *kapu* sometimes invited insurrection (Davenport 1969; Gailey 1983).

7. The ideology of meaning being created independently of engagement in the world is familiar. It derives from the emergence of class relations. The irony is that now both Geertz and Sahlins have adopted what is at base an assertion found in all precapitalist state societies and have presented it as an analysis of state formation. (Geertz 1980; Sahlins 1981).

8. Certain occupations were available to both *mu'as* and *tu'as*; others were open to both *mu'as* and *matāpules*; but no occupations were open to both *matāpules* and *tu'as*.

4. Reproduction of Ambiguity

1. Father's sister/brother's son rivalry also occurred in Hawaii, but for different reasons. In Tonga, the father's sister was a potential disruption because of her superior rank and greater *tapu*; in Hawaii she was a contender because of her equivalent rank and degree of *kapu* or sacredness. In Hawaii, if a brother and sister had the same parents, each was allowed, on the basis of parallel rank, to contract the same degree of sacred marriage (Davenport 1969:7). Thus, their children would have similar sacredness and, so, similar claims to title.

2. The dates are reckoned from a combination of chiefly genealogies which are notable for accuracy in terms of chronology, related accounts from Samoa, and myths and legends from Tonga that concern the actions of early chiefs, corroborated by archaeological remains (Lātūkefu 1968; Krämer 1902; Ve'ehala and Tupou Posesi Fanua 1977). The chronology is approximate, but the sequence is consistent in most accounts.

3. The first of the major tombs, or *langi*, is said to have been built for the daughter of the eleventh Tu'i Tonga, the sacred paramount chief who ordered the construction of a monumental structure called the Ha'amonga supposedly to preserve his memory (Bain 1954:73). His sister, Fatafehi, bore the name of the sacred paramount kin group; the name could have been a title as well.

Burial mounds also were constructed in later times (e.g., the 1700's) for the Tu'i Tonga Fefines by their brothers (Gifford 1923:199). Two other mounds exist, in different places, in which are buried the umbilical cords of two children of Tu'i Tongas: one a son, one a daughter (ibid.:192, 201). Thus, even if the Tu'i Tonga Fefine title did not exist, it is clear that the women who would later be so titled were named and were accorded birth and burial treatment similar to their brothers'.

The sister burials of this early period may be indirect evidence for a type of co-chieftainship on a brother-sister basis. Archaeologists frequently assume, when a female body is found in the same tomb as a male body, that the female is either a spouse or a concubine. In Tonga, concubines at times were strangled upon the death of a paramount male chief (see Chapter 7). But, there is also another explanation for the female bodies. When the daughter of Queen Salote died in 1938, she was buried outside of the family vault. When her father died some years later, she was reburied in his vault (Bain 1967 : 134). I do not know whether this was an unusual practice. If the daughter of a paramount chief became the next female paramount chief, this type of burial would be consistent. In any case, we should question the ready identification of younger female skeletons as wives or concubines, in the absence of other forms of identification.

4. In the same generation, the administrative paramount (Tu'i Ha'a Takalaua) was married to a Samoan chiefly woman. She would have become the mother of the Tu'i Kanokupolu, but the marriage can be seen as, in part, a denial of the usual obligation to marry the daughter of the male sacred paramount. On the other hand, it could also be an attempt by the sacred paramount house (*ha'a*) to limit the growing power of the administrative paramount house, by refusing the marriage and, thus, support.

5. Lévi-Strauss first discussed this type of marriage system in *Elementary Structures of Kinship* (1969). Leach refined the pattern and described the different implications for social stratification of open- and closed-ended forms in his study of the Kachin and Shan in Burma (1954).

6. Younger daughters frequently accompanied their eldest sister as secondary co-wives, or they married into other chiefly houses to forge other alliances. One difference between younger sons and younger daughters is notable: younger sons did not share their brother's chiefly title. Younger sisters were politely addressed by the title of their eldest sister. This sharing of title, albeit in a lesser degree, would serve to make marriages into high-ranking chiefly houses more possible for them than for their brothers. None of the sons of the highest-ranking female chiefs would fare as well as the women's eldest daughters. In theory, at some point the sons would "drop out" of contention because of their Fijian father.

7. Another early European traveler claimed that the Tu'i Tonga Fefine also had this responsibility, but he may have been referring to the younger sisters of the principal Tu'i Tonga Fefine (J. Wilson 1799/1968).

Attempts to remove high-ranking women from political contention through marriage arrangements have been reported from many state formative situations; the situation where high-ranking women leave no potential successors to title has a direct analogy in precolonial Dahomey (Diamond 1951).

8. Lower-ranking male relatives could either resign themselves to a gradually declining status or marry *matāpule* women and see their children become *matāpule*. If lower-ranking chiefly people were deprived of their functions as attendants, their association with higher-ranking chiefs became one of rank alone. Even though any chiefly person outranked any *matāpule*—even a titled *matāpule*—their rank decreased with each generation (Gifford 1929 : 112). Rank devoid of privileges emerged where *matāpules* were interposed. The injection of administrative persons to replace those with high

rank is reminiscent of the decline in the Tu'i Tonga's authority after administrative functions were divorced from sacred rank.

5. Division of Labor

1. Erskine (1853/1967:156) first pointed out this quality of the Tongan *fono*.

2. Mariner vacillates between referring to the ranks as classes and denying the existence of classes (as in the quote at the heading of this chapter). In part this is due to the plural meanings of "class" in English at the time—ranked status, occupational group, and so on. While "class" in the United States is typically defined in either a vague or an absurd fashion (e.g., by income level), the meaning is precise in the Marxist tradition: a social group with a distinctive relationship to the resources and labor needed for production. *Mu'as* would thus not constitute a class, since their relationship to tools, resources, and labor was similar to that of other social groups, particularly the *tu'as* and *matāpules*, as well as lower-ranking chiefly people.

3. The abolition of the *'inasi* can be compared with the abolition of the *kapu* (*tapu*) system in Hawaii, also in the first years after contact (see Davenport 1969). Both were related to the consolidation of political power by one chiefly group at the expense of another. In Tonga, the sacred paramounts were denied their embodiment—literally in terms of corpulence—of social prosperity. In Hawaii, the priestly/brother group lost its similar fertility-assurance functions.

4. Captain Wilson, of the missionary ship *Duff*, commented about local response to the missionaries' rat trap. The rats "were given to the women at their request, and eaten raw as relishing foods" (1799/1968:271).

5. Erskine claims that *tapa* was a Tongan term and that it referred to the undecorated variety (1853/1967:115). Kooijman, basing his references to Tonga on the M.A. thesis by Maxine Tamahori (University of Auckland, 1963), says that the term *tapa* is today applied only to the unpainted edge of a piece of *ngatu*. *Ngatu* is the stamped, dyed, and painted variety. Smaller sheets of undecorated bark cloth, before they are joined together, are called *feta'aki* (Kooijman 1972:319).

In the precontact period there were many more varieties, including washable, glazed, smoked, and water-resistant types. *Masi* appears to have been a traditional generic term for *tapa*, which is made from the inner bark of the paper mulberry tree.

6. Fine mats, or *ngafi ngafi*, were used for special occasions. Different types of fine mats were used as apparel and to make pathways during ceremonies. They were intricately plaited; those associated with the highest chiefs incorporated dyed fibers and exotic feathers. Mats worn about the waist to show respect for higher-ranking people were and still are known as *ta'ovala* (Bain 1967:206). *Vala* referred to an underskirt in general, not the several sorts of *ta'ovala* (ibid.:77).

7. It is unclear if *kava* was reserved for chiefly consumption, or if it was occasionally available for nonchiefly use. The *tu'as* grew the root, and

chiefly people could claim the roots, but whether nonchiefly people were prohibited from drinking the brew is not clear.

8. The process is described in Mariner 1827:2:202–207; Erskine 1853/ 1967:115; Beaglehole and Beaglehole 1941; Neill 1955, and especially Kooijman 1972.

9. Women of high rank no longer are responsible for making the sewn sinnet (coconut fiber rope) and pandanus stamps, known as *kobechi*. As chiefly women have become less involved in the everyday production of *tapa* and *ngatu* in particular, the structure of the women's association to make this type of *koloa* also has changed. The *kautaha* appears to have become more "democratic," according to Kooijman (1972:319). The work groups are cooperative; the leader is selected by the participants. This implies that the woman who presided over the *kautaha* and *kokanga* was chiefly in former times (ibid.:301).

10. The missionary translation of *ngāue* as "work" has encouraged the identification of wage labor with men in the twentieth century: women should not be doing "work"; so if they do, they should be paid less.

11. By the 1930's, cooking arrangements had changed somewhat. Baking and cooking meat were still considered men's tasks, but boiling foods was not gender-specific (Beaglehole and Beaglehole 1941:39).

12. Mother's brother's daughter/father's sister's son marriage seems to have been rare for nonchiefly people (Gifford 1929:189). It may have been *tapu* for lower-ranking people to contract such close-in marriages, as it was forbidden in Hawaii (and in Incaic Peru). The close-in marriages may have been considered incestuous for all but the highest-ranking people and, thus, a marker of high rank. Cross-cousin marriage is a violation of the avoidance *tapus* for brothers and sisters (Collocott 1923b:227; Gifford 1929:22) and was not considered a promising match for nonchiefly people in the 1930's (Beaglehole and Beaglehole 1941).

6. Exchange and Value

1. "Production for exchange" is a term originating in Marx's work. It refers to the sphere of commodities, not to gifts, presentations, or other kin-associated exchanges. Many anthropologists have conflated the two. For example, Weiner (1976) uses the term to refer to goods used to fulfill kin obligations or to extend networks of kin relations. *Commodity* has a specific meaning in the Marxist tradition: it is an item which, being transformed in some way through human labor, both has a use-value (it helps to satisfy wants) and—by virtue of being transferred by a person who possesses it to another—manifests the value of the labor embedded in it, in relation to the item received in the exchange (see Marx 1881/1967:1:40–41, 47).

2. Things changing hands do not create commodity circulation. The social relations embedded in commodity production and exchange are distinctive. Marx was clear on this point: "The circulation of commodities differs from the direct exchange of products (barter), not only in form, but in substance. . . . the exchange of commodities breaks through all local and per-

sonal bounds inseparable from direct barter, and . . . develops a whole network of social relations spontaneous in their growth and entirely beyond the
control of the actors. . . . The process of circulation [of commodities], therefore, does not, like direct barter of products, become extinguished upon the
use-values changing places and hands" (1881/1967:1:112).

3. Weiner (1978) considers the Trobrianders to "fetishize" yams. These
yams are publicly displayed and allowed to rot over the year as a symbol of
prosperity. But this form of "fetishizing" differs markedly from the concept
of "commodity fetishism" as used in the Marxist tradition.

Where the commodity form dominates the economy, as in capitalism and
as nowhere in the kin-based world, the relations among people—and, indeed, the sense of self—become mediated by the commodity forms. People
are described in terms of consumption patterns, clothing, automobile types,
purchasing power, and so on. The Trobrianders symbolize personal relations—claims to one another's labor and products—through the yams on
display. The commodities of capitalist society are not fetishes in the strictest anthropological sense, since the commodities replace the content of personal relations, rather than embody it. But the term chosen by Weiner is
unfortunate, because the connotation of obsessiveness or idolatry that
"fetishize" has in English derives from our commodity universe, and so does
not suit the interpersonal relations and claims embodied in yams for the
Trobrianders.

7. Gender Relations at Contact

1. This contradicts Lévi-Strauss' view of etiquette as reflecting an
underlying social code (Lévi-Strauss 1979). I am arguing that customary
ranking was being challenged or upheld through the way in which etiquette
was expressed by different constituencies in the society.

2. The fact that women used such spears contradicts Marvin Harris'
contention that women in "band and village level societies" do not control
weapons (1977; see also Divale and Harris 1976).

3. Even in recent years, women continue to pride themselves on the accomplishment of laborious and intricate tasks. A traveler reported the following incident. A woman was struggling to loose an octopus from one of
the deep tidal pools. After half an hour, the European man asked why none
of the male spectators helped her. One man replied, "But she will get it. . . .
She will not give up . . . she is a sister of my wife and she comes from
Ha'apai" (Ruhen 1966:37–38). The incident also reveals men's confidence
in the competence of women in their work.

4. Perhaps the only model for deferent behavior of men toward women
for Euro-Americans continues to be chivalry. It must have been difficult for
early travelers (and evidently recent ones as well) to comprehend Tongan
gender relations. The accounts are brimming with apparent contradictions.
The observations probably were accurate and seem contradictory only when
placed in the context of European or American gender relations. Deference

without subservience, and authority restricted to given contexts, must have been puzzling.

5. In recent years, a favor-seeking father could secretly bring an unmarried daughter by night to a male chief and take her away in the morning (Bain 1967:82). The context has changed: the chiefs now are part of a land tenure system that includes the right to exclude, and there are needs for favors to retain economic security.

6. The same young woman recognized the racism of Englishmen. She pointed out in the course of her conversation that if she went to England, in all likelihood no Englishman would marry her, because her skin would be considered too brown (Mariner 1827:2:49). She did not say that her skin was too brown.

7. Ortner uses a foggy definition of stratification. She lumps caste and "aristocratic," that is, estate-type, stratification as one (cf. Jérome Rousseau 1978). This is impermissible, since caste is directly linked to the division of labor and estates are not.

8. Early Contact

1. The term derives from the way in which Tasman arrived. Tongans exclaimed that his ships were *Ko e vaka no papa langi*, which Tasman translated as "ships burst from the sky". Basil Thomson received a different variation on this theme. He was told *papālangi* came from an old Tongan chief's witticism. When someone asked from where Cook's vessels arrived in 1773, he is said to have remarked, "Why, from the land of riches—from Babalangi [an imaginary land]!" Another chief of Thomson's acquaintance said that the word referred to the masts of the ships, which went *ba-ki-langi*, "shooting up to the sky" (B. Thomson 1902:206). Beaglehole claims that Tongans transferred the word *papālangi* from the goods brought by the strangers— notably cotton and linen—to the people themselves (1969:3:178n). Cook said ". . . they call our ships *Towacka no papalangie* and us *Tangata no papalangie*; that is cloth ships and cloth men" (Cook in Beaglehole, ed. 1969: 3:178). Given the appearance of sailing vessels—with white sheets the color of a type of *tapa* used only on special occasions, such as marriage—and their cargoes of cloth and valuables, the epithet seems appropriate. The derivation may be simpler. *Papa* refers to a coarse mat, including the type once used as sails. *Langi* were the rectangular slabs used for chiefly tombs. Tongan sails were not rectangular.

2. The punishments meted to Tongans were comparable to those for sailors on the ships. It is of note in this context that the mutiny on Bligh's ship took place in Tongan waters.

3. Sahlins makes this error in his monograph on the early Hawaiian kingdom (1981). Because Europeans tailored goods for the Hawaiian market, he speaks of a "Hawaiian mode of production" to which the "European mode of production" had to accommodate itself. He misses the imposition of commodity production of sandalwood on lower-ranking Hawaiians by the

nascent Hawaiian ruling class, in collusion with merchants and representatives of the United States and Britain. By focusing solely on the items exchanged, he completely obscures the production process, which by that time involved forced labor and was oriented toward commodities in both Hawaii and Europe. What the Europeans brought to the Islands was tailored to the local elite, but the local elite was dependent upon the merchants' weaponry and exotic goods for their continued dominant position (Gailey 1983).

4. Recently, Sahlins (1981) has interpreted the sexual liaisons between lower-ranking Hawaiian women and sailors as an attempt to attach themselves to a chiefly personage, "finding a lord" in his words. There is no evidence of this motivation in Tonga and, indeed, other interpretations of Hawaiian women's activities are possible, as I have discussed elsewhere (Gailey 1983).

5. It is well recognized, for instance, that early Portuguese accounts of West African peoples speak of separate but equivalent cultures.

6. For the most part, only nonchiefly men would be engaged in agricultural production. Higher-ranking captives could be set to making war clubs, as the manufacture of these implements was in the province of *matāpule*, *mu'a*, and *'eiki* men. Male captives, then, could be used productively or reproductively: the latter by making the weapons used to acquire more captives. Terray makes the argument for the importance of captives in reproducing class relations in the precolonial Abron kingdom of Gyaman (1979a).

7. Muller describes a transition to class relations of this sort for the Germanic tribes. Non-kin-related military retinues could retain spoils from raiding without kin having access to the goods (1985).

8. The LMS missionaries were offered a young man by two chiefs, "his hands tied together with sinnet," in return for an axe. The term the chiefs used for the transaction was *fakatau*, the word used to describe all transactions with the Europeans. The young man was not a gift. His sellers described him as "Good for roasting yams and running errands" (J. Wilson 1799/1968:256–257). In other words, he was a lower-ranking cook, the most menial of tasks being cooking. The missionaries were horrified (ibid.). This might indicate one possible use for male prisoners, apart from torture or killing. Farmer claimed that the *populas* were slaves, and that they were either prisoners of war or gifts from one chief to another from the ranks of those who had offended him (1855:140).

9. Missionaries

1. Mumui was probably Tu'i Kanokupolu. According to both Vason and Wilson, he was Tu'i Kanokupolu (Vason 1810:71; J. Wilson 1799/1968). According to John Singleton, one of the men spared from the *Port-au-Prince* in 1806, he was Tu'i Ha'a Takalaua (Dumont D'Urville 1834:4:94).

2. The missionaries may have been the first to bring tobacco to Tonga: Cook did not mention it and Tasman commented that it was unknown at Tongatapu (in Dalrymple, ed. 1770/1967:79).

3. Mariner cited a case of a resident Hawaiian directed by one chief to kill a madwoman.

4. Vason said, ". . . man, left to himself without the restraints of law and civilized life, will, unless the grace of God prevent, soon degenerate into a savage, through the corrupt tendency of his nature to yield to the influence of bad example" (1810:70).

5. *Monucka* expresses yearning or lust, not love. It could be said of things one wanted or of sexual arousal.

6. This spelling of "Tubou" reflects the orthography of the Wesleyan Methodists, the religion of these converts. In other places, I have used *p* in place of *b*.

7. "Taoufa comprit vite le parti qu'il pouvait tirer de la religion protestante."

8. In late 1986, for example, a sales tax was announced by the central government. In Vava'u, there was universal outrage about the manner in which the tax was imposed and the lack of information about how the revenues would be spent. Merchants and marketpeople in Vava'u refused to collect the tax, and when government agents were sent to the island to investigate, they were asked to leave. They did.

Whenever I asked older commoners why Vava'u was part of Tonga, they responded that the chiefs bowed to the threat of bloodshed, but that Vava'u could have defeated George's forces. The absence of conquest in Vava'u, far from indicating compliance and accommodation to the state, provided a structure for preserving a sense of independence, a background for resistance. The pride and autonomy of Vava'uans is noted widely in the islands, with begrudging admiration or resentment.

9. Nick Blatchley, personal communication, 1977.

10. A Native Kingdom

1. A similar situation occurred in the Hawaiian Islands during political centralization. Far from being in line with chiefly practice, the *kapu* was used to further capital accumulation. I take issue with Sahlins' interpretation of how customarily everyone was acting (Sahlins 1981; Gailey 1983; cf. Davenport 1969).

2. Derek Freeman has considered a similar practice in Samoa as rape (1984). For the precontact period in Samoa, his claims appear dubious. For precontact Tonga it certainly is not the case. Rape was rare, and when it occurred outside of warfare, it was "in the bush," perpetrated as a rule by marauding young chiefly men.

3. Even if the children were adopted by their natural father, their inheritance rights would be limited to movable property (Im Thurn 1905:55).

11. Changing Production

1. Sandalwood was important in the Asian trade. Extraction usually was conducted through the use of forced labor. Most expeditions were by companies from the United States or New South Wales. The trade expanded rapidly after 1804 (Ward 1948:17), but by 1815, sandalwood regions were depleted. Extraction continued in some areas, using forced labor of indigenous peoples or "blackbird" labor, which pretended to contractual legality (Foreign Office Papers 1872–1873; Report to the House of Lords 1873). Conditions for workers were extremely oppressive, even murderous (Erskine 1853/1967:145; Report to the House of Lords 1873).

2. In the mid-twentieth century, Ledyard reported children helping women grate the coconut meat (1956:203).

3. The Beagleholes noted that women still made the oil in the late 1930's (Beaglehole and Beaglehole 1941:20).

4. The enthusiasm with which local people participated in mission donations may indicate a formal resemblance to older customs. It is possible that the prestige accruing to those with the greatest amount of agricultural products was formally similar to that obtained through the first fruits ceremonial, the *'inasi*, but there is no evidence. It is highly unlikely that the fervor of people's amassing of mission donations would be due to their attachment to the Wesleyan Methodists.

5. Women found smoking were to pay $2.50 plus $1.50 court costs.

6. Lātūkefu disagrees with Rutherford and Cumming about the mission involvement in the law (1974). There is no direct proof of their involvement in the case of *tapa*, but there is evidence of collusion with Godeffroy's on other occasions (Maudslay 1878/1930:225, 240).

7. An old chief, Tungi, spoke before Parliament, saying, "Don't let us talk about it. Let us sweep it away without another thought." He told a European observer later that people shouted, "We are Tongans, although we have hidden ourselves under whiteman's clothes" (Maudslay 1930:230).

8. Bananas were introduced as a commercial crop by Roman Catholic priests in the mid-1800's (Erskine 1853/1967:163). They have grown in importance as an export crop in the twentieth century, but in the nineteenth century coconut oil and copra were the only significant export crops. Copra still is by far the most important export product; bananas now are second (Colonial Office 1909–1914; 1920–1938; 1956–1963). Sweet bananas, as opposed to cooking bananas, have never been a significant part of Tongans' diets, but rejected bunches are used as pig feed (Shephard 1945:162).

9. A recent incident reveals the function of mothers as bankers. In the early 1960's, a European was selling a car for £895 to a young Tongan man. They had to wait until the man's mother arrived from the countryside.

She carried a plaited basket over which was draped a tattered piece of brown paper. With a smile, she handed it to me. . . . Beneath the brown paper lay a haphazard pile of £1 Government of Tonga Treasury notes. (Bain 1967:49)

10. Land scarcity is primarily due to political arrangements, not population growth. The precontact population estimate most scholars agree upon is twenty-five thousand for all island groups. In the early nineteenth century, the introduction of European diseases, particularly colds and measles, reduced the population to an estimated sixteen thousand in 1834 (Seed 1874 : 3). Following the initial decimation, the insistence on European clothing, the decline in sanitary conditions for the direct producers, the reduction of time between children, inadequate foods after early weaning, and demands for labor time led to an increase in both infant mortality and tuberculosis. Lieutenant Meade of the HMS *Curacao* held that population was from nine to ten thousand in 1865 (ibid.: 4). This probably was an underestimate, because British officials in 1878 estimated the population at nineteen thousand (Cumming 1882 : 1 : 34). By 1915, the British reported a marked increase in tuberculosis (Colonial Office 1914–1915 : 10). Infant mortality ranged from 11 percent to 20 percent from 1927 to 1945 (Colonial Office 1920–1939; 1945–1954).

Nevertheless, by 1945, the population had grown to 32,761 (Shephard 1945 : 160). Today, the population is around 110,000. Reasons for the population growth can be sought in changes in the cash-cropping and land tenure system, making it difficult for peasants to obtain adequate lands. The leasing of lands to foreigners, coupled with commercial farming by estate-holders, has forced many tenants to find alternative means of employment. Wherever this forced migration without social security occurs, those in the most insecure income group must try to have more children, given childhood mortality rates and the shift from community to familial old-age care. In the Tongan case, population growth is tied to the increasing penetration by capitalist relations, leading to increasing economic insecurity for more people.

11. The increasing need for wage labor and cash income has had consequences for public health. Some of the "diseases of development" have emerged as widespread problems in Tonga in the past thirty years: obesity, diabetes, hypertension, and dental caries (cf. Bodley 1982). These health problems are related in part to vastly increased sugar, tinned beef and fish, and fatty mutton consumption—all of which are imported and prestigious. As land has become scarce, and wage work demands migration overseas, landless relatives have come to rely, via gifts and remittances, on purchased foods. The very expense of imported foods creates prestige in consumption: tinned corned beef, mutton flaps, and extremely sweet fruit drinks have become standard fare for Sunday meals.

12. Mats and *tapa*, like other goods made autonomously by a people, are termed folklore by Flores (1978). These creations are essential for social reproduction. Flores uses the example of quilting in the United States: quilts were made to mark significant life-events, such as births and marriages. This parallels the customary uses of women's wealth objects in Tonga. Like quilts, they were necessary for local continuity in the narrow sense of needed household furnishings, blankets, clothing, and the like, but they also embodied the continuity of generational and status changes. All these forms recorded history from a women's perspective—in the Tongan case,

history from both chiefly and nonchiefly women's perspectives.

Tapa and mats were history as continuously and consciously constructed by women. In contrast, material objects that represent interclass relations—such as samplers in the United States—are not historical. Such accomplishments have as an end the denial of the natal kin: upward mobility through marriage. The debasement of *tapa* and mats in the last century perhaps shows this tendency. For elite women who participate, the action is seen as an accomplishment. For the regular producers, the objects represent a way of making a living in a setting where women have unequal access to wage labor.

12. Dialectics of Class and State Formation

1. Marx used the term "village community" to define kin- or quasi-kin-defined groups with hereditary rights to resources; thus, Tongan local kindreds would qualify as "village communities," although the settlement pattern was dispersed prior to contact. For clarity, I have used "kin community."

Glossary: Tongan Terms

'api.	acreage for use issued from either Crown lands or a hereditary estate; a tax-allotment; a household.
'eiki.	of chiefly status: included both titled and untitled people.
fa'ahinga.	in modern Tonga, an extended family.
fahu.	literally, "above custom"; the prerogatives of sisters and their children vis-à-vis brothers and their children, derived from the higher rank of sisters.
faka-Tonga (fakatonga).	in the Tongan way; customary; Tongan culture.
fāmili.	a modern term describing a mutual aid and labor exchange unit similar to the traditional *kāinga*; also, a nuclear family.
feta'aki.	smaller sheets of undecorated bark cloth, before they are joined together.
fetokoni'aki.	helping one another; cooperation.
fokonofo.	co-wife; secondary wives brought with a chiefly woman upon marriage.
fono.	traditionally, an assembly called by a chief to relay instructions or harangue people in a district. Today, mandatory assemblies called by the King or his representatives, a local estate-holder, or a mayor.
ha'a.	"house," a group of related chiefly lineages; a chiefly corporate kindred.
Ha'a Fale Fisi.	House of Fiji; the chiefly kindred into which the female sacred paramount chief usually married.
Ha'a Moheofo.	kindred of the administrative paramount chief and his sister, the primary wife of the male sacred paramount chief.
Ha'apai.	the middle island group of Tonga.
hau.	the highest rank of titled chiefs; paramount chiefs.
hia.	murder; adultery with the wife of a higher-ranking man.
'inasi.	the first fruits ceremony in precontact Tonga.
kāinga.	the cognatic kindred in precontact Tonga; unit having hereditary use-rights to land and other resources; now, a cognatic kindred.
kato.	generically, a basket; often, a large carrying basket woven of coconut palm leaves.

kautaha.	the group of women who beat *tapa*; now, a cooperative work group of women.
kava.	fermented beverage consumed in gatherings, the order of drinking reflecting rank.
kie.	a type of finely plaited mat, especially an heirloom mat.
kobechi.	a sewn and embroidered bundle of pandanus and coconut sinew, used to stamp designs for *ngatu*.
kokanga.	group of women who decorate and finish bark cloth.
koloa.	traditionally, products made by women, considered as valuables. Today, any wealth.
mana.	impersonal, supernatural power, said to be associated with high rank.
mana'ai.	handsome young men used by chiefly people to attract sexual partners.
masi.	the paper mulberry tree; Tongan term for bark cloth.
matāpule.	one of a group of kindreds, mostly of foreign origin, who acted as assistants or attendants for chiefly people. Foreigners usually were incorporated into Tongan society as *matāpules*.
mehikitanga.	father's sister.
Moheofo.	the primary wife of the Tu'i Tonga; female chiefly title of the Tu'i Kanokupolu line.
monucka.	yearning, desire, lust; said of goods or sexual attraction.
mu'a.	according to some, a rank between chiefly and non-chiefly people; according to others, a nonchiefly rank between *matāpule* and *tu'a*.
ngafi ngafi.	a variety of finely plaited mat.
ngatu.	the stamped, dyed, and painted variety of bark cloth.
ngāue.	traditionally, the production of men, considered less valuable than that of women. Today, wage labor.
nōpele.	the modern nobility, consisting of certain chiefly patrilineages, or a member of the nobility.
Nuku'alofa.	the capital city of Tonga, situated on Tongatapu.
oanna.	husband or wife.
'ofa.	compassion, lasting affection, enduring friendship.
pālangi.	current word for European or white person.
papālangi.	older word for European or white person.
popula (*bobula*).	captives, prisoners of war.
Sina'e.	branch of the house of the Tu'i Tonga, possibly composed of descendants of the female sacred paramounts; name of several Tu'i Tonga Fefines.

sinifu.	a chiefly husband's relationship to concubines; temporary wives of a paramount chief.
Tamaha.	the "sacred child"; the eldest daughter of the female sacred paramount chief, Tu'i Tonga Fefine; the highest-ranking person in traditional Tongan society.
tamao'eiki.	slave, literally "chief's boy"; used to describe people sentenced to life terms of penal servitude.
ta'ovala.	woven mats worn about the waist to show one's respect for higher-ranking persons.
tapa.	generic term for bark cloth; also, the plain or monochromatic varieties.
tapu.	sacred, forbidden, reserved for chiefly use; anything so designated.
tofi'a.	in modern Tonga, a hereditary estate.
Tongatapu.	the largest island in Tonga.
tu'a.	the lowest rank of nonchiefly people.
Tu'i Ha'a Takalaua.	formerly, the administrative paramount chief, replaced in that capacity by the Tu'i Kanokupolu.
Tu'i Ha'a Teiho.	a paramount chiefly title of the Ha'a Fale Fisi; often chosen as the husband of the Tu'i Tonga Fefine.
Tu'i Kanokupolu.	the administrative paramount chief.
Tu'i Lakepa.	one of the paramount titles of the Ha'a Fale Fisi; often chosen as the husband of the Tu'i Tonga Fefine.
Tu'i Tonga.	the male sacred paramount chief.
Tu'i Tonga Fefine.	the female sacred paramount chief, sister of the Tu'i Tonga.
'ulumotu'a.	designated head of a kindred.
vala.	generic term for an underskirt, as distinguished from *ta'ovala.*
Vava'u.	the northernmost island group in Tonga.

References

Abélès, Marc
  1981. "Sacred kingship" and formation of the state. In *The Study of the State*, edited by H. J. M. Claessen and Peter Skalník, pp. 1–15. The Hague: Mouton.
Allen, Percy S.
  1920, 1921. *Stewart's Handbook of the Pacific Islands*. Sydney: McCarron, Stewart and Co., Ltd.
Alpers, Anthony
  1970. *Legends of the South Sea*. London: John Murray.
Althusser, Louis
  1969. *For Marx*. London: Allen and Unwin.
Amin, Samir
  1976. *Unequal Development*. New York: Monthly Review.
Aoyagi, M.
  1966. Kinship organization and behavior in a contemporary Tongan village. *Journal of the Polynesian Society* 75:141–176.
Ardrey, Robert
  1966. *The Territorial Imperative*. New York: Atheneum.
  1970. *The Social Contract*. New York: Atheneum.
  1976. *The Hunting Hypothesis*. New York: Atheneum.
Arendt, Hannah
  1958. *The Human Condition*. Chicago: University of Chicago Press.
Arnold, Rosemary
  1957a. Port of trade: Whydah on the Guinea coast. In *Trade and Market in the Early Empires*, edited by Karl Polanyi et al., pp. 154–176. Chicago: Henry Regnery.
  1957b. Separation of trade and market. In *Trade and Market in the Early Empires*, edited by Karl Polanyi et al., pp. 177–187. Chicago: Henry Regnery.
Asad, Talal
  1973. *Anthropology and the Colonial Encounter*. Atlantic Heights, N.J.: Humanities.
Bachofen, Johann J.
  1859/1967. *Myth, Religion and Mother Right*. Translated by Ralph Manheim. Princeton, N.J.: Princeton University Press.
Bain, K. R.
  1954. *Official Record of the Royal Visit to Tonga, 1953*. Nuku'alofa, Tonga: Government Printer.
  1967. *The Friendly Islanders*. London: Hodder and Stoughton.
Baker, John
  1977. Contemporary Tonga: An economic survey. In *Friendly Islands*, edited by Noel Rutherford, pp. 228–246. Melbourne: Oxford University Press.

Baker, L., and Shirley Baker
   1951. *Memoirs of the Rev. Dr. Shirley Waldeman Baker.* London.
Banaji, Jairus
   1972. For a theory of colonial modes of production. *Economic and Political Weekly* 7(52):2498–2502.
   1977. Modes of production in a materialist conception of history. *Capital and Class* 3:1–44.
Barrau, Jacques
   1963. *Plants and Migrations of Pacific Peoples.* Honolulu: B. P. Bishop Museum.
Barrow, T., and H. Sieben
   1967. *Women of Polynesia.* Wellington, New Zealand: Seven Seas.
Bateson, Gregory
   1970. Bali: The value system of a steady state. In *Traditional Balinese Culture,* edited by Jane Belo, pp. 384–402. New York: Columbia University Press.
   1972. Culture contact and schismogenesis. In *Steps to an Ecology of Mind,* pp. 61–72. San Francisco: Chandler.
Beaglehole, Ernest, and Pearl Beaglehole
   1941. *Pangai.* Wellington, New Zealand: Polynesian Society.
Beaglehole, John Cawte
   1934/1966. *The Exploration of the Pacific.* London: A. and C. Black.
Beaglehole, John Cawte, ed.
   1969. *The Journals of Captain James Cook.* 3 vols. Cambridge: Cambridge University Press for the Hakluyt Society.
Bell, Diane
   1980. Desert politics: Choices in the "marriage market." In *Women and Colonization,* edited by Mona Etienne and Eleanor Leacock, pp. 239–269. New York: J. F. Bergin/Praeger.
Bell, Diane, and Pam Ditton
   1980. *Law: The Old and the New.* Canberra: Aboriginal History/Central Australian Legal Aid Service.
Benderly, Beryl
   1982. Rape free or rape prone. *Science* 82 (October).
Best, Elsdon
   1909. Maori forest lore . . . part III. *Transactions of the New Zealand Institute* 42:433–481.
Blackburn, Julia
   1979. *The White Men.* London: Orbis Books.
Blacket, J.
   1914. *Missionary Triumphs among the Settlers of Australia and the South Seas.* London.
Blamires, G. G.
   1939. *Little Island Kingdom of the South.* London.
Bodley, John
   1982. *Victims of Progress.* Palo Alto, Calif.: Mayfield.

Bonte, Pierre

1981. Kinship and politics. In *The Study of the State*, edited by H. J. M. Claessen and Peter Skalník, pp. 35–58. The Hague: Mouton.

Boserup, Esther

1970. *Women's Role in Economic Development*. New York: Allen and Unwin.

Boutilier, James, Daniel Hughes, and Sharon Tiffany, eds.

1978. *Mission, Church and Sect in Oceania*. Ann Arbor: University of Michigan Press.

British Museum

1979. *Yearbook 3: Captain Cook and the South Pacific*. London.

Bunzel, Ruth

1938. The economic organization of primitive peoples. In *General Anthropology*, edited by Franz Boas, pp. 327–408. New York: Heath.

Burrows, Edwin

1970. *Western Polynesia*. Dunedin, Scotland: University Book Shop.

Cabral, Amilcar

1969. *Revolution in Guinea*. New York: Monthly Review.

Cardoso, C. F. S.

1975. On the colonial modes of production in the Americas. *Critique of Anthropology* 4(5): 1–36.

Carroll, Vernon, ed.

1970. *Adoption in Eastern Oceania*. Honolulu: University of Hawaii Press.

Chapman, Anne

1957. Port of trade enclaves in Aztec and Maya civilizations. In *Trade and Market in the Early Empires*, edited by Karl Polanyi et al., pp. 114–153. Chicago: Henry Regnery.

Chayanov, Aleksandr V.

1922/1966. *The Theory of Peasant Economy*. Homewood, Ill.: Irwin.

Childe, V. Gordon

1950. The urban revolution. *Town Planning Review* 21(1): 3–17.

1951a. *Man Makes Himself*. New York: New American Library.

1951b. *Social Evolution*. London: Watts.

1952. The birth of civilization. *Past and Present* 2: 1–10.

Churchward, Clerk Maxwell

1953. *Tongan Grammar*. New York: Oxford University Press.

1959. *Tongan Dictionary*. London: Oxford University Press.

Claessen, H. J. M.

1979. The balance of power in primitive states. In *Political Anthropology: The State of the Art*, edited by S. Lee Seaton and H. J. M. Claessen, pp. 183–196. The Hague: Mouton.

Claessen, H. J. M., and Peter Skalník, eds.

1978. *The Early State*. The Hague: Mouton.

1981. *The Study of the State*. The Hague: Mouton.

Clastres, Pierre

1977. *Society against the State*. New York: Urizen.

Cohen, Yehudi
 1969. Ends and means in political control: State organization and the punishment of adultery, incest and the violation of celibacy. *American Anthropologist* 71:658–688.
Cohn, Bernard
 1981. Anthropology and history in the 1980's. *Journal of Interdisciplinary History* 12(2):227–252.
Collocott, E. E. V.
 1923a. An experiment in Tongan history. *Journal of the Polynesian Society* 32:166–184.
 1923b. Marriage in Tonga. *Journal of the Polynesian Society* 32:221–228.
 1928. *Tales and Poems of Tonga.* Honolulu: B. P. Bishop Museum.
 1929. *Kava Drinking in Tonga.* Honolulu: B. P. Bishop Museum.
 n.d. Papers on Tonga, 1845–19 . . . , Folios 1–5. Mitchell Library, Sydney. ML MSS.207.
Collocott, E. E. V., and John Havea
 1922. *Proverbial Sayings of the Tongans.* Honolulu: B. P. Bishop Museum Press.
Colonial Office, Great Britain
 1908–1915, 1920–1939, 1945–1954. *Annual Reports.* London: H. M. Stationery Office.
 1946, 1948–1955, 1956–1963. *Reports on Tonga.* London: H. M. Stationery Office.
Condliffe, J. B.
 1930. The economic and social movements underlying antagonisms in the Pacific. *Journal of the Royal Institute of International Affairs* 4(July):519–530.
Cook, Captain James
 1777. *A Voyage towards the South Pole and round the World.* 2 vols. London: W. Strahan and T. Cadell.
 1784. *A Voyage to the Pacific Ocean.* 2 vols. London: W. and A. Strahan.
Coquery-Vidrovich, Catherine
 1975. Research on an African mode of production. *Critique of Anthropology* 4(5):37–71.
Coult, Allan D.
 1959. Tongan authority structure. *Kroeber Anthropological Society Papers* 20:56–70.
Couper, A. D.
 1968. Protest movements and proto-cooperatives in the Pacific islands. *Journal of the Polynesian Society* 77:263–274.
Cowgill, George
 1975. On causes and consequences of ancient and modern population changes. *American Anthropologist* 77(3):505–525.
Crane, E. A.
 1978. *The Tongan Way.* Auckland, New Zealand: Heinemann Educational Books.
 1979. *Geography of Tonga.* Nuku'alofa: Government of Tonga.

Crocombe, R. G.
  1973. *The New South Pacific.* Canberra: Australian National University Press.
Cumming, Constance F. Gordon
  1882. *A Lady's Cruise in a French Man of War.* 2 vols. Edinburgh.
Cummins, H. G.
  1977a. Holy war: Peter Dillon and the 1837 massacres in Tonga. *Journal of Pacific History* 12(1): 25–39.
  1977b. Tongan society at the time of contact. In *Friendly Islands*, edited by Noel Rutherford, pp. 63–89. Melbourne: Oxford University Press.
Dalrymple, Alexander, ed.
  1770/1967. *A Historical Collection of the Several Voyages and Discoveries in the South Pacific Ocean*, vol. 2. Amsterdam: N. Israel.
Dalton, R. W.
  1919. *Trade of Western Samoa and the Tongan Islands.* London: H. M. Stationery Office.
Davenport, W. H.
  1969. The "Hawaiian Cultural Revolution": Some political and economic considerations. *American Anthropologist* 71(1): 1–20.
Davidson, J. W.
  1971. The decolonization of Oceania. *Journal of Pacific History* 6: 133–150.
Davidson, James W.
  1975. *Peter Dillon of Vanikoro.* Melbourne: Oxford University Press.
Deere, Carmen Diana
  1979. Rural women's subsistence production in the capitalist periphery. In *Peasants and Proletarians: The Struggles of Third World Workers*, edited by Robin Cohen, Peter C. W. Gutkind, and Phyllis Brazier, pp. 133–148. New York: Monthly Review.
Diamond, Stanley
  1951. *Dahomey: A Proto-State in West Africa.* Ann Arbor: University Microfilms.
  1966. Introduction: Africa in the perspective of political anthropology. In *The Transformation of East Africa: Studies in Political Anthropology*, edited by Stanley Diamond and Fred Burke. New York: Basic Books.
  1970. Un Ethnocide. *Les Temps Modernes*, vol. 238.
  1974. *In Search of the Primitive: A Critique of Civilization.* New Brunswick, N.J.: E. P. Dutton–Transaction.
  1975. The Marxist tradition as dialectical anthropology. *Dialectical Anthropology* 1(1): 1–5.
  1979. *Toward a Marxist Anthropology.* The Hague: Mouton.
Diener, Paul, Eugene Robkin, and Donald Nonini
  1978. The dialectics of the sacred cow in India. *Dialectical Anthropology* 3(3): 221–241.

Dillon, Peter
> 1829. *Narrative of the Discovery of the Fate of La Pérouse (1813, 1827)*. 2 vols. London: Hurst, Chance and Co.

Divale, William, and Marvin Harris
> 1976. Population, warfare and the male supremacist complex. *American Anthropologist* 78(3): 521–538.

Douglas, Mary
> 1966. *Purity and Danger*. London: Routledge and Kegan Paul.
> 1973. *Natural Symbols*. New York: Random House.

Dumont d'Urville, J. S. C.
> 1834. *Voyage . . . de la Corvette l'Astrolabe*. 4 vols. Paris: Ministère de la Marine.

Durkheim, Emile
> 1964. *The Division of Labor in Society*. New York: Free Press.

Edholm, Felicity, Olivia Harris, and Kate Young
> 1977. Conceptualising women. *Critique of Anthropology* 3(9–10): 101–130.

Edwards, Cpt. Edward, and George Hamilton
> 1915. *Voyage of H.M.S. "Pandora."* London: Francis Edwards.

Egan, Fred
> 1965. Comparative method in anthropology. In *Context and Meaning in Cultural Anthropology*, edited by Melford Spiro, pp. 357–372. New York: Free Press.

Elkin, A. P.
> 1948. Review of Beaglehole and Beaglehole, Pangai. *Oceania* 18(4): 359–360.

Engels, Frederick
> 1884/1972. *The Origins of the Family, Private Property and the State*. Edited by Eleanor B. Leacock. New York: International Books.

Erskine, Cpt. John E.
> 1853/1967. *Journal of a Cruise among the Islands of the Western Pacific*. London: Dawsons.

Etienne, Mona
> 1979. The case for social maternity: Adoption of children by urban Baulé women. *Dialectical Anthropology* 4: 237–242.
> 1980. Women and men, cloth and colonization. In *Women and Colonization*, edited by Mona Etienne and Eleanor Leacock, pp. 214–238. New York: J. F. Bergin/Praeger.

Etienne, Mona, and Eleanor Leacock
> 1980. Introduction. In *Women and Colonization*, edited by idem. New York: J. F. Bergin/Praeger.
> ———, eds. *Women and Colonization*. New York: J. F. Bergin/Praeger.

Fairbairn, I. J.
> 1971. Pacific island economies. *Journal of the Polynesian Society* 80: 74–118.

Fanning, Edmund

1838. *Voyages to the South Seas, Indian and Pacific Oceans.* New York: William Vermilye.

1924. *Voyages and Discoveries in the South Seas, 1792–1832.* Salem, Mass.: Marine Research Society.

Fanon, Frantz

1967. *Black Skin, White Masks.* New York: Grove.

Farmer, Sarah Stock

1855. *Tonga and the Friendly Islands, with a Sketch of Their Mission History.* London: Hamilton Adams.

Firestone, Shulamith

1971. *The Dialectic of Sex.* New York: Bantam.

Firth, Raymond

1936. *We, the Tikopia.* London: Allen and Unwin.

1959a. *Economics of the New Zealand Maori.* Wellington: Owen.

1959b. *Social Change in Tikopia.* New York: Macmillan.

1965. *Primitive Polynesian Economy.* London: Routledge.

1967. Themes in economic anthropology: A general comment. In *Themes in Economic Anthropology,* edited by idem, pp. 1–28. London: Tavistock.

1968. A note on descent groups in Polynesia. In *Kinship and Social Organization,* edited by Paul Bohannan and John Middleton, pp. 213–224. Garden City, N.Y.: Natural History Press.

Fison, Lorimer

1907. *Tales from Old Fiji.* London: De La More.

Flores, Toni

1978. Undefining art. *Dialectical Anthropology* 3(2): 129–138.

Fonua, Pesi, and Mary Fonua

1981. *A Walking Tour of Neiafu, Vava'u.* Neiafu, Tonga: Vava'u Press, Ltd.

Foreign Office Papers

1872. *The Deportation of South Sea Islanders.* London: William Clowes and Sons.

1873. *Polynesian Labourers: Correspondence Relative to the Introduction of Polynesian Labourers into Queensland.* London: William Clowes and Sons.

1883. *Correspondence respecting the Natives of the Western Pacific and the Labour Traffic.* London: George Eyre and William Spottiswoode.

Forman, Charles W.

1978. Tonga's tortured venture in church unity. *Journal of Pacific History* 13(1): 3–21.

Fortune, Reo

1963. *Sorcerers of Dobu.* New York: E. P. Dutton.

Freeman, Derek

1984. *Margaret Mead and Samoa.* Cambridge, Mass.: Harvard University Press.

Freeman, J. D.
  1968. On the concept of the kindred. In *Kinship and Social Organiza-tion*, edited by Paul Bohannan and John Middleton, pp. 253–272. Garden City, N.Y.: Natural History Press.
Fried, Morton
  1957. The classification of corporate unilineal descent groups. *Journal of the Royal Anthropological Institute* 87:1–29.
  1960. On the evolution of social stratification and the state. In *Culture in History: Essays in Honor of Paul Radin*, edited by Stanley Diamond, pp. 713–731. New York: Columbia University Press.
  1967. *The Evolution of Political Society.* New York: Random House.
  1975. *The Notion of Tribe.* Menlo Park, Calif.: Cummings.
Friedl, Ernestine
  1978. Society and sex roles. *Human Nature* (April).
Friedman, Jonathan
  1974. Marxism, structuralism and vulgar materialism. *Man* 9(3): 444–469.
  1975. Tribes, states and transformations. In *Marxist Analyses and Social Anthropology*, edited by Maurice Bloch, pp. 161–202. ASA Studies No. 3. New York: Halsted.
Fusitu'a, 'Eseta, and Noel Rutherford
  1977. George Tupou II and the British Protectorate. In *Friendly Islands*, edited by Noel Rutherford, pp. 173–189. Melbourne: Oxford University Press.
Gailey, Christine Ward
  1980. Putting down sisters and wives: Tongan women and colonization. In *Women and Colonization*, edited by Mona Etienne and Eleanor Leacock, pp. 294–322. New York: J. F. Bergin/Praeger.
  1981. *"Our History Is Written . . . in Our Mats": State Formation and the Status of Women in Tonga.* Ann Arbor: University Microfilms.
  1983. Categories without culture: Structuralism, ethnohistory and ethnocide. *Dialectical Anthropology* 8(4):241–250.
  1984. Women and warfare: Shifting status in precapitalist state formation. *Culture* 4(1):61–70.
  1985a. The state of the state in anthropology. *Dialectical Anthropology* 9(1–2):65–89.
  1985b. The kindness of strangers. *Culture* 5(2):3–16.
  1987. Evolutionary perspectives on gender hierarchy. In *Analyzing Gender*, edited by Beth Hess and Myra Ferree. Beverly Hills, Calif.: Sage.
Gailey, Christine Ward, and Thomas Patterson
  In press State formation and uneven development. In *State and Society*, edited by Barbara Bender, John Gledhill, and Mogens Larsen. London: Allen and Unwin.
Geertz, Clifford
  1980. *Negara: The Theatre-State in 19th Century Bali.* Princeton, N.J.: Princeton University Press.

Gerstle, Donna, and Helen Raitt
1974. *Tongan Pictorial/Kupesi 'O Tonga*. San Diego, Calif.: Tofua Press.
Geschiere, Peter
1982. *Village Communities and the State*. London: Routledge and Kegan Paul.
Gifford, Edward Winslow
1923. *Tongan Place Names*. Honolulu: B. P. Bishop Museum Press.
1924a. *Tongan Myths and Tales*. Honolulu: B. P. Bishop Museum.
1924b. Euro-American acculturation in Tonga. *Journal of the Polynesian Society* 33:281–292.
1929. *Tongan Society*. Honolulu: B. P. Bishop Museum.
Gill, Rev. William W.
1876. *Myths and Songs from the South Pacific*. London: Henry S. King.
Gluckman, Max
1963. *Order and Rebellion in Tribal Africa*. New York: Free Press.
Godelier, Maurice
1964. Economie politique et anthropologie économique. *L'Homme* 4(3): 118–132.
1977. *Perspectives in Marxist Anthropology*. Cambridge: Cambridge University Press.
1979. The appropriation of nature. *Critique of Anthropology* 4(13–14): 17–27.
1980. Processes of the formation, diversity and bases of the state. *International Social Sciences Journal* 32(4):609–623.
Goldman, Irving
1970. *Ancient Polynesian Society*. Chicago: University of Chicago Press.
Goodale, Jane
1971. *Tiwi Wives*. Seattle: University of Washington Press.
Goodenough, Ward
1968. A problem in Malayo-Polynesian social organization. In *Kinship and Social Organization*, edited by P. Bohannan and J. Middleton, pp. 195–212. Garden City, N.Y.: Natural History Press.
Goody, Jack
1966. Introduction. In *Succession to High Office*, edited by idem, pp. 1–56. Cambridge: Cambridge University Press.
1971. *Technology, Tradition and the State in Africa*. London: Oxford University Press.
1976. *Production and Reproduction in Society*. London: Cambridge University Press.
Goody, Jack, and S. J. Tambiah
1973. *Bridewealth and Dowry*. Cambridge Papers in Social Anthropology No. 7. Cambridge: Cambridge University Press.
Gough, Kathleen
1968. The Nayars and the definition of marriage. In *Marriage, Family and Residence*, edited by Paul Bohannan and John Middleton, pp. 49–73. Garden City, N.Y.: Natural History Press.
1971. Nuer kinship: A re-examination. In *The Translation of Culture*,

edited by Thomas Beidelman, pp. 79–122. London: Tavistock.

Government of Tonga (*see also* N. Horne 1929; Tukuaho and Thomson 1891)

    1907. *The Law of the Government of Tonga*. Auckland, New Zealand: Brett Printing Co.

    1967. *The Law of Tonga, Revised Edition*. Edited by Sir Cambell Wylie. 3 vols. London: Sweet and Maxwell; Nuku'alofa: Government Printer.

    1973. *Lands and Survey Report*. Nuku'alofa: Government Printer.

Gramsci, Antonio

    1971. *Selections from the Prison Notebooks of Antonio Gramsci*, edited and translated by Quentin Hoare and G. N. Smith. London: Lawrence and Wishart.

Grattan, C. Hartley

    1961. *The United States and the Southwest Pacific*. Cambridge, Mass.: Harvard University Press.

    1963. *The Southwest Pacific to 1900*. Ann Arbor: University of Michigan Press.

Griffin, John

    1822. *Memoirs of Captain James Wilson*. Boston: Armstrong.

Grosvenor, Melville, and E. S. Grosvenor

    1968. South Seas' Tonga hails a king. *National Geographic* 133(3): 322–344.

Habermas, Jürgen

    1975. Toward a reconstruction of historical materialism. *Theory and Society* 2(3):287–300.

Harris, Marvin

    1974. *Cows, Pigs, Wars and Witches*. New York: Random House.

    1977. Why men dominate women. *New York Times Magazine*, November 13.

Hart, C. W., and A. R. Pilling

    1960. *The Tiwi of Northern Australia*. New York: Holt.

Hervier, R. P. Jean

    1902. L'archipel des Iles Tonga. In *Les Missions catholiques françaises aux XIXᵉ siècle*, edited by Père J.-B. Piolet, pp. 125–148. Paris: Armand Colin.

Hindess, Barry, and Paul Hirst

    1975. *Precapitalist Modes of Production*. London: Routledge and Kegan Paul.

Hinton, William

    1966. *Fanshen: A Documentary of Revolution in a Chinese Village*. New York: Random House/Vintage.

Hobbes, Thomas

    1651/1958. *Leviathan, Parts I and II*. Indianapolis: Bobbs-Merrill.

Hobsbawm, Eric

    1959. *Primitive Rebels*. New York: Norton.

1964. Introduction. In *Pre-Capitalist Economic Formations*, by Karl Marx, edited by Eric Hobsbawm. New York: International Publishers.

Hocart, A. M.
1915. Chieftainship and the sister's son in the Pacific. *American Anthropologist* 17:631–646.

Hogbin, H. Ian
1934. *Law and Order in Polynesia*. London: Christophers.
1970. *An Experiment in Civilization*. New York: Schocken.

Hogbin, H. Ian, and L. R. Hiatt, eds.
1963. *Readings in Australian and Pacific Anthropology*. Melbourne: Melbourne University Press.

Horne, C. Silvester
1904. *The Story of the L.M.S.* London: London Missionary Society.

Horne, William K.
1929. *Revised Edition of the Law of Tonga*. Nuku'alofa: Government Printing Office.

Huizer, Gerritt
1970. Resistance to change and radical peasant mobilization. *Human Organization* 29(4):303–313.

Im Thurn, Everard
1905. *Report on Tongan Affairs (December 1904–January 1905)*. Suva, Fiji: Edward John March, Government Printer.

Kaberry, Phyllis
1939. *Aboriginal Woman: Sacred and Profane*. London: Routledge and Kegan Paul.

Kaeppler, Adrienne
1971. Rank in Tonga. *Ethnology* 10:174–193.

Kahn, Joel
1980. *Minangkabau Social Formations: Indonesian Peasants and the World Economy*. Cambridge: Cambridge University Press.

Kelly, J. L.
1885. *South Sea Islands: Possibilities of Trade*. Auckland.

Khaldun, Ibn
1377/1958. *An Introduction to History*. Translated by Franz Rosenthal. 3 vols. New York: Pantheon.

Kirchhoff, Paul
1959. Principles of clanship in human society. In *Readings in Anthropology*, vol. 2, edited by Morton Fried, pp. 259–270. New York: Crowell.

Kohl, Philip, and Rita Wright
1977. Stateless cities: The differentiation of societies in the Near Eastern Neolithic. *Dialectical Anthropology* 2(4):271–284.

Kooijman, Simon
1972. Tonga. In *Tapa in Polynesia*, pp. 297–341. Honolulu: B. P. Bishop Museum Press.

Korn, Shulamit Decktor
  1974. Tongan kin groups: The noble and the common view. *Journal of the Polynesian Society* 83: 5–13.
  1978. After the missionaries came: Denominational diversity in the Tongan Islands. In *Mission, Church, and Sect in Oceania*, edited by James Boutilier, D. T. Hughes, and Sharon Tiffany, pp. 395–422. Ann Arbor: University of Michigan Press.
Krader, Lawrence
  1968. *State Formation*. Englewood Cliffs, N.J.: Prentice-Hall.
  1975. *The Asiatic Mode of Production*. Assen, Netherlands: Vangorcum.
  1978. The origin of the state among the nomads of Asia. In *The Early State*, edited by H. J. M. Claessen and Peter Skalník. The Hague: Mouton.
Krämer, Augustin
  1902. *Die Samoa-Inseln*. 2 vols. Stuttgart: E. Nagele.
Kreniske, John
  1984. Sociobiology: The Runcible Science. Ph.D. dissertation, Columbia University.
Krige, Eileen Jenson, and J. D. Krige
  1943. *The Realm of a Rain Queen*. London: Oxford University Press.
Labilliardière, Jacques Julien Houtou de
  1797. *Relation du voyage . . . La Pérouse*. 2 vols. Paris.
  1800. *Voyage in Search of La Pérouse, 1791–1794*. London: John Stockdale.
Laclau, Ernesto.
  1971. Feudalism and capitalism in Latin America. *New Left Review*, vol. 71.
Lamphere, Louise
  1974. Strategies, cooperation, and conflict among women in domestic groups. In *Women, Culture and Society*, edited by Michelle Rosaldo and Louise Lamphere, pp. 97–112. Stanford: Stanford University Press.
Landes, Ruth
  1971. *The Ojibwa Woman*. New York: Norton.
Lappé, Frances, and Joseph Collins
  1977. *Food First: Beyond the Myth of Scarcity*. New York: Random House.
Lattimore, Owen
  1937/1962. Origins of the Great Wall of China. In *Studies in Frontier History*, edited by idem, pp. 97–118. London: Oxford University Press.
Lātūkefu, Sione
  1968. Oral traditions. *Journal of Pacific History* 3: 135–143.
  1974. *Church and State in Tonga*. Canberra: Australian National University Press.
  1977. The Wesleyan mission. In *Friendly Islands*, edited by Noel Rutherford, pp. 114–135. Melbourne: Oxford University Press.

Laughlin, William
 1968. Hunting: An integrating biobehavioral system and its evolutionary importance. In *Man the Hunter*, edited by Richard Lee and Irven DeVore, pp. 304–320. Chicago: Aldine.
Lawry, Rev. Walter
 1850. *Friendly and Feejee Islands: A Missionary Visit*. London: Elijah Hoole.
 1851. *A Second Missionary Visit*. London.
 1852. *Missions in the Tonga and Feejee Islands*, edited by Daniel Kidder. New York: Lane and Scott.
Leach, Edmund R.
 1951. The structural implications of matrilateral cross-cousin marriage. *Journal of the Royal Anthropological Institute* 81:23–55.
 1954. *Political Systems of Highland Burma*. Boston: Beacon.
 1966. The structural implications of cross-cousin marriage. In idem, *Rethinking Anthropology*, pp. 54–104. New York: Humanities Press.
Leacock, Eleanor Burke
 1954. *The Montagnais "Hunting Territory" and the Fur Trade*. American Anthropological Association Memoir 78.
 1972. Introduction. In *The Origin of the Family, Private Property and the State*, by Frederick Engels, edited by Eleanor B. Leacock, pp. 7–67. New York: International Publishers.
 1977. The changing family and Lévi-Strauss, or whatever happened to fathers? *Social Research* 44(2):235–259.
 1978. Women's status in egalitarian society: Implications for social evolution. *Current Anthropology* 19(2):247–275.
 1979. Class, commodity and the status of women. In *Toward a Marxist Anthropology*, edited by Stanley Diamond, pp. 185–199. The Hague: Mouton.
 1981. *Myths of Male Dominance*. New York: Monthly Review.
 1983. The origins of gender inequality: Conceptual and historical problems. *Dialectical Anthropology* 7(4):263–284.
Leacock, Eleanor B., and Richard Lee, eds.
 1982. *Politics and History in Band Societies*. Cambridge: Cambridge University Press.
Leacock, Eleanor, and June Nash
 1977. *Ideology of Sex: Archetypes and Stereotypes*. Annals, New York Academy of Sciences, vol. 285.
Leakey, Richard, and Roger Lewin
 1977. Is it our culture, not our genes, that makes us killers? *Smithsonian* (November).
Ledyard, Patricia
 1956. *A Tale of the Friendly Islands*. New York: Appleton-Century-Crofts.
Lee, Richard
 1982. Politics, sexual and non-sexual, in an egalitarian society. In *Politics*

and *History in Band Societies*, edited by Eleanor B. Leacock and Richard Lee, pp. 37–60. Cambridge: Cambridge University Press.

Lee, Richard, and Irven DeVore, eds.
1968. *Man the Hunter*. Chicago: Aldine.

Leibowitz, Lila
1975. Perspectives on the evolution of sex differences. In *Toward an Anthropology of Women*, edited by Rayna Rapp Reiter, pp. 20–35. New York: Monthly Review.

Lerner, Gerda
1986. *The Origin of Patriarchy*. New York: Oxford University Press.

Levine, Andrew
1981. Althusser's Marxism. *Economy and Society* 10(3): 243–283.

Lévi-Strauss, Claude
1966. *The Savage Mind*. Chicago: University of Chicago Press.
1969. *The Elementary Structures of Kinship*. Translated by James Bell and John Von Sturmer. Edited by Rodney Needham. Boston: Beacon.
1979. *The Origin of Table Manners*. Translated by John and Doreen Weightman. New York: Harper and Row.

Linton, Sally
1971. Woman the gatherer: Male bias in anthropology. In *Women in Perspective*, edited by Sue-Ellen Jacobs. Urbana: University of Illinois Press.

Lips, Julius
1966. *The Savage Strikes Back*. New Hyde Park, N.Y.: University Books.

Lonsdale, John
1981. The state and social processes in Africa. *African Studies Review* 24(2–3): 139–225.

Lowie, Robert Harry
1927. *The Origin of the State*. New York: Harcourt, Brace and World.

Luke, Sir Harry
1945. *From a South Seas Diary, 1938–1942*. London: Nicholson and Watson.

MacKinnon, Catharine
1982. Feminism, Marxism, method and the state: Part 1. *Signs* 7(3): 515–544.
1983. Feminism, Marxism, method and the state: Part 2. *Signs* 8(4): 635–658.

McNickle, D'Arcy
1973. *North American Tribalism*. New York: Oxford University Press.

Maine, Sir Henry
1861/1963. *Ancient Law*. Boston: Beacon.
1872. *Village Communities, East and West*. London: John Murray.

Malia, Soane, and Joseph-Félix Blanc
1934. *A History of Tonga or Friendly Islands*. Translated by C. S. Ramsey. Vista, Calif.: Vista Press.

Malinowski, Bronislaw
1961. *Argonauts of the Western Pacific*. New York: E. P. Dutton.

Malo, David
  1951. *Hawaiian Antiquities*. Honolulu: B. P. Bishop Museum.
Mander, Linden
  1954. *Some Dependent Peoples of the South Pacific*. New York: Macmillan.
Marcus, George
  1977a. Succession disputes and the position of the nobility in modern Tonga. *Oceania* 47(3):220–241; 47(4):284–299.
  1977b. Contemporary Tonga—the background of social and cultural change. In *Friendly Islands*, edited by Noel Rutherford, pp. 210–227. Melbourne: Oxford University Press.
  1980. The Nobility and the Chiefly Tradition in Modern Tonga. Honolulu: University of Hawaii Press for the Polynesian Society.
Marden, Luis
  1968. The friendly isles of Tonga. *National Geographic* 133(3):345–367.
Maretina, Sofia
  1978. The Kachari state. In *The Early State*, edited by H. J. M. Claessen and Peter Skalník, pp. 339–358. The Hague: Mouton.
Mariner, William
  1827. *An Account of the Natives of the Tongan Islands*. Edited by Dr. John Martin. 2 vols. Edinburgh: John Constable.
Marx, Karl
  1852/1972. *The Eighteenth Brumaire of Louis Bonaparte*. New York: International Publishers.
  1858/1964. *Pre-Capitalist Economic Formations*. Edited by Eric Hobsbawm. New York: International Publishers.
  1881/1967. *Capital*. 3 vols. New York: International Publishers.
  1881/1974. *The Ethnological Notebooks*. Edited by Lawrence Krader. Assen, Netherlands: Vangorcum.
Maude, Alaric
  1971. Tonga: Equality overtaking privilege. In *Land Tenure in the Pacific*, edited by Ronald G. Crocombe, pp. 106–127. Melbourne: Oxford University Press.
Maudslay, Alfred P.
  1878/1930. *Life in the Pacific Fifty Years Ago*. London: G. Routledge and Sons.
Mauss, Marcel
  1967. *The Gift: Forms and Functions of Exchange in Archaic Societies*. New York: Norton.
Mead, Margaret
  1928/1973. *Coming of Age in Samoa*. New York: Museum of Natural History/William Morrow.
Meigs, Anna
  1976. Male pregnancy and the reduction of sexual opposition in a New Guinea Highlands Society. *Ethnology* 15(4):393–408.
Meillassoux, Claude
  1960. Essai d'interprétation du phénomène économique dans les sociétés

traditionelles d'autosubsistence. *Cahiers d'Etudes Africaines* 4:38–67.

1972. From production to reproduction. *Economy and Society* 1(1): 93–105.

1975. *Femmes, greniers et capitaux*. Paris: Maspéro.

1979. The historical modalities of the exploitation and over-exploitation of labour. *Critique of Anthropology* 4(13–14):7–27.

Melville, Herman

1846/1964. *Typee: A Peep at Polynesian Life*. New York: New American Library.

Memmi, Alfred

1967. *The Colonizer and the Colonized*. Boston: Beacon.

Mintz, Sydney

1977. The so-called world system: Local initiative and local response. *Dialectical Anthropology* 2:253–270.

Missionary Voyage

1799. *A Missionary Voyage to the South Pacific Ocean Performed in the Years 1796, 1797, 1798 in the Ship "Duff" Commanded by Captain James Wilson*. London: Chapman.

Monfat, A.

1893. *Les Tonga*. Lyon: Emmanuel Vitte.

Montagu, Ashley

1980. *Sociobiology Examined*. Oxford: Oxford University Press.

Montaigne, Michel de

1580/1946. *The Essays*. Translated by George Ives. New York: Heritage.

Morgan, Lewis Henry

1877/1964. *Ancient Society*. Cambridge, Mass.: Harvard University Press.

Morrell, W. P.

1946. The transition to Christianity in the South Pacific. *Transactions of the Royal Historical Society* 28:101–120.

1960. *Britain in the Pacific Islands*. Oxford: Clarendon.

Mosley, Henry N.

1879. *Notes by a Naturalist on the "Challenger," 1872–1876*. London: John Murray.

Moulton, Rev. James Egan

1921. *Moulton of Tonga*. London: Epworth.

Muller, Jean-Claude

1980. On the relevance of having two husbands: Polygynous/polyandrous marriage forms of the Jos plateau. *Journal of Comparative Family Studies* 11(3):359–369.

Muller, Viana

1977. The formation of the state and the oppression of women: A case study in England and Wales. *Review of Radical Political Economics* 9(3):7–21.

1979. The revolutionary fate of the peasantry. *Dialectical Anthropology* 4:225–235.

1985. Origins of class and gender stratification in northwest Europe. *Dialectical Anthropology* 10(1–2):93–106.

Murdock, George P.
1968. Cognatic forms of social organization. In *Kinship and Social Organization*, edited by Paul Bohannan, and John Middleton, pp. 233–253. Garden City, N.Y.: Natural History Press.

Murra, John
1962. Cloth and its function in the Inca state. *American Anthropologist* 64(4):710–728.

Naval Staff, Naval Intelligence Division, Great Britain
1944. *Pacific Islands*, vol. 3, *Western Pacific*. London: H.M. Stationery Office.

Neill, James Scott
1955. *Ten Years in Tonga*. London: Hutchinson.

Nonini, Donald
1985. Varieties of materialism. *Dialectical Anthropology* 9(1–4):7–64.

Oakley, Ann
1972. *Sex, Gender and Society*. New York: Harper and Row.

Oliver, Douglas
1961. *The Pacific Islands*. New York: Doubleday.

Orange, Rev. James
1840. *Life of the Late George Vason of Nottingham*. Derby: Henry Mozley and Sons.

Ortner, Sherry
1974. Is female to male as nature is to culture? In *Women, Culture and Society*, edited by Michelle Rosaldo and Louise Lamphere, pp. 67–88. Stanford: Stanford University Press.
1978. The virgin and the state. *Feminist Studies* 4(3):19–36.
1981. Gender and sexuality in hierarchical societies. In *Sexual Meanings*, edited by Sherry Ortner and Harriet Whitehead, pp. 359–409. New York: Cambridge University Press.

Parrish, Timothy C.
1984. *Agrarian Politics and Regional Class Formation: La Rioja, Spain, 1860–1975*. Ann Arbor: University Microfilms.

Patterson, Thomas C.
1985. The first fifty years. *American Anthropologist* 88:7–26.

Paulmé, Denise, ed.
1971. *Women of Tropical Africa*. Berkeley: University of California Press.

Poewe, Karla
1978. Matriliny and capitalism: The development of incipient classes in Luapula, Zambia. *Dialectical Anthropology* 3(4):331–348.
1980. Universal male dominance: An ethnological illusion. *Dialectical Anthropology* 5:110–125.

Polanyi, Karl
1957/1968. The semantics of money-uses. In *Primitive, Archaic and*

Modern Economies: Essays of Karl Polanyi, edited by George Dalton. New York: Doubleday.

1968. *Primitive, Archaic and Modern Economies*, edited by George Dalton. New York: Doubleday.

Polanyi, Karl, Conrad Arensberg, and Harry Pearson, eds.

1971. *Trade and Market in the Early Empires*. Chicago: Henry Regnery.

Pomeroy, Sarah

1976. *Goddesses, Whores, Wives and Slaves*. New York: Schocken.

Potash, Betty

1986. Introduction. In *Widows in African Societies*. Stanford: Stanford University Press.

Poulantzas, Nicos

1975. *Political Power and Social Classes*. Translated by T. O'Hagan. London: New Left Books.

Radin, Paul

1971. *The World of Primitive Man*. New York: E. P. Dutton.

1973. *The Trickster*. New York: Schocken.

Ralston, Caroline

1978. *Grass Huts and Warehouses: Pacific Beach Communities of the Nineteenth Century*. Honolulu: University Press of Hawaii.

Rapp, Rayna

1978a. Gender and class: An archaeology of knowledge concerning the origin of the state. *Dialectical Anthropology* 2(4): 309–316.

1978b. Review of Claude Meillassoux, *Femmes, greniers et capitaux*. *Dialectical Anthropology* 2(4): 317–324.

Redfield, Robert

1971. *The Little Community and Peasant Society and Culture*. Chicago: University of Chicago Press.

Reeves, Edward

1898. *Brown Men and Women, or, The South Sea Islands in 1895 and 1896*. London: Swan Sonnenschein.

Reiter, Rayna Rapp, ed.

1975. *Toward an Anthropology of Women*. New York: Monthly Review.

Report to the House of Lords

1873. South Sea Islands: Outrages on Natives. Folio 14804. Foreign and Commonwealth Office Library, London.

Rey, Pierre Philippe

1973. *Les Alliances des classes*. Paris: Maspéro.

1979. Class contradiction in lineage societies. *Critique of Anthropology* 4(13–14): 41–60.

Ribeiro, Darcy

1968. *The Civilizational Process*. Washington, D.C.: Smithsonian Institute.

Rickman, John

1781/1966. *Journal of Captain Cook's Last Voyage to the Pacific Ocean*. Readex Microprint.

Rigby, Peter
   1983. Time and historical consciousness: The case of Ilparakuyo Maasai. *Comparative Studies in Society and History* 25(3):428–456.
Rohrlich, Ruby
   1980. State formation in Sumer and the subjugation of women. *Feminist Studies* 6(1):76–102.
Rohrlich-Leavitt, Ruby, Barbara Sykes, and Elizabeth Weatherford
   1975. Aboriginal woman: Male and female perspectives. In *Toward an Anthropology of Women*, edited by Rayna Rapp Reiter, pp. 110–126. New York: Monthly Review.
Rosaldo, Michelle
   1974. Women, culture and society: A theoretical overview. In *Women, Culture and Society*, edited by Michelle Rosaldo and Louise Lamphere, pp. 17–42. Stanford: Stanford University Press.
Rosaldo, Michelle, and Louise Lamphere, eds.
   1974. *Women, Culture and Society*. Stanford: Stanford University Press.
Roseberry, William
   1978a. Peasants as proletarians. *Critique of Anthropology* 3(11):3–18.
   1978b. Peasants in primitive accumulation. *Dialectical Anthropology* 3(3):243–260.
Rousseau, Jean-Jacques
   1754, 1762/1950. *The Social Contract and Discourses*. Translated by G. D. H. Cole. New York: E. P. Dutton.
Rousseau, Jérome
   1978. On estates and castes. *Dialectical Anthropology* 3(1):85–96.
Rubin, Gayle
   1975. The traffic in women. In *Toward an Anthropology of Women*, edited by Rayna Rapp Reiter, pp. 157–210. New York: Monthly Review.
Ruhen, Olaf
   1966. *Harpoon in My Hand*. Sydney: Angus and Robertson.
Russell, Rt. Rev. M.
   1845. *Polynesia*. Edinburgh: Oliver and Boyd.
Rutherford, Noel
   1971. *Shirley Baker and the King of Tonga*. Melbourne: Oxford University Press.
   1977. George Tupou I and Shirley Baker. In *Friendly Islands*, edited by idem, pp. 154–172. Melbourne: Oxford University Press.
Sacks, Karen
   1975. Engels revisited. In *Toward an Anthropology of Women*, edited by Rayna Rapp Reiter, pp. 211–234. New York: Monthly Review.
   1976. State bias and women's status. *American Anthropologist* 78:565–569.
   1979. *Sisters and Wives*. Westport, Conn.: Greenwood.
Sahlins, Marshall
   1958. *Social Stratification in Polynesia*. Seattle: University of Washington Press.

1963. Poor man, rich man, big-man, chief: Political types in Melanesia and Polynesia. *Comparative Studies in Society and History* 5(3): 285–303.

1972. *Stone Age Economics*. Chicago: Aldine.

1976. *Culture and Practical Reason*. Chicago: University of Chicago Press.

1981. *Historical Metaphors and Mythical Realities*. Ann Arbor: University of Michigan Press.

St. Julian, Charles

1857. *Official Report on Central Polynesia*. Sydney: Fairfax and Sons.

Scarr, Derek

1967. *Fragments of Empire: A History of the Western Pacific High Commission, 1877–1914*. Canberra: Australian National University Press.

Schneider, Thomas

1977. *Functional Tongan-English, English-Tongan Dictionary*. Suva, Fiji: Oceania Printers.

Scott, James

1985. *Weapons of the Weak*. New Haven: Yale University Press.

Seaton, S. Lee, and H. J. M. Claessen, eds.

1979. *Political Anthropology: The State of the Art*. The Hague: Mouton.

Seddon, R. J.

1900. *Visit to Tonga, Fiji, Savage Island, and the Cook Islands, May 1900*. Wellington, New Zealand: John Mackay, Government Printer.

Seed, W.

1874. Area, population, trade, etc., of the principal groups of islands. In *Papers Relating to the South Seas Islands, Part 2*, p. 3. Wellington, New Zealand: George Didsbury, Government Printer.

Servet, Jean-Michel

1982. Primitive order and archaic trade: Part 2. *Economy and Society* 11(1):22–59.

Service, Elman

1971. *Cultural Evolutionism*. New York: Holt, Rinehart and Winston.

1975. *Origins of the State and Civilization*. New York: Norton.

Service, Elman, and Marshall Sahlins, eds.

1960. *Evolution and Culture*. Ann Arbor: University of Michigan Press.

Shadbolt, Maurice, and Olaf Ruhen

1968. *Isles of the South Pacific*. Washington, D.C.: National Geographic Society Special Publication.

Sharp, Andrew

1968. *The Voyages of Abel Janszoon Tasman*. Oxford: Clarendon.

Sharp, Nonie

1976. Nationalism and cultural politics. *Arena* 43.

Shephard, C. Y.

1945. Tonga. *Tropical Agriculture* 22(9):160–163. Port-of-Spain, Trinidad: Government Printer.

Shostak, Marjorie
1981. *Nisa*. Cambridge, Mass.: Harvard University Press.
Shumway, Eric
1971. *An Intensive Course in Tongan*. Honolulu: University of Hawaii Press.
Shutz, Albert J., ed.
1977. *The Diaries and Correspondence of David Cargill, 1832–1843*. Canberra: Australian National University Press.
Sider, Gerald
1976. Lumbee Indian cultural nationalism and ethnogenesis. *Dialectical Anthropology* 1(2): 161–172.
Silverblatt, Irene
1978. Andean women in the Inca empire. *Feminist Studies* 4(3): 37–61.
1980. "The Universe has turned inside out . . . there is no justice for us here": Andean women under Spanish rule. In *Women and Colonization*, edited by Mona Etienne and Eleanor Leacock, pp. 149–185. New York: J. F. Bergin/Praeger.
1987. *Sun, Moon and Witches*. Princeton, N.J.: Princeton University Press.
Siskind, Janet
1973. *To Hunt in the Morning*. London: Oxford University Press.
Skalník, Peter
1979. The dynamics of early state development in the Voltaic area. In *Political Anthropology: The State of the Art*, edited by S. Lee Seaton and H. J. M. Claessen, pp. 197–214. The Hague: Mouton.
1981. Some additional thoughts on the concept of the early state. In *The Study of the State*, edited by H. J. M. Claessen and Peter Skalník, pp. 339–352. The Hague: Mouton.
Skinner, G. W.
1971. Chinese peasants and the closed community. *Comparative Studies in Society and History* 13(3): 270–281.
Small, Cathy
1985. The powers and limits of women's cooperative organizations in Tonga. Paper presented at the Association for Women and International Development Conference, "Women Creating Wealth," Washington, D.C.
Smith, Adam
1776/1937. *An Inquiry into the Nature and Causes of the Wealth of Nations*. Edited by Edwin Camon. New York: Modern Library.
Smith, M. G.
1960. *Government in Zazzau, 1800–1950*. London: Oxford University Press.
Somerville, Adm. H. B. T.
1936. *Will Mariner*. London: Faber and Faber.
Spencer, Herbert
1896/1967. *The Evolution of Society*. Edited by Robert Carneiro. Chicago: University of Chicago Press.

Stack, Carol
   1974. *All Our Kin*. New York: Harper and Row.
Sterndale, H. B.
   1874. Memoranda on some of the South Sea islands. In *Papers Relating to the South Sea Islands*, part 3, pp. 1–6. Wellington, New Zealand: George Didsbury, Government Printer.
Steward, Julian
   1972. *Theory of Culture Change*. Urbana: University of Illinois Press.
Strauss, W. P.
   1963. *Americans in Polynesia*. East Lansing: Michigan State University Press.
Sullivan, L. R.
   1921. A contribution to Tongan somatology. *B. P. Bishop Museum Memoirs* 8(4):234–260.
Susser, Ida
   1982. *Norman Street*. New York: Oxford University Press.
Szombati, Ilona, and Johannes Fabian
   1976. Art, history and society: Popular painting in Shaba, Zaire. *Studies in the Anthropology of Visual Communication* 3:1–21.
Tamahori, Maxine
   1963. Cultural Change in Tongan Bark-Cloth Manufacture. M.A. thesis, University of Auckland, New Zealand.
Terray, Emmanuel
   1972. *Marxism and "Primitive" Societies*. New York: Monthly Review.
   1979a. Long-distance trade and the formation of the state: The case of the Abron kingdom of Gyaman. In *Toward a Marxist Anthropology*, edited by Stanley Diamond, pp. 291–320. The Hague: Mouton.
   1979b. On exploitation: Elements of an autocritique. *Critique of Anthropology* 4(13–14):29–39.
Thapar, Romila
   1981. The state as empire. In *The Study of the State*, edited by H. J. M. Claessen and Peter Skalník, pp. 409–426. The Hague: Mouton.
Thompson, Edward P.
   1975. The grid of inheritance. In *Family and Inheritance: Rural Society in Western Europe, 1200–1800*, edited by Jack Goody, Joan Thirsk, and Edward P. Thompson, pp. 328–360. Cambridge: Cambridge University Press.
   1977. Folklore, anthropology and social history. *Indian Historical Review* 3:247–266.
   1979. *The Poverty of Theory and Other Essays*. New York: Monthly Review.
Thomson, Basil
   1902. *Savage Island*. London: John Murray.
   1904. *Diversions of a Prime Minister*. London: William Blackwood and Sons.

Thomson, George

　1949. *Studies in Ancient Greek Society: The Prehistoric Aegean*. London: Lawrence and Wishart.

　1955. *Studies in Ancient Greek Society*. London: Lawrence and Wishart.

Tiger, Lionel

　1969. *Men in Groups*. New York: Random House.

　1971. *The Imperial Animal*. New York: Holt, Rinehart and Winston.

Tremblay, Rev. Edward

　1954. *When You Go to Tonga*. Derby, N.Y.: Daughters of St. Paul.

Tukuaho, J. U., and Basil Thomson

　1891. *Criminal and Civil Code of the Kingdom of Tonga*. Auckland, New Zealand: Brett, for the Tongan Government.

Turnbull, Colin

　1962. *The Forest People*. New York: Simon and Schuster.

　1965. *Wayward Servants*. Garden City, N.Y.: Natural History Press.

Tyler, David B.

　1968. *The Wilkes Expedition*. Philadelphia: American Philosophical Society.

Tylor, Edward B.

　1888. On a method of investigating the development of institutions: Applied to the laws of marriage and descent. *Journal of the Anthropological Institute* 18:245–269.

　1904. *Anthropology: An Introduction to the Study of Man and Civilization*. New York: D. Appleton.

Urbanowicz, Charles

　1979. Change in rank and status in the Polynesian Kingdom of Tonga. In *Political Anthropology: The State of the Art*, edited by S. Lee Seaton and H. J. M. Claessen, pp. 225–242. The Hague: Mouton.

Valeri, Valerio

　1972. Le Fonctionnement du système des rangs à Hawaii. *L'Homme* 12(1):29–66.

Van Allen, Judith

　1972. "Sitting on a man": Colonization and the lost political institutions of Igbo women. *Canadian Journal of African Studies* 6:165–181.

Van Binsbergen, Wim, and Peter Geschiere, eds.

　1985. *Old Modes of Production and Capitalist Encroachment*. London: Routledge and Kegan Paul.

van Teeffelen, T.

　1978. The Manchester School in Africa and Israel. *Dialectical Anthropology* 3(1):67–84.

Vason, George

　1810. *An Authentic Narrative of Four Years of Tongatapu*. London: Longman, Hurst, Rees and Orme.

Ve'ehala and Tupou Posesi Fanua

　1977. Oral tradition and prehistory. In *Friendly Islands*, edited by Noel Rutherford, pp. 27–38. Melbourne: Oxford University Press.

314 References

Wallace, Anthony
   1965. Driving to work. In *Context and Meaning in Cultural Anthropology*, edited by Melford Spiro, pp. 277–292. New York: Free Press.
Ward, John M.
   1948. *British Policy in the South Pacific*. Sydney: Australasian Publishing Co.
Washburn, Sherwood, and C. S. Lancaster
   1968. The evolution of hunting. In *Man the Hunter*, edited by Richard Lee and Irven DeVore, pp. 293–303. Chicago: Aldine.
Webb, Malcolm
   1965. The abolition of the taboo system in Hawaii. *Journal of the Polynesian Society* 74(1):21–39.
Weiner, Annette B.
   1976. *Women of Value, Men of Renown: New Perspectives in Trobriand Exchange*. Austin: University of Texas Press.
   1978. The reproductive model in Trobriand society. *Mankind* 11:175–186.
   1979. A fine mat is a fine mat is a fine mat: Reproduction, regeneration, and replacement in the Pacific. Paper prepared for the Pacific Congress, Khabarovsk, U.S.S.R. (August–September 1979).
   1980. Stability in banana leaves: Colonization and women in Kiriwina, Trobriand Islands. In *Women and Colonization*, edited by Mona Etienne and Eleanor Leacock, pp. 270–293. New York: J. F. Bergin/Praeger.
West, Rev. Thomas
   1846/1865. *Ten Years in South-Central Polynesia*. London: James Nisbet.
White, Leslie
   1959. *The Evolution of Culture*. New York: McGraw-Hill.
Wickham, Chris
   1981. *Early Medieval Italy: Central Power and Local Society, 400–1000*. Totowa, N.J.: Barnes and Noble.
   1984. The other transition: From the ancient world to feudalism. *Past and Present* 104(May):1–36.
Wilkes, Charles
   1852. *The United States Exploring Expedition during the Years 1838, 1839, 1840–1842*. 2 vols. London: Ingram, Cooke and Co.
Willey, Gordon R., and Demitri Shimkin
   1973. The Maya collapse. In *The Classic Maya Collapse*, edited by T. Patrick Culbert, pp. 457–492. Albuquerque: University of New Mexico Press.
Williamson, Robert W.
   1924. *The Social and Political Systems of Central Polynesia*. 3 vols. Cambridge: Cambridge University Press.
Wilson, Edmund O.
   1975. *Sociobiology: The New Synthesis*. Cambridge, Mass.: Belknap Press, Harvard University Press.
   1978. *On Human Nature*. Cambridge, Mass.: Harvard University Press.

Wilson, James
   1799/1968. *A Missionary Voyage to the Southern Pacific Ocean, 1796–1798*. New York: Praeger.
Wittfogel, Karl
   1957. *Oriental Despotism*. New Haven: Yale University Press.
Wolf, Eric
   1959. *Sons of the Shaking Earth*. Chicago: University of Chicago Press.
   1966. *Peasants*. Englewood Cliffs, N.J.: Prentice-Hall.
   1969. *Peasant Wars of the Twentieth Century*. New York: Harper and Row.
   1982. *Europe and the People without History*. Berkeley: University of California Press.
Wood, A. H.
   1945. *History and Geography of Tonga*. Auckland, New Zealand: Wilson and Horton.
   1975. *Overseas Missions of the Australian Methodist Church*, vol. 1, *Tonga and Samoa*. Melbourne: Aldersgate Press.
Wright, Henry T.
   1977. Recent research on the origin of the state. *Annual Review of Anthropology* 6:379–397.
Wright, Henry T., and Greg Johnson
   1975. Population, exchange and early state formation in southwestern Iran. *American Anthropologist* 77:267–289.
Wright, L. B., and M. I. Fry
   1936. *Puritans in the South Seas*. New York: Henry Holt.
Wright, Olive
   1955. *The Voyage of the Astrolabe, 1840*. Wellington, New Zealand: A. H. and A. W. Reed.
Wrigley, E. A.
   1969. *Population and History*. New York: McGraw-Hill.
Yonge, C. M.
   1932. The kingdom of Tonga. *Empire Review* (London) 55(375):245–249.

Index

212–213, 227, 232, 256; arrivals, 146, 171–172, 178; collections and tithing, 192–193, 218, 222, 227–228, 236, 247, 256, 284n.4; and commerce, 172–173, 176, 180, 194, 212–213, 217–218, 220–224, 226–228, 231–236, 246, 253, 255; and gender roles, 170, 173, 176, 186–191, 226, 264; mistrust of, 171–172, 175, 177; and resident Europeans, 171, 174–178, 182–183, 223–224, 269; and sexuality, 153, 186–191. *See also* Christianity; Conversion; Holy Wars; London Missionary Society; Roman Catholic Church; Warfare; Wesleyan Methodist Church
Mode of production: definition of, 31, 281n.3; slave-based, 33–34. *See also* Capitalist mode of production; Communal mode of production; Tribute-based mode of production
Moheofo, 61–62, 69, 73–75, 77–78, 137, 174, 180
Money, 149, 151, 228, 234–238, 261
Monogamy, 128–130, 187. *See also* Marriage
Mothers, 16, 59, 109, 115, 125, 239; and managing finances, 235, 284n.9; and rank, 48, 50, 57, 59, 61, 141, 214. *See also* Adoption; Birth
Mu'as, 56–59, 89, 95, 141, 202, 278n.2. *See also* Estates, non-chiefly

Nationality, 71
Native kingdom, xiii, 193–194, 212
Ngatu, xv, 93, 101, 165, 219, 228, 230, 241, 243–245, 278n.5, 279n.9. *See also* Tapa; Textiles
Ngāue. See Wage labor; Work, men's
Nobility, modern. *See Nōpeles*
Nōpeles, 50, 85, 194, 196–197, 199–203, 208, 212–213, 215, 243, 248,

254, 256, 258–259, 263, 265

Objectification, 85–86, 126–127, 157. *See also* Representations
Occupations. *See* Class; Part-time specialization
Orders. *See* Estates

Pālangis. See Papālangis
Papālangis 146, 157, 174–175, 231, 248, 281n.1. *See also* Europeans
Part-time specialization: artisans, 86, 88, 90, 98, 100, 174, 246; attendants, 86–88; cooks, 89–90, 101, 191; medical practitioners, 90; peasants, 86, 89, 93, 95, 101, 246; petty marketing, 239, 261, 264; precontact, 85–91; priesthood, 90–91, 96; warriors (*see also* Warfare), 101. *See also* Commodity production, petty; Division of labor
Patriarchy, xi, 21, 140, 179, 185, 187, 192
Patrilineality: in chiefly kindreds, 49–50, 109, 250–251; in inheritance and succession, 49–51, 63–65, 74, 191, 197, 210, 214, 262; and land tenure, 53, 197, 202; and marriage, 128, 207
Penal servitude, 185, 194, 204–207, 213, 218, 228, 231–235, 247, 250, 256, 263. *See also* Punishments
Polygyny: chiefly, 60, 128–130; co-wives, 61, 128–130, 135, 139, 263, 277n.6; vs. monogamy, attitudes toward, 187, 206. *See also* Marriage
Production: for civil sphere, 18, 28, 32, 255–256; for use, 31, 85, 91, 104, 106–107, 152, 217–219, 230, 235, 241–242, 246–247, 249, 255–256, 258–259, 261, 265–266, 271n.1; socially necessary, 104, 244, 262, 265, 271n.5. *See also* Commodity production; Subsistence